DISCOVER COSTA RICA

San José (p51) Costa Rica's frenetic capital serves as an urban complement to more far-flung, rural locales.

Central Valley (p73) The country's heartland is home to colonial cities, coffee plantations and half the population.

Northern Costa Rica (p97) A tourist-packed region of cloud forests and hot springs, and home to a fiery volcano.

Península de Nicoya (p165) This Pacific peninsula is a slice of paradise for surfers and beachcombers alike.

Central Pacific Coast (p199) The most developed stretch of coastline in Costa Rica is also the most cosmopolitan.

Southern Costa Rica (p227) Get off the beaten path and venture into the depths of pure wilderness.

Caribbean Coast (p269) Mellow vibes radiate to the tune of steel drums along this Afro-Caribbean-influenced coast.

D1425903

↘CONTENTS

6

NORTHERN
COSTA RICA
p97

PENÍNSULA
DE NICOYA
p165

CENTRAL VALLEY
p73

CARIBBEAN
COAST
p269

SAN JOSÉ
p51

CENTRAL
PACIFIC COAST
p199

SOUTHERN
COSTA RICA
p227

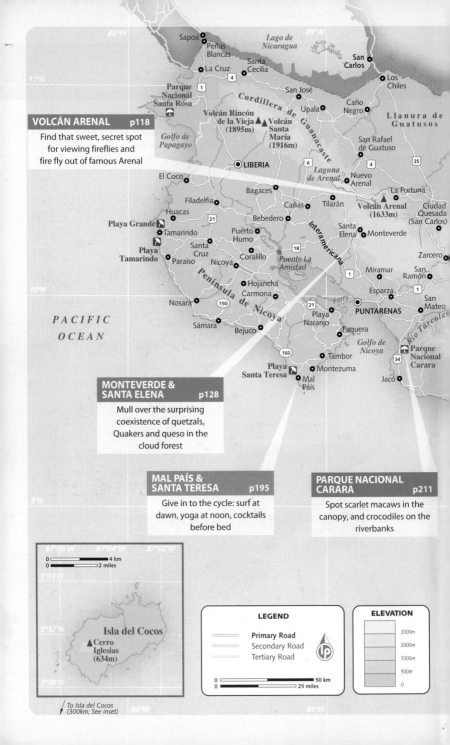

VOLCÁN ARENAL p118

Find that sweet, secret spot for viewing fireflies and fire fly out of famous Arenal

MONTEVERDE & SANTA ELENA p128

Mull over the surprising coexistence of quetzals, Quakers and queso in the cloud forest

MAL PAÍS & SANTA TERESA p195

Give in to the cycle: surf at dawn, yoga at noon, cocktails before bed

PARQUE NACIONAL CARARA p211

Spot scarlet macaws in the canopy, and crocodiles on the riverbanks

LEGEND

Primary Road
Secondary Road
Tertiary Road

0 ——————— 50 km
0 ——————— 25 miles

ELEVATION

3000m
2000m
1000m
500m
0

0 ———— 4 km
0 ———— 2 miles

Isla del Cocos

▲ Cerro Iglesias (634m)

To Isla del Cocos (300km; See inset)

PACIFIC OCEAN

SAN JOSÉ p51

Take in some culture at the capital's magnificent Teatro Nacional

PARQUE NACIONAL TORTUGUERO p287

Stay up all night on the beach while spying on egg-hatching turtles

CARIBBEAN SEA

VOLCÁN IRAZÚ p91

Allow your jaw to hit volcanic earth after taking in the view from the summit

TURRIALBA p93

Ride your adrenaline high after rafting some of the world's fiercest rapids

PARQUE NACIONAL CHIRRIPÓ p262

Climb to the lofty heights of Costa Rica's highest peak

PARQUE NACIONAL MANUEL ANTONIO p222

Get up close and personal with rare squirrel monkeys

PUERTO VIEJO DE TALAMANCA p292

Slink like a sloth into a hammock and gently rock away the days

PARQUE NACIONAL CORCOVADO p251

Endure the multiday trek across the country's last great wilderness

↘ THIS IS COSTA RICA

Costa Rica is sometimes referred to as the Switzerland of Central America because of its comfortable lifestyle, peaceful democracy and overwhelming natural beauty.

Indeed, this tiny mountainous country gave birth to one of the world's most progressive environmental movements. The Green Revolution kicked off in the 1970s when the unpredictable nature of the global coffee market created a rather unusual alliance between economic developers and environmental conservationists.

If wealth could not be sustained through exports, what about imports – of tourists? By 1985 tourism was contributing US$100 million annually to the Costa Rican economy, and today almost one-third of the entire country is under some form of environmental protection.

With economic empowerment came tremendous social change. As recently as 1980, Ticos (Costa Ricans) lived on family farms, listened to state radio and shopped at the neighborhood *pulpería* (corner grocery store). Today, shopping at supermarkets is a matter of course, satellite TV and wireless internet are the norm, and North American–style malls are all the rage.

Given the rise in quality of life throughout the country, Ticos are generally self-content and passive about politics, but underneath the easygoing veneer is discernible pride and support for their unarmed democracy. As stated by former President Oscar Arias Sánchez in his Nobel Peace Prize acceptance speech, 'we seek peace and democracy together, indivisible, an end to the shedding of human blood, which is inseparable from an end to the suppression of human rights.' This is a unique point of view – not only in Central America, but in the whole world.

On top of its lifestyle and democracy, Costa Rica is also mind-bendingly beautiful. Although there are certainly other countries in the world that enjoy divinely inspired natural landscapes, Costa Rica boasts a higher biodiversity than Europe and the USA combined. Its small size also means that traveling from cloud forest to coastline and from summit to savanna is quick, easy and enjoyable.

> 'Costa Rica boasts a higher biodiversity than Europe and the USA combined.'

↘ COSTA RICA'S TOP 25 EXPERIENCES

1

⬎ MONTEVERDE & SANTA ELENA

The neighboring towns of **Monteverde** and **Santa Elena** (p128), which edge iconic cloud forests, are the birthplace of the country's ecotourism movement. Here you can go trekking at high altitudes, search for rare resplendent quetzals and straddle your feet across the continental divide.

↘ HOT SPRINGS

Lying on the flanks of Arenal, one of the world's most active volcanoes, La Fortuna is a tourist-friendly town with an incredible list of activities on offer. Adventure types can organize an expedition in search of lava flows, while hedonists can soak their cares away in luxurious natural **hot springs** (p112).

↘ VOLCÁN ARENAL

By day you'll hear it rumbling and quaking, and if the smoke clouds above clear, you can gaze precariously at its near-perfect conical shape, but it's during the night that **Arenal** (p118) reveals its true power with almost constant eruptions of red-hot lava and tumbling avalanches of flaming rocks.

1 Reserva Biológica Bosque Nuboso Monteverde (p143); 2 Thermal bath, La Fortuna (p112); 3 Volcán Arenal (p118)

↘ PARQUE NACIONAL MANUEL ANTONIO

4

One of the country's most famous national parks, Manuel Antonio (p222) is the Costa Rica you imagined in your dreams. Here you can watch all manner of monkeys bounding through the forest canopy as you take leisurely hikes along palm-fringed shores lapped by tropical waves.

5

↘ REGGAE IN PUERTO VIEJO

Puerto Viejo de Talamanca (p292) is where you can feast on coconut-scented rice and spice-rubbed jerk chicken, then burn off the calories while dancing the night away to reggae beats (p296). This is the so-called 'other Costa Rica,' where English trumps Spanish, Rastafarians praise 'I and I,' and Afro-Caribbean culture thrives.

⬆ WILDLIFE

With a remarkable natural **environment** (p313) that fosters one of the world's highest concentrations of biodiversity, Costa Rica is quite simply a wildlife-watcher's paradise. Home to charismatic avian species, such as toucans and trogons, higher primates including spider monkeys and capuchins, and the impossibly cute sloths, this is a truly wild place.

6

4 CHRISTER FREDRIKSSON; 5 CHRISTER FREDRIKSSON; 6 CHRISTER FREDRIKSSON

4 Parque Nacional Manuel Antonio (p222); 5 Puerto Viejo de Talamanca (p292); 6 Two-toed sloth, Parque Nacional Manuel Antonio (p222)

⬎ SURFING

Costa Rica proudly rests on its laurels as one of the world's top **surfing** (p304) destinations. And why shouldn't it? On the same day, you can ride barreling breaks over Pacific beaches and Caribbean reefs. If you happen to be a beginner, there are a couple of places where you can practice standing up before tackling meaner swells.

7

8

⇘ PARQUE NACIONAL CORCOVADO

An off-the-beaten-path destination that caters exquisitely to seasoned trekkers, Corcovado (p251) is a gem of a national park that harbors an incredible complement of wildlife. Here you'll find jaguar footprints, scurrying tapirs, herds of peccaries and more species of birds than you can shake a stick at.

⇘ MAL PAÍS & SANTA TERESA

9

At the tip of the Península de Nicoya is this destination duo, which offers some of the country's best surf. Mal País and Santa Teresa (p195) were once far-flung locales that took serious determination to reach, but better road access and improved tourist infrastructure have brought about an increasingly sophisticated scene.

7 CHRISTIAN ASLUND; 8 LUKE HUNTER; 9 CHRISTIAN ASLUND

7 Surfer, Mal País (p195); 8 Parque Nacional Corcovado (p251); 9 Beachlife, Mal País (p195)

10

⬎ SAN JOSÉ

The bustling capital city of **San José** (p51) gives most travelers their first glimpse of Costa Rica. While the sprawling cityscape differs drastically from the lush rainforest and ocean-swept coast just around the corner, San José is nevertheless a rich cultural hub that warrants exploration.

⬎ PARQUE NACIONAL CARARA

11

Despite its comparatively small size, **Carara** (p211) is one of the country's most vitally important national parks. In addition to protecting a rare and unique intersection of biomes, Carara is occupied by a large and healthy population of vibrantly colored scarlet macaws.

⬏ COSTA RICAN COFFEE

12

One of the pleasures of traveling around Costa Rica is sampling its wonderful **coffee** (p322). Shade-grown and organic varietals are predictably on the menu everywhere, but you can visit Café Britt Finca in Barva (p89) if you want to drink right from the source.

13

⬏ CENTRAL VALLEY

Costa Rica gets top billing for coasts and cloud forests, but don't overlook the **Central Valley** (p73). As the country's major population center, this is where you'll get to know Costa Rica's true heart and soul.

10 RICHARD CUMMINS; 11 RALPH HOPKINS; 12 CHRISTOPHER BAKER; 13 RICHARD CUMMINS

10 Teatro Nacional (p61), San José; 11 Scarlet macaws, Puntarenas (p210); 12 Coffee-plantation worker; 13 Traditional *carreta* (oxcart), Sarchí (p86)

14

↘ WHITE-WATER RAFTING

The tiny town of Turrialba in the Central Valley might not look like much on the map, but the surrounding area is home to some of the most intense white-water rafting (p95 and p304) in the whole of Central America. If you're searching for a serious adrenaline rush, a day of fierce paddling should definitely be on your agenda.

⇘ NOSARA AREA

The collection of all-star wilderness beaches at **Nosara** (p186) attract surfers and nature-lovers alike. The area is blissfully lacking in tourist infrastructure – here, you'll find the Costa Rica of yesteryear.

15

14 ADRIAN HEPWORTH/HEPWORTHIMAGES; 15 KUNZ ROLF E/AGE FOTOSTOCK

14 White-water rafting, Río Pacuare (p95); 15 Beachside wilderness, Nosara (p186)

↘ JACÓ

Something of an obligatory stop for travelers along the central Pacific coast, Jacó (p211) is the country's most developed enclave for mass tourism. While the vibe is definitely more gringo than local, you can enjoy cosmopolitan eateries, upmarket resort hotels, decent surf and some seriously frenetic nightlife.

16

17

⬊ HIKING CHIRRIPÓ

From the lofty heights of Costa Rica's highest peak, **Cerro Chirripó** (p263), you can bask in panoramic views of both the Pacific Ocean and the Caribbean Sea. Of course, if you want to enjoy this visual feast, you're going to have to endure the arduous – but highly rewarding – slog to the top.

⬊ DOMINICAL

18

Lying at the central Pacific coast's southern end, **Dominical** (p222) is a tiny town fronted by not-so-tiny waves. Surfers are predictably well catered for, as are beachcombers and sun-worshippers alike.

16 IMAGEBROKER/HANS ZAGLITSCH; 17 LUKE HUNTER; 18 IMAGEBROKER/MICHAEL ZEGERS

16 Jacó (p211); 17 Parque Nacional Chirripó (p262); 18 Mountain landscape around Dominical (p222)

↘ PLAYA TAMARINDO

Costa Rica's most famous party town, **Tamarindo** (p180) is rambunctious and self-assured. You can live it up with a boozy drink in hand, and cut loose with travelers from all corners of the world. Even if you're a teetotaler, the Pacific sunsets here are about as bright and beautiful as they come.

19

20

⇘ CANOPY TOURS

Costa Rica's most famous activity, the **canopy tour** (p302) is a homegrown attraction that involves donning a harness and clipping into a system of zip lines strung across the treetops. Assuming you have a need for speed and a healthy respect for heights, no other pursuit can give you such a clear bird's-eye view of the forest.

19 AARON MCCOY; 20 PAUL KENNEDY

19 Playa Tamarindo (p180); 20 Zipping through the rainforest on a canopy tour (p302)

21

⬎ PLAYA SÁMARA

Among the country's most picture-perfect beaches, Sámara (p187) is an angelic strip of powder-white sand that lies between gently rolling turquoise seas and a string of trendy restaurants and cafes. An ideal destination for vacationing families in search of a quiet retreat, Sámara is peaceful yet sophisticated.

⬎ PARQUE NACIONAL TORTUGUERO

One of Costa Rica's top eco-destinations, Tortuguero (p287) is an elaborate network of narrow canals that wind their way through pristine jungle and coastal wetlands. From the safety and comfort of your own canoe, you can paddle along the shrouded waterways in search of hidden wildlife.

22

⬎ BIRD-WATCHING

23

Be sure to save space in your luggage for binoculars – and a spotting scope, if you want to go hard-core. Indeed, Costa Rica boasts some of the world's best **birdwatching** (p306), with literally hundreds of species on the checklist.

COSTA RICA'S TOP 25 EXPERIENCES

24

⬎ PARQUE INTERNACIONAL LA AMISTAD

It takes a bit of commitment to access this remote **binational park** (p267). However, Parque Internacional La Amistad offers up nothing less than true wilderness at soaring elevations.

21 Family fun at the beach, Playa Sámara (p187); 22 Parque Nacional Tortuguero (p287); 23 Quetzal, Reserva Biológica Bosque Nuboso Monteverde (p143); 24 Parque Internacional La Amistad (p267)

↘ MONTEZUMA

An eternally relaxed, hippie beach town at the tip of the Península de Nicoya, **Montezuma** (p190) is the sort of place you work hard to get to, then quickly dismiss the idea of ever leaving. Days here revolve around a blissful cycle of sea, sun, sand and sleep.

25

25 COREY WISE

25 Montezuma (p190), Península de Nicoya

COSTA RICA'S TOP ITINERARIES

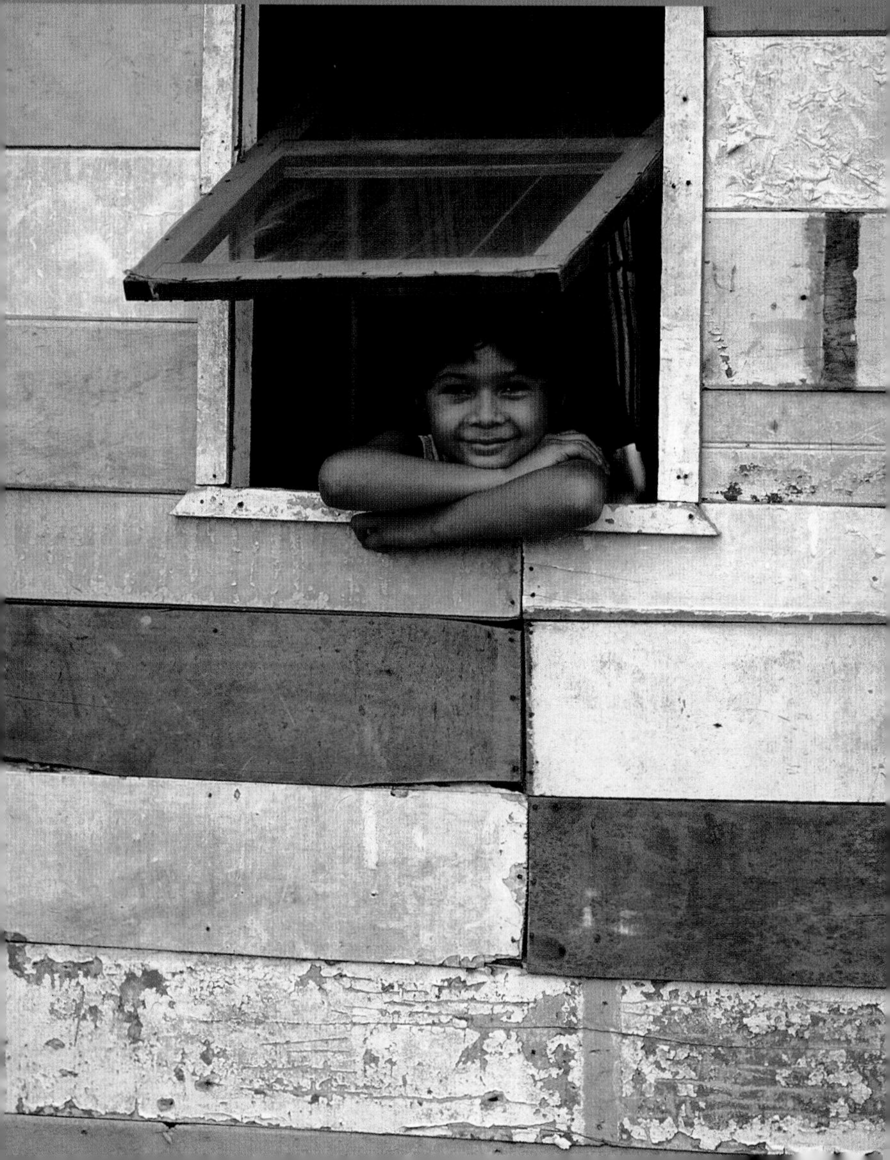

NORTHERN HIGHLIGHTS

FIVE DAYS SAN JOSÉ TO MONTEVERDE & SANTA ELENA

For a taste of the north, this classic route will take you through
the capital's hidden charms and colonial flourishes and into
the mountains of the interior, passing by bubbling volcanoes,
hot springs and tranquil cloud forests.

❶ SAN JOSÉ

Touching down in the sprawling capital of Costa Rica can be a shock
to the senses, but there is plenty to do here before embarking for
greener pastures. A great introduction to the Latin American lifestyle
is a trip to the bustling **Mercado Central** (p66), or Central Market,
where you can bargain-hunt for anything from a kilo of coffee to a
sack of mangoes. If you're in need of a quick respite from the street
crowds and tropical heat, head indoors to the **Museo de Jade** (p62),
where you can admire centuries-old pre-Columbian jade carvings.
Architecture and culture buffs alike shouldn't miss out on the **Teatro
Nacional** (p61), a stunning colonial construction that is the beating
heart of San José's theater scene.

❷ LA FORTUNA

Just a few hours away by bus on the flanks of Volcán Arenal, the tourist-
friendly town of **La Fortuna** (p112) is a world away from the hustle and
bustle of San José. Your first destination is obvious, namely the dark and
brooding volcano in the distance that is **Volcán Arenal** (p118). Ample
daylight is conducive to long hikes through the surrounding forests,
while nighttime allows for stunning views of exploding lava showers.

CHRISTER FREDRIKSSON

The mountains of the interior provide endless stunning vistas

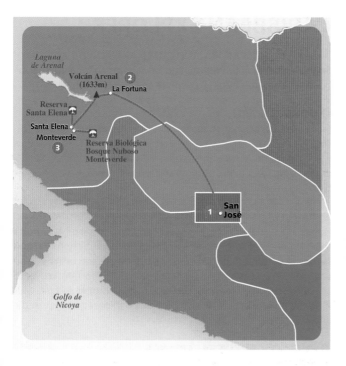

If the weather isn't cooperating and clouds obscure the summit, you can wait it out in any number of the town's luxurious and therapeutic **hot springs** (p112). With a fruity cocktail in hand and steam rolling off your toes, it doesn't take long to slip into the *pura vida* (literally 'pure life') frame of mind.

❸ MONTEVERDE & SANTA ELENA
After you towel-dry, take a boat across Laguna de Arenal, followed by a shuttle bus to the rural retreat of Monteverde and Santa Elena. Founded by Quakers and famous for dairy, the peaceful town of Santa Elena comprises cute cafes, eclectic restaurants, attractive galleries and some of the country's best ice cream. Of course, the main billing is the adjacent **Reserva Biológica Bosque Nuboso Monteverde** (p143), where you can search for the elusive quetzal. Nearby **Reserva Santa Elena** (p144) and the **Children's Eternal Rainforest** (p133) offer equally misty cloud-forest experiences.

CARIBBEAN EXPLORER

10 DAYS VOLCÁN IRAZÚ TO TORTUGUERO

Spanish gives way to English, and Latin beats change into Caribbean vibes as you begin to explore the 'other Costa Rica.'

❶ VOLCÁN IRAZÚ

This itinerary is all about nature, so take the round-trip bus from San José for a worthwhile day trip to **Volcán Irazú** (p91). On a clear day, you'll be rewarded with an amazing view of the Caribbean (as well as the Pacific), but hold onto your swimsuit – the ocean is a lot closer than you think.

❷ CAHUITA

Hop on the first eastbound bus out of San José and get off at **Cahuita** (p289), capital of Afro-Caribbean culture and gateway to **Parque Nacional Cahuita** (p291). Here along the white-sand beaches, you can watch in awe as hungry mammals dash out of the forest cover to snack on scurrying crabs. Stick around Cahuita proper and get your fill of this mellow little village where the air is thick with reggae music and the scent of coconut rice.

❸ PUERTO VIEJO DE TALAMANCA

If Cahuita starts to feel too small, it's just a quick bus or taxi ride south to **Puerto Viejo de Talamanca** (p292), the Caribbean coast's center for surfing, nightlife and Rasta. Fronting the beach is Salsa Brava, an epic surf break that first put the town on the map. Even if you're not a proficient short-boarder, you can easily spend a few days here bar-hopping

Red-eyed tree frogs are well camouflaged in the rainforest

CHRISTER FREDRIKSSON

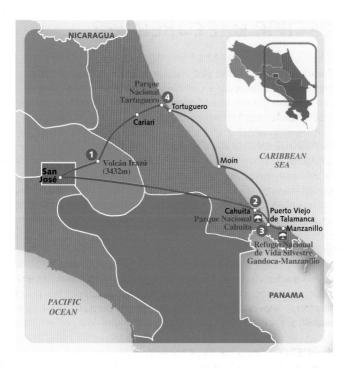

with the backpacker set. If you feel the need to stretch your legs, rent a good old-fashioned push-bike and ride to nearby **Manzanillo** (p296), from where you can snorkel, kayak and hike in the **Refugio Nacional de Vida Silvestre Gandoca-Manzanillo** (p298).

❹ PARQUE NACIONAL TORTUGUERO

For the adventurous at heart, head north to grab a boat from **Moín** (p282) and travel the canal-lined coast to the village of **Tortuguero** (p284), where you can watch nesting green and leatherback turtles. You can also access the region via **Cariari** (p284), if you're coming from San José. Of course, the real reason you're here is to arrange a canoe trip through the mangrove-lined canals of **Parque Nacional Tortuguero** (p287), Costa Rica's mini-Amazon.

PACIFIC EXPLORER

TWO WEEKS CARARA TO CORCOVADO

For days on end of sun, surf and sand, head south along the central Pacific coast for a combination of beach towns dedicated to the pursuit of hedonism, and scenic national parks where wilderness and wildlife abound.

❶ PARQUE NACIONAL CARARA

Before settling in to Jacó, take a quick bus or taxi ride to this nearby coastal **national park** (p211), home to the country's largest population of scarlet macaws. While sightings of these flaming-red avians are rare elsewhere, Carara is one spot where we can guarantee that you'll need to dust off the binoculars or spotting scope.

❷ JACÓ

Well, this is it, the unofficial party capital of Costa Rica's central Pacific coast – **Jacó** (p211) isn't for everybody, but if you're looking to kick back with the bold and the brash, welcome to paradise. Even if you take pride in being one who goes easy on the drink, don't miss the beach town's motley assortment of international-inspired eateries. If you prefer to dial it down a notch, head a bit further south along the coastal highway to **Playa Hermosa** (p215). And bring a board – surf's up!

❸ QUEPOS & MANUEL ANTONIO

Continuing south, public transportation leads to **Quepos** (p216), a tiny Tico town bordering a chart-topping national park. At **Parque**

Sunset horseback ride, Parque Nacional Manuel Antonio (p222)

CHRISTER FREDRIKSSON

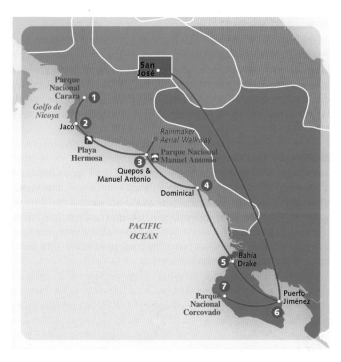

Nacional Manuel Antonio (p222), monkeys descend from the tree-tops to frolic in troops along the palm-fringed coastline. If you want to get a monkey's-eye view, arrange a guided tour to the nearby **Rainmaker Aerial Walkway** (p220), which lets you stroll from platform to platform across the canopy.

❹ DOMINICAL

If you haven't had enough of the postcard-perfect Pacific coast, keep heading south by public transportation to **Dominical** (p222) to catch some more waves, soak up some more rays and consider delaying your return trip home. Indeed, you don't have to try very hard to get stuck in this terminally chilled-out beach town where time passes to the rhythm of the crashing surf.

❺ BAHÍA DRAKE

Home to Costa Rica's most pristine nature, Península de Osa is an undeniable draw for anyone wanting some rugged wilderness exploration. However, before you penetrate the heart of the peninsula, spend a couple of days at an all-inclusive ecoresort in **Bahía Drake** (p241), where you can revel in nature while living it up in the lap of luxury. Book in advance, and have all your transportation arranged for you.

❻ PUERTO JIMÉNEZ

A bit further down the peninsula is the official gateway to Corcovado, **Puerto Jiménez** (p246) – or Port Jim, as it's affectionately called by locals. Here you can spend a day or so kayaking around the mangroves or soaking up the charm of this tiny town. And, of course, don't forget to stock up on supplies for the big adventure ahead. Port Jim can be reached by bus or plane, though most people press onward by foot.

❼ PARQUE NACIONAL CORCOVADO

The undisputed highlight of the Península de Osa is **Parque Nacional Corcovado** (p251), one of the country's top wildlife-watching spots. It's worth spending a few days exploring the trails with a backpack of supplies, and particularly well-equipped travelers can even trek across the entirety of the park. If you're getting close to the end of your time in Costa Rica (and you're not put off by small prop planes), it's just a quick flight from Port Jim to San José.

RALPH HOPKINS

Parque Nacional Corcovado (p251)

COSTA RICA'S BEST

TROPICAL BEACHES

- **Manzanillo** (p296) The Caribbean coast's most scenic stretch of sand.
- **Playa Conchal** (p179) Crushed shells and turquoise water.
- **Montezuma** (p190) White sands, rocky coves and killer sunrises.
- **Mal País** (p195) Huge, crashing surf for kilometers in each direction.
- **Playa Sámara** (p187) A destination for sophisticated beach-goers and fun-loving families.

IDYLLIC SUNSETS

- **Cerro Chirripó** (p262) Take in the panoramic views from the Crestones Base Lodge atop Costa Rica's highest point.
- **Playa Tamarindo** (p180) Sail on the deep-blue Pacific and watch the sun dip below the jagged coastline.
- **Tortuguero Village** (p284) Sip an ice-cold *cerveza* (beer) while kickin' back to soothing reggae beats.

- **Bosque Eterno de los Niños** (p133) Hike at twilight through the Children's Eternal Rainforest – just in time to see the nocturnal creatures come out.
- **Plaza de la Democracia** (p61) Relax on colonial steps in the heart of downtown San José.

NATIONAL PARKS

- **Monteverde & Santa Elena** (p128) Cloud forests straddling both sides of the continental divide.
- **Parque Nacional Manuel Antonio** (p222) Monkeys bounding across palm-fringed Pacific beaches.
- **Parque Nacional Corcovado** (p251) A true wilderness destination, home to the country's densest concentration of wildlife.
- **Parque Nacional Tortuguero** (p287) Sea turtles and caimans complement the Caribbean environs.

CHRISTIAN ASLUND

Surfers, Mal País (p195)

- **Parque Internacional La Amistad** (p267) Often forgotten, but wild, rugged and impossible to tame.

SURF BREAKS

- **Parque Nacional Santa Rosa** (p155) Costa Rica's surfing mecca for experienced board-riders with time to kill.
- **Puerto Viejo de Talamanca** (p292) Centered on Salsa Brava, one of the country's gnarliest breaks.
- **Mal País & Santa Teresa** (p195) Huge swaths of prime beachfront are shaped by lefts, rights and point breaks.
- **Playas Avellanas & Negra** (p183) This is where the magic happened in the on-screen surf epic, *Endless Summer II*.
- **Playa Tamarindo** (p180) Rather developed, but a good place to get your feet on the board for the first time.

ADRENALINE RUSHES

- **La Fortuna** (p112) Costa Rica's center for adventure sports, from bungee jumping to zip lining.
- **Turrialba** (p93) Home to the fiercest white water that Costa Rica has on tap.
- **La Virgen** (p157) Head to this northern destination if kayaking floats your boat.
- **Nosara** (p186) Home to the world's longest zip-line canopy tour.
- **Volcán Arenal** (p118) Nothing gets the blood boiling like hot, molten lava.

OFF-THE-BEATEN-PATH SPOTS

- **Pavones** (p257) Record-breaking waves, yet only a handful of other surfers to share them with.
- **Parque Nacional Volcán Tenorio** (p153) Ample hiking trails, a bright-blue waterfall and little more than a few scattered footprints.
- **Reserva Indígena Boruca** (p265) Difficult to access, but worth the trip if you want insight into the country's pre-Columbian past.
- **Isla del Cocos** (p258) The inspiration for Isla Nublar in Michael Crichton's *Jurassic Park*.
- **Punta Mona** (p299) Extremely remote, but the lodge is home to an amazing ongoing experiment in sustainable living.

CHILL-OUT SPOTS

- **Dominical** (p222) A classic backpackers' beach town where surfing and partying complement long spells of doing nothing.
- **Bahía Drake** (p241) An upscale collection of luxurious ecolodges lines this scenic bay.
- **Cahuita** (p289) A low-key Caribbean beach destination where good times are by no means in short supply.
- **Nosara** (p186) A magical collection of remote wilderness beaches and raging surf.
- **Uvita** (p225) Far-flung, but on the edge of a tranquil marine park.

THINGS YOU NEED TO KNOW

AT A GLANCE

- **ATMs** Widely available; machines dispense both colones and US dollars.
- **Bargaining** Only in markets.
- **Credit cards** Visa and Mastercard widely accepted, others less so.
- **Language** English is spoken in tourist areas and along the Caribbean, but Spanish prevails elsewhere.
- **Money** Colones (₡).
- **Tipping** Leave a small tip to show your appreciation, but it is not required.
- **Visas** Most visitors receive short-stay visas on arrival.

ACCOMMODATIONS

- **B&Bs** Midrange to top-end affairs typically run by North American and European expats (p340).
- **Hostels** Good-value accommodations with the needs of the modern backpacker in mind (p340).
- **Hotels** Highly variable in range, including everything from budget crash pads to lavish five-star resorts (p340).

ADVANCE PLANNING

- **Car rental** Booking online before your departure date will enable you to pick up your rental car at the airport and make the most of your time in Costa Rica.
- **Reservations** Make accommodations reservations a couple of months in advance if you're traveling during Semana Santa or the Christmas holiday season.

BE FOREWARNED

- **Climate** Tropical sun along the coasts, frequent precipitation in the rainforests and evening chills at high altitude – be prepared with the proper attire.

COSTS

- **Up to US$50 per day** Budget hotels and backpacker hostels, meals in simple restaurants or self-catering, and local transportation.
- **US$50 to US$150 per day** Upmarket hotels, great restaurants, an activity or two and private transportation.
- **More than US$150 per day** Luxury hotels, fine dining, private 4WD rental and/or charter flights.

EMERGENCY NUMBERS

- **Emergency** ☎ 911
- **Fire** ☎ 118
- **Police** ☎ 117

GETTING AROUND

- **Air** Domestic airlines and private charters can help you squeeze the most into your travels (p356).
- **Bus** Depending on your desired level of comfort, you can choose from air-conditioned private shuttles and more economical local coaches (p359).
- **Car** Renting a private vehicle is the best way to explore Costa Rica at your own pace (p360).

PLANNING YOUR TRIP

- **Taxi** In San José as well as in rural areas, a quick taxi ride is worth the cash if you don't have time to waste (p362).

GETTING THERE & AWAY

- **Air** A long list of major carriers service Aeropuerto Internacional Juan Santamaría in San José (p66) and – to a lesser extent – Aeropuerto Internacional Daniel Oduber Quirós in Liberia (p149).

TECH STUFF

- **Computers and internet** Nearly all B&Bs, hostels and upmarket hotels have internet access; wi-fi is surprisingly widespread, particularly in tourist towns.
- **Cell phones** Costa Rica uses GSM phones; rental phones are available through car-rental agencies.

- **Plugs and voltage** Electrical current is 110V AC at 60Hz. Plugs are two flat prongs – same as in the USA.

WHAT TO BRING

- **Insect repellent** Make sure it contains DEET, especially if you're planning large-scale jungle adventures.
- **Spanish phrasebook** Learning a little of the local lingo makes all the difference.
- **Anti-diarrheal pills** Because sometimes you never know when nature's gonna call.
- **Sunblock** Take precautions as you don't want to get cooked by the tropical sun.
- **Proper footwear** Bring along a pair of waterproof sandals and sturdy jungle boots.
- **Binoculars** These are requisite for proper bird-watching – a field guide also helps.

THINGS YOU NEED TO KNOW

CHRISTOPHER BAKER

Swimming pool, Florblanca (p197), Santa Teresa

PLANNING YOUR TRIP

THINGS YOU NEED TO KNOW

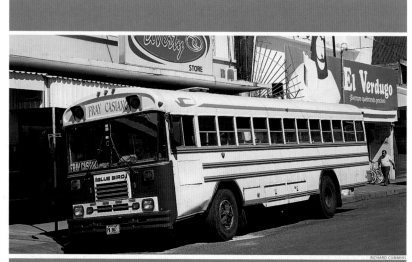

Local bus, Puntarenas (p210)

RICHARD CUMMINS

- **Miscellaneous necessities** A flashlight (torch), poncho, padlock, alarm clock, matches and a pocketknife.

WHEN TO GO

- **Dry season (December to April)** Referred to by locals as *verano* (summer), this is the best time to visit. Note that dry season does not mean that it doesn't rain – it just rains less.

- **Wet season (May to November)** The early months of *invierno* (winter) are a wonderful time to travel to Costa Rica: you can avoid the tourist bustle and lodging is slightly cheaper.

GET INSPIRED

⇲ BOOKS

- **Naturalist in Costa Rica** (Dr Skutch) The author weaves his philosophies into his beautiful descriptions of flora and fauna in this enchanting memoir and natural history guide.
- **Green Phoenix** (William Allen) An absorbing and inspiring account of the author's efforts to conserve and restore the rainforest in Guanacaste.
- **Around the Edge** (Peter Ford) A story of the author's travels along the Caribbean coast from Belize to Panama, on foot and by boat.
- **Green Dreams: Travels in Central America** (Stephen Benz) An astute analysis that questions the impact visitors are having on the region and its people.

⇲ FILMS

- **Endless Summer II** Surfers Pat O'Connell and Robert 'Wingnut' Weaver touch down in Costa Rica to see how far the sport has spread.
- **Agua Fría de Mar (Cold Water of the Sea)** A story of a young couple and a seven-year-old girl from contrasting social backgrounds who spend Christmas together along the Pacific coast.
- **Jurassic Park** Michael Crichton's modern literary classic about the genetic resurrection of dinosaurs puts the fictional Costa Rican island of Isla Nublar on the silver screen.

- **1492: Conquest of Paradise** Ridley Scott's epic re-enactment of Christopher Columbus' voyage to the New World was largely filmed in Costa Rica.

⇲ MUSIC

- **Paloma Negra** A legendary ballad by Chavela Vargas, a folkloric singer with a hauntingly beautiful voice.
- **Los Brillanticos** The self-titled album of Costa Rica's much-loved salsa group.
- **Ramses Araya** A popular hit from the Tico salsa orchestra Timbaleo.
- **La Fiesta** The classic album from the Taboga Band, which plays jazz-influenced salsa and merengue.

⇲ WEBSITES

- **Costa Rica Tourism Board** (www.visitcostarica.com) The official website of the Instituto Costarricense de Turismo (ICT).
- **Tico Times** (www.ticotimes.net) The online edition of Costa Rica's excellent English-language weekly newspaper.
- **Lanic** (http://lanic.utexas.edu/la/ca/cr) An exceptional collection of links to the websites (mostly in Spanish) of many Costa Rican organizations, from the University of Texas.
- **Guías Costa Rica** (www.guias costarica.com) Links that connect you to everything you'd ever need to know – from entertainment to health to government websites.

CALENDAR

JAN   FEB   MAR   APR

AARON MCCOY

Fiesta de Santa Cruz (p185)

↘ JANUARY

FIESTA DE SANTA CRUZ
During the second week of January in Nicoya's cultural capital of Santa Cruz (p185), revelers line the streets to watch religious processions, rodeos, bullfights, traditional dances and a beauty pageant, all set to a soundtrack of live marimba music.

LAS FIESTAS DE PALMARES
Ten days of continuous beer drinking, horse shows and carnival events in mid-January transform the tiny town of Palmares (p87) into the country's largest outdoor spectacle, drawing annual crowds of more than 10,000 people and garnering complete TV coverage.

↘ FEBRUARY

FIESTA DE LOS DIABLITOS   FEB 5–8
At the village of Curré in the Reserva Indígena Boruca (p265), men wear woodcarved devil masks and burlap masks to re-enact the fight between the indigenous people and the Spanish. In this one, the Spanish lose badly.

FIESTAS DE LA FORTUNA
In mid-February the town of La Fortuna (p112) boasts two weeks of bullfights, carnival rides, greasy food, craft stands and temporary tents featuring live performances of *ranchera,* salsa and reggaetón.

| MAY | JUN | JUL | AUG | SEP | OCT | NOV | DEC |

↘ MARCH–APRIL

DÍA DEL BOYERO

San José's suburb of **Escazú** (p71) honors oxcart drivers on the second Sunday of March, as dozens of *boyeros* from all over the country decorate traditional, brightly painted carts and form a colorful (if slow) parade.

DÍA DE SAN JOSÉ   MAR 19

St Joseph's Day honors the patron saint of **San José** (p51). All across the capital, churches open their doors and hold masses to mark the life and death of the father of the Holy Family.

FESTIVAL DE ARTE

For two weeks in March, **San José** (p51) hosts a biennial citywide arts showcase featuring theater, music, dance and film.

FERIA DE LA MASCARADA

Typically held during the last week in March, this festival in **Barva** (p89) is celebrated by donning massive masks (which can weigh up to 20kg) and dancing around the town square for days on end.

SEMANA SANTA

Costa Rica shuts down and goes on holiday during the Christian Holy Week, which typically falls in late March and/or early April. Semana Santa includes the holidays of Palm Sunday, Holy Thursday and Good Friday, all of which lead up to Easter Sunday.

DÍA DE JUAN SANTAMARÍA APR 11

This nationwide public holiday commemorates the national hero who was martyred in 1856 at the Battle of Rivas, which was fought against the North American invader William Walker.

DAFLAI/WIKIMEDIA COMMONS

Street festival, Liberia (p145), Guanacaste

CALENDAR

JAN   FEB   MAR   APR

JULY

FIESTA DE LA VIRGEN DEL MAR
Held in Playa del Coco (p176) in mid-July, the Festival of the Virgin of the Sea is celebrated in true Nicoya style with colorful regattas and boat parades.

DÍA DE GUANACASTE   JUL 25
Santa Cruz (p185) garners the country's spotlight as local loyalists take to the streets to commemorate the annexation of Guanacaste from Nicaragua in 1824.

AUGUST

SURF COMPETITION
Every August the central Pacific coastal town of Playa Hermosa (p215) hosts one of the country's top-rated surf-

ing competitions, attracting amateurs and pros from around the world.

SEPTEMBER

**DÍA DE LA
INDEPENDENCIA   SEP 15**
Costa Rica's big birthday bash unfurls with patriotic parades in towns and cities across the country to mark the gaining of independence from Spanish colonial rule in 1821.

NOVEMBER

DÍA DE LOS MUERTOS   NOV 2
Tico families celebrate All Souls' Day by visiting graveyards and holding festive religious parades in honor of the deceased.

ADRIAN HEPWORTH/HEPWORTHIMAGES

Día de la Independencia parade, Cartago (p90)

MAY	JUN	JUL	AUG	SEP	OCT	NOV	DEC

Catedral Metropolitana (p60), San José

PAUL KENNEDY

⚲ DECEMBER–JANUARY

FESTIVAL DE LUZ
In San José (p51), the first week in December hosts the Festival of Light, a Christmas-themed parade that sees enormous quantities of plastic snow hurled through the air.

FIESTA DE LOS NEGRITOS
At the village of Boruca in the Reserva Indígena Boruca (p265), the Virgin of the Immaculate Conception is honored in mid-December with traditional drumming, piping and costumed dancing.

CHRISTMAS   DEC 24–25
After Christmas Eve mass, Tico families eat a large and festive midnight meal to celebrate the birth of Jesus Christ. Christmas Day witnesses an exodus to the beach for plenty of sand and sun.

LAS FIESTAS DE ZAPOTE   DEC 25–JAN 1
A weeklong celebration of even more rodeos, cowboys, carnival rides, fried food and a whole lot of drinking takes hold of the district of Zapote in southeastern of San José (p51).

FIESTA DE LOS DIABLITOS   DEC 31–JAN 2
In the village of Boruca in the Reserva Indígena Boruca (p265) men wear woodcarved devil masks and burlap masks in a performance akin to Curré's February festivities.

ADRIAN HEPWORTH/HEPWORTHIMAGES

Día de Guanacaste, Nicoya (p185)

↘ SAN JOSÉ

LEE FOSTER

Some of San José's hotels are housed in beautiful early-20th-century mansions

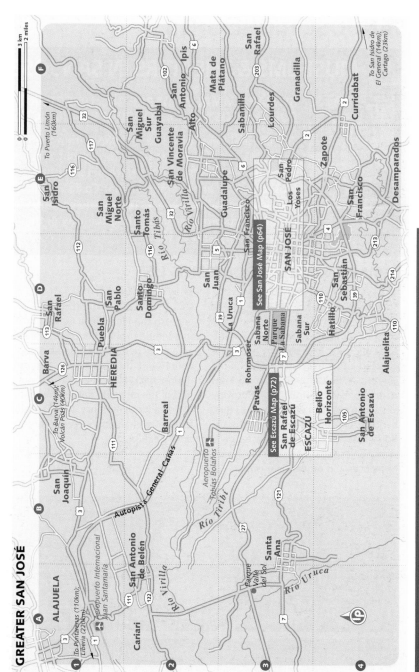

GREATER SAN JOSÉ

SAN JOSÉ HIGHLIGHTS

1   MUSEUMS & THEATERS IN SAN JOSÉ

BY MARIA AMALIA, MARKETING DIRECTOR FOR THE COSTA RICA TOURISM BOARD (ICT)

The cultural heart of Costa Rica lies within the museums and theaters spread throughout San José. Venues like the Teatro Nacional and the Museo de Oro are a reminder that Costa Rica is a country of varied history. Today, the country continues to progress by leading the way in the contemporary arts as well.

↘ MARIA AMALIA'S DON'T MISS LIST

❶ TEATRO NACIONAL

The stately **national theater** (p61) is an architectural masterpiece, and a key component in the capital's bevy of cultural offerings. The building was constructed in the neoclassical style at the very end of the 19th century, and houses a series of lavish paintings that provide visual commentary on Costa Rica's rural heritage. On the cultural front, the national theater hosts plays, dance, opera, symphonies, Latin American music performances and other major events.

❷ MUSEO DE ORO PRE-COLOMBINO Y NUMISMÁTICA

Beneath the Plaza de la Cultura is this three-in-one **museum** (p61), centered on a collection of pre-Columbian gold containing hand-tooled ornaments dating back to AD 400. The second part of the museum details the history of Costa Rican currency, while another features a changing selection of temporary exhibitions.

Clockwise from top: Museo de Jade (p62); Foyer of the Teatro Nacional (p61)

❺ MUSEO DE ARTE Y DISEÑO CONTEMPORÁNEO

This **art museum** (p62) is focused on showing the works of contemporary Costa Rican and Latin American artists. It also occasionally features temporary exhibits devoted to interior design, fashion and graphic art.

❸ MUSEO DE JADE

The world's largest **collection of jade** (p62) has display cases full of elaborate carvings depicting everything from frogs and serpents to shamans and fertility goddesses. The craftsmanship is superb, and the pieces are in a fine state of conservation given their pre-Columbian origins.

❹ MUSEO NACIONAL DE COSTA RICA

The **national museum** (p62) is located inside the Bellavista Fortress, which served as the old army headquarters, and saw fierce fighting (hence the pockmarks) in the civil war of 1948. It was here that President José Figueres announced the following year that he would abolish the country's military.

❶ Teatro Nacional
❷ Museo de Oro Precolombino y Numismática
❸ Museo de Jade
❹ Museo Nacional de Costa Rica
❺ Museo de Arte y Diseño Contemporáneo

❯ THINGS YOU NEED TO KNOW

Access Aeropuerto Internacional Juan Santamaría (p66) is the country's main international airport **More information** The Instituto Costarricense de Turismo website (ICT; www.visitcostarica.com) provides a detailed overview of tourism in Costa Rica **See the author's reviews, p61**

SAN JOSÉ HIGHLIGHTS

↘ MERCADO CENTRAL

San José is a magnet for shoppers in search of a great deal. The action is centered on the **Central Market** (p66), a sprawling complex of stalls and shops selling everything from bulk produce and butchered meats to secondhand clothes and tourist souvenirs. As this is Latin America, you'll need good bargaining skills to keep the prices low – fortunately, haggling in Spanish with smiling vendors is half the fun.

↘ PUBLIC PARKS

San José may be lacking in tree-lined promenades, but fortunately there is no shortage of leafy green **parks** (p62). Two of the capital's best escapes are Parque Nacional, which is studded with myriad monuments devoted to key figures in Latin American history, and Parque Metropolitano La Sabana, a perfect place for a quiet stroll, a relaxed jog or a picnic with the entire family.

4

↘ PLAZA DE LA CULTURA

Both the spiritual and the physical heart of the city, the **Plaza of Culture** (p60) is little more than a slab of concrete in the middle of downtown. But for the residents of San José, this is the city's greatest public space for gathering with friends and family, and indulging in a bout of people-watching.

5

↘ ESCAZÚ

A trendy suburb that is often associated with wealth and status, **Escazú** (p71) makes for a pleasant day trip from the capital proper. As an alternative to the urban hustle and bustle, this is where you can also bed down and dine out in relative peace and comfort.

6

↘ LOS YOSES & SAN PEDRO

Two more San José suburbs that definitely merit a glimpse are **Los Yoses** and **San Pedro** (p71), each with their own distinct character. Los Yoses is prim and proper, offering Escazú a run for its money, while the university district of San Pedro has noticeably more bohemian leanings.

2 ADRIAN HEPWORTH/HEPWORTHIMAGES; 3 IMAGEBROKER/OLIVER GERHARD; 4 CHRISTER FREDRIKSSON; 5 CHRIS FREDRIKSSON/ALAMY; 6 PETER LANGER/DANITADELIMONT.COM

2 Mercado Central (p66); **3** Parque Morazán in downtown San José; **4** Street game of chess, San José; **5** Tranquil accommodations, Escazú (p71); **6** Students, San José

SAN JOSÉ'S BEST...

⤣ SPLURGES

- **Hotel Grano de Oro** (p63) Bed down in an early-20th-century Tropical Victorian mansion complete with period furniture.
- **Restaurante Grano de Oro** (p64) Chow down in an early-20th-century Tropical Victorian mansion centered on a formal dining hall decked out in fresh flowers.
- **Casa Cristal** (p72) A boutique hotel high up in the hills of Escazú that elegantly lords over San José.

⤣ SHOPPING

- **Mercado Central** (p66) A traditional Latin American shopping extravaganza.
- **Galería Namu** (p65) A fair-trade gallery showcasing indigenous artwork.
- **Biesanz Woodworks** (p72) Arguably the country's best woodcrafting studio, located in Escazú.

⤣ ENTERTAINMENT

- **Teatro Nacional** (p61) Catch a performance in the city's most historic theater.
- **Jazz Café** (p71) Los Yoses and San Pedro boast the top spot for live musical performances.
- **Centro Comercial El Pueblo** (p65) A complex of dozens of bars and clubs that attracts serious revellers.

⤣ EATS

- **Churrería Manolo's** (p63) Home to the delicious *churro* (doughnut tube).
- **Machu Picchu** (p64) This Peruvian food spot is one of the city's best restaurants.
- **La Casona de Laly** (p72) Down-to-earth home cooking in high-falutin Escazú.

A huge choice of spices on offer at the Mercado Central (p66)

ADRIAN HEPWORTH/HEPWORTHIMAGES

THINGS YOU NEED TO KNOW

⬎ VITAL STATISTICS

- **Area** 2366 sq km
- **Population** City 346,000, greater metro area more than 1.5 million
- **Best time to visit** Día del Boyero (mid-March), Festival de Luz (Christmas), Las Fiestas de Zapote (late December)

⬎ NEIGHBORHOODS IN A NUTSHELL

- **Downtown** The city center is very pedestrian-friendly.
- **La Sabana** Centered on an expansive public park.
- **Escazú** (p71) The capital's glitziest suburb.
- **Los Yoses & San Pedro** (p71) A wealthy neighborhood and the university district, respectively.

⬎ ADVANCE PLANNING

- **Car rental** Travelers touching down at Aeropuerto Internacional Juan Santamaría can pick up their rental car from the agencies based at the airport, and then head out immediately on the open road.

⬎ RESOURCES

- **Costa Rica Tourism Board** (www. visitcostarica.com)
- **Tico Times** (www.ticotimes.net)

⬎ EMERGENCY NUMBERS

- **Emergency** (☎ 911)
- **Fire** (☎ 118)
- **Police** (☎ 117)
- **Red Cross** (☎ 128, 2221-5818)
- **Traffic Police** (☎ 2222-9330)

⬎ GETTING AROUND

- **Air** San José is the gateway to Costa Rica for the vast majority of international arrivals.
- **Bus** The intercity bus network is comprehensive, cheap and relatively reliable.
- **Taxi** Taxis are a safe and convenient way to move quickly between neighborhoods, especially at night.
- **Walk** The compact city center is perfect for a leisurely stroll during the daytime hours.

⬎ BE FOREWARNED

- **Crime** San José is a big city with rough areas like any other, so be sure to exercise a measure of street sense.
- **Traffic** If you've picked up a rental car at the airport, it's not recommended that you drive in the city proper. Dense traffic and a lack of public parking can quickly add up to a serious headache.

SAN JOSÉ

THINGS YOU NEED TO KNOW

DISCOVER SAN JOSÉ

Over the last century, the transformation from prewar agrarian coffee town to 21st-century urban sprawl has been unkind to the city's physical form. San José is not a pretty city. On some days, it is sensory overload: walk its teeming streets and you'll get jostled by businessmen grunting into cell phones and street vendors hawking fried bananas, all set to a soundtrack of tooting horns and roaring bus engines. But linger long enough and 'Chepe' – as San José is affectionately known – will begin to reveal its charms.

Duck into an anonymous-looking restaurant and you might find yourself in the middle of a garden, sipping wine beside a gushing fountain. A vintage house might conceal a cutting-edge contemporary art space. An unremarkable-looking hotel may have been the place where presidents once slept. It is a place rife with history. San José, after all, is where forward-thinking leaders once gathered to decide that this would be a country without an army.

ORIENTATION

San José's center is arranged in a grid with avenidas (avenues) running east to west and calles (streets) running north to south. The central area is home to innumerable businesses, bus terminals, hotels and cultural sites. West of the city center is La Sabana, named after the park. Further west is the affluent outer suburb of Escazú. Immediately east (and within walking distance) of the downtown area are the contiguous neighborhoods of Los Yoses and San Pedro.

INFORMATION

Instituto Costarricense de Turismo (ICT; Costa Rica Tourism Board; ☎ 2299-5800; www.visitcostarica.com; ☉ 9am-5pm with flexible lunch Mon-Fri) Correo Central (Map p68; Calle 2 btwn Avs 1 & 3); Plaza de la Cultura (Map p68; ☎ 2222-1090; Calle 5 btwn Avs Central & 2) The government tourism office is good for a copy of the master bus schedule and handy free maps of San José and Costa Rica.

SIGHTS
PLAZA DE LA CULTURA

For many Ticos, Costa Rica begins here. This architecturally unremarkable concrete **plaza** (Map p68; Avs Central & 2 btwn Calles 3 & 5) in the heart of downtown gets packed with locals slurping ice-cream cones and admiring the wide gamut of San José street life.

CATEDRAL METROPOLITANA

The **cathedral** (Map p68; Avs 2 & 4 btwn Calles Central & 1) was built in 1871 after the previous one was destroyed in an earthquake. The interiors, in keeping with the period, are a graceful neoclassic style, with colorful Spanish tile floors, stained-glass windows, and a Christ figure that was produced by a Guatemalan workshop in the late 17th century.

BARRIO AMÓN

North and west of the Jade Museum lies this pleasant, historic **neighborhood** (Map p64), home to a cluster of *cafetalero*

ADRIAN HEPWORTH/HEPWORTHIMAGES

Teatro Nacional, San José's cultural hub

◥ TEATRO NACIONAL

On the southern side of the Plaza de la Cultura resides the National Theater, San José's most revered public building. Constructed in 1897, it features a columned neoclassical facade that is flanked by statues of Beethoven and Calderón de la Barca, a 17th-century Spanish dramatist. The lavish marble lobby and auditorium are lined with paintings depicting various facets of 19th-century life. The most famous is *Alegoría al café y el banano*, an idyllic canvas showing coffee and banana harvests. The painting was produced in Italy and shipped to Costa Rica for installation in the theater, and the image was reproduced on the old ₡5 note (now out of circulation). As an interesting aside, it is clear that the painter never witnessed a banana harvest because of the way the man in the center is awkwardly grasping a bunch (actual banana workers hoist the stems onto their shoulders).

Things you need to know: Map p68; ☎ 2221-1329; Calles 3 & 5 btwn Avs Central & 2; admission US$7; ☺ 9am-4pm Mon-Sat

(coffee baron) mansions constructed during the late 19th and early 20th centuries.

PLAZA DE LA DEMOCRACIA

This stark **plaza** (Map p68; Avs Central & 2 btwn Calles 13 & 15) was constructed by President Oscar Arias Sánchez in 1989 to commemorate 100 years of Costa Rican democracy. Some of its elevated terraces provide decent views of the mountains surrounding San José.

MUSEUMS
MUSEO DE ORO PRECOLOMBINO Y NUMISMÁTICA

This **museum** (Map p68; ☎ 2243-4221; www.museosdelbancocentral.org; basement, Plaza de la Cultura; admission US$9; ☺ 9am-4:45pm Tue-Sun) is an important repository of Costa Rica's most priceless pieces of pre-Columbian gold, in addition to rare coins and temporary exhibitions. Look for intricate depictions of regional fauna.

MUSEO DE JADE

You will find the world's largest collection of American jade (pronounced 'ha-day' in Spanish) at this small **museum** (Map p68; ☎ 2287-6034; 1st fl, Edificio INS, Av 7 btwn Calles 9 & 11; adult/child under 11yr US$7/free; ⏱ 8:30am-3:30pm Mon-Fri, 9am-1pm Sat) on the 1st floor of the Instituto Nacional de Seguros (INS; National Insurance Institute).

MUSEO NACIONAL DE COSTA RICA

The **National Museum** (Map p64; ☎ 2257-1433; www.museocostarica.go.cr; Calle 17 btwn Avs Central & 2; adult/child US$6/3; ⏱ 8:30am-4:30pm Tue-Sun) provides a quick survey of Costa Rican history.

MUSEO DE ARTE Y DISEÑO CONTEMPORÁNEO

Commonly referred to as MADC, the **Contemporary Art and Design Museum** (Map p68; ☎ 2257-7202; www.madc.ac.cr; Av 3 btwn Calles 13 & 15; admission US$3; ⏱ 9am-4:45pm Mon-Sat) is the largest and most important contemporary art museum in the region.

MUSEO DE LOS NIÑOS & GALERÍA NACIONAL

If you were wondering how to get your young tykes interested in art and science, this unusual **museum** (Map p64; ☎ 2258-4929; www.museocr.com; Calle 4, north of Av 9; adult/child US$2/1.50; ⏱ 8am-4:30pm Tue-Fri, 9am-5pm Sat & Sun; 🐾) is an excellent place to start. Housed in an old penitentiary built in 1909, it is part children's museum and part art gallery.

PARKS

PARQUE NACIONAL

One of the nicest of San José's green spaces is the **Parque Nacional** (Map p64; Avs 1 & 3 btwn Calles 15 & 19), a shady spot where retirees arrive to read newspapers and young couples smooch coyly on concrete benches.

PARQUE METROPOLITANO LA SABANA

Known simply as **Parque La Sabana** (Map p53), this 72-hectare green space at the west end of the Paseo Colón was once the site of the country's main airport.

SAN JOSÉ FOR CHILDREN

Small children might enjoy a ride on the **Tico Train** (Map p68; adult/child US$2/1; ⏱ Sun), which picks up riders from the eastern side of the Plaza de la Cultura and takes them on a 45-minute joyride through the city.

The **Museo de los Niños** (see left) is a hit with children who just can't keep their hands off the exhibits, while teens might dig checking each other out at the **Plaza de la Cultura** (p60), which has a number of fast-food outlets and ice-cream shops nearby.

FESTIVALS & EVENTS

Festival de Arte Every even year, San José becomes host to a citywide arts showcase that features theater, music, dance and film. It's held for two weeks in March. Keep an eye out for information in the daily newspapers.

Día de San José (St Joseph's Day; March 19) San José marks the day of its patron saint with mass in some churches.

Festival de Luz (Festival of Light) A month after Paseo Colón's oxcart parade is the Christmas parade, marked by an absurd amount of plastic 'snow.'

Las Fiestas de Zapote (December 25 to January 1) The celebration, which annually draws in tens of thousands of Ticos, takes place at the bullring in the suburb of Zapote, just southeast of the city.

SAN JOSÉ

SLEEPING

SLEEPING

Hotel Aranjuez (Map p64; ☎ 2256-1825; www.hotelaranjuez.com; Calle 19 btwn Avs 11 & 13; s/d/tr from US$29/42/49, s/d without bathroom US$22/25, all incl breakfast; P 🖳 🛜 👪) This rambling hotel in Barrio Aranjuez consists of several nicely maintained vintage homes that have been strung together with connecting gardens. The breakfast buffet is served in the lush garden patio.

Kaps Place (Map p64; ☎ 2221-1169; www.kapsplace.com; s US$25-40, d US$50-60, tr US$70, apt US$80-115, all incl breakfast; P 🖳 🛜 👪) Calle 19 (Calle 19 btwn Avs 11 & 13); Av 11 (Av 11 btwn Calles 19 & 21) A colorful little guesthouse on a residential street in Barrio Aranjuez, Kaps has 24 small, homey rooms of various configurations spread over two buildings.

Rosa del Paseo (Map p64; ☎ 2257-3258; www.rosadelpaseo.com; Paseo Colón btwn Calles 28 & 30; s/d/ste from US$76/88/93; P 🖳) This sprawling Victorian mansion (built in 1897 by a family of coffee exporters) reaches into an interior garden courtyard that provides a respite from city noise.

Raya Vida Villa (Map p64; ☎ 2223-4168; www.rayavida.com; Calle 15, off Av 11; s/d incl breakfast US$85/95, extra person US$20; P) This longtime B&B, housed in a secluded hilltop villa, reflects owner Michael Long's interest in art and antiques.

Gran Hotel Costa Rica (Map p68; ☎ 2221-4000; www.grandhotelcostarica.com; Calle 3 btwn Avs Central & 2; d standard/superior US$96/121, junior ste/ste/master ste US$168/260/283, all incl breakfast; P 🕱 🖳) The city's first prominent hotel was constructed in 1930 and is today recognized as a national landmark.

Hotel Grano de Oro (Map p64; ☎ 2255-3322; www.hotelgranodeoro.com; Calle 30 btwn Avs 2 & 4; d US$115-165, f/garden/vista-del-oro ste US$175/210/305; P 🕱) Built around a sprawling early-20th-century Victorian mansion, this elegant inn has 40 demure 'Tropical Victorian' rooms furnished with wrought-iron beds and rich brocade linens.

EATING

Churrería Manolo's (Map p68; churros ₡200-275, mains ₡2400-3500, casados ₡2420; ✌ 7am-10pm) Av Central (Av Central btwn Calles Central

Gran Hotel Costa Rica has been declared a national landmark

IMAGEBROKER/OLIVER GERHARD

SAN JOSÉ

EATING

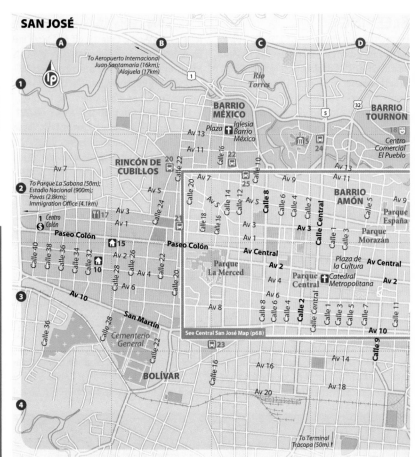

& 2); Av Central (**Av Central btwn Calles 9 & 11**) This San José institution is famous for its cream-filled *churros*, which draw crowds of hungry *josefinos* in search of a quick sugar rush.

Machu Picchu (Map p64; ☎ 2255-1717; Calle 32 btwn Avs 1 & 3; mains ₡4200-11,000; ⏰ 10am-10pm Mon-Sat, 11am-6pm Sun; ⚙) This locally renowned Peruvian restaurant will do you right if you have a hankering for all things Andean.

Nuestra Tierra (Map p68; cnr Av 2 & Calle 15; mains ₡5200-10,000; ⏰ 24hr; ⚙) Cheery waiters deliver wooden platters piled with heaping *casados* to hordes of hungry tourists and Tico families seated at rustic picnic-style tables.

El Patio (Map p68; ☎ 2221-1700; www. elpatiodelbalmoral.com; mains ₡5200-11,000; sandwiches ₡1400-2200; ⏰ 6am-10:30pm) Filled with chattering gringos and suited Ticos, this all-purpose cafe/restaurant is a good place to chill out while taking in the pedestrian action on Av Central. Bonus: on sunny days, the restaurant opens its retractable roof.

Restaurante Grano de Oro (Map p64; ☎ 2255-3322; Calle 30 btwn Avs 2 & 4; lunch

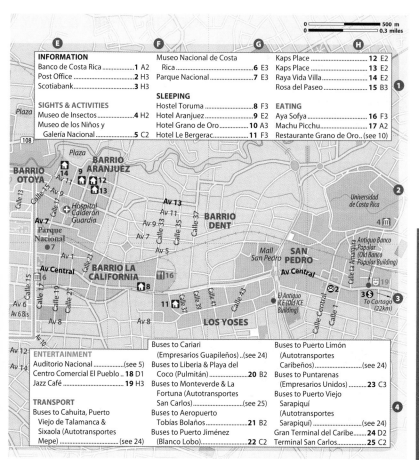

The map legend contains:

INFORMATION
Banco de Costa Rica **1** A2
Post Office **2** H3
Scotiabank...............................**3** H3

SIGHTS & ACTIVITIES
Museo de Insectos...................**4** H2
Museo de los Niños y
Galería Nacional **5** C2

Museo Nacional de Costa
Rica **6** E3
Parque Nacional **7** E3

SLEEPING
Hostel Toruma **8** F3
Hotel Aranjuez **9** E2
Hotel Grano de Oro **10** A3
Hotel Le Bergerac **11** F3

Kaps Place **12** E2
Kaps Place **13** E2
Raya Vida Villa **14** E2
Rosa del Paseo **15** B3

EATING
Aya Sofya **16** F3
Machu Picchu.........................**17** A2
Restaurante Grano de Oro..(see 10)

ENTERTAINMENT
Auditorio Nacional ....(see 5)
Centro Comercial El Pueblo ..**18** D1
Jazz Café **19** H3

TRANSPORT
Buses to Cahuita, Puerto
Viejo de Talamanca &
Sixaola (Autotransportes
Mepe) ....(see 24)

Buses to Cariari
(Empresarios Guapileños) ..(see 24)
Buses to Liberia & Playa del
Coco (Pulmitán) **20** B2
Buses to Monteverde & La
Fortuna (Autotransportes
San Carlos) ....(see 25)
Buses to Aeropuerto
Tobías Bolaños **21** B2
Buses to Puerto Jiménez
(Blanco Lobo).....................**22** C2

Buses to Puerto Limón
(Autotransportes
Caribeños) ....(see 24)
Buses to Puntarenas
(Empresarios Unidos) **23** C3
Buses to Puerto Viejo
Sarapiquí
(Autotransportes
Sarapiquí) ....(see 24)
Gran Terminal del Caribe........**24** D2
Terminal San Carlos................**25** C2

mains ₡5900-12,000, dinner mains ₡7500-15,600; noon-2pm & 6-10pm Mon-Sat) One of San José's top dining destinations is the stately, flower-filled restaurant at the Hotel Grano de Oro.

ENTERTAINMENT
NIGHTCLUBS
Centro Comercial El Pueblo (Map p64; P) This Spanish Mediterranean outdoor mall is a warren of bars, clubs and music venues, and a density of human activity on weekends. Things usually get going at about 9pm and shut down by 3am.

THEATER
Teatro Nacional (Map p68; ☎ 2221-5341; www.teatronacional.go.cr; Calles 3 & 5 btwn Avs Central & 2) Costa Rica's most important theater stages plays, dance, opera, symphonies, Latin American music performances and other major events.

SHOPPING
Galería Namu (Map p68; ☎ 2256-3412; www.galerianamu.com; Av 7 btwn Calles 5 & 7; 9:30am-6:30pm Mon-Sat, 9am-1:30pm Sun) A longtime fair-trade gallery run by Aisling French does a wonderful job of bringing

SAN JOSÉ

IMAGEBROKER/OLIVER GERHARD

Teatro Melico Salazar

⤷ IF YOU LIKE...

If you like the **Teatro Nacional** (p65), we think you'll like these other theaters in San José:

- **Auditorio Nacional** (Map p64; ☎ 2256-5876; www.museocr.com; Museo de los Niños, Calle 4, north of Av 9) A grand stage for concerts, dance theater and plays.
- **Little Theatre Group** (☎ 2289-3910; www.littletheatregroup.org) This English-language performance troupe has been around since the 1950s.
- **Teatro La Máscara** (Map p68; ☎ 2222-4574; Calle 13 btwn Avs 2 & 6) Dance performances as well as repertory theater.
- **Teatro Melico Salazar** (Map p68; ☎ 2233-5424; www. teatromelico.go.cr; Av 2 btwn Calles Central & 2) The restored 1920s theater has regular fine-arts performances.

together artwork and crafts from a diverse population of regional ethnicities.

Mercado Central (Map p68; Avs Central & 1 btwn Calles 6 & 8; ☺ 6am-6pm Mon-Sat) The bustling central market is the best place in the city for just about anything you'd want. It is lined with vendors hawking everything from cheese and spices to export-quality coffee beans and obligatory *pura vida* souvenir T-shirts.

GETTING THERE & AWAY

GETTING THERE & AWAY
AIR
Aeropuerto Internacional Juan Santamaría (Map p53; ☎ 2437-2400; Alajuela) handles international air traffic in its main terminal. For domestic and charter flights, head to **Aeropuerto Tobías Bolaños** (Map p53; ☎ 2232-2820; Pavas).

BUS
Dozens of private companies operate out of stops scattered throughout the city. Bus schedules change regularly – get a useful but not always up-to-date master schedule from the ICT office (p60).

TO THE CENTRAL VALLEY
Alajuela Tuasa (Map p68; Av 2 btwn Calles 12 & 14) ₡400; 40 minutes; departs every 10 minutes from 4am to 11pm, every 30 minutes after 11pm.

Cartago (Map p68; Calle 13 btwn Avs 6 & 8) ₡500; 40 minutes; departs hourly between 5:15am and 10pm.

Heredia (Map p68; Calle 1 btwn Avs 7 & 9) ₡400; 20 minutes; departs every 10 minutes from 5am to 11pm.

Sarchí (Map p68; Av 5 btwn Calles 18 & 20) ₡1000; 1½ hours; departs every 30 minutes from 5am to 10pm.

Turrialba (Map p68; Calle 13 btwn Avs 6 & 8) ₡1100; two hours; departs hourly from 5am to 10pm.

Volcán Irazú (Map p68; Av 2 btwn Calles 1 & 3) Round-trip ₡2500; two hours; departs at 8am.

TO NORTHERN COSTA RICA
La Fortuna Autotransportes San Carlos (Map p64; Terminal San Carlos) ₡2900; four hours; departs at 6:15am, 8:30am and 11:30am.

Liberia Pulmitán (Map p64; ☎ 2666-0458; Calle 24 btwn Avs 5 & 7) ₡2800; four hours; departs hourly from 6am to 8pm.

Monteverde & Santa Elena Autotransportes San Carlos (Map p64; Calle 12 btwn Avs 7 & 9) ₡3200; 4½ hours; departs at 6:30am and 2:30pm. (This bus fills up quickly – book ahead.)

Puerto Viejo de Sarapiquí Autotransportes Sarapiquí (Map p64; Gran Terminal del Caribe) ₡1400, two hours, departs at 6:30am, 7:30am, 10am, 11:30am, 1:30pm, 2:30pm, 3:30pm, 4:30pm, 5:30pm and 6pm.

TO THE PENÍNSULA DE NICOYA

Montezuma & Mal País (Map p68; Terminal Coca-Cola) ₡6800; six hours; departs at 6am and 2pm.

Playa Brasilito Tralapa (Map p68; Calle 20 btwn Avs 3 & 5) ₡4600; six hours; departs at 8am, 10:30am and 2pm.

Playa del Coco Pulmitán (Map p64; Calle 24 btwn Avs 5 & 7) ₡3300; five hours; departs at 8am, 2pm and 4pm.

Playa Nosara Empresas Alfaro (Map p68; ☎ 2256-7050; Av 5 btwn Calles 14 & 16) ₡3900; six hours; departs at 5am.

Playa Sámara Empresas Alfaro (Map p68; ☎ 2256-7050; Av 5 btwn Calles 14 & 16) ₡3600; five hours; departs at noon.

Playa Tamarindo Empresas Alfaro (Map p68; ☎ 2256-7050; Av 5 btwn Calles 14 & 16) ₡4400; five hours; departs at 11:30am and 3:30pm.

Santa Cruz Empresas Alfaro (Map p68; ☎ 2256-7050; Av 5 btwn Calles 14 & 16) ₡4200; five hours; departs at 6am, 8am, 9:45am, 11am, noon, 12:30pm, 2pm, 4:30pm, 5:30pm and 7pm.

TO THE CENTRAL PACIFIC COAST

Dominical & Uvita Transportes Morales (Map p68; Terminal Coca-Cola) ₡2500; seven hours; departs at 6am and 3pm.

Jacó Transportes Jacó (Map p68; ☎ 2290-2922; Terminal Coca-Cola) ₡2000; three hours; departs at 6am, 7am, 9am, 11am, 1pm, 3pm, 5pm and 7pm.

Puntarenas Empresarios Unidos (Map p64; ☎ 2222-8231; cnr Av 12 & Calle 16) ₡1500; 2½ hours; departs hourly at 6am and 7pm.

Quepos & Manuel Antonio Transportes Morales (Map p68; Terminal Coca-Cola) ₡3500 to ₡3700; four hours; departs approximately every 90 minutes from 6am to 7:30pm.

TO SOUTHERN COSTA RICA

The following buses depart from Terminal Tracopa bus stop (off Map p64) unless otherwise indicated.

ADRIAN HEPWORTH/HEPWORTHIMAGES

Herb seller, Mercado Central (p66)

↘ IF YOU LIKE...

If you like the **Mercado Central** (p66), we think you'll like these other markets in San José:

- **Mercado Borbón** (Map p68; cnr Av 3 & Calle 8) Adjacent to the Mercado Central, the Borbón is more focused on fresh produce.
- **Mercado Central Annex** (Map p68; Avs 1 & 3 btwn Calles 6 & 8) This market is less touristy, and crowded with butchers, fishmongers and informal food counters.
- **Mercado Artesanal** (Map p68; Plaza de la Democracia; Avs Central & 2 btwn Calles 13 & 15; ☻ midmorning-sunset) This touristy open-air market sells typical handicrafts and souvenirs.

CENTRAL SAN JOSÉ

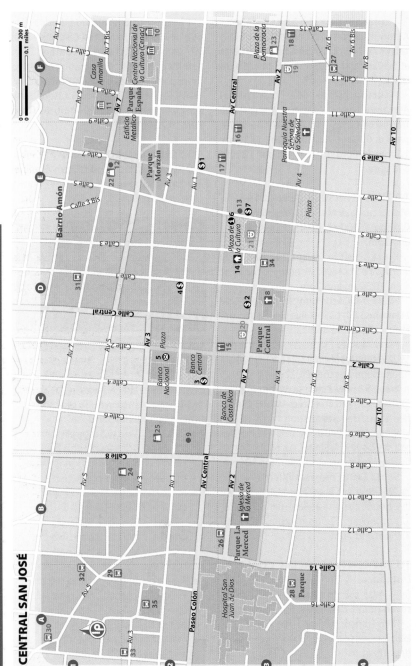

Ciudad Neily Tracopa (☎ 2221-4214; Calle 5 btwn Avs 18 & 20) ₡5000; eight hours; departs at 5am, 1pm, 4:30pm and 6:30pm.

Golfito Tracopa (☎ 2221-4214; Calle 5 btwn Avs 18 & 20) ₡4700; eight hours; departs at 7am, 3:30pm and 10:15pm.

Palmar Norte Tracopa (☎ 2221-4214; Calle 5 btwn Avs 18 & 20) ₡2800; five hours; departs at 5am, 7am, 8:30am, 10am, 1pm, 2:30pm and 4:30pm.

Paso Canoas Tracopa (☎ 2221-4214; Calle 5 btwn Avs 18 & 20) ₡5000; six hours; departs at 5am, 1pm, 4:30pm and 6:30pm.

Puerto Jiménez Blanco Lobo (Map p64; ☎ 2221-4214; Calle 12 btwn Avs 9 & 11) ₡5900; eight hours; departs at 6am and noon. (This bus fills up quickly in high season; buy tickets in advance.)

San Isidro de El General Tracopa (☎ 2221-4214; Calle 5 btwn Avs 18 & 20) ₡2100; three hours; departs hourly from 5am to 6:30pm; Transportes Musoc (Calle Central btwn Avs 22 & 24) ₡2100, three hours, departs hourly from 5:30am to 5:30pm.

San Vito Tracopa (☎ 2221-4214; Calle 5 btwn Avs 18 & 20) ₡4200; seven hours; departs at 6am, 8:15am, noon and 4pm.

TO THE CARIBBEAN COAST

Cahuita Autotransportes Mepe (Map p64; Gran Terminal del Caribe) ₡3700; four hours; departs at 6am, 10am, noon, 2pm and 4pm.

Cariari Empresarios Guapileños (Map p64; Gran Terminal del Caribe) ₡1400; 2¼ hours; departs at 6:30am, 9am, 10:30am, 1pm, 3pm, 4:30pm, 6pm and 7pm.

Puerto Limón Autotransportes Caribeños (Map p64; Gran Terminal del Caribe) ₡2500; three hours; departs roughly every 30 minutes from 5am to 7pm.

Puerto Viejo de Talamanca Autotransportes Mepe (Map p64; Gran Terminal del Caribe) ₡4300; 4½ hours; departs at 6am, 10am, noon, 2pm and 4pm.

Sixaola Autotransportes Mepe (Map p64; Gran Terminal del Caribe) ₡5300; six hours; departs at 6am, 10am, noon, 2pm and 4pm.

TOURIST BUSES

Grayline's Fantasy Bus (☎ 2220-2126; www.graylinecostarica.com) and **Interbus** (☎ 2283-5573; www.interbusonline.com) run air-con minivans to many places around Costa Rica. They cost more than standard buses, but offer faster, door-to-door service.

SAN JOSÉ

GETTING THERE & AWAY

INFORMATION		
Banco de Costa Rica	**1**	E2
Banco de San José	**2**	D3
Banco Nacional de Costa Rica		
Exchange House	**3**	C2
Citibank	**4**	D2
Correo Central	**5**	C2
ICT (Tourist Office)	(see 5)	
ICT (Tourist Office)	**6**	E3
Scotiabank	**7**	E3

SIGHTS & ACTIVITIES		
Catedral Metropolitana	**8**	D3
Mercado Central	**9**	C2
Museo de Arte y Diseño		
Contemporáneo	**10**	F2
Museo de Jade	**11**	F1
Museo de Oro Precolombino		
y Numismática	(see 6)	
Rainforest Aerial Tram Office	**12**	E1
Teatro Nacional	(see 21)	
Tico Train	**13**	E3

SLEEPING		
Gran Hotel Costa Rica	**14**	D3

EATING		
Churrería Manolo's	**15**	C3
Churrería Manolo's	**16**	E3
El Patio	**17**	E3
Mercado Central	(see 9)	
Nuestra Tierra	**18**	F3

ENTERTAINMENT		
Teatro La Máscara	**19**	F3
Teatro Melico Salazar	**20**	D3
Teatro Nacional	**21**	D3

SHOPPING		
Galería Namu	**22**	E1
Mercado Artesanal	**23**	F3
Mercado Borbón	**24**	B2
Mercado Central	(see 9)	
Mercado Central Annex	**25**	C2

TRANSPORT		
Buses to Alajuela,		
Volcán Poás & Airport		
(Tuasa)	**26**	B3
Buses to Cartago &		
Turrialba	**27**	F4

Buses to Dominical &		
Uvita (Transportes		
Morales)	(see 35)	
Buses to Escazú	**28**	A3
Buses to Escazú	**29**	A1
Buses to Sarchí	**30**	A1
Buses to Heredia	**31**	D1
Buses to Jacó		
(Transportes Jacó)	(see 35)	
Buses to Montezuma &		
Mal País	(see 35)	
Buses to Península de		
Nicoya, Playa Nosara,		
Playa Sámara, Santa		
Cruz & Playa		
Tamarindo		
(Empresas Alfaro)	**32**	A1
Buses to Playa Brasilito		
(Tralapa)	**33**	A2
Buses to Quepos &		
Manuel Antonio		
(Transportes		
Morales)	(see 35)	
Buses to Volcán Irazú	**34**	D3
Terminal Coca-Cola	**35**	A2

GETTING AROUND
TO/FROM THE AIRPORTS
TO/FROM AEROPUERTO INTERNACIONAL JUAN SANTAMARÍA

You can reserve a pickup with **Taxi Aeropuerto** (☎ 2221-6865; www.taxiaeropuerto.com), which charges a flat rate of between US$21 and US$30 for trips to and from most parts of San José. (These are a bright orange color.) You can also take a street taxi, but the rates may vary wildly. Plan on spending at least ₡11,000 to ₡14,000 (roughly US$20 to US$25), more in heavy traffic.

Interbus (☎ 2283-5573; www.interbusonline.com) runs an airport shuttle service that will pick you up at your hotel (US$10 per person), good value if you're traveling alone. The cheapest option is the red **Tuasa bus** (Map p68; cnr Calle 10 & Av 2; ₡400) bound for Alajuela. Be sure to tell the driver that you are getting off at the airport (say: *Voy al aeropuerto, por favor.*).

From downtown, the drive to the airport can take anywhere from 20 minutes to an hour (more if you take the bus) – and vice versa. Plan accordingly.

TO/FROM AEROPUERTO TOBÍAS BOLAÑOS

Buses to Tobías Bolaños (see Map p64) depart every 30 minutes from Av 1, 250m west of the Terminal Coca-Cola. A taxi to the airport from downtown starts at about ₡6600 (or about US$12). **Interbus** (☎ 2283-5573; www.interbusonline.com) also has an airport shuttle service for US$10.

CAR

It is not advisable to rent a car just to drive around San José. The traffic is heavy and the streets narrow – hire one of the plentiful taxis instead. If you are renting a car to travel throughout Costa Rica, however, you will not be short of choices: there are more than 50 car-rental agencies – including many of the global brands – in and around San José. The travel desks at travel agencies and upmarket hotels can arrange rentals; likewise, you can arrange rentals online and at the airport.

TAXI

Red taxis can be hailed on the street day or night, or you can have your hotel call one for you. You can also hire taxis at the stands at the Parque Nacional, Parque Central and near the Teatro Nacional.

Short rides downtown cost ₡1000 to ₡2000. A taxi to Escazú from downtown will cost roughly ₡4500, while a ride to Los Yoses or San Pedro will generally cost about ₡2000. There's a 20% surcharge after 10pm that may not appear on the *maría*.

You can hire a taxi and a driver for half a day or longer if you want to do some touring around the area, but rates vary wildly depending on the destination and the condition of the roads. For these trips, it is best to negotiate a flat fee in advance.

ROBERTO GEROMETTA

Typical city bus, San José

AROUND SAN JOSÉ

LOS YOSES & SAN PEDRO

Los Yoses is a charming residential district dotted with modernist structures, historic homes, cozy inns and chilled-out neighborhood eateries. San Pedro, on the other hand, which houses the university district, is more boisterous. Both of these areas provide an enticing (and convenient) alternative to staying in San José.

SIGHTS

The **Museo de Insectos** (Insect Museum; Map p64; ☎ 2511-5318; admission US$2; ☺ 1-5pm Mon-Fri; ♿), also known as the Museo de Entomología, has a fine collection of insects assembled by the Facultad de Agronomía at the Universidad de Costa Rica.

SLEEPING & EATING

Hostel Toruma (Map p64; ☎ 2234-8186; www.hosteltoruma.com; Av Central btwn Calles 29 & 33, Los Yoses; dm/s/d US$12/35/45; P ☐ ☎ ☒) Overlooking Av Central from a small hill, this graceful neoclassical home once belonged to José Figueres. While there are four dormitories, it feels much more like an inn, with 17 large private rooms.

Hotel Le Bergerac (Map p64; ☎ 2234-7850; www.bergerachotel.com; Calle 35 btwn Avs Central & 8, Los Yoses; d standard/superior/deluxe/grande US$90/115/135/145, all incl breakfast; P ☐) A whitewashed building contains a bright lobby accented with fresh flowers and 25 rooms that overlook a tropical garden at this Los Yoses standard-bearer.

Aya Sofya (Map p64; ☎ 2224-5050; cnr Calle 33 & Av 1, Los Yoses; dishes ₡2600-7900; ☺ 7am-7pm Mon-Sat; Ⓥ) A hidden gem with a diminutive outdoor patio serves a variety of Mediterranean specialties, including fresh hummus, green salads with feta cheese, chicken sandwiches with tangy yogurt sauce, and changing daily specials.

ENTERTAINMENT

Jazz Café (Map p64; ☎ 2253-8933; www.jazzcafecostarica.com; ☺ 6pm-2am) is *the* destination in San José for live music, with a different band every night. Countless performers have taken to the stage here, including legendary Cuban bandleader Chucho Valdés and Colombian pop star Juanes. Admission charges vary, but plan on spending about ₡4000 for local groups. It's 50m east of the Antiguo Banco Popular.

GETTING THERE & AWAY

From the Plaza de la Cultura in San José, take any bus marked 'Mall San Pedro.' A taxi from downtown costs about ₡2000, depending on traffic. Otherwise, to get into San José, buses make stops all along Av Central heading west into the city.

ESCAZÚ

You can find an unusual juxtaposition of gringo expats, moneyed aristocrats and old-world Tico village life in this sprawling suburb that climbs a steep hillside overlooking San José and Heredia. The area consists of three adjoining neighborhoods: San Rafael de Escazú, Escazú Centro and San Antonio de Escazú, each of which has its own unique character.

SIGHTS

The best spot for a walk are the narrow, gridded streets of Escazú Centro, which contains at its heart a small park and the **Iglesia Escazú** (Map p72; cnr Av Central & Calle Central).

FESTIVALS & EVENTS

On the second Sunday of March, Escazú is home to **Día del Boyero**, a celebration in honor of oxcart drivers. The country's *boyeros* join in a procession with their traditional, colorful oxcarts.

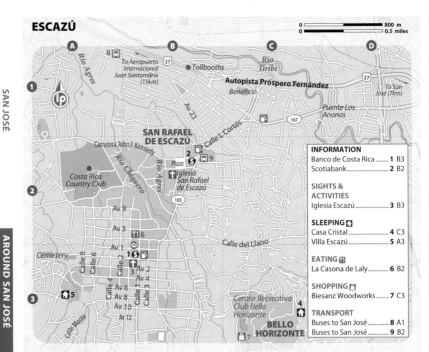

INFORMATION
Banco de Costa Rica **1** B3
Scotiabank **2** B2

SIGHTS & ACTIVITIES
Iglesia Escazú **3** B3

SLEEPING
Casa Cristal **4** C3
Villa Escazú **5** A3

EATING
La Casona de Laly **6** B2

SHOPPING
Biesanz Woodworks **7** C3

TRANSPORT
Buses to San José **8** A1
Buses to San José **9** B2

SLEEPING & EATING

Villa Escazú (Map p72; ☎ 2289-7971; www.hotels
.co.cr/vescazu.html; Escazú Centro; s/d/tr without
bathroom incl breakfast US$50/60/75, 2-night mini-
mum; P 🛜) This two-story wood chalet
with a wraparound veranda is surrounded
by gardens and fruit trees.

Casa Cristal (Map p72; ☎ 2289-2530; www.
casacristalcr.com; Bello Horizonte; d incl breakfast US$130-225; P ⊠ ⊠ 🛜 ⊠) This chic,
whitewashed boutique hotel is situated
on what has to be the best piece of real
estate in Escazú: at the end of a winding
mountain road, on a hillside overlooking
several dozen hectares of uninhabited
parkland, with the twinkling lights of San
José in the distance.

La Casona de Laly (Map p72; cnr Av 3 & Calle
Central, Escazú Centro; bocas ₡1000-2200, casados
₡1900, mains ₡2200-7000; 🕙 11am-12:30am Tue-
Sat, 11am-6pm Sun) At the heart of Escazú

Centro, this much loved restaurant-tavern
specializes in country-style Tico fare.

SHOPPING

Biesanz Woodworks (Map p72; ☎ 2289-
4337; www.biesanz.com; 🕙 8am-5pm Mon-Fri,
10am-4pm Sat & Sun) Located in the hills of
Bello Horizonte in Escazú, this shop is
one of the finest woodcrafting studios
in the nation, run by celebrated artisan
Barry Biesanz. His bowls and other decorative containers are exquisite and take
their inspiration from pre-Columbian
techniques.

GETTING THERE & AWAY

Frequent buses between San José and
Escazú cost about ₡300 and take about
25 minutes. All depart San José (Map p68)
from east of the Coca-Cola Terminal or
south of the Hospital San Juan de Dios.

CENTRAL VALLEY

CENTRAL VALLEY

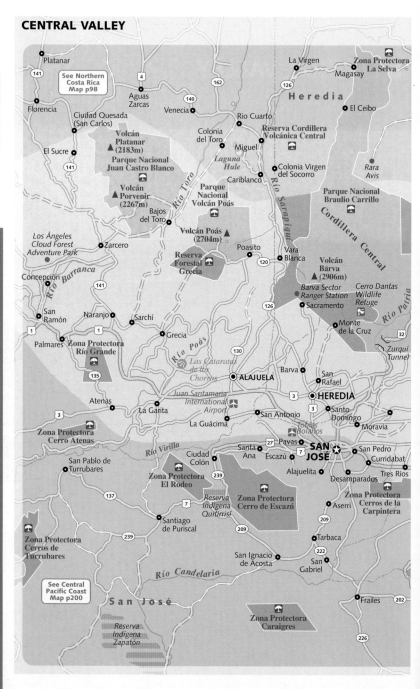

Platanar
141
See Northern Costa Rica Map p98
4
162
126
La Virgen
Zona Protectora La Selva
Magasay
Florencia
Aguas Zarcas
140
H e r e d i a
Ciudad Quesada (San Carlos)
Venecia
Río Cuarto
El Ceibo
141
Volcán Platanar (2183m)
Colonia del Toro
Reserva Cordillera Volcánica Central
El Sucre
Parque Nacional Juan Castro Blanco
Miguel
Laguna Hule
Colonia Virgen del Socorro
Rara Avis
Volcán Porvenir (2267m)
Parque Nacional Volcán Poás
Cariblanco
Parque Nacional Braulio Carrillo
Bajos del Toro
Río Toro
Cordillera Central
Los Ángeles Cloud Forest Adventure Park
Zarcero
Volcán Poás (2704m)
Poasito
Vara Blanca
Volcán Barva (2906m)
Cerro Dantas Wildlife Refuge
Concepción
Río Barranca
141
Reserva Forestal Grecia
120
Río Patria
San Ramón
Naranjo
Sarchí
Barva Sector Ranger Station
126
Sacramento
Monte de la Cruz
32
1
1
Grecia
130
Zurquí Tunnel
Palmares
Zona Protectora Río Grande
Río Poás
Las Cataratas de los Chorros
Barva
San Rafael
135
Atenas
La Garita
Juan Santamaría International Airport
ALAJUELA
3
HEREDIA
Santo Domingo
3
Moravia
San Antonio
3
Zona Protectora Cerro Atenas
La Guácima
Tobías Bolaños
San Pablo de Turrubares
Río Virilla
Ciudad Colón
Santa Ana
Pavas
27
SAN JOSÉ
San Pedro
Curridabat
Tres Ríos
Zona Protectora El Rodeo
239
Escazú
7
Alajuelita
Desamparados
137
Reserva Indígena Quitirrisí
7
Zona Protectora Cerro de Escazú
209
Aserri
Zona Protectora Cerros de la Carpintera
Zona Protectora Cerros de Turrubares
Santiago de Puriscal
239
209
Tarbaca
222
San Ignacio de Acosta
San Gabriel
Río Candelaria
See Central Pacific Coast Map p200
S a n   J o s é
Frailes
202
Reserva Indígena Zapatón
Zona Protectora Caraigres
226

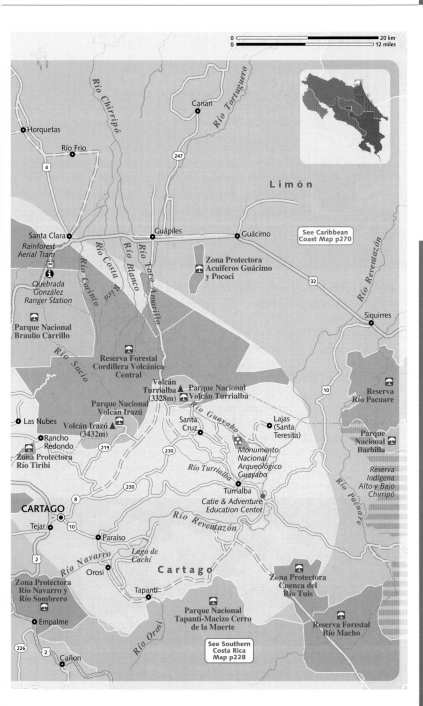

0   20 km
0   12 miles

Cariari

Río Chirripó

Río Tortuguero

Horquetas

Río Frio

4

247

L i m ó n

Santa Clara

Guápiles

Guácimo

See Caribbean
Coast Map p270

Rainforest
Aerial Tram

Río Costa Rica

Río Blanco

Río Toro Amarillo

Río Corinto

Zona Protectora
Acuiferos Guácimo
y Pococi

32

Río Reventazón

Quebrada
González
Ranger Station

Siquirres

Parque Nacional
Braulio Carrillo

Río Sucio

Reserva Forestal
Cordillera Volcánica
Central

Reserva
Río Pacuare

10

Volcán
Turrialba
(3328m)

Parque Nacional
Volcán Turrialba

Parque Nacional
Volcán Irazú

Río Guayabo

Las Nubes

Volcán Irazú
(3432m)

Santa
Cruz

Lajas
(Santa
Teresita)

Parque
Nacional
Barbilla

Rancho
Redondo

219

230

Monumento
Nacional
Arqueológico
Guayabo

Zona Protectora
Río Tiribi

Río Turrialba

Reserva
Indígena
Alto y Bajo
Chirripó

230

Turrialba

Río Pacuare

8

Catie & Adventure
Education Center

CARTAGO

Tejar

10

Paraíso

Río Reventazón

2

Río Navarro

Lago de
Cachí

Orosi

C a r t a g o

Zona Protectora
Río Navarro y
Río Sombrero

Tapantí

Zona Protectora
Cuenca del
Río Tuis

Empalme

Parque Nacional
Tapantí-Macizo Cerro
de la Muerte

Río Orosi

Reserva Forestal
Río Macho

226

2

Cañón

See Southern
Costa Rica
Map p228

CENTRAL VALLEY HIGHLIGHTS

1 RAFTING IN TURRIALBA

BY DANIEL BUSTOS ARAYA, RIVER GUIDE FOR EXPLORNATURA

Turrialba is a beautiful town in Costa Rica's Central Valley. The geography of this region caters to people who like real white-water rafting. With big mountains and a long rainy season, Turrialba lies close to an excellent group of fast and furious rivers. Another reason to come here on a rafting trip are the very professional and friendly local guides.

⬎ DANIEL BUSTOS ARAYA'S DON'T MISS LIST

❶ RÍO REVENTAZÓN FOR BEGINNERS

The Río Reventazón (p95) is divided into four sections between the dam and the take-out point in Siquirres. Las Máquinas (Power House) is a Class II–III float that's perfect for families, while Florida, the final and most popular segment, is a scenic Class III with a little more white water to keep things interesting.

❷ RÍO REVENTAZÓN FOR THRILL-SEEKERS

If you've gone white-water rafting before, or you're confident in your physical prowess and quick reflexes, you might want to consider some of the more advanced runs on the Río Reventazón (p95). The Pascua section has 15 Class IV rapids – featuring names like 'The Abyss' – and is widely considered to be the most classic run in the area. The Class V Peralta segment is extremely challenging and not for

Clockwise from top: Paddling the white water of Río Pacuare (p95); Down the rapids of Río Pacuare (p95)

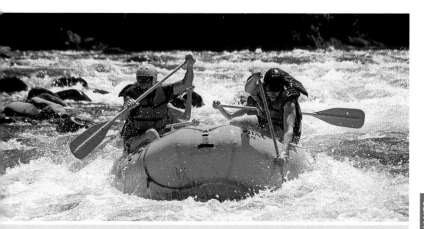

CENTRAL VALLEY

CENTRAL VALLEY HIGHLIGHTS

the faint of heart. Tours do not always run it due to safety concerns.

❸ LOWER PACUARE

Not to be outdone by its top competitor, the **Río Pacuare** (p95) is divided into lower and upper stretches, both of which are home to an excellent variety of white-water runs. The Class III–IV Lower Pacuare is the more accessible bit: 28km through rocky gorges and isolated canyons, past an indigenous village, untamed jungle and lots of wildlife curious as to what the screaming is all about.

❹ UPPER PACUARE

The upper reaches of the **Río Pacuare** (p95) are also classified as Class III–IV, but there are a few sections that can go to Class V depending on conditions. It's about a two-hour drive to the put-in, so you need a bit more time to access this remote stretch. It's most definitely worth the trip though, especially since you'll be able to paddle alongside the area's densest jungles.

↘ THINGS YOU NEED TO KNOW

Access Turrialba (p93) is the preferred base for white-water rafting in the Central Valley **Best time to visit** The rainy season runs from June through October, and makes for exhilarating rafting conditions **See the author's coverage, p95**

CENTRAL VALLEY

CENTRAL VALLEY HIGHLIGHTS

CENTRAL VALLEY HIGHLIGHTS

⬎ VOLCÁN IRAZÚ

The roof of the Central Valley is this 3432m-tall active **volcano** (p91), which in the country's brief history has unleashed its liquid fury more than 15 times. These days, things have temporarily quietened down, meaning that hiking around the summit is safer than you might imagine. When the weather is clear, you can soak up impressive views reaching out to both the Pacific Ocean and the Caribbean Sea.

⬎ MONUMENTO NACIONAL ARQUEOLÓGICO GUAYABO

Although not comparable to the elaborate temple complexes elsewhere in Central America, this **archaeological site** (p95) is Costa Rica's clearest window into the past. The modest remains of a pre-Columbian city, Guayabo was once inhabited by sophisticated urban dwellers more than 20,0000 strong. You can still see evidence wrought in stone, including cisterns, cobbled roads and sunken foundations.

4

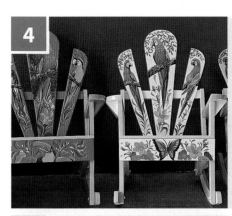

↘ SARCHÍ

Something of a shopper's paradise for authentic souvenirs, Sarchí (p86) is the birthplace of the *carreta* (painted oxcart). Beyond these colorful symbols of the Costa Rican working class, this tiny town in the Central Valley is also home to dozens of woodworking studios that fashion richly hued hardwoods into elaborate handicrafts.

5

↘ BARVA

Lying on the edge of the city of Heredia, the historic colonial town of Barva (p89) was first settled in 1561 by the Spanish conquistadors, though many of the present buildings were constructed in the 19th century. Architecture aside, Barva is also the home of the most famous coffee roaster in Costa Rica, namely Café Britt.

6

↘ CARTAGO

Costa Rica's second city and long-term rival to San José, Cartago (p90) has weathered its fair share of natural disasters over the centuries. Today it plays second fiddle to the capital, though it does remain the guardian of La Negrita, a venerated religious artifact that is housed in the city's grand basilica.

2 PATRICK HORTON; 3 STEVE BLY/ALAMY; 4 RICHARD CUMMINS; 5 CHRISTOPHER BAKER; 6 IMAGEBROKER/SIEPMANN

2 Parque Nacional Volcán Irazú (p91); 3 Monumento Nacional Arqueológico Guayabo (p95); 4 Colorful handicrafts, Sarchí (p86); 5 Barva (p89); 6 Basílica de Nuestra Señora de los Ángeles, Cartago (p92)

THE CENTRAL VALLEY'S BEST...

⬎ HISTORICAL SITES

- **Museo Juan Santamaría** (p84) Here you can learn about Costa Rica's most famous drummer boy.
- **El Fortín** (p89) The remains of a Spanish fortress is the symbol of Heredia.
- **Basílica de Nuestra Señora de los Ángeles** (p92) The country's most celebrated religious monument.
- **Guayabo** (p95) Costa Rica's most prominent pre-Columbian site.

⬎ SPLURGES

- **Xandari Resort Hotel & Spa** (p85) Bed down in a working coffee plantation before grabbing your flight home.
- **Casa Turire** (p94) An exceedingly elegant throwback to the colonial era.
- **Sarchí** (p86) Bring your cash and shop 'til you drop for woodworks.

⬎ VISTAS

- **Palmares** (p87) Few can forget the sight of tens of thousands of raging festival-goers.
- **Cartago** (p90) The annual pilgrimage attracts devotees who walk to the basilica on their knees.
- **Volcán Irazú** (p91) The top panorama in the region takes in both coastlines.

⬎ EATS & DRINKS

- **Restaurante Betico Mata** (p94) Home to Costa Rica's version of the taco.
- **Café Britt Finca** (p89) The best spot for a freshly brewed cup of shade-grown coffee.
- **La Mansarda** (p85) A neighborhood eatery offering excellent people-watching.

IMAGEBROKER/JAN KRIMMER

Mountain vistas, Orosi (p87)

THINGS YOU NEED TO KNOW

⬎ VITAL STATISTICS

- **Population** Alajuela 43,000; Heredia 33,000; Cartago 24,000; Turrialba 27,000
- **Best time to visit** Las Fiestas de Palmares (mid-January), Feria de la Mascarada (March), pilgrimage to Cartago (August 2), peak white-water (June through October)

⬎ CITIES IN A NUTSHELL

- **Alajuela** (p84) The largest city in the Central Valley is a convenient port of entry and subsequent departure point for international flights.
- **Heredia** (p88) A relaxed city with colonial airs that serves as a jumping-off point for the town of Barva and its famous coffee roaster.
- **Cartago** (p90) Costa Rica's first settlement is home to some of the country's most historic structures including the Basílica de Nuestra Señora de los Ángeles.
- **Turrialba** (p93) Home to the country's best white-water rafting.

⬎ ADVANCE PLANNING

- **Car rental** Travelers touching down at Aeropuerto Internacional Juan Santamaría can pick up their rental car from the agencies based at the airport, and then head out immediately on the open road.

⬎ RESOURCES

- **Costa Rica Tourism Board** (www.visitcostarica.com)
- **Tico Times** (www.ticotimes.net)

⬎ EMERGENCY NUMBERS

- **Emergency** (☎ 911)
- **Fire** (☎ 118)
- **Police** (☎ 117)

⬎ GETTING AROUND

- **Air** Alajuela – not San José – is actually the closest city to the international airport.
- **Bus** Intercity bus connections are fast and frequent.
- **Car** Winding mountain roads offer expansive views over the valley.
- **Walk** All of the major cities in the region are relatively safe to walk around by day.

⬎ BE FOREWARNED

- **Signage** Roads in the Central Valley are poorly signed, so it's best to bring along a good road map when setting out.

CENTRAL VALLEY

THINGS YOU NEED TO KNOW

CENTRAL VALLEY ITINERARIES

TURRIALBA & AROUND Three Days

If your time is limited, this itinerary is perfect for getting a quick taste of what the region has to offer. Furthermore, if your travels started in San José, you need only hop a quick bus to Turrialba, and then use the town as a base for exploring a couple of the Central Valley's top highlights.

After spending some time getting your bearings in (1) **Turrialba** (p93), your first order of business is to arrange a white-water rafting trip with any of the town's recommended operators. Depending on the time of year and your skill level, your next destination will be one of the stretches along the (2) **Ríos Reventazón & Pacuare** (p95). Day trips can take in a good sampling of rapids, though you can always extend your time out on the water with an overnight. When you're ready to dial things down a notch, the (3) **Monumento Nacional Arqueológico Guayabo** (p95) provides a rich cultural perspective on the pre-Columbian inhabitants of the area.

CITY-HOPPING Five Days

Costa Rica's beaches and rainforests may garner most of the spotlight, but to truly understand the country, you need to understand its people. Considering that the vast majority of Ticos live in the cities of the Central Valley, spending a few days here will enable you to put your finger on the pulse of the modern nation. Plus, frequent bus connections mean that moving back and forth is a snap.

As the closest city to the airport, (1) **Alajuela** (p84) provides a soft landing for bleary-eyed travelers, but it's also home to an attractive city park that invites long bouts of people-watching. Home to a large university, (2) **Heredia** (p88) bustles with activity, and has a few storied buildings that retell Costa Rica's history as a Spanish colony. The original capital and long-time rival of San José (especially on the soccer field!), (3) **Cartago** (p90) is centered on one of the most impressive basilicas in the whole of Central America. Finally, though it's not much more than an oversized town in comparison to the big three, (4) **Turrialba** (p93) offers up some bucolic charm in addition to stunning natural surrounds.

CENTRAL VALLEY EXPLORER One Week

If you have a full week to devote to exploring the Central Valley, consider picking up a rental car at the airport when you arrive. In addition to freeing you from the clutches of bus timetables, you'll also be able to move around at your own pace, and stop at a whole slew of tiny towns and villages that give the region its charming character.

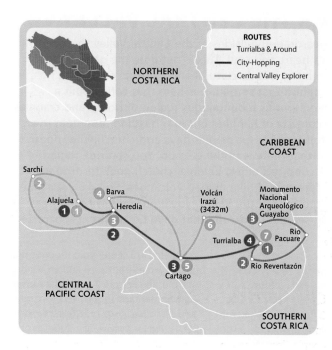

Starting in (1) Alajuela (p84), take a quick detour to the shopper's paradise that is (2) Sarchí (p86). Next stop on the itinerary is (3) Heredia (p88), but be sure to get out of the city and visit the attractive colonial town of (4) Barva (p89) for some of the country's best coffee. The trip continues to (5) Cartago (p90), but the emphasis should be on the city's nemesis, namely the hulking (6) Volcán Irazú (p91). You can wind things down in (7) Turrialba (p93), using the remainder of your time to go rafting, visiting ruins or just soaking up the beautiful countryside.

DISCOVER THE CENTRAL VALLEY

It is on the coffee-draped hillsides of the Central Valley that you will find Costa Rica's heart and soul. This is not only the geographical center of the country, it is its cultural and spiritual core. It is here that the Spanish first settled. It is here that coffee built a prosperous nation. In this mountainous region of nooks and crannies, entertainment consists of hanging out in a bustling mountain town, and watching folks gather for market days and church. That doesn't mean, however, that there is nothing to do. You can ride raging rapids, visit the country's oldest colonial church, look for trogons in mist-shrouded forests and hike myriad volcanoes. So take your time. When you explore the Central Valley, you'll not only witness great beauty, but also see the landscape that gave Costa Rica its character.

ALAJUELA

pop 43,000

Alajuela is by no means a tourist 'destination.' But it's an inherently Costa Rican city. And, in its more relaxed moments, can unveil a few charms – a spot where Tico families have leisurely Sunday lunches and teenagers steal kisses in the park. It's also an ideal base if you are flying into or out of the international airport.

INFORMATION

Instituto Costarricense de Turismo (ICT; Costa Rica Tourism Board; ☎ 2442-1820) There's no tourist office in Alajuela proper, but the ICT has a desk at the international airport.

SIGHTS

The shady **Parque Central** is a pleasant place to relax beneath a cluster of mango trees. Several 19th-century buildings, including a spacious and elegant **cathedral**, surround the park.

Six blocks to the east, a Renaissance-inspired structure, built in 1941, houses the **Iglesia La Agonía**, a popular local spot for mass.

Situated in a century-old structure that has served as both a jail and an armory, north of the Parque Central, the **Museo Juan Santamaría** (☎ 2441-4775; www.museo juansantamaria.go.cr; cnr Av 3 & Calle 2; admission free; ☺ 10am-5:30pm Tue-Sun) chronicles the life and history of Juan Santamaría, the legendary drummer boy who helped route American filibuster William Walker in 1856 by torching the building that he and his men were hiding out in.

SLEEPING

Alajuela Backpackers Boutique Hostel & Hotel (☎ 2441-7149; www.alajuelaback packers.com; cnr Av 4 & Calle 4; dm US$15, s/d standard US$30/45, s/d deluxe US$38/58, s/d junior ste US$48/68; ✂ 🖳 ☜) This brand new 21-room inn facing the Parque de los Niños is less a hostel than a full-blown hotel equipped with a smattering of dormitory rooms.

Hotel 1915 (☎ 2441-0495; www.1915hotel. com; Calle 2 btwn Avs 5 & 7; d US$55-85; 🅿 ✂ 🖳 ☜) Step through the front door and you'll find yourself in a quaint 16-room inn built around a century-old home. Rooms have adobe walls, wood-beam ceilings, period-style furnishings and a graceful living room with a stained-glass window and vintage Spanish tiles.

Trapp Family Lodge (☎ 2431-0776; www.trappfam.com; d US$95, additional person US$15, child 3-11yr US$6; P 🖳 🐕 🐕) A bright, mustard-yellow Spanish country inn houses 20 terra-cotta-tiled rooms with comfortable polished-wood beds and a graceful hacienda vibe.

Xandari Resort Hotel & Spa (☎ 2443-2020; www.xandari.com; d villa US$230-315; P 🕱 🐕 🛜 🐕) Set in a coffee plantation overlooking the Central Valley, about 6km north of Alajuela, this romantic spot

has postcard-perfect views and modern bungalows painted in tropical colors.

EATING

Ambrosia (☎ 2201-5057; Av 5 btwn Calles Central & 2; mains ₡1350-2200; 🕙 10am-9pm Mon-Sat) This pretty, open-air cafe housed in a yellow building is good for a pick-me-up espresso. The menu features a mix of Italian-influenced options.

La Mansarda (☎ 2441-4390; 2nd fl, Calle Central btwn Avs Central & 2; meals ₡2600-7500; 🕙 11am-11pm) An old standby for traditional Costa Rican fare is this casual

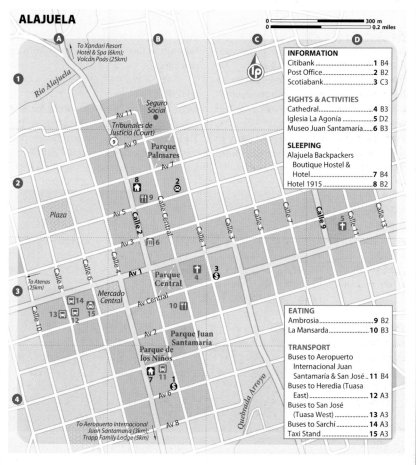

ALAJUELA

To Xandari Resort Hotel & Spa (6km); Volcán Poás (25km)

Río Alajuela

Seguro Social

Av 11

Tribunales de Justicia (Court)

Av 9

Parque Palmares

Av 7

Plaza

Av 5

Calle 2

Calle Central

Av 3

Av 1

Parque Central

Mercado Central

To Atenas (25km)

Av Central

Av 2

Parque Juan Santamaría

Parque de los Niños

Av 6

To Aeropuerto Internacional Juan Santamaría (3km); Trapp Family Lodge (5km)

Av 8

Quebrada Arroyo

0 ——————— 300 m
0 ——————— 0.2 miles

INFORMATION
Citibank.................................1 B4
Post Office............................2 B2
Scotiabank...........................3 C3

SIGHTS & ACTIVITIES
Cathedral.............................4 B3
Iglesia La Agonía.................5 D2
Museo Juan Santamaría......6 B3

SLEEPING
Alajuela Backpackers
 Boutique Hostel &
 Hotel....................................7 B4
Hotel 1915...........................8 B2

EATING
Ambrosia...............................9 B2
La Mansarda.......................10 B3

TRANSPORT
Buses to Aeropuerto
 Internacional Juan
 Santamaría & San José..11 B4
Buses to Heredia (Tuasa
 East)..................................12 A3
Buses to San José
 (Tuasa West)...................13 A3
Buses to Sarchí.................14 A3
Taxi Stand..........................15 A3

balcony restaurant overlooking the street. Grilled fish and chicken dishes are the specialty, and can be complemented by a good selection of wine.

GETTING THERE & AWAY
Buses go to the following destinations:

Heredia (Tuasa Terminal East; Calle 8 btwn Avs Central & 1) ₡300; 30 minutes; departs every 15 minutes from 5am to 11pm.

San José (Tuasa Terminal West; Calle 8 btwn Avs Central & 1) ₡400; 45 minutes; departs from Alajuela bus terminal every 10 minutes from 5am to 11pm; some of these stop at the international airport.

San José via Aeropuerto Internacional Juan Santamaría (Station Wagon; Av 4 btwn Calles 2 & 4) ₡400; 45 minutes; departs every 15 to 20 minutes during the day, less frequently at night; operates 24 hours a day. Locally, these buses are referred to as *los buses amarillos de la liga* (the league's yellow buses).

Sarchí (Calle 8 btwn Avs Central & 1) ₡300; 30 minutes; departs every 30 minutes from 5am to 10pm.

SARCHÍ
Welcome to Costa Rica's most famous crafts center, where artisans produce the ornately painted oxcarts and leather-and-wood furnishings for which the Central Valley is known. Most folks come in for an afternoon of shopping and call it a day, but there are more than 200 artisanal workshops in the area. If you have time on your hands, it is possible to meet different artisans and custom-order a creation.

ORIENTATION
Sarchí is divided by the Río Trojas into Sarchí Norte and Sarchí Sur, and is rather spread out, straggling for several kilometers along the main road from Grecia to Naranjo. In fact, it's easiest to explore by private car.

SHOPPING
Most travelers come to Sarchí for one thing and one thing only: *carretas*, the elaborate, colorfully painted oxcarts that are the unofficial souvenir of Costa Rica – and the official symbol of the Costa Rican

Topiary garden, Iglesia de San Rafael, Zarcero (p87)

IMAGEBROKER/HANS ZAGLITSCH

worker. Workshops are usually open from 8am to 4pm daily, and accept credit cards and US dollars. For shipping, you'll find a **UPS office** (☎ 2454-5555) in Sarchí Sur.

Below is a list of some of the most respected and popular shopping spots.

Coopearsa (☎ 2454-4196/4050; www.coopearsa.com) In Sarchí Norte, 200m west of the soccer field, is this kitsch-filled paradise of *carretas,* woodwork and painted feathers.

Fábrica de Carretas Joaquín Chaverri (☎ 2454-4411) The oldest and best-known factory in Sarchí Sur. In the back, a small studio is a good spot for watching artisans emblazon those incredible patterns on the oxcarts by hand.

Taller Lolo Alfaro (☎ 2454-4131) One block north of the Palí supermarket in Sarchí Norte, this renowned workshop (the country's oldest) produced the massive oxcart in Sarchí's main plaza.

Los Rodríguez (☎ 2454-4097), **El Arte Sarchiseño** (☎ 2454-1686) and **Muebles El Artesano** (☎ 2454-4422) are all located along the main road and specialize in rocking chairs and other furniture.

GETTING THERE & AWAY
If you're driving from San José, from the Interamericana take the signed exit to Grecia and from there follow the road north to Sarchí.

Buses arrive and depart from Sarchí Norte.

Alajuela ₡300; 30 minutes; departs every 30 minutes from 6am to 11pm.

San José ₡1000; 1½ hours; departs every 30 minutes from 5am to 10pm.

PALMARES
Palmares' claim to fame is the annual **Las Fiestas de Palmares**, a 10-day beer-soaked extravaganza that takes place in mid-January and features carnival rides, a *tope* (horse parade), fireworks, big-name

Orosi
ADRIAN HEPWORTH/HEPWORTHIMAGES

CENTRAL VALLEY

PALMARES

↘ IF YOU LIKE...
If you like **Sarchí** (opposite), you might also like these other small towns in the Central Valley:

- **Zarcero** The center for Costa Rica's organic-farming movement, not to mention a park full of bizarrely shaped topiary.
- **Bajos del Toro** This 250-person town is rural idyll at its finest, and the mountain air couldn't possibly be any fresher.
- **San Ramón** The 'City of Presidents and Poets' has sent five men to the country's highest office.
- **Orosi** Famous for its mountain vistas and coffee – lots and lots of coffee – with the additional perk of hot springs.

bands, small-name bands, exotic dancers, fried food, *guaro* (the local firewater made from sugarcane) tents and the densest population of drunk Ticos you've ever seen. It is one of the biggest events in the country – crowds can reach upwards of 10,000 people – and is covered widely on national TV. For the other 355 days of the year, Palmares is a tumbleweed town, where life is centered on the ornate stained-glass **church** in the central plaza.

Buses run continuously from San José to Palmares throughout the festival. For information on the musical line-up, visit **Fiestas Palmares** (www.fiestaspalmares.com).

HEREDIA

pop 33,000

During the 19th century, *La Ciudad de las Flores* (The City of the Flowers) was home to a *cafetalero* (coffee growers) aristocracy that made its fortune exporting Costa Rica's premium blend. Today, the historic center retains some of this well-bred air, with a leafy main square that is overlooked by a stocky cathedral,

and low-lying buildings that channel the architecture of the Spanish colony.

SIGHTS

Heredia was founded in 1706, and in true Spanish-colonial style it has several interesting old landmarks arranged around the **Parque Central**. To the east is **Iglesia de la Inmaculada Concepción**, built in 1797 and still in use. Opposite the church steps you can take a break and watch old men playing checkers at the park tables while weddings and funerals come and go.

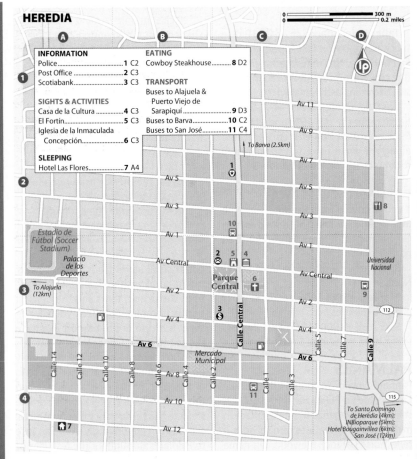

HEREDIA

INFORMATION	
Police	1 C2
Post Office	2 C3
Scotiabank	3 C3

SIGHTS & ACTIVITIES	
Casa de la Cultura	4 C3
El Fortín	5 C3
Iglesia de la Inmaculada Concepción	6 C3

SLEEPING	
Hotel Las Flores	7 A4

EATING	
Cowboy Steakhouse	8 D2

TRANSPORT	
Buses to Alajuela & Puerto Viejo de Sarapiquí	9 D3
Buses to Barva	10 C2
Buses to San José	11 C4

To Barva (2.5km)

Estadio de Fútbol (Soccer Stadium)

Palacio de los Deportes

To Alajuela (12km)

Parque Central

Mercado Municipal

Universidad Nacional

To Santo Domingo de Heredia (4km); INBioparque (5km); Hotel Bougainvillea (6km); San José (12km)

0   300 m
0   0.2 miles

To the north of the park is an 1867 guard tower called simply **El Fortín**, the last remaining turret of a Spanish fortress and the official symbol of Heredia – and a national historic site.

At the park's northeast corner, in a low-lying Spanish structure that dates back to the 18th century, is the **Casa de la Cultura** (☎ 2261-4485; cnr Calle Central & Av Central; admission free; ⏰ hours vary), which once served as the residence of President Alfredo González Flores, who governed from 1913–17. It is beautifully maintained and now houses permanent historical displays as well as changing art exhibits.

About 4km southeast of town, in the neighborhood of Santo Domingo, is **INBioparque** (☎ 2507-8107; www.inbioparque.com/en; adult/student/child US$23/17/13; ⏰ 8:30am-2pm Tue-Fri, 9:30am-3:30pm Sat & Sun; 🅿 ♿), a wildlife park and botanical garden run by the nonprofit INBio (National Biodiversity Institute), which catalogs Costa Rica's biodiversity and promotes its sustainable use.

SLEEPING & EATING

Hotel Las Flores (☎ 2261-8147; www.hotel-lasflores.com; Av 12 btwn Calles 12 & 14; s/d/tr US$14/28/42; 🅿 🛜) On the southern end of town – and a bit of a walk from the action – this spotless family-run spot has 29 rooms painted bright sky blue and key-lime green.

Hotel Bougainvillea (☎ 2244-1414; www.hb.co.cr; d incl breakfast US$103-140; 🅿 🍽 📶 🛜 🏊) In Santo Domingo de Heredia, this efficient hotel is set on 4 hectares of land and is surrounded by a well-manicured garden dotted with old-growth trees, stunning flowers and plenty of statuary.

Cowboy Steakhouse (☎ 2237-8719; Calle 9 btwn Avs 3 & 5; dishes ₡1900-7400; ⏰ 5-11pm Mon-Sat) This yellow-and-red joint with two bars has patio seating and the best cuts of beef in town.

GETTING THERE & AWAY

Buses go to the following destinations:

Alajuela (cnr Av Central & Calle 9) ₡400; 20 minutes; departs every 15 minutes from 6am to 10pm.

Barva (Calle Central btwn Avs 1 & 3) ₡300; 20 minutes; departs every 30 minutes from 5:15am to 11:30pm.

Puerto Viejo de Sarapiquí (cnr Av Central & Calle 9) ₡1200; 3½ hours; departs at 11am, 1:30pm and 3pm.

San José (Av 8 btwn Calles Central & 1) ₡300; 20 minutes; departs every 20 to 30 minutes from 4:40am to 11pm.

BARVA

Just 2.5km north of Heredia is the historic town of Barva, a settlement that dates back to 1561 and which has been declared a national monument. The town center is dotted with low-lying 19th-century buildings and is centered on the towering **Iglesia San Bartolomé**, which was constructed in 1893. Surrounded by picturesque mountains, it oozes colonial charm.

SIGHTS

The most famous coffee roaster in Costa Rica is **Café Britt Finca** (☎ 2277-1600; www.coffeetour.com; adult with/without lunch US$35/20, student US$30/16; ⏰ tours 11am; ♿), headquartered just 1km south of Barva. On offer here is a 90-minute bilingual tour of its plantation area. Naturally, there's plenty of coffee tasting and gift-shop browsing. For an extra US$10, you can make a one-hour trip to a *beneficio* (processing plant).

Located in Santa Lucía de Barva, about 1.5km southeast of Barva, the small **Museo de Cultura Popular** (☎ 2260-1619; admission US$3; ⏰ 9am-4pm) is located in a restored 19th-century farmhouse that exhibits period pieces, such as domestic and agricultural tools.

FESTIVALS & EVENTS

Every March the town is home to the famous **Feria de la Mascarada**, a tradition with roots in the colonial era, in which people don massive colorful masks (some of which weigh up to 20kg), and gather to dance and parade around the town square. Demons and devils are frequent subjects, but celebrities and politicians also figure in the mix of characters.

GETTING THERE & AWAY

Half-hourly buses travel between Heredia and Barva (₡400, 20 minutes), picking up and dropping off in front of the church.

CARTAGO

pop 24,000

After the rubble was cleared, in the early 20th century, nobody bothered to rebuild Cartago to its former quaint specifications. As in other commercial towns, expect plenty of functional concrete structures. One exception is the bright white Basílica de Nuestra Señora de los Ángeles, which is visible from many parts of the city, standing out like a snowcapped mountain above a plane of one-story edifices. It is considered to be the holiest religious shrine in Costa Rica and has been unquestionably rebuilt after each of the city's natural disasters.

SLEEPING & EATING

Los Ángeles Lodge (☎ 2551-0957, 2591-4169; Av 4 btwn Calles 14 & 16; d incl breakfast US$50; P ✗) With its balconies overlooking the Plaza de la Basílica, this decent B&B stands out with spacious and comfortable rooms, hot showers and a big breakfast made to order by the cheerful owners.

La Puerta del Sol (Av 4 btwn Calles 14 & 16; casados ₡2600-3000, mains ₡2400-5000; ✗ 8am-midnight) Downstairs from Los Ángeles Lodge, this pleasant *soda* has been around since 1957 and serves myriad Tico specialties, as well as burgers and sandwiches.

GETTING THERE & AWAY

Catch a bus to the following destinations:

San José (Calle 5, north of Av 6) ₡500; 45 minutes; departs every 15 minutes.

Traveling by bus near Cartago

IMAGEBROKER/JAN KRIMMER

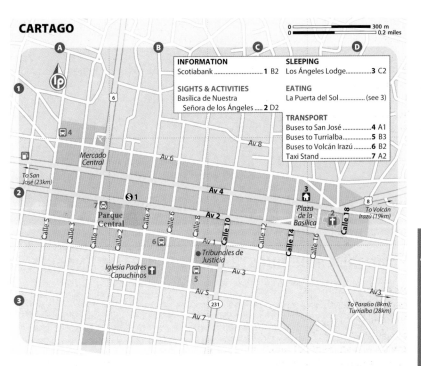

CARTAGO

INFORMATION
Scotiabank **1** B2

SIGHTS & ACTIVITIES
Basílica de Nuestra
   Señora de los Ángeles **2** D2

SLEEPING
Los Ángeles Lodge **3** C2

EATING
La Puerta del Sol .... (see 3)

TRANSPORT
Buses to San José **4** A1
Buses to Turrialba **5** B3
Buses to Volcán Irazú **6** B2
Taxi Stand **7** A2

Turrialba (Av 3 btwn Calles 8 & 10) ₡600; 1½ hours; departs every 45 minutes from 6am to 10pm weekdays, 8:30am, 11:30am, 1:30pm, 3pm and 5:45pm weekends.

Volcán Irazú (Calle 6 btwn Avs 1 & 3) ₡2000; one hour; the bus originates in San José at 8am, stops in Cartago at about 8:30am and returns from Irazú at 12:30pm. Get there early.

PARQUE NACIONAL VOLCÁN IRAZÚ

Looming on the horizon, 19km northeast of Cartago, **Volcán Irazú** (☎ 2551-9398, 2200-5025; park admission US$10, parking ₡600; ☻ 8am-3:30pm), which derives its name from the indigenous word *ara-tzu* (thunderpoint), is the largest and highest (3432m) active volcano in Costa Rica. In 1723 the Spanish governor of the area, Diego de la Haya Fernández, watched helplessly as

the volcano unleashed its destruction on the city of Cartago. Rather ironically, one of the craters is named in his honor. Since the 18th century, no fewer than 15 major eruptions have been recorded.

The national park was established in 1955 to protect 23 sq km around the base of the volcano. The summit is a bare landscape of volcanic-ash craters. The principal crater is 1050m in diameter and 300m deep; the Diego de la Haya Crater is 690m in diameter, 100m deep and contains a small lake; and the smallest, Playa Hermosa Crater, is slowly being colonized by sparse vegetation. There is also a pyroclastic cone, which consists of rocks that were fragmented by volcanic activity.

At the summit it is possible to see both the Pacific and the Caribbean, but it is rarely clear enough. The best chance for a clear view is in the very early morning

Cartago's Basílica de Nuestra Señora de los Ángeles, home of La Negrita

↘ BASÍLICA DE NUESTRA SEÑORA DE LOS ÁNGELES

The most venerated religious site in the country, the Basilica of Our Lady of the Angels channels any airy Byzantine grace with fine stained-glass windows and ornate side chapels that feature carved-wood altars. Though the structure has changed many times since 1635, when it was first built, the relic that it protects remains unharmed inside. La Negrita, 'the Black Virgin,' is a small (less than 1m tall), probably indigenous representation of the Virgin Mary, found on this spot on August 2, 1635, by a native woman. The story goes that when she tried to take the statuette with her, it miraculously reappeared back where she'd found it. Twice. So the townspeople built a shrine around her. In 1824 she was declared Costa Rica's patron Virgin. She now resides on a gold, jewel-studded platform at the main altar. Each August 2, on the anniversary of the statuette's miraculous discovery, pilgrims from every corner of the country (and beyond) walk the 22km from San José to the basilica. Many of the penitent complete the last few hundred meters on their knees.

Things you need to know: located on the corner of Av 2 & Calle 16

during the dry season (January through April). It tends to be cold and windy up here and there's an annual rainfall of 2160mm – come prepared with warm, rainproof clothes.

From the parking lot, a 200m trail leads to a viewpoint over the craters; a longer, steeper trail leaves from behind the toilets and gets you closer to the craters (note that this trail is intermittently closed). While hiking, be on the lookout for high-altitude bird species, such as the volcano junco.

To get to the volcano, drivers can take Hwy 8 from Cartago, which begins at the northeast corner of the plaza and continues 19km to the summit. The road is well-signed.

The only public transportation to Irazú departs from San José (₡2500 round-trip) at 8am, stops in Cartago (₡2000) to pick up passengers at about 8:30am and arrives at the summit a little after 9:30am. The bus departs from Irazú at 12:30pm.

TURRIALBA

pop 27,000

When the railway shut down in 1991, Turrialba ceased to be an important commercial pit-stop on the San José–Limón trade route. Commerce slowed down, but the town nonetheless remained a regional agricultural center, where local coffee-growers could bring their crops to market. Things didn't remain quiet for long, however. With tourism on the rise in the 1990s, it wasn't long before this modest mountain town became known for having access to some of the best white-water rafting on the planet. By the early 2000s, Turrialba was a simmering hotbed of international rafters looking for Class-V thrills.

SIGHTS

About 4km east of Turrialba, **Catie** (Centro Agronómico Tropical de Investigación; Center for Tropical Agronomy Research & Education; ☎ 2556-6431; www.catie.ac.cr; admission US$1, guided tours US$15-20; ☺ 7am-4pm) consists of 1000 hectares dedicated to tropical agricultural research and education. Agronomists from all over the world recognize this as one of the most important centers in the tropics.

About 10km east of Turrialba, in the village of Pavones, **Parque Viborana** (☎ 2538-1510; admission US$7; ☺ 9am-4pm Mon-Fri) is a small serpentarium run by a local family. Here you can see (and even handle) a variety of Costa Rican snakes, including some very large boas. It's 500m east of the cemetery.

TOURS

Costa Rica Ríos (☎ in USA 888-434-0776; www.costaricarios.com; Calle 1, north of Av 6)

Offers weeklong rafting trips that must be booked in advance. It's located 25m north of Parque Central.

Explornatura (☎ 2556-2070; www.explor natura.com) This long-time outfitter also runs reader-recommended canyoning expeditions, among other tours.

Río Locos (☎ 2556-6035; www.whiteh2o. com) This popular local company does rafting – as well as other area tours.

Tico's River Adventures (☎ 2556-1231; www.ticoriver.com) Another good local outfit offering all manner of rafting trips; also runs a kayaking school.

TOM BOYDEN

Parque Nacional Volcán Poás

↘ IF YOU LIKE...

If you like **Parque Nacional Volcán Irazú** (p91), we think you'll like these other national parks in the Central Valley:

- **Los Ángeles Cloud Forest Adventure Park** Offers the chance to whiz through the treetops on a canopy tour or trot through hills on horseback.
- **Parque Nacional Tapantí-Macizo Cerro de la Muerte** This little-visited park is a perfect outpost for dedicated bird-watchers.
- **Parque Nacional Volcán Poás** Easily accessible, this park has a shimmering crater lake and plenty of surrounding cloud forest.

TURRIALBA

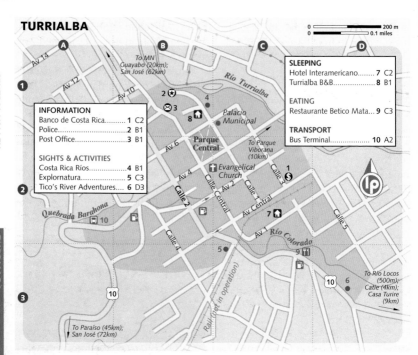

INFORMATION
Banco de Costa Rica.......... 1 C2
Police.................................2 B1
Post Office........................3 B1

SIGHTS & ACTIVITIES
Costa Rica Ríos.................4 B1
Explornatura.....................5 C3
Tico's River Adventures.... 6 D3

SLEEPING
Hotel Interamericano........ 7 C2
Turrialba B&B.................. 8 B1

EATING
Restaurante Betico Mata... 9 C3

TRANSPORT
Bus Terminal.................. 10 A2

SLEEPING & EATING

Hotel Interamericano (☎ 2556-0142; www.hotelinteramericano.com; Av 1; s/d/tr/q with bathroom US$25/35/45/55, without bathroom US$11/20/30/40; P 🛜) On the south side of the old train tracks is this simple 22-room hotel, regarded by rafters as *the* meeting place in Turrialba.

Turrialba B&B (☎ 2556-6651; www.turrialbahotel.com; Calle 1, north of Av 6; s/d/tr incl breakfast US$40/60/80; P ⛖ 🛜) This charming and tranquil spot has clean, bright, well-appointed rooms, a cozy living room area and a lovely garden patio equipped with a hot tub spa.

Casa Turire (☎ 2531-1111; www.hotelcasaturire.com; d standard/ste/master ste incl breakfast US$135/210/350, additional person US$25-55, child under 6yr free; P ⛖ 🖳 ⛲ ♨) South of town is this elegant three-story plantation inn with graceful well-appointed rooms with high ceilings, wood floors and wrought-iron beds.

Restaurante Betico Mata (Hwy 10; gallos ₡600-800; ⏰ 11am-midnight, until late Sat & Sun) This carnivore's paradise at the southern end of town specializes in *gallos* (open tacos on corn tortillas) piled with succulent, fresh-grilled meats all soaked in the special house marinade.

GETTING THERE & AWAY

The bus terminal is on the western edge of town off Hwy 10.

Monumento Nacional Arqueológico Guayabo ₡400; one hour; departs at 11:15am, 3:10pm and 5:30pm Monday through Saturday, and at 9am, 3pm and 6:30pm on Sunday.

San José via Cartago ₡1200; two hours; departs every 45 minutes from 5am to 6:30pm.

Siquirres, for transfer to Puerto Limón ₡1000; 1¾ hours; departs every 60 to 90 minutes from 6am to 6pm.

MONUMENTO NACIONAL ARQUEOLÓGICO GUAYABO

Nestled into a patch of stunning hillside forest 20km northeast of Turrialba is the largest and most important archaeological site in the country. **Guayabo** (☎ 2559-1220; admission US$7; ❦ 8am-3:30pm) is composed of the remains of a pre-Columbian city that was thought to have peaked at some point in AD 800, when it was inhabited by as many as 20,000 people. Today, visitors can examine the remains of old petroglyphs, residential mounds, an old roadway and an impressive aqueduct system – built with rocks that were hauled in from the Río Reventazón along a cobbled, 8km road. Amazingly, the cisterns still work, and (theoretically) potable water remains available onsite.

It's easy to get here by car. Head north out of Turrialba and make a right after the metal bridge. The road is well-signed from there. It's mostly paved, but the last

WHITE-WATER RAFTING IN THE CENTRAL VALLEY

There are two major rivers in the Turrialba area that are popular for rafting – the Río Reventazón and the Río Pacuare. The following is a quick guide to the ins and outs (and ups and downs) of each.

Río Reventazón

This storied rock-lined river has its beginnings at the Lago de Cachí, an artificial lake created by a dam of the same name. It begins here, at 1000m above sea level, and splashes down the eastern slopes of the cordilleras to the Caribbean lowlands. It is one of the most difficult, adrenaline-pumping runs in the country – and with more than 65km of rapids, you can get as hardcore as you like. Water levels stay fairly constant year-round because of releases from the dam. There are no water releases on Sunday however, and although the river is runnable, it's generally considered the worst day.

Río Pacuare

The Río Pacuare is the next major river valley east of the Reventazón, and has arguably the most scenic rafting in Costa Rica, if not Central America. The river plunges down the Caribbean slope through a series of spectacular canyons clothed in virgin rainforest, through runs named for their fury and separated by calm stretches that enable you to stare at near-vertical green walls towering hundreds of meters above. The Pacuare can be run year-round, though June through October are considered the best months.

Trips & Prices

For day trips (many of which originate in San José), you can expect to pay anywhere from US$85 to US$120 depending on transportation, accessibility and amenities. It is generally less expensive to leave from Turrialba (from US$75). For two-day trips, prices vary widely depending on accommodations, but expect to pay between US$195 to US$300 per person. Children must be at least nine years old for most trips, and older for tougher runs.

Tomb on main trail, Monumento Nacional Arqueológico Guayabo (p95)

CHRISTOPHER BAKER

3km of the drive is not; 4WD is recommended.

Buses from Turrialba (₡400, one hour) depart at 11:15am, 3:10pm and 5:30pm Monday through Saturday, and at 9am, 3pm and 6:30pm on Sunday.

Buses travel from Guayabo to Turrialba at 5:15am, 6:30am, 12:30pm and 4pm Monday through Saturday, and at 6:30am, 12:30pm and 4pm on Sunday. You can also take a taxi from Turrialba (from ₡8000).

↘ NORTHERN COSTA RICA

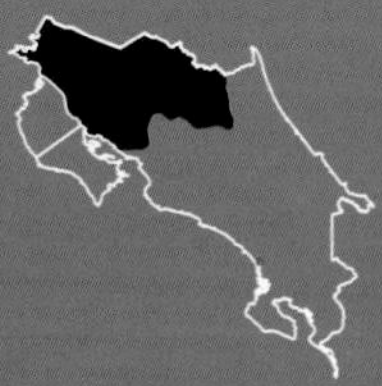

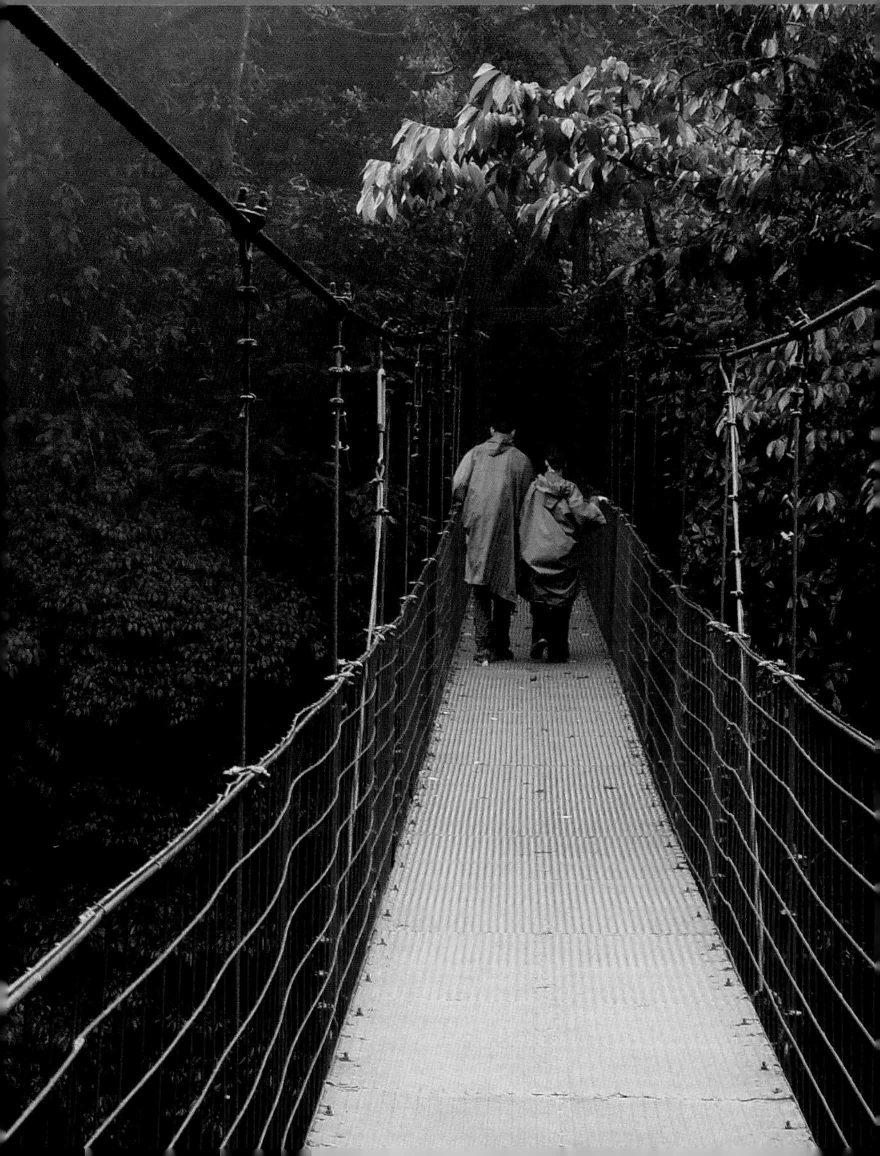

NORTHERN COSTA RICA

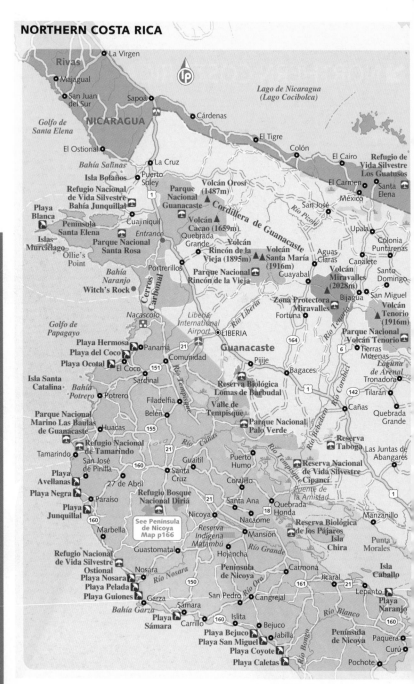

La Virgen

Rivas

Majagual

San Juan del Sur

Sapoá

Cárdenas

Lago de Nicaragua
(Lago Cocibolca)

Golfo de
Santa Elena

NICARAGUA

El Tigre

Colón

El Cairo

El Ostional

Bahía Salinas

La Cruz

El Carmen

México

Refugio de
Vida Silvestre
Los Guatusos

Santa
Elena

Isla Bolaños

Puerto
Soley

Refugio Nacional
de Vida Silvestre
Bahía Junquillal

Parque
Nacional
Guanacaste

Volcán Orosí
(1487m)

San José

Upala

Playa
Blanca

Cuajiniquil

Cordillera de Guanacaste

Río Pizote

Colonia
Puntarenas

Península
Santa Elena

Entrance

Volcán
Cacao (1659m)

Quebrada
Grande

Volcán
Rincón de la
Vieja (1895m)

Volcán
Santa María
(1916m)

Aguas
Claras

Canalete

Santo
Domingo

Islas
Murciélago

Parque Nacional
Santa Rosa

Volcán
Miravalles
(2028m)

San Miguel

Volcán
Tenorio
(1916m)

Ollie's
Point

Portrerillos

Parque Nacional
Rincón de la Vieja

Guayabal

Bijagua

Bahía
Naranjo

Witch's Rock

Cerros Carbonal

Nacascolo

Liberia
International
Airport

Río Liberia

LIBERIA

Zona Protectora
Miravalles

Fortuna

Río Tenorio

Parque Nacional
Volcán Tenorio

Golfo de
Papagayo

Playa Hermosa

Playa del Coco

Playa Ocotal

El Coco

Panamá

Comunidad

21

Guanacaste

Pijije

164

6

Tierras
Morenas

Laguna
de Arenal

Tronadora

Isla Santa
Catalina

Bahía
Potrero

Potrero

Sardinal

151

Río Tempisque

Filadelfia

Belén

Bagaces

Reserva Biológica
Lomas de Barbudal

Valle de
Tempisque

1

142

Tilarán

Cañas

Quebrada
Grande

Parque Nacional
Marino Las Baulas
de Guanacaste

Huacas

155

Río Cañas

Parque Nacional
Palo Verde

Río Bebedero

Reserva
Taboga

Las Juntas de
Abangares

Tamarindo

Refugio Nacional
de Tamarindo

San José
de Pinilla

160

Guaitil

Santa
Cruz

Puerto
Humo

Río Tempisque

Reserva Nacional
de Vida Silvestre
Cipancí

Puente de
la Amistad

1

Playa
Avellanas

27 de Abril

21

Corralillo

Playa Negra

Paraíso

Refugio Bosque
Nacional Diriá

21

Santa Ana

18

Quebrada
Honda

Manzanillo

Playa
Junquillal

160

Marbella

Nicoya

Nacaome

Mansión

Reserva Biológica
de los Pájaros
Isla
Chira

Punta
Morales

See Península
de Nicoya
Map p166

Guastomatal

Reserva
Indígena
Matambú

Río Grande

Isla
Caballo

Refugio Nacional
de Vida Silvestre
Ostional

Hojancha

Península
de Nicoya

Carmona

161

Jicaral

21

Lepanto

Playa Nosara

Playa Pelada

Playa Guiones

Nosara

Garza

Río Nosara

150

San Pedro

Río Oro

Cangrejal

Playa
Naranjo

160

Bahía Garza

Playa
Sámara

Sámara

Carrillo

160

Islita

Bejuco

Jabilla

Península
de Nicoya

Paquera

Curú

Playa Bejuco

Playa San Miguel

Río Bongo

Playa Coyote

Río Blanco

Pochote

Playa Caletas

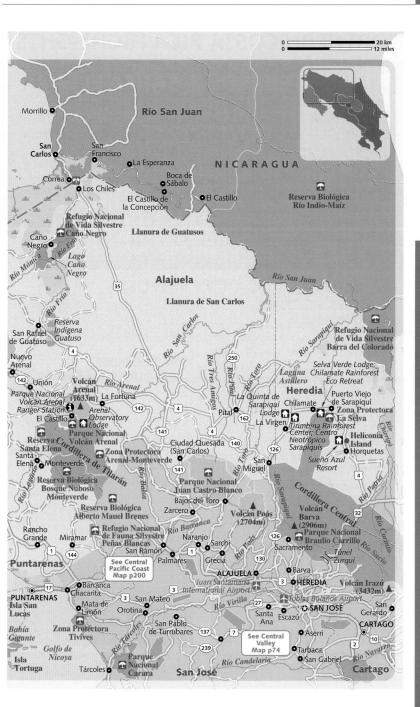

0 — 20 km
0 — 12 miles

Morrillo

Río San Juan

San Carlos
San Francisco

Correa
Los Chiles

La Esperanza

Boca de Sábalo

El Castillo de la Concepción
El Castillo

NICARAGUA

Reserva Biológica Río Indio-Maíz

Refugio Nacional de Vida Silvestre Caño Negro

Caño Negro

Lago Caño Negro

Llanura de Guatusos

Río San Juan

Alajuela

Llanura de San Carlos

35

Refugio Nacional de Vida Silvestre Barra del Colorado

Reserva Indígena Guatuso

San Rafael de Guatuso

Nuevo Arenal

4

142
Unión

Volcán Arenal (1633m)
La Fortuna

Río Arenal

250

Río Peñas

Río Toro

Río Tres Amigos

Laguna Astillero

Selva Verde Lodge; Chilamate Rainforest Eco Retreat

Heredia

Puerto Viejo de Sarapiquí

La Quinta de Sarapiquí Lodge

Chilamate

Parque Nacional Volcán Arenal Ranger Station
El Castillo

Arenal Observatory Lodge

142

4

Pital

162
La Virgen

Zona Protectora La Selva

Tirimbina Rainforest Center; Centro Neotrópico Sarapiquís

Heliconia Island
Horquetas

Parque Nacional Volcán Arenal

141

Ciudad Quesada (San Carlos)

140

126

Río Chirripó

4

Reserva Santa Elena
Santa Elena
Monteverde

Zona Protectora Arenal-Monteverde

Cordillera de Tilarán

141

Río Balsa

San Miguel

Sueño Azul Resort

4

Reserva Biológica Bosque Nuboso Monteverde

Parque Nacional Juan Castro Blanco

Bajos del Toro
Zarcero

Río Toro

Cordillera Central

Río Patria

Río Sucio

Reserva Biológica Alberto Manuel Brenes

Rancho Grande
Miramar

Refugio Nacional de Fauna Silvestre Peñas Blancas
San Ramón

1

144

Palmares

Río Barranca

Naranjo
Sarchí

Grecia

Río Poás

Volcán Poás (2704m)

126

130

Sacramento

Volcán Barva (2906m)

Parque Nacional Braulio Carrillo

Túnel Zurquí

32

Río Carrío

Puntarenas

Barranca
Chacarita

17
PUNTARENAS

Isla San Lucas

Mata de Limón

3
San Mateo
Orotina

See Central Pacific Coast Map p200

1

ALAJUELA

Juan Santamaría International Airport

Río Virilla

27

Barva

3
HEREDIA

Tobías Bolaños Airport

Santa Ana
Escazú

SAN JOSÉ

San Gerardo

Volcán Irazú (3432m)

CARTAGO

10

2

Bahía Gigante

Zona Protectora Tivives

San Pablo de Turrubares

137

7

See Central Valley Map p74

Aserrí

Tarbaca

San Gabriel

Río Navarro

Cartago

Isla Tortuga

Golfo de Nicoya

239

Parque Nacional Carara

Tárcoles

Río Tárcoles

Río Candelaria

San José

NORTHERN COSTA RICA HIGHLIGHTS

1 MONTEVERDE & SANTA ELENA

BY J ANDRÉS VARGAS, DIRECTOR OF EUFORIA EXPEDITIONS

Monteverde and Santa Elena are a hot spot for biologists, and ongoing research has broadened our understanding of tropical ecosystems. These towns are also two of Costa Rica's most popular tourist destinations, with lodgings and restaurants to suit every taste. Activities range from family-oriented tours and wilderness treks to cloud-forest zip lines.

↘ J ANDRÉS VARGAS' DON'T MISS LIST

❶ RESERVA BIOLÓGICA BOSQUE NUBOSO MONTEVERDE

One of the country's most famous **biological reserves** (p143), Monteverde is a bird-watching paradise. Although the list of recorded species tops out at more than 400, the one most visitors want to see is the resplendent quetzal. The Maya bird of paradise is most often spotted during the March and April nesting season, but you could get lucky anytime of year. For mammal-watchers, commonly sighted species

(especially in the backcountry) include coatis, howler monkeys, capuchins, sloths, agoutis and squirrels.

❷ MONTEVERDE BACKCOUNTRY TREKKING

Longer, less developed trails stretch out east across the **reserve** (p144) and down the Peñas Blancas river valley to lowlands north of the Cordillera de Tilarán and into the **Children's Eternal Rainforest** (p133). If you are strong enough and have the time to spare,

Clockwise from top: Canopy tour, Parque Nacional Rincón de la Vieja (p152); Reserva Biológica Bosque Nuboso Monteverde (p143); Heliconian butterfly, Monteverde (p128)

these hikes are highly recommended as you'll maximize your chances of spotting wildlife. If you're serious about visiting the backcountry, hire a reliable guide – you'll be entering some fairly rugged terrain.

❸ RESERVA SANTA ELENA

This **community-managed reserve** (p144) is slightly higher in elevation than Monteverde. Since some of the forest is secondary growth, there are sunnier places for spotting birds and other animals throughout. This place is moist, and almost all the water comes as fine mist. More than 25% of all the biomass in the forest consists of epiphytes (mosses and lichens) for which this is a humid haven. Interestingly, 10% of species here aren't found in Monteverde, which is largely on the other side of the continental divide.

❹ CANOPY TOURS

Wondering where the whole **zip line** (p136) craze was born? Santa Elena is the site of Costa Rica's first canopy tour. You won't be spotting any quetzals or coatis as you whoosh your way over the canopy, but this is the best way to burn your holiday buck on some adrenaline-soaked thrills.

⬎ THINGS YOU NEED TO KNOW

Access The sights and activities mentioned above are easily accessed from the towns of Monteverde and Santa Elena (p128) **Fitness level** Trails in these reserves range from 300m to 4.8km, which means almost everyone will find a suitable length of hike **See the author's coverage, p143 and p144**

NORTHERN COSTA RICA HIGHLIGHTS

2 BOSQUE ETERNO DE LOS NIÑOS

BY GISELLE RODRÍGUEZ, ADMINISTRATOR OF THE MONTEVERDE CONSERVATION LEAGUE

Costa Rica is proud to have the Children's Eternal Rainforest, its largest private reserve. The idea to conserve and protect it was inspired by children from all over the world. Just walking around, seeing the butterflies fluttering, the birds singing, the grandeur of its trees and its crystalline waters shows that the forest is life and we should enjoy it.

↘ GISELLE RODRÍGUEZ' DON'T MISS LIST

❶ SENDERO BAJO DEL TIGRE

This hiking trail (p134) is the primary route for visitors to the Children's Eternal Rainforest. Comprising premontane forest, this habitat is largely unique in Costa Rica, and offers some of the area's best wildlife-watching. The entire route is just under 4km in length, and has stunning views that stretch as far as the Gulf of Nicoya.

❷ WILDLIFE-WATCHING

The Children's Eternal Rainforest is home to six of the 12 biomes found in Costa Rica, which results in an impressive amount of biodiversity. In total, the reserve is home to 60 species of amphibian, 101 species of reptile, 425 species of bird, and 121 species of mammal; more than 50% of the country's terrestrial vertebrates are found here.

Clockwise from top: Dorm-style accommodations, Monteverde; Best not to disturb the local stink bug; Trail leading deeper into Reserva Biológica Bosque Nuboso Monteverde (p143)

CLOCKWISE FROM TOP: TOM BOYDEN; CHRISTER FREDRIKSSON; CHRISTER FREDRIKSSON

❸ NIGHT HIKES

One of the most popular activities for tourists visiting the Children's Eternal Rainforest is participating in a **night hike** (p134). Every day from 5:30pm to 7:30pm, guided tours of the Bajo del Tigre trail offer a glimpse of nocturnal wildlife. Highlights include everything from lowly tarantulas to sloths in the treetops, not to mention some truly stunning sunsets.

❹ VOLUNTEERING

The Monteverde Conservation League offers a wide range of **volunteer placements** (p135) for anyone interested in helping protect the Children's Eternal Rainforest.

❺ OFF THE BEATEN PATH

The reserve is home to two **field stations** (p134) that are accessible by hiking or 4WD from Monteverde and La Fortuna, and offer overnight accommodations and full board as well as access to more than 5km of trails. Each is located in a distinctive rainforest habitat – perfect for those who want to get away from the main tourist attractions.

↘ THINGS YOU NEED TO KNOW

Access The Children's Eternal Rainforest is easily accessed from the towns of Monteverde and Santa Elena (p128) **More information** The reserve is administered by the Monteverde Conservation League (www.acmcr.org) **See the author's coverage, p133**

NORTHERN COSTA RICA HIGHLIGHTS

3 | PARQUE NACIONAL VOLCÁN ARENAL

BY CHRISTIAN CAMPOS, NATURALIST GUIDE FOR THE ARENAL OBSERVATORY LODGE

The most obvious reason to visit this national park is its most prominent landmark, the Volcán Arenal. Since erupting in 1968, it has become one of the world's most active volcanoes. The surrounding area is home to jungle hiking, hardened lava flows and waterfalls, not to mention more than 350 species of birds, abundant mammals and fascinating insect life.

➢ CHRISTIAN CAMPOS' DON'T MISS LIST

❶ VOLCÁN ARENAL
The degree of activity varies from year to year and week to week – even day to day. Sometimes there can be a spectacular display of flowing red-hot lava and incandescent rocks flying through the air; at other times the **volcano** (p118) subsides to a gentle glow. During the day, the lava isn't easy to see, but you might still see a great cloud of ash thrown up by a massive explosion. During the night, assuming the clouds of ash have lifted, you'll have the best opportunity to see the full fury of Mother Nature in action.

❷ WILDLIFE-WATCHING
This area is rugged and varied, and the biodiversity is high; roughly half the species of land-dwelling vertebrates known in Costa Rica can be found here. Birdlife is very rich in the park, and includes species such as trogons, rufous motmots, fruitcrows and lancebills. Commonly sighted mammals include howler monkeys, white-faced capuchins and coatis.

Clockwise from top: White-throated capuchin monkey; Volcán Arenal (p118)

CLOCKWISE FROM TOP: PAUL KENNEDY; CHRISTER FREDRIKSSON

NORTHERN COSTA RICA

NORTHERN COSTA RICA HIGHLIGHTS

❸ ARENAL OBSERVATORY LODGE

Even if you're not staying here, the lodge (p119) is worth visiting as there are 6km of trails in total. A handful of short hikes include views of a nearby waterfall, while sturdy souls could check out recent lava flows (2½ hours), old lava flows (three hours) or climb to Arenal's dormant partner, Volcán Chato (four hours) whose crater holds an 1100m-high lake. The lodge also has a 4.5km bike trail that winds through secondary forest, as well as a 1km sidewalk trail that is completely wheelchair-accessible.

❹ HIKING IN THE NATIONAL PARK

From the ranger station and the park headquarters there is an extensive network of trails (p118). Independent exploration is permitted, but you'll get the most out of the experience if you bring along a knowledgeable guide.

⬎ THINGS YOU NEED TO KNOW

Access Parque Nacional Volcán Arenal is easily accessed from the town of La Fortuna (p112) **More information** Check out all things Arenal at www. arenal.net **See the author's review, p118**

NORTHERN COSTA RICA HIGHLIGHTS

4

↘ LA FORTUNA

The closest town to the smoking-hot volcano that is Arenal, **La Fortuna** (p112) welcomes visitors with its well-developed tourist infrastructure. After a good night's sleep and a delectable meal, check out the incredible number of activities on offer. True hedonists can spend days soaking in the hot springs, while adventure buffs will want to go bungee jumping, canyoning, horseback riding and zip lining.

5

↘ LAGUNA DE ARENAL

Although you're going to need a car to make the most of this stunningly beautiful region, **Lake Arenal** (p125) has all the makings of a classic road trip. First of all, there is the incredible nature on display, prompting many to make the comparison to Switzerland. Add to the mix boutique hotels and gourmet restaurants, and suddenly you have a multistop itinerary that can take a couple of days to complete.

6

↘ PARQUE NACIONAL VOLCÁN TENORIO

One of the region's hidden treasures, this **national park** (p153) is centered on a series of volcanoes, but the undisputed highlight is the Río Celeste, a milky-blue river complete with a dramatic cascade. The vibrant hues are the result of the rich mineral deposits that collect in high concentrations in the waterway.

7

↘ LA VIRGEN

If you're an avid kayaker – or if you've ever thought about going kayaking – the far-flung town of **La Virgen** (p157) in the northern lowlands should make an appearance on your itinerary. With a whole slew of crisscrossing rivers to choose from, the area around La Virgen has the country's most diverse offering of kayak runs.

8

↘ PARQUE NACIONAL SANTA ROSA

Lying just south of the Nicaraguan border, this remote **national park** (p155) takes some serious commitment to access. But if you're interested in surfing two legendary breaks, namely Witch's Rock and Ollie's Point, it's most definitely worth the long boat ride out to the country's extreme northwestern corner.

4 AARON MCCOY; 5 IMAGEBROKER/SIEPMANN; 6 CARVERMOSTARDI/ALAMY; 7 ROBERTO GEROMETTA; 8 LUKE HUNTER

4 La Catarata de la Fortuna (p112); 5 Laguna de Arenal (p125); 6 Río Celeste, Parque Nacional Volcán Tenorio (p153); 7 Kayaking through Costa Rica's estuaries; 8 Low tide at Parque Nacional Santa Rosa (p155)

NORTHERN COSTA RICA'S BEST...

⬏ SPLURGES

- **Tabacón Grand Spa Thermal Resort Lodge** (p116) Admire a background of tropical rainforest while you soak in a Jacuzzi bathtub.
- **Arenal Observatory Lodge** (p119) The only lodge smack-dab in the middle of Parque Nacional Volcán Arenal.
- **Hidden Canopy Treehouses** (p140) Indulge your inner child by bedding down in a luxury tree house.

⬏ VISTAS

- **Monteverde & Santa Elena** (p128) The cloud-forest panoramas are everything you expect them to be – lush, misty and full of wildlife.
- **Volcán Arenal** (p118) It's hard to top the dramatic sight of bursting cones of molten lava.
- **Laguna de Arenal** (p125) Find a Switzerland-like vista in the middle of Central America.

⬏ EATS

- **Restaurant Don Rufino** (p117) A formal La Fortuna eatery that blends continental and Tico influences.
- **Gingerbread Restaurant** (p124) The menu changes weekly at this place in the Unión area, ensuring nothing but the freshest fare.
- **Sofia** (p141) A Nuevo Latino hot spot that is transforming the Monteverde restaurant scene.

⬏ ACTIVITIES

- **Hiking** (p133) Monteverde and Santa Elena are within easy walking distance of some of the country's greatest hiking trails.
- **Kayaking** (p158) Head to La Virgen with oar in hand.
- **Surfing** (p156) Parque Nacional Santa Rosa is an undisputed surfing mecca.

LEFT: CHRISTER FREDRIKSSON; RIGHT: PHILIP & KAREN SMITH

Left: Reserva Biológica Bosque Nuboso Monteverde (p143); Right: *Pura vida*, Liberia (p145)

THINGS YOU NEED TO KNOW

⬊ VITAL STATISTICS

- **Population** Liberia 45,000; La Fortuna 10,000
- **Best time to visit** Guanacaste gets little to no rain during the months of November through April, and bakes in the tropical sun. At higher elevations, in places such as Monteverde and Santa Elena, temperatures are cooler and rainfall is fairly constant year-round.

⬊ TOWNS & CITIES IN A NUTSHELL

- **Liberia** (p145) The capital of Guanacaste, and home to Aeropuerto Internacional Daniel Oduber Quirós, a major international airport that competes with San José's airport.
- **La Fortuna** (p112) A thriving tourist town in the shadow of Volcán Arenal that caters to international visitors.
- **Monteverde & Santa Elena** (p128) A side-by-side Quaker settlement and Tico town sandwiched between the country's most iconic cloud-forest reserves.

⬊ ADVANCE PLANNING

- **Car rental** Having a rental car increases your ability to move around this large and fairly spread-out region.

⬊ RESOURCES

- **Costa Rica Tourism Board** (www.visitcostarica.com)
- **Tico Times** (www.ticotimes.net)

⬊ EMERGENCY NUMBERS

- **Emergency** (☎ 911)
- **Fire** (☎ 118)
- **Police** (☎ 117)

⬊ GETTING AROUND

- **Air** An increasing number of international flights are touching down at and taking off from Liberia's Aeropuerto Internacional Daniel Oduber Quirós.
- **Bus** Distances are long, but intercity bus connections are reliable.
- **Car** The roads surrounding Laguna de Arenal are perfectly conducive to road-tripping.
- **Jeep-Boat-Jeep** This unique transportation combination connects La Fortuna to Monteverde.
- **Walk** The cloud forests of the northern reaches attract casual hikers and serious trekkers alike.

⬊ BE FOREWARNED

- **Signage** Roads in northern Costa Rica are poorly signed, so it's best to bring along a good road map before setting out.

NORTHERN COSTA RICA ITINERARIES

MONTEVERDE & SANTA ELENA Three Days

Northern Costa Rica is an enormous region that takes time to access, though three days is just long enough to visit the top highlight that is Monteverde and Santa Elena. Truth be told, you could easily spend a week here and not exhaust the incredible number of hiking and trekking opportunities on offer, not to mention activities galore and plenty of boutique hotels, restaurants and galleries.

Base yourself in the adjacent towns of **(1) Monteverde & Santa Elena** (p128), though save time for coming and leaving as the access roads are largely unpaved and very slow-going. Make the most of your brief time here by staying busy around the clock – night tours through the Children's Eternal Rainforest provide face-to-face encounters with nocturnal wildlife. During the daylight hours, a diverse range of hiking is available at both the **(2) Reserva Biológica Bosque Nuboso Monteverde** (p143) and **(3) Reserva Santa Elena** (p144), two of the country's most famous protected spaces.

LA FORTUNA & AROUND Five Days

Monteverde and Santa Elena garner their fair share of the spotlight, but the area around La Fortuna is a close contender when it comes to the country's top attractions. This tiny Tico town has one of the country's best tourist infrastructures, as well as a remarkable number of luxurious hot-spring resorts. Of course, the main reason why you're here is to observe the lava flows from Volcán Arenal, one of the world's most active volcanoes.

Everything centers on **(1) La Fortuna** (p112), but with good reason – even if the weather isn't cooperating and Arenal is shrouded in clouds, you'll still enjoy yourself immensely here. Hedonists can't seem to pry themselves away from Tabacón Hot Springs, while more outdoorsy types can hike to waterfalls or zip line through the forest canopy. If the weather is good, clear your agenda and make a beeline to **(2) Parque Nacional Volcán Arenal** (p118). By day, you can hike along hardened lava flows, while nighttime viewing focuses on new ones. As an added bonus, the roads surrounding the nearby **(3) Laguna de Arenal** (p125) are perfect for road-tripping.

NORTHERN PARKS One Week or More

Liberia is on its way to equaling – and possibly topping – San José when it comes to international arrivals and departures by plane. Touching down in the capital of Guanacaste not only gives you quick and easy access to the Península de Nicoya, but also puts the northern parks within easy reach. This itinerary focuses on these off-the-

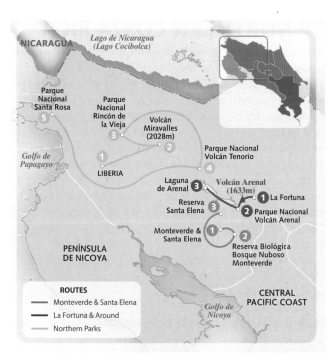

beaten-path destinations, which are a welcome alternative to the tourist hordes encountered elsewhere.

(1) Liberia (p145) is an interesting enough destination in its own right, but don't let the urban conveniences and comforts distract you from the stunning nature lying just beyond the city limits. The (2) Volcán Miravalles (p151) area is home to a collection of therapeutic hot springs, while (3) Parque Nacional Rincón de la Vieja (p152) boasts a great assortment of hiking trails catering to various skill levels. For something completely different, (4) Parque Nacional Volcán Tenorio (p153) has a cascading waterfall of pure milky-blue hues. If you have a bit more time to devote to this itinerary, (5) Parque Nacional Santa Rosa (p155) offers extreme surfing far from the trappings of civilization.

DISCOVER NORTHERN COSTA RICA

Iconic Costa Rica lives in the northwest. Whether it's for a glimpse of Volcán Arenal spitting fiery lava, the flash of green from a quetzal's wing or the perfect barrel ride at Witch's Rock, this region is heavily traveled for these and a wealth of other reasons. The landscape ranges from the blazing, dry beaches of the Guanacaste coast to the mist-shrouded heights of Volcán Miravalles (2028m) along the region's chain of volcanoes. The number and diversity of national parks and reserves alone sums up northwestern Costa Rica's classic eco-destination status.

And then there are the northern lowlands, where plantations of bananas, sugarcane and pineapples roll across the humid plains from the Cordillera Central to the Nicaraguan border. These plantations are fringed by tropical forest out of which arable soil has been slashed. This is real-life Costa Rica, where the balance of agricultural commerce and ecological conservation converge to create a contemporary work in green progress.

LA FORTUNA & AROUND

pop 10,000

The influx of tourism has altered the face, fame and fortunes of this former one-horse town. On the morning of July 29, 1968, Volcán Arenal erupted violently after nearly 400 years of dormancy, and buried the small villages of Pueblo Nuevo, San Luís and Tabacón. Since then, La Fortuna has served as the principal gateway for visiting Arenal, and it's one of the top destinations for travelers in Costa Rica. And yet, La Fortuna has managed to retain an underlying, small-town *sabanero* (cowboy) feel, with all the bustling action still centered on the attractive church and Parque Central.

SIGHTS

HOT SPRINGS

If Spielberg ever needed a setting for the Garden of Eden sequence in Genesis, **Tabacón Hot Springs** (Map p120; ☎ 2519-1900; www.tabacon.com; day pass adult/child incl lunch or dinner US$85/40, evening pass incl dinner

US$70/35; ☻ 10am-10pm) would be it. Enter through the gratuitously opulent ticket counter, flanked by an outrageous buffet on one side and glittering gift shop on the other. Then, with a thundering announcement, rare orchids and more florid tropical blooms part to reveal, oh yes, a 40°C (104°F) waterfall pouring over a cliff, concealing natural-looking caves complete with camouflaged cup holders. And lounged across each well-placed stone, in various stages of sweat-induced exhaustion, relax reddening tourists all enjoying what could be called a hot date.

WATERFALLS

La Catarata de la Fortuna (Map p120; admission US$10; ☻ 8am-5pm) is a sparkling 70m ribbon of clear water pouring through a sheer canyon of dark volcanic rock arrayed in bromeliads and ferns. It's photogenic, and you don't have to descend the canyon – a short, well-maintained and almost-vertical hike – to get the shot, but you do have to pay the steep entry fee.

LA FORTUNA

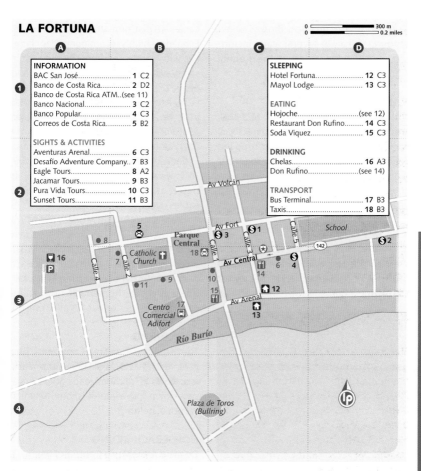

0 — 300 m
0 — 0.2 miles

INFORMATION
BAC San José...................... **1** C2
Banco de Costa Rica............ **2** D2
Banco de Costa Rica ATM..(see 11)
Banco Nacional.................... **3** C2
Banco Popular...................... **4** C3
Correos de Costa Rica........... **5** B2

SIGHTS & ACTIVITIES
Aventuras Arenal.................. **6** C3
Desafío Adventure Company.. **7** B3
Eagle Tours........................... **8** A2
Jacamar Tours....................... **9** B3
Pura Vida Tours.................. **10** C3
Sunset Tours....................... **11** B3

SLEEPING
Hotel Fortuna.................... **12** C3
Mayol Lodge...................... **13** C3

EATING
Hojoche...........................(see 12)
Restaurant Don Rufino......... **14** C3
Soda Viquez...................... **15** C3

DRINKING
Chelas.............................. **16** A3
Don Rufino.......................(see 14)

TRANSPORT
Bus Terminal...................... **17** B3
Taxis................................ **18** B3

The falls are also the trailhead for the steep, five- to six-hour **Cerro Chato** climb, a seriously strenuous but rewarding trek to a beautiful lake-filled volcanic crater, where you can have a swim once you summit Cerro Chato.

Can't handle the hike? Just past the turnoff to the *catarata* (waterfall), at the third bridge (Río Fortuna) as you leave La Fortuna for San Ramón, there's a short trail on the left leading to a pretty **swimming hole** (Map p120) just under the road, with a rope swing and a little waterfall of its own.

ECOCENTRO DANAUS

Ecocentro Danaus (Map p120; ☎ 2479-7019; www.ecocentrodanaus.com; admission with/without guide US$12/7; ⏰ 8am-4pm Mon-Sat, 9am-3:30pm Sun) has a well-developed trail system that's good for bird-watching, and there are frequent sightings of sloths, coatis and howler monkeys.

ACTIVITIES
BUNGEE JUMPING

Arenal Bungee (Map p120; ☎ 2479-7440; www.arenalbungee.com; jump US$50; ⏰ 9:30am-9:30pm), safety-certified by the Costa Rica

Tourism Board, lets you fling yourself through the air in several ways, including launching upwards from the ground. Confused? Try it for yourself.

CANOEING

Canoa Aventura (Map p120; ☎ 2479-8200; www.canoa-aventura.com; ◷ 6:30am-9:30pm) specializes in canoe and float trips led by bilingual naturalist guides. The most popular paddle is to the northern rainforest for an opportunity to spot the great green macaw.

CANOPY TOURS

Ecoglide (Map p120; ☎ 2479-7120; www. arenalecoglide.com; adult/student/child 5-12yr $45/35/22.50; ◷ 8am-4pm; ⚑) is the newest and biggest game in town, featuring 15

cables, 18 platforms and a 'Tarzan' swing. Ecoglide is highly recommended for families with young children; the dual-cable safety system provides extra security and peace of mind.

Try **Arenal Paraíso Canopy Tours** (Map p120; ☎ 2479-1100; www.arenalparaiso.com; adult/student & child US$45/35) for two-hour tours along 12 zip lines.

Canopy Los Cañones (Map p120; ☎ 2479-1000; www.canopyloscanones.com; US$45) is based at the Hotel Los Lagos, with 15 cables over the rainforest.

There's also **Arenal Mundo Aventura** (Map p120; ☎ 2479-9762; www.arenalmundo aventura.com; canopy tour adult/child US$65/33), an ecological park where you can take a canopy tour over La Fortuna Waterfall, go rappelling, horseback riding and catch Maleku performances all in one go.

CANYONING

The reputable **PureTrek Canyoning** (Map p120; ☎ 2479-1313, 2479-1315; www.puretrek. com; US$85; ◷ 7am-10pm) leads guided rappels down four waterfalls, one of which is 50m in height.

HORSEBACK RIDING

Desafío Adventure Company (Map p113; ☎ 2479-9464; www.desafiocostarica.com; Calle 2; ◷ 6:30am-9pm) treats its horses well and has been recommended for the trek to Monteverde (US$75).

FESTIVALS & EVENTS

The big annual bash is **Fiestas de la Fortuna**, held in mid-February and featuring two weeks of Tico-rules bullfights, colorful carnival rides, greasy festival food, craft stands and unusual gambling devices. It's free, except for the beer (which is cheap) and you'll have a blast trying to decide between the temporary disco with go-go dancers getting down to reggaetón

IMAGEBROKER/HANS ZAGLITSCH
Boat trip on the Laguna de Arenal (p125)

or the rough and wild tents next door with live *ranchera* and salsa.

SLEEPING
IN TOWN

Mayol Lodge (Map p113; ☎ 2479-9110; www.mayollodge.com; Av Arenal; s/d with fan US$20/35, with air-con US$35/50; P ⏚ 🐾) Small, bright rooms done up in cheery blue-and-yellow tile are centered around a cool, refreshing pool with volcano views.

Hotel Fortuna (Map p113; ☎ 2479-9197; www.lafortunahotel.com; cnr Av Arenal & Calle 3; s/d incl breakfast US$68/79, with volcano views add US$10; P ✗ ⏚ 🐾 ♿) The tallest building in town, this 5-story, 44-room hotel is the newest and most modern hotel in downtown La Fortuna. The well-appointed rooms have balconies (some with volcano views) and even room service.

Hotel Cabañitas (Map p120; ☎ 2479-9343; www.hotelcabanitas.com; standard cabins s/d/tr US$80/95/115, superior cabins US$100/115/135, ste US$110/125/145; P ✗ ⏚ 🐾 ♿) Located about 1km east of downtown, this quiet complex of 43 private cabins surrounding lush gardens is a great place to get away from it all, but still close enough to walk to town. Each cabin features dark polished wood from floor to ceiling.

OUTSIDE TOWN

Cerro Chato Lodge (Map p120; ☎ 2479-9522; www.cerrochato.com; r incl breakfast US$35-65; P ⏚ 🐾 🐾) Owned by Miguel Zamora, an avid naturalist who delights in leading travelers on nature tours. Rooms here are simple and sweet, with hot-water bathrooms and great views of the volcano.

Erupciones Inn B&B (Map p120; ☎ 2479-1400; www.erupcionesinn.com; s/d incl breakfast US$80/90; P ✗) The colorful *cabinas* at this appealing B&B are adorned with ornamental tiles and windows facing the

Relaxing in a thermal bath, La Fortuna (p112)

⬎ IF YOU LIKE...

If you like **Tabacón Hot Springs** (p112), why not try these other hot springs in the La Fortuna area:

- **Springs Resort & Spa** (Map p120) Eighteen free-form pools with various temperatures, volcano views, landscaped gardens, waterfalls and swim-up bars, including a jungle bar with a water slide.

- **Baldi Hot Springs Hotel Resort & Spa** (Map p120) Twenty-five thermal pools here range in temperature from 32°C (90°F) to a scalding 67°C (153°F), while the ambience of these springs falls somewhere between Caesar's Palace and Epcot Center.

- **Eco Thermales Hot Springs** (Map p120) The theme is minimalist elegance, and everything from the natural circulation systems in the pools to the soft, mushroom lighting is understated yet luxurious.

volcano. Each one comes with its own private patio with chairs, looking onto the green scenery or the volcano, and there's even a Jacuzzi at this sweet spot.

Chachagua Rainforest Hotel (Map p120; ☎ 2468-1010; www.chachaguarainforesthotel.com; s/d incl breakfast US$87/103;

(P) (X) (R)) This hotel is a naturalist's dream, situated on a private reserve that abuts the Children's Eternal Rainforest. Part of the property is a working orchard, cattle ranch and fish farm, while the rest is humid rainforest that can be accessed either through a series of hiking trails or on horseback. Request the older, Frank Lloyd Wright–esque wooden cabins, which have low windows for watching the birds.

Lomas del Volcán (Map p120; ☎ 2479-9000; www.lomasdelvolcan.com; s/d/tr/q incl breakfast US$97/105/135/165; (P) (X) (旦) (令) (R)) At Lomas del Volcán, one of the original resorts lining this stretch of road, you'll find comfy, hardwood cabins with stained-glass accents. There are also plenty of opportunities for hiking through the surrounding primary forest.

Arenal Nayara Hotel & Gardens (Map p120; ☎ 2479-1600; www.arenalnayara. com; r US$232, ste US$309, both incl breakfast; (P) (X) (旦) (令) (R)) This intimate hotel has 24 casitas with Asian-inspired architecture and minimalist decor. All rooms have exquisite furnishings and bedding, rich woods, flat-screen TV, DVD player, iPod dock and an indoor and separate outdoor shower. But the best feature is outside: your own private balcony with a Jacuzzi where you can soak up surreal views of Volcán Arenal.

Tabacón Grand Spa Thermal Resort Lodge (Map p120; ☎ 2256-1500; www.tabacon.com; d incl breakfast US$245-450; (P) (X) (X) (旦) (令) (R)) The original and still one of the finest luxury resorts in the area, the classy complex features 114 recently remodeled rooms and suites, spread out over several buildings that tastefully blend into the tropical rainforest background. All rooms have all the upscale amenities you'd expect, while suites add spacious Jacuzzi tubs.

EATING & DRINKING

Soda Viquez (Map p113; ☎ 2479-7132; mains ₡1500-4000; ⏱ 7am-10pm) Locals swear this is the best *soda* in town, and we won't dispute their opinion. Located just left of

La Catarata de la Fortuna (p112)

the Rainforest Café, this cute, open-air, family place serves great Tico favorites.

Chelas (Map p113; ☎ 2479-9594; bocas ₡1600-2600; ⏰ 5pm-2am Mon-Fri, noon-midnight Sat) This popular, open-air local bar has great *bocas* (small, savory dishes), including *chicharrones* (stewed pork) and *ceviche de pulpo* (raw octopus marinated in lemon juice). The best nights of the week to visit are Monday (karaoke) and Thursday (disco).

Vagabondo (Map p120; ☎ 2479-9565; mains ₡3000-8000; ⏰ noon-11pm) Of the many Italian restaurants in the region, Vagabondo has the best wood-fired pizzas around, plus great pasta dishes. There's also a popular sports bar.

Hojoche (Map p113; ☎ 2479-9197; www.lafortunahotel.com; cnr Av Arenal & Calle 3; mains ₡4000-10,000; ⏰ 7am-11pm; 🛜) Named for the gorgeous dark wood liberally used throughout the decor (check out the ceiling!), this open-air restaurant at Hotel Fortuna is one of our favorite new dining spots. The international menu specializes in fresh seafood dishes. There's live music on weekends, sports and movies on TV and even a Wii video game corner.

Ginger Sushi (Map p120; ☎ 2401-3310; www.thespringscostarica.com; mains ₡6000-10,000; ⏰ 2-11pm) Who's in the mood for sushi? This fabulous, open-air restaurant on the ground level of the Springs Resort & Spa has fantastic sushi rolls.

Restaurant Don Rufino (Map p113; ☎ 2479-9997; www.donrufino.com; cnr Av Central & Calle 3; mains ₡5000-23,000; ⏰ 10am-11pm) Fortuna's best restaurant is formal enough to justify buttoning up your shirt and putting on a little lipstick. Continental cuisine with judiciously applied Tico flavor makes up the menu here. The half-in and half-out bar is also a prime place to chill out with a cocktail

(as late as 2:30am, if you're in that kind of mood).

GETTING THERE & AWAY
BUS
Monteverde ₡1400; six to eight hours; departs at 8am (change at Tilarán at 12:30pm for Monteverde).

San José (Autotransportes San José–San Carlos) ₡1955; 4½ hours; departs at 12:45pm & 2:45pm. Alternatively, take a bus to Ciudad Quesada and change to frequent buses to the capital.

Tilarán (Autotransportes Tilarán) ₡1100; 3½ hours; departs at 8am and 5:30pm.

HORSEBACK
Several tour companies offer horseback-riding trips between La Fortuna and Monteverde. The trip (a combination of horse, taxi or boat) takes about five to seven hours and costs about US$85, including separate transportation of your luggage. One recommended company is Desafío Adventure Company (p114).

JEEP-BOAT-JEEP
The fastest route between Monteverde and Santa Elena and La Fortuna is the sexy-sounding jeep-boat-jeep combo (US$18 to US$25, three hours) – the 'jeep' is actually a minivan with the requisite yellow 'turismo' emblazoned on the side. Jeep or not, it's a terrific transportation option and can be arranged through almost any hotel or tour operator in either town. The minivan from La Fortuna takes you to Laguna de Arenal, meeting a boat that crosses the lake, where a 4WD taxi on the other side continues to Monteverde. This is increasingly becoming the primary transportation between La Fortuna and Monteverde as it's incredibly scenic,

reasonably priced and it'll save you half a day of travel over rocky roads.

PARQUE NACIONAL VOLCÁN ARENAL

Arenal was just another dormant volcano surrounded by fertile farmland from about AD 1500 until July 29, 1968, when something snapped. Huge explosions triggered lava flows that destroyed three villages, killing about 80 people and 45,000 cattle. The surrounding area was evacuated and roads throughout the region were closed. Eventually, the lava subsided to a relatively predictable flow and life got back to normal. Sort of.

Although it occasionally quietens down for a few weeks or even months, Arenal has been producing menacing ash columns, massive explosions and streamers of glowing molten rock almost daily since 1968 (it was particularly active between 1998 and 2000). Miraculously, the volcano has retained its picture-perfect conical shape despite constant volcanic activity, though its slopes are now ashen instead of green.

INFORMATION

The **ranger station** (Map p120; ☎ 2461-8499; park admission US$10; ☉ 8am-4pm) is on the western side of the volcano.

ACTIVITIES

From the ranger station (which has trail maps available), you can hike the 1km circular **Sendero Los Heliconias**, which passes by the site of the 1968 lava flow (vegetation here is slowly sprouting back to life). A 1.5km-long path branches off this trail and leads to an overlook, where you might hear the growling sounds of Arenal volcano.

The **Sendero Las Coladas** also branches off the Heliconias trail, and wraps around the volcano for 2km past the 1993 lava flow before connecting with the **Sendero Los Tucanes** (US$4). This trail extends for another 3km through the tropical rainforest at the base of the volcano. To return to the car-parking area, you will have to turn back. You'll get good views of the summit on the way back since you're now at a better angle to view it.

ADRIAN HEPWORTH/HEPWORTHIMAGES

Volcán Arenal at dusk (p118)

From the park headquarters (not the ranger station), there is also the 1.2km **Sendero Los Miradores**, which leads you down to the shores of the lake, and provides a good angle for viewing the volcano.

Near the highway turnoff to the park, there are two other trail systems worth checking out. The newest is **Arenal 1968** (Map p120; ☎ 2462-1212; www.arenal1968.com; adult/child under 10yr US$7/free; ⏰ 7am-10pm), a system of trails and lookouts along the original 1968 lava flow. It's located 1.2km from the turnoff, just before the ranger station.

Just before the turnoff, **Mirador El Silencio** (Map p120; adult/child under 7yr US$6/free;

Waterfall on the grounds of the Arenal Observatory Lodge

IMAGEBROKER/SIEPMANN

🔽 ARENAL OBSERVATORY LODGE

The Arenal Observatory Lodge was built in 1987 as a private observatory for the Universidad de Costa Rica. Scientists chose to construct the lodge on a macadamia-nut farm on the south side of Volcán Arenal due to its proximity to the volcano (only 2km away) and its relatively safe location on a ridge. Since its creation, volcanologists from all over the world, including researchers from the Smithsonian Institute in Washington, DC, have come to study the active volcano. Today, the majority of visitors are tourists, though scientists regularly visit the lodge, and a seismograph in the hotel continues to operate around the clock. The lodge is also the only place inside the park where you can legally bed down.

The lodge offers massages (from US$60), guided hikes and all the usual tours at good prices. You can swim in the pool, wander around the macadamia-nut farm or investigate the pine forest that makes up about half of the 347-hectare site. You can also rent horses for US$8 per hour. A tiny **museum** (admission free) on the old observation deck has a seismograph and some cool newspaper clippings.

Things you need to know: Map p120; ☎ reservations 2290-7011, lodge 2479-1070; www.arenalobservatorylodge.com; day pass per person US$4; ℗

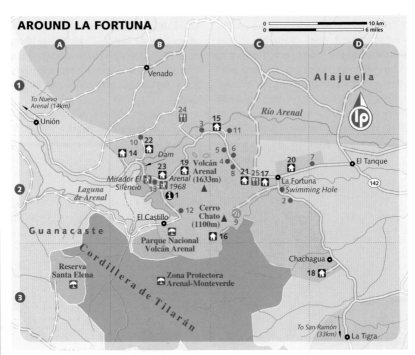

AROUND LA FORTUNA

7am-9pm; US$3) is a private 556-acre private nature reserve with four hiking trails.

TOURS

The tour operators listed in this section are a few of the more established agencies in La Fortuna.

Aventuras Arenal (Map p113; ☎ 2479-9133; www.arenaladventures.com; Av Central; 7am-8pm) Has been around for over 15 years, organizing a variety of local day tours by bike, boat and horseback.

Desafío Adventure Company (Map p113; ☎ 2479-9464; www.desafiocostarica.com; Calle 2; 6:30am-9pm) This highly recommended company offers a variety of tours including rafting, lava-viewing hikes, horseback riding, mountain biking, spelunking and more. Look for the castle-like building.

Eagle Tours (Map p113; ☎ 2479-9091; www.eagletours.net; 6:30am-9pm) Budget travelers rave about this professionally run tour agency.

Jacamar Tours (Map p113; ☎ 2479-9767; www.arenaltours.com; 7am-9pm) Recommended for its incredible variety of naturalist hikes. It's located on the ground level of Hotel Arenal Carmela.

Pura Vida Tours (Map p113; ☎ 2479-9045; www.puravidatrips.com; cnr Calle 1 & Av Central; 7am-10pm) Personalized nature tours.

Sunset Tours (Map p113; ☎ 2479-9800; www.sunsettourcr.com; Calle 2; 6:30am-9pm) This is La Fortuna's most established tour company, recommended for high-quality tours with bilingual guides.

SLEEPING & EATING

Arenal Observatory Lodge (Map p120; ☎ 2479-1070, 2290-7011; www.arenalobservatorylodge.com; La Casona s/d/tr/q US$74/87/103/116, standard r US$104/118/125/147, Smithsonian r

US$134/154/163/174, junior ste US$167/175/183/193, White Hawk Villa for 8 people US$511, all incl breakfast; P ✗ 🖥 🐾 ♿) Although most of the lava flows are on the southwest side of Arenal (the lodge is positioned to the west), the views of the eruptions are excellent, and the constant rumbling is enough to make you sleep a bit uneasily at night. The lodge has a variety of rooms spread throughout the property. Rates include a buffet breakfast and guided hike. The restaurant (lunch/dinner mains ₡6000 to ₡25,000) has a good variety of international dishes, and is decorated with jars of venomous snakes in formaldehyde.

GETTING THERE & AWAY
Most people arrive as part of a group tour, but you can reach the park independently if you have a rented vehicle.

EL CASTILLO
The tiny mountain village of El Castillo is a wonderful alternative to staying in La Fortuna – it's bucolic, untouristed and perfectly situated to watch the southwesterly lava flows. There are also some delightful accommodation options, and a number of worthwhile sights. Unfortunately you'll need your own wheels as no buses serve this lovely little enclave.

SIGHTS & ACTIVITIES
On the road to El Castillo, **SkyTrek** (Map p120; ☎ 2645-7070; www.skytrek.com; adult/student/child tram only US$55/44/28, canopy tour US$66/52/42; ⏰ 7:30am-4pm) runs canopy tours on the south side of Arenal. This canopy tour gives stellar views of Laguna de Arenal, the volcano and the lush rainforest. A silent gondola (the SkyTram) slowly conveys visitors up above the canopy, and at the top you can either tram it back down or fly down the zip lines.

On the only road in town, you'll find two noteworthy ecological attractions. The **El Castillo-Arenal Butterfly Conservatory** (☎ 2479-1149; www.butterflyconservatory.org; admission with/without guide US$10/8; ⏰ 8am-4pm) is run by an American expat named Glenn, whose conservation project far exceeds your normal butterfly garden. He is seeking to understand life cycles and hatching times for different species, and routinely works with students and volunteers to rigorously catalog every scrap of data. Here you'll find seven different gardens pertaining to each habitat as well as a ranarium, an insect museum, a medicinal herb garden, botanic garden trails and a river walk.

Next door is the **Arenal EcoZoo** (El Serpentario; ☎ 2479-1059; www.arenalecozoo.com; adult/child US$13/10; ⏰ 8:30am-5:30pm), where local snake-handler Victor Hugo Quesada will introduce you to some of the most dangerous snakes in the world,

NORTHERN COSTA RICA

EL CASTILLO

such as Eliza, a 3.8m-long Burmese python. Victor will also demonstrate how to handle and milk a venomous snake.

SLEEPING & EATING

Essence Arenal (☎ 2479-1131; www.essence arenal.com; dm US$16, d with/without bathroom; US$43/32; P 🖳 🛜 🐾 V) Perched on a 100-acre hilltop with incredible volcano and lake views, this new 'boutique hostel' is one of the most exciting new projects in the Arenal region. Essence owners Nico and Kelly have created the perfect budget resort. Common area amenities include a fireplace and Japanese soaking tub, cable TV, video games, movie nights, laundry service, cafeteria, hiking trails and small pool with killer views of the lava flows.

Hummingbird Nest B&B (☎ 8835-8711, 2479-1174; www.hummingbirdnestbb.com; s/d incl breakfast US$50/75, 2-night minimum; P) At the entrance to town, you'll see a small path that leads up the (steep) hill to one of our favorite B&Bs in all of Costa Rica. It's owned by Ellen, a former Pan Am stewardess and all-round world traveler who has

finally found a small slice of paradise to call her own. Her quaint little home has two guest bedrooms with private hot-water showers and enough frilly pillows to make you miss home – but that's not even the best part! In her immaculately landscaped front garden, you can soak the night away in a huge outdoor Jacuzzi while watching the lava flow down Arenal.

Essence Demo Cuisine (☎ 2479-1131; www.essencearenal.com; V) On the grounds of Essence Arenal, resident gourmet chef Isaac Weliver of Chicago lovingly prepares all-vegetarian meals (US$10) right before your eyes. Guests are encouraged to take part in the creation of dishes that will delight even the most hardcore carnivore.

Pizza John's Jardín Escondido (☎ 2479-1155; mains ₡2500-4250; ⏱ noon-9pm) Owner John DiVita of Los Angeles is lively and entertaining, and he'll have you in stitches with stories about his past life as a punk rocker and his escape from corporate America. John – a second-generation pizza-maker – cooks up an awesome pizza

TOM BOYDEN

Nymphalid butterfly

pie and also whips up delicious home-made ice cream.

DAM TO TILARÁN

This beautiful stretch of road is lined on both sides with cloud forest, and there are a number of fantastic accommodations strung along the way.

AROUND THE DAM

Unlike the fly-by view you'll get on a zip-line canopy tour, a walk through **Puentes Colgantes de Arenal** (Map p120; Arenal Hanging Bridges; ☎ 2479-1128; www.hangingbridges.com; adult/student/child under 12yr US$22/12/free; ☼ 7:30am-4:30pm) allows you to explore the rainforest and canopy from trails and suspended bridges at a more natural and peaceful pace.

If you want to stay in the area, **Arenal Lodge** (Map p120; ☎ 2290-4232; www.arenallodge.com; d standard US$88, superior US$124, junior ste US$155, chalet US$161, matrimonial ste US$185, all incl breakfast; P ✄ ⏏) is 400m west of the dam, at the top of a steep 2.5km ascent, though the entire lodge is awash with views of Arenal and the surrounding cloud forest. Standard rooms are just that, but junior suites are spacious, tiled and have wicker furniture, a big hot-water bathroom and a picture window or balcony with volcano views. Ten chalets sleep four and have kitchenette and good views.

Alternatively, **Lost Iguana Resort** (Map p120; ☎ 2267-6148, 2479-1331; www.lostiguanaresort.com; r US$215-300, ste US$300-535, casitas US$460, all incl breakfast; P ✄ ⏏) is easily the area's most stylish place to lay your head. This resort occupies a serene mountainside that affords phenomenal volcano views, sequestered far from the activity in La Fortuna. Even the standard rooms have private balconies looking out on Arenal, beds boasting Egyptian cot-ton sheets, satellite TV, and an invaluable sense of peace and privacy.

UNIÓN AREA

Places in this section are listed in order of their distance from the dam.

You can't miss **Hotel Los Héroes** (☎ 2692-8012/3; www.hotellosheroes.com; d with/without balcony US$65/55, tr US$80, apt US$115, all incl breakfast; P ⏏), a slightly in-congruous alpine chalet 13.5km west of the dam, complete with carved wooden balconies and Old World window shut-ters – and that's just on the outside. Large, immaculate rooms with wood paneling and private hot-water bathrooms are decorated with thickly hewn wood fur-niture that may make Swiss-Germans a little homesick, particularly when view-ing paintings of tow-headed children in lederhosen smooching innocently.

The owners have even built a mini-ature train (₡5500) that brings you up a hill to an underground station beneath the **Rondorama Panoramic Restaurant** (mains ₡5000-10,000), a revolving restaurant (seriously!) that's reportedly one-of-a-kind in Central America. There's also a hiking trail that leads to the restaurant and is great for wildlife-watching. English, German, French, Spanish and Portuguese are spoken.

Rates for the simply gorgeous two-person cottages – works of art, really – at **La Mansion Inn Arenal** (☎ 2692-8018; www.lamansionarenal.com; cottages incl breakfast US$204-640; P ⏏ ⏏) also include a cham-pagne breakfast, fruit basket, welcome cocktail, canoe access and horse rides, all conspiring with the magnificent views to make this the most romantic inn in the re-gion. The cottages feature huge split-level rooms with private terraces, lake views, high ceilings, Italianate painted walls and arched bathroom doors.

A serene, German-run escape, **La Ceiba Tree Lodge** (☎ 2692-8050, 8814-4004; www.ceibatree-lodge.com; d US$84; P) is 22km west of the dam and centered on a 500-year-old ceiba tree. Its five spacious, cross-ventilated rooms are entered through Maya-inspired carved doors and decorated with original paintings. Views of Laguna de Arenal, the lush, tropical gardens and utterly lovely dining-hangout area make this mountaintop spot a tranquil retreat from whatever ails you.

Another accommodation option is **Villa Decary B&B** (☎ 2694-4330, in US or Canada 1-800-556-0505; www.villadecary.com; r US$99, casitas with kitchen US$129-149, extra person US$15, all incl breakfast; P ⏾ ♿), an all-round winner with bright, spacious, well-furnished rooms, delicious full breakfasts and fantastic hosts. Paths into the woods behind the house give good opportunities for bird-watching and wildlife-watching, and there's a good chance that howler monkeys will wake you in the morning. The American-owned B&B is family-friendly and gay-friendly.

If you're a gourmand, make absolutely sure to book dinner reservations at the **Gingerbread Hotel & Restaurant** (☎ 2694-0039, 8351-7815; www.gingerbreadarenal.com; r incl breakfast US$100; ⏾ 5-9pm Tue-Sat, lunch by reservation only), arguably the best restaurant in northern Costa Rica. Better yet, stay at the charming boutique hotel, where the beds are sumptuous and the rooms adorned with murals by renowned local artists – this way, you'll get homemade preserves and pastries at breakfast. With the freshest local fare providing the foundation of his weekly menus, Chef Eyal turns out transcendent meals (mains US$9 to US$40, wines US$30 to US$200) and is choosy about his wine list, emphasizing top Chilean and Spanish *vino*. And come prepared – credit cards are not accepted.

NUEVO ARENAL

The only good-sized town between La Fortuna and Tilarán is the small Tico settlement of Nuevo Arenal, which is 27km west of the dam, or one hour drive from La Fortuna. In case you were wondering

Black-necked stilts, Parque Nacional Palo Verde (p146)

LAGUNA DE ARENAL AREA

About 18km west of La Fortuna, you'll arrive at a 750m-long causeway across the dam that created Laguna de Arenal, an 88-sq-km lake that is the largest in the country. Although a number of small towns were submerged during the lake's creation, the lake currently supplies valuable water to Guanacaste, and produces hydroelectricity for the region. High winds also produce power with the aid of huge, steel windmills, though windsurfers and kitesurfers frequently steal a breeze or two.

If you have your own car (or bicycle), this is one of the premier road trips in Costa Rica. The road is lined with odd and elegant businesses, many run by foreigners who have fallen in love with the place, and the scenic views of lakeside forests and Volcán Arenal are about as romantic as they come. Strong winds and high elevations give the lake a temperate feel, and you'll be forgiven if you suddenly imagine yourself in the English Lakes District or the Swiss countryside.

what happened to the old Arenal (no, it wasn't wiped out by the volcano, but good guess), it's about 27m below the surface of Laguna de Arenal.

Tom's Pan (☎ 2694-4547; mains ₡4500-8000; ⏲ 7am-4pm Mon-Sat; P), better known as 'the German Bakery,' is a famous rest stop for road-trippers heading to Tilarán. Its breads, strudels and cakes are all homemade and delicious, though heartier eaters will rave about the big German breakfasts, goulash with homemade noodles, spätzle, bratwurst, weisswurst and real German beer.

NUEVO ARENAL TO TILARÁN

Continue west and around the lake from Nuevo Arenal, where the scenery becomes even more spectacular just as the road gets progressively worse. Tilarán is the next 'big' city, with a reasonable selection of hotels and restaurants, plus roads and buses that can take you to Liberia, Monteverde or beyond.

ACTIVITIES

Some of the world's most consistent winds blow across northwestern Costa Rica, and this consistency attracts windsurfers from all over the world. Laguna de Arenal is rated one of the three best windsurfing spots in the world, mainly because of the predictability of the winds. From December to April, the winds reliably provide great rides for board sailers who gather on the southwest corner of the lake for long days of fun on the water. Windsurfing is possible in other months, too, but avoid September and October, which are considered the worst.

The best company for windsurfing is **Tico Wind** (☎ 2692-2002, 8813-7274; www. ticowind.com; rentals half-day US$42, full-day incl lunch US$78, lessons per hr US$50), which sets up camp on the western shores of the lake each year from late November to late April. It has state-of-the-art boards and sails that are replaced every year, with different equipment to suit different wind conditions and client experience. First-timers should consider the 'Get on Board' package (US$120). Lessons are offered in English, Spanish, German, Italian and Portuguese.

Hotel Tilawa (see p127) has emerged as a popular destination for windsurfers (and increasingly kitesurfers, too), and has an excellent selection of sailboards for rent at comparable rates. Although some folks think that the high winds, waves and world-class conditions are too much for a beginner to handle, the folks at Tilawa disagree. It runs the reader-recommended **Tilawa Windsurf Center** (www.windsurf costarica.com; half-/full-day US$100/150), offering windsurfing and kitesurfing lessons.

SLEEPING & EATING

All attractions in this section are listed in order of their distance from Nuevo Arenal.

Agua Inn (☎ 2694-4818, 8981-4735; www. aguainn.com; d incl breakfast US$78, apt US$141; ⓟ 🛜 🐾) The sounds of nature will lull you to sleep at this intimate B&B on the banks of the raging Río Cote that overlooks a primary rainforest and beautiful pool. Four rooms in a kaleidoscope of colors all feature full-sized comfy beds, fans, hot-water bathrooms and tiled floors. There's also a one-bedroom apartment with full kitchen (three-night minimum) and a studio with a kitchen.

Nearby, a great hiking trail follows the old road to Laguna de Arenal. Ask Californian owner Trent Deushane about his days as a tour bus driver for such acts as the Rolling Stones and Alicia Keys! It's 2.5km west of Nuevo Arenal down a very steep dirt road.

Chalet Nicholas (☎ 2694-4041; www. chaletnicholas.com; d incl breakfast US$79, extra person US$15; ⓟ 🚫) This attractive mountain chalet 2.7km west of Nuevo Arenal is owned by Catherine and John Nicholas, though their co-owners, five very playful Great Danes (don't be alarmed when they come bounding out to greet you), really know how to steal the show. Two downstairs rooms have private bathroom, while the upstairs loft has two linked bedrooms (for families or groups) and shares a downstairs bathroom. On clear days, all rooms have views of the volcano at the end of the lake. The owners enjoy natural history and have a living collection of dozens of orchids, which attract numerous species of birds. This place has many repeat guests.

Laguna de Arenal (p125)

CHRISTER FREDRIKSSON

Lago Coter Ecolodge (☎ 2440-6768; www.ecolodgecostarica.com; s/d/tr standard US$76/87/99, cabins US$93/105/122, all incl breakfast; P ⊠) This environmentally friendly lodge caters mostly to visitors that come on a complete package, including meals, rental equipment and guided naturalist hikes. Built in 1990 with an endowment from the World Bank, the hotel is committed to preserving its 250 hectares of primary-forest private reserve and 50 hectares of secondary-growth forest and pastures. Standard rooms with private hot-water showers are in a handsome wood-and-stone lodge that has a large fireplace and a relaxation area.

Café y Macadamia de Costa Rica (☎ 2692-2000; cafeymacadamia@yahoo.com; pastries & coffee ₡1000-2000, mains ₡1200-4500; ⊗ 8:30am-5pm) Pull over for a cup of coffee – and maybe a salad or Thai chicken curry, and leave room for a tasty pastry – all best savored along with the spectacular views of the lake (or clouds and fog, as the weather dictates).

Hotel Tilawa (☎ 2695-5050; www.hotel-tilawa.com; d US$68-98; P ⊠ ⊠ ⬛ ⬛) This place is something of a legend among windsurfers and kitesurfers, and whether you're semiprofessional or just starting out, you'll find a great community of wind warriors here. As for the rooms, well, they're definitely spacious and they cater to different budgets, though the Grecian theme – frescoes and all – is sort of over-the-top. Tilawa also has the best collection of amenities on the lake, including a huge skateboard park, pool, tennis courts and free bike rental.

TILARÁN

Near the southwestern end of Laguna de Arenal, the small town of Tilarán has a prosperous air to it – probably because it has served as a regional ranching center since long before there was a lake to speak of.

SIGHTS
If you're passing through here on your way to Monteverde, take a detour to visit **Viento Fresco Waterfalls** (☎ 2695-3434; www.vientofresco.net; adult/student/child 6-12yr US$15/12/10; ⊗ 7:30am-5pm), a series of five cascades including the amazing Arco Iris (Rainbow Falls) that drops 75m into a refreshing shallow pool that's perfect for swimming.

SLEEPING & EATING
Hotel La Carreta (☎ 2695-6593; www.lacarretacr.com; s/d incl breakfast US$40/55; P ⊛) Owners Rita and Ed have beautifully refurbished these skylit rooms, installing orthopedic beds, reading lights and hand-painted murals by local artists. In addition to the indoor dining area, there's a pleasant garden terrace for sipping coffee and reading something you've picked up from the book exchange in the front room.

Five Corners Grill (☎ 8887-7175; mains ₡2800-4000; ⊗ 8am-2pm; ⊛) You'll smell the wonderful barbecue aroma long before you even see this new restaurant. The menu specializes in what owner Jim Aoki calls 'Gringo comfort food' – eggs Benedict, nachos, bratwurst, peanut butter and jelly milkshakes, French fries and the best flame-grilled burgers on Laguna de Arenal.

GETTING THERE & AWAY
Buses service the following destinations:

Puntarenas ₡1530; two hours; departs at 6am and 1pm.

San José (Autotransportes Tilarán) ₡3650; four hours; departs at 5am, 7am, 9:30am, 2pm and 5pm.

Santa Elena/Monteverde ₡1200; 2½ hours; departs at 7am and 4pm.

NORTHERN COSTA RICA

MONTEVERDE & SANTA ELENA

MONTEVERDE & SANTA ELENA

Strung between two lovingly preserved cloud forests is this slim corridor of civilization, which consists of the Tico village of Santa Elena and the Quaker settlement of Monteverde. A 1983 feature article in *National Geographic* described this unique landscape and subsequently billed the area as *the* place to view one of Central America's most famous birds – the resplendent quetzal. Since then, the cloud forests near Monteverde and Santa Elena have become Costa Rica's premier destination for everyone from budget backpackers to well-heeled retirees. Indeed, this is a place where you can be inspired about the possibility of a world where organic farming and alternative energy sources help to salvage the fine mess we've made of the planet.

HISTORY

The history of these settlements dates back to the 1930s when a few Tico families left the gold-mining settlement of Juntas, and headed up the mountain to try to make a living through logging and farming. In a completely unrelated turn of events, four Quakers (a pacifist religious group also known as the 'Friends') were jailed in Alabama in 1949 for their refusal to be drafted into the Korean War. Since Quakers are obligated by their religion to be pacifists, the four men were eventually released from prison. However, in response to the incarceration, 44 Quakers from 11 families left the US and headed for greener pastures – namely Monteverde.

The Quakers chose Monteverde (Green Mountain) for two reasons – a few years prior, the Costa Rican government had abolished its military and the cool, mountain climate was ideal for grazing cattle. The Quakers found their isolated refuge from the ills of the world, and adopted a simple, trouble-free life of dairy farming and cheese production amid a new-found world of religious freedom. In an effort to protect the watershed above its 15-sq-km plot in Monteverde, the Quaker commu-

Reserva Biológica Bosque Nuboso Monteverde (p143)

IMAGEBROKER/ARCO IMAGES/RUEGNER, MARTIN

nity agreed to preserve the mountaintop rainforests.

SIGHTS
EL JARDÍN DE LAS MARIPOSAS
One of the most interesting activities is visiting El Jardín de las Mariposas (Butterfly Garden; ☎ 2645-5512; www.monte verdebutterflygarden.com; adult/student $10/8; ☾ 9:30am-4pm). Admission entitles you to a naturalist-led tour (in Spanish or English) that begins with an enlightening discussion of butterfly life cycles and the butterfly's importance in nature. A variety of eggs, caterpillars, pupae and adults are examined. Visitors are taken into the greenhouses, where the butterflies are raised, and on into the screened garden, where hundreds of butterflies of many species are seen.

RANARIO
The Ranario (Frog Pond; ☎ 2645-6320; www. ranario.com; adult/student & child US$10/8; ☾ 9am-8:30pm) houses about 30 species of Costa Rica's colorful array of frogs and toads in terraria lining the winding indoor-jungle paths. Sharp-eyed guides lead informative tours in English or Spanish, pointing out frogs, eggs and tadpoles with flashlights. You'll get to see the brilliantly fake-looking red-eyed tree frog, the glass frog and a variety of poison-dart frogs.

SERPENTARIO
Biologist Fernando Valverde has collected about 40 species of snake, plus a fair number of frogs, lizards, turtles and other cold-blooded critters at his serpentario (serpentarium; ☎ 2645-6002; adult/student/ child US$8/6/5; ☾ 9am-8pm). The venomous snake displays are awesome, and you'll get to see your first (and hopefully last) fer-de-lance.

BAT JUNGLE
Learn about echolocation, bat-wing aerodynamics and other amazing facts about the (incredibly cute) flying mammal, the bat. The stellar Bat Jungle (☎ 2645-6566; adult/child US$10/8; ☾ 9:30am-7:30pm), a labor of love realized by biologist Richard Laval, has terrific exhibits including a free-flying bat habitat, beautiful sculptures and a lot of bilingual educational displays.

MUNDO DE LOS INSECTOS
The Mundo de los Insectos (World of Insects; ☎ 2645-6859; adult/student US$10/6; ☾ 9am-8pm) goes beyond just butterflies with its collection of creepy cloud-forest crawlies, from hermaphroditic walking sticks to notoriously venomous banana spiders.

JARDÍN DE ORQUÍDEAS
This sweet-smelling Jardín de Orquídeas (Orchid Garden; ☎ 2645-5308; www.monteverde orchidgarden.com; adult/child under 12yr US$10/ free; ☾ 8am-5pm) has shady trails winding past more than 400 types of orchid organized into taxonomic groups.

MONTEVERDE CHEESE FACTORY
Until the recent upswing in ecotourism, Monteverde's number-one employer was this cheese factory (☎ 2645-5522; tours adult/child US$10/8; ☾ tours 9am & 2pm Mon-Sat, store 7:30am-5pm Mon-Sat, to 4pm Sun), also called La Lechería (The Dairy). Started in 1953 by Monteverde's original Quaker settlers, the factory produces everything from a creamy Gouda to a very nice sharp, white cheddar, sold all over the country, as well as other dairy products such as yogurt and, most importantly, ice cream. If you've got a hankering for something sweet, our favorite treat is the coffee milk shake. Reservations are required for the two-hour tour of the factory.

MONTEVERDE & SANTA ELENA

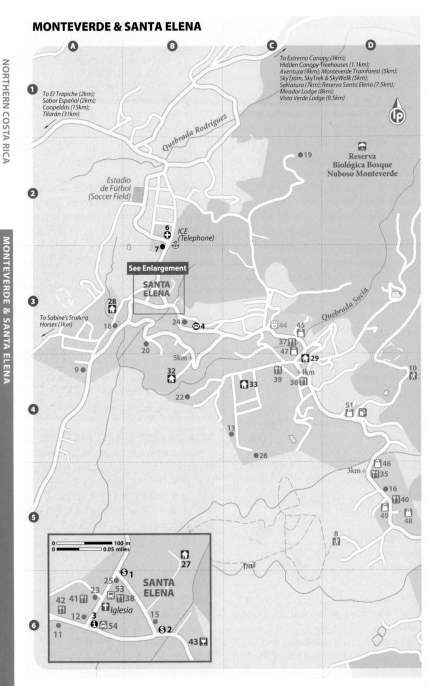

To El Trapiche (2km);
Sabor Español (2km);
Coopeldós (15km);
Tilarán (31km)

To Extremo Canopy (1km);
Hidden Canopy Treehouses (1.1km);
Aventura (4km); Monteverde Trainforest (5km);
SkyTrám, SkyTrek & SkyWalk (5km);
Selvatura (7km); Reserva Santa Elena (7.5km);
Mirador Lodge (8km);
Vista Verde Lodge (9.5km)

Quebrada Rodríguez

Reserva
Biológica Bosque
Nuboso Monteverde

Estadio
de Fútbol
(Soccer Field)

ICE
(Telephone)

See Enlargement

SANTA
ELENA

Quebrada Sucia

To Sabine's Smiling
Horses (3km)

5km

4km

3km

0   100 m
0   0.05 miles

SANTA
ELENA

Iglesia

Trail

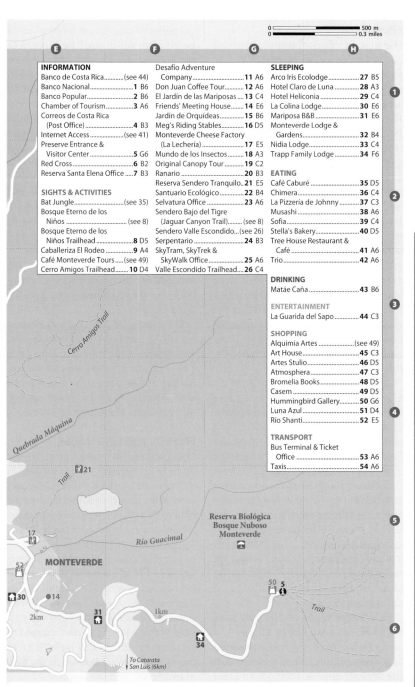

0   500 m
0   0.3 miles

INFORMATION
Banco de Costa Rica............(see 44)
Banco Nacional............................**1** B6
Banco Popular..............................**2** B6
Chamber of Tourism....................**3** A6
Correos de Costa Rica
  (Post Office)..............................**4** B6
Internet Access....................(see 41)
Preserve Entrance &
  Visitor Center...........................**5** G6
Red Cross......................................**6** B2
Reserva Santa Elena Office.......**7** B3

SIGHTS & ACTIVITIES
Bat Jungle.............................(see 35)
Bosque Eterno de los
  Niños....................................(see 8)
Bosque Eterno de los
  Niños Trailhead.......................**8** D5
Caballeriza El Rodeo..................**9** A4
Café Monteverde Tours......(see 49)
Cerro Amigos Trailhead........**10** D4

Desafío Adventure
  Company.................................**11** A6
Don Juan Coffee Tour............**12** A6
El Jardín de las Mariposas....**13** C4
Friends' Meeting House.........**14** E6
Jardín de Orquídeas..............**15** B6
Meg's Riding Stables.............**16** D5
Monteverde Cheese Factory
  (La Lechería)...........................**17** E5
Mundo de los Insectos.........**18** A3
Original Canopy Tour............**19** C2
Ranario......................................**20** B3
Reserva Sendero Tranquilo..**21** E5
Santuario Ecológico..............**22** B4
Selvatura Office......................**23** A6
Sendero Bajo del Tigre.........(see 8)
Sendero Valle Escondido...(see 26)
Serpentario.............................**24** B3
SkyTram, SkyTrek &
  SkyWalk Office.......................**25** A6
Valle Escondido Trailhead....**26** C4

SLEEPING
Arco Iris Ecolodge..................**27** B5
Hotel Claro de Luna..............**28** A3
Hotel Heliconia.......................**29** C4
La Colina Lodge......................**30** E6
Mariposa B&B.........................**31** E6
Monteverde Lodge &
  Gardens..................................**32** B4
Nidia Lodge.............................**33** C4
Trapp Family Lodge...............**34** F6

EATING
Café Caburé.............................**35** D5
Chimera....................................**36** C4
La Pizzería de Johnny...........**37** C3
Musashi....................................**38** A6
Sofía...**39** C4
Stella's Bakery........................**40** D5
Tree House Restaurant &
  Café..**41** A6
Trio...**42** A6

DRINKING
Matáe Caña.............................**43** B6

ENTERTAINMENT
La Guarida del Sapo...............**44** C3

SHOPPING
Alquimia Artes....................(see 49)
Art House.................................**45** C3
Artes Stulio.............................**46** D5
Atmosphera.............................**47** C3
Bromelia Books.......................**48** D5
Casem.......................................**49** D5
Hummingbird Gallery............**50** G6
Luna Azul.................................**51** D4
Río Shanti................................**52** E5

TRANSPORT
Bus Terminal & Ticket
  Office......................................**53** A6
Taxis..**54** A6

Cerro Amigos Trail

Quebrada Máquina

Trail

21

17

52

MONTEVERDE

30   14

2km

31

1km

Río Guacimal

**Reserva Biológica
Bosque Nuboso
Monteverde**

50 5

Trail

34

To Catarata
San Luis (6km)

SELVATURA

The makers of eco-fun really went all out at Selvatura (☎ 2645-5929, 2645-6200; www.selvatura.com; hummingbird garden US$5, butterfly garden US$12, reptile museum US$12, hanging bridges adult/student/child under 12yr US$25/20/15, canopy tour US$45/35/30; 🕑 7:30am-4pm), a huge ecocomplex complete with butterfly and hummingbird gardens, a herpetarium (reptiles and amphibian museum), a canopy tour and a series of hanging bridges. The star attraction is the slightly overwhelming Jewels of the Rainforest Exhibition. This exhibition brings together the world's largest private collection of the strangest and most stunning insects you've ever seen. The exhibit is the life's work of entomologist Richard Whitten (with a little help from his wife, Margaret), and is masterfully presented using a combination of art, video and music. If you only have time for one sight in Monteverde, this is the one.

COFFEE PLANTATIONS

Coffee lovers will be excited to find some of the finest coffee in the world right here. Late April is the best time to see the fields in bloom, while the coffee harvest (done entirely by hand) takes place from December through February. Anytime is a good time to see how your favorite beverage makes the transition from ruby-red berry to smooth black brew. Advance reservations are required for all tours, which you can book direct by phone or through many hotels. Most charge about US$30 for adults, including transportation to the fincas (plantations).

Café Monteverde (☎ 2645-5901; www.monteverde-coffee.com) Run by Cooperative Santa Elena, this highly recommended tour takes visitors to coffee fincas that use entirely organic methods to grow the perfect bean. You can help pick some beans, after which you'll be brought to the beneficio (processing plant), where you can watch as the beans are washed and dried, roasted and then packed. Of course, you'll also get to taste the final product with a snack. The cafe (open from 7:30am to 6pm) itself offers free samples of six roasts, or buy some beans to take home.

Coopeldós (☎ 2693-8441; www.coopeldos.com) This cooperative of 450 small- and medium-sized organic coffee growers is Fairtrade-certified. One of its main clients is Starbucks. It's about halfway between Tilarán and Monteverde.

Don Juan Coffee Tour (☎ 2645-7100; www.donjuancoffeetour.com) Book this two-hour tour at its downtown shop near the SuperCompro.

El Trapiche (☎ 2645-5834; www.eltrapichetour.com; 🕑 tours 10am & 3pm Mon-Sat, 3pm Sun) This reader-recommended, family-run coffee plantation also grows sugarcane. Besides coffee, you can also sample the area's other famous beverage, saca de guaro, a liquor made from sugarcane.

FRIENDS MEETING HOUSE

The Quakers (or more correctly, the Society of Friends) who settled in Monteverde played a direct role in preserving the cloud forest, and they remain extremely active in the local community, though they're not recognizable by any traditional costume. Quakerism began as a breakaway movement from the Anglican Church in the 1650s, founded by the young George Fox, who in his early 20s heard the voice of Christ, and claimed that direct experience with God was possible without having to go through the sacraments. Today, this belief is commonly described by Quakers as the 'God in everyone,' and the community continues to lead a peaceful lifestyle in the Monteverde area.

If you're interested in learning more about the Society of Friends, prayer meetings at the **Friends Meeting House** in Monteverde are held on Sunday at 10:30am and Wednesday at 9am. If you're willing to give at least a six-week commitment, there are numerous volunteer opportunities available. For more information, contact the **Monteverde Friends School** (www.mfschool.org).

ACTIVITIES

Don't forget your hiking boots, bug spray and a hat – there's plenty to do outdoors around here, including lots of action either on horseback or in the jungle canopy.

HIKING

Two of the best hikes are at the cloud-forest reserves bookending the main road, Reserva Biológica Bosque Nuboso Monteverde (p143) and Reserva Santa Elena (p144).

For advice on deep-jungle trekking and reputable local guides, contact trekking guide J Andrés Vargas (www.euforia expeditions.com), a socially responsible, superknowledgeable adventure specialist.

CHILDREN'S ETERNAL RAINFOREST

If you've ever felt cynical about schoolchildren asking for money to save the rainforest, then you really must stop by **Bosque Eterno de los Niños** (BEN; ☎ 2645-5003; www.acmcr.org; adult/student day use US$8/5, guided night hike US$15/10; ☺ 7:30am-5:30pm) and see what they purchased with all that spare change. Keep in mind, however, that this enormous 220-sq-km reserve, which dwarfs both the Monteverde and Santa Elena reserves, is largely inaccessible. The international army of children who paid the bills decided that it was more important to provide a home for local wildlife among the primary and secondary forest (and to allow former agricultural land to be slowly reclaimed by the jungle) than develop a lucrative tourist infrastructure. Kids today, what can you do?

ADRIAN HEPWORTH/HEPWORTHIMAGES

Olive ridley sea turtle

The effort has allowed for one fabulous trail that hooks into a system of unimproved trails that are primarily for researchers, the 3.5km **Sendero Bajo del Tigre** (Jaguar Canyon Trail), which offers more open vistas than those in the cloud forest, so spotting birds tends to be easier. The reason is that a good portion of the surrounding area was clear-cut during the mid-20th century, though there has been significant regrowth since it was granted protected status. The resulting landscape is known as premontane forest, which is unique in Costa Rica as most things that are cut down stay cut down. Visitors also report that wildlife-watching tends to be better here than in the reserves at Monteverde or Santa Elena since the tourist volume is considerably lower.

Make reservations in advance for the popular **night hikes**, which set off at 5:30pm for a two-hour trek by flashlight (bring your own) through a sea of glowing red eyes.

The **Estación Biológica San Gerardo** (San Gerardo Biological Station; ☎ 2645-5200; http://acmcr.org/sangerardo_biological_station.htm; per person incl full board US$48) is located on the Atlantic slope of the Tilarán mountain range (1200m), and features a rustic lodge that is rented out to overnight visitors in addition to research scientists and student groups. The 1st floor consists of a kitchen, dining area and meeting rooms, while the 2nd floor is home to ensuite rooms facing Volcán Arenal and Laguna de Arenal. There are also more than 5km of trails that wind through the surrounding primary and secondary forest, some of which is regenerating pastureland. Bird-watching is predictably excellent, particularly between April and June when the courtship displays of the bare-necked umbrella bird captivate local residents. Advance reservations, which can be made through the visitors center at the entrance to the Sendero Bajo del Tigre, are highly recommended. Access on foot is via a 3.5km trail that starts from the parking lot of the Reserva Santa Elena.

The **Estación Biológica Pocosol** (Pocosol Biological Station; ☎ 2468-8382,

Hundreds of butterflies can be seen at El Jardín de las Mariposas (p129), Santa Elena

http://acmcr.org/pocosol_biological_station.htm; per person incl full board US$48) is also on the Atlantic slope of the Tilarán mountain range (720m), though it's decidedly more remote, which is indeed the main attraction. The station is divided into three parts: a recently inaugurated building that can accommodate up to 28 people, classrooms and meetings spaces for students, tourists and researchers, and a full kitchen and dining hall. The station is surrounded by 10km of trails that wind through an evergreen forest with a canopy at 30m to 40m in height, abundant epiphytes and a dense understory. Due to its lower altitude and proximity to a transitional forest, Pocosol offers unique biological diversity and forest structure that is markedly different from other parks and reserves in the region. As with San Gerardo, advance reservations are a very good idea. Access is by 4WD from La Fortuna, though it's best to inquire at the time of booking about specific directions as it's a bit tricky to find.

Finally, if you're looking to participate in a **volunteer program**, the administration of the Children's Eternal Rainforest is always looking for help.

OTHER HIKES

Offering hikes of varying lengths, **Santuario Ecológico** (Ecological Sanctuary; ☎ 2645-5869; adult/student/child US$10/8/6, guided night tour US$15/12/10; ☉ 7am-5:30pm) has four loop trails (the longest takes about 2½ hours at a slow pace) through private property comprising premontane and secondary forest, coffee and banana plantations, and past a couple of waterfalls and lookout points. Coatis, agoutis and sloths are seen on most days, and monkeys, porcupines and other animals are also common. There are also good bird-watching opportunities here.

Guided tours are available throughout the day, but you'll see even more animals on the guided night tours (5:30pm to 7:30pm).

An 81-hectare private reserve, **Reserva Sendero Tranquilo** (Tranquil Path Reserve; ☎ 2645-5010; admission US$20; ☉ tours 7:30am & 1pm) is located between the Reserva Biológica Bosque Nuboso Monteverde and the Río Guacimal. Trails here are narrow to allow for minimal environmental impact, and the group size is capped at six people, which means you won't have to worry about chattering tourists scaring away all the animals. The trails pass through four distinct types of forest, including a previously destroyed area that's starting to bud again.

Sendero Valle Escondido (Hidden Valley Trail; ☎ 2645-6601; day use US$5, night tour adult/child US$20/10; ☉ 7am-4pm) begins behind the Pensión Monteverde Inn and slowly winds its way through a deep canyon into an 11-hectare reserve. In comparison with the more popular reserves, Valle Escondido is quiet during the day and relatively undertouristed, so it's a good trail for wildlife-watching. However, the reserve's two-hour guided night tour (departing at 5:30pm) is very popular, so it's best to make reservations for this in advance.

Take a free hike up **Cerro Amigos** (1842m) for good views of the surrounding rainforest and, on a clear day, of Volcán Arenal, 20km away to the northeast. Near the top of the mountain, you'll pass by the TV towers for channels 7 and 13. The trail leaves Monteverde from behind Hotel Belmar and ascends roughly 300m in 3km. From the hotel, take the dirt road going downhill, then the next left. Note that this trail does not connect to the trails in the Monteverde reserve, so you will have to double back.

Another popular (but strenuous) hike is to visit the **Catarata San Luis**, a gorgeous ribbon of water streaming from the cloud forests into a series of swimming holes just screaming for a picnic. The distance from the parking area to the falls is only a few kilometers, but it's steeply graded downhill, and the rocky, mud-filled terrain can get very slick. Readers report that their entire families have been OK on the trail, but it's important to go slow and turn back if it becomes too difficult. However, your efforts will be worth it as the waterfall is simply breathtaking.

CANOPY TOURS

Before you tighten your harness and clip in for the ride, you're going to have to choose which canopy tour will get your hard-earned cash – this is more challenging than you might think!

Aventura (☎ 2645-6388; www.monteverdeadventure.com; adult/student US$40/30; ☀ 7am-4pm) Aventura has 16 platforms that are spiced up with a Tarzan swing and a 15m rappel. It's about 3km north of Santa Elena

on the road to the reserve, and transportation from your hotel is included in the price.

Extremo Canopy (☎ 2645-6058; www.monteverdeextremo.com; adult/child US$40/30; ☀ 8am-4pm) The newest player on the Monteverde canopy scene, this outfit runs small groups and doesn't bother with extraneous attractions if all you really want to do is fly down the zip lines. There's also a new Superman canopy ride (US$5 extra), allowing you to fly Superman-style through the air.

Original Canopy Tour (☎ 2645-6950; www.canopytour.com; adult/student/child US$45/35/25; ☀ 7:30am-4pm) On the grounds of Cloud Forest Lodge, this has the fabled zip lines that started an adventure-tourism trend of questionable ecological value. These lines aren't as elaborate as the others, but with 14 platforms, a rappel through the center of an old fig tree and 5km of private trails worth a wander afterward, you can enjoy a piece of history that's far more entertaining than many museums.

LACEY ANN JOHNSON/AURORA PHOTOS

Zip lining through the mist, Reserva Biológica Bosque Nuboso Monteverde (p143)

Selvatura (☎ 2645-5929; www.selvatura. com; adult/child US$45/30; ☺ 7:30am-4pm) One of the bigger games in town, Selvatura has 3km of cables, 18 platforms and one Tarzan swing through primary forest. The office is across the street from the church in Santa Elena.

SkyTrek (☎ 2645-5238; www.skywalk.co.cr; adult/student/child US$75/60/48; ☺ 7:30am-5pm) If you're not buying the whole 'eco' element of canopy tours, this is definitely for you. This seriously fast canopy tour consists of 11 platforms attached to steel towers that are spread out along a road. We're talking serious speeds of up to 64km/h, which is probably why SkyTrek is the only canopy tour that has a real brake system. The price includes admission to the SkyTram gondola and SkyWalk hanging bridges; cheaper ticket options are available.

HANGING BRIDGES, TRAMS & TRAINS
OK, so you're too scared to zip through the canopy on a steel cable, but fear not: the makers of eco-fun have something special for you – hanging bridges and trams, the safe and slightly less expensive way to explore the tree tops and live out your Indiana Jones fantasies.

Monteverde Trainforest (☎ 2645-5700; www.trainforest.com; adult/student/child under 12yr US$65/33/free; ♿) is a miniature train system that travels six kilometers through the forest, crossing one tunnel and four bridges. The scenic railroad offers amazing views of Monteverde and Arenal lake and volcano. This is a great option for families with young children, as kids under 12 are free. It's located 5km north of downtown Santa Elena, on the road to Reserva Santa Elena.

SkyTram (☎ 2645-5238; www.skywalk.co.cr; ♿), also owned by SkyTrek, is a cable car

that is handicapped-accessible, and leads you on a gentle ride through the cloud forest; tickets can only be purchase in conjunction with SkyWalk or SkyTrek.

HORSEBACK RIDING
Until recently, this region was most easily traveled on horseback, and considering the roads around here, that's probably still true. Several operators offer you the chance to test this theory, with guided horse rides ranging from two-hour tours to five-day adventures. Shorter trips generally run about US$15 per hour, while an overnight trek including meals and accommodations runs between US$150 and US$200.

Some outfitters also make the trip to La Fortuna (US$60 to US$100), an intriguing transportation option with several caveats, including only going in the dry season. Though a few operators will charge less, remember you (or more likely, the horse) get what you pay for.

Caballeriza El Rodeo (☎ 2645-5764, 2645-6306; elrodeo02@gmail.com) Does local tours on private trails, as well as trips to San Luis Waterfall and a sunset tour to a spot overlooking the Golfo de Nicoya. Average price is US$30 for two hours.

Desafío Adventure Company (☎ 2645-5874; www.monteverdetours.com) Does local treks for groups and individuals around town, day trips to San Luis waterfall (six hours, per person including admission US$60) and several multiday rides. This established outfitter will arrange rides to La Fortuna for US$85, usually on the Lake Trail. The company also arranges white-water rafting trips on the Ríos Toro, Sarapiquí and others, and can help with transportation and hotel reservations. Located next door to Morpho's Restaurant.

Meg's Riding Stables (☎ 2645-5560, 2645-5052; ♿) Takes folks on private trails nearby plus treks to Catarata San Luis.

Kid-sized saddles and gentle horses are also available. The horses are well looked after, and this is the longest-established operation in Monteverde.

Mirador Lodge (☎ 2645-5354; Monteverde to Arenal ride US$70) The Quesada family at this isolated cloud-forest lodge takes riders on horseback tours as well as to Arenal, starting from the lodge. If the weather and trail conditions are not perfect, they will arrange a taxi-boat-taxi transfer as an alternative.

Sabine's Smiling Horses (☎ 2645-6894, 8385-2424; www.horseback-riding-tour.com) Run by Sabine, who speaks English, French, Spanish and German, Smiling Horses offers a variety of treks, from US$15 per-hour day-trips to specialty tours, including a Full Moon Ride (per person US$50, three hours). Several multiday treks are also on offer, and Sabine may also take experienced riders on the Castillo Trail, weather permitting. This outfitter has been highly recommended by readers year after year.

FESTIVALS & EVENTS

The **Monteverde Music Festival** is held annually on variable dates from late January to early April. It's gained a well-deserved reputation as one of the top music festivals in Central America. Music is mainly classical, jazz and Latin, with an occasional experimental group to spice things up. Concerts are held on Thursday, Friday and Saturday, at different venues all over town and at Monteverde Institute, which sponsors it. Some performances are free, but most events ask US$5 to US$15 – proceeds go toward teaching music and the arts in local schools.

SLEEPING

Arco Iris Ecolodge (☎ 2645-5067; www.arcoirislodge.com; s US$30-64, d US$40-128, cabins US$107-200, honeymoon ste US$193; P 🖥)

This clutch of pretty cabins is on a little hill overlooking Santa Elena and the surrounding forests, and has the privacy and intimacy of a mountain retreat. The lodge features a system of private trails that wind throughout the property, including one that leads to a lookout point where you can see the Pacific on a clear day.

Mariposa B&B (☎ 2645-5013; vmfamilia@costarricense.cr; s/d incl breakfast US$35/55; P)
Just 1.5km from the Monteverde reserve, this friendly family-run place has simple but very nice rooms with private hot showers, all nestled into the forest. In addition to breakfast (a *real* breakfast of fruit, pancakes, eggs and tortillas), there's also a little balcony for observing wildlife.

La Colina Lodge (☎ 2645-5009; www.lacolinalodge.com; campsite per person US$5, d with/without bathroom incl breakfast US$52/44; P) This is the former Flor Mar opened in 1977 by Marvin Rockwell, one of the area's original Quakers, who was jailed for refusing to sign up for the draft in 1949 and then spent three months driving down from Alabama. All of the rambling rooms on this peaceful property are hand-painted in cheery colors with unique furniture and decor.

Nidia Lodge (☎ 2645-5236, 2645-6082; www.nidialodge.com; s/d standard US$58/76, deluxe US$81/99, junior ste US$93/116, all incl breakfast; P 🖥 📶) The area is peaceful and just steps away from the Santuario Ecológico, so there's a good chance that wildlife will grace your front doorstep and the motmots will hang out in the trees out back. Nidia provides a superchill presence around the inn, and the owner Eduardo, an expert naturalist, clearly revels in offering guided walks of the area's forests.

Hotel Claro de Luna (☎ 2645-5269; www.clarodelunahotel.com; s standard/deluxe US$59/68, d standard/deluxe US$68/88, all incl breakfast; P) This sweet mountain chalet just southwest of Santa Elena is the perfect getaway for lovers. If you squint your eyes just a bit while staring at the hotel's Swiss-inspired architecture, you could convince yourself you're summering high up in the Alps. All nine rooms have hardwood floors and ceilings, and feature luxurious, hot-water bathrooms with regal tiles.

Vista Verde Lodge (☎ 8380-1517; www.info-monteverde.com; s/d standard US$87/107, junior ste US$93/116, extra person US$14, all incl breakfast; P) When you really want to get away from it all, this marvelous lodge lets you fall asleep to the sounds of the surrounding rainforest. Wood-paneled rooms with picture windows take in views of Volcán Arenal, and the current direction of the lava flow means that on a clear night you will see plenty of fireworks. There's also a great common area where you can unwind in front of the TV and warm your feet beside the fire.

Trapp Family Lodge (☎ 2645-5858; www.trappfam.com; d superior/ste US$96/113, extra person US$17; P ⚔ 🖳 👶) The closest lodge to the reserve entrance (just under 1km away) has 20 spacious rooms with high wooden ceilings, big bathrooms and fabulous views from the picture windows (which overlook either gardens or cloud forest). The emphasis here is on creating a family atmosphere, so bring the kids along and teach them a thing or two about nature.

Hotel Heliconia (☎ 2645-5109; www.hotelheliconia.com; d standard/junior ste/family ste/master ste incl breakfast US$100/112/137/155; P 🖳) Located in Cerro Plano, this attractive, wooden, family-run hotel consists of the main lodge and several bungalows that are spread out across a mountainside. Standard rooms have breezy views while junior suites are ridiculously luxurious with stained-glass windows. Owners arrange all the usual tours, and operate a spa and aesthetic center where you can soak your stresses away in the Jacuzzi, or indulge in an endless list of beauty treatments.

Monteverde Lodge & Gardens (☎ 2257-0766; www.costaricaexpeditions.com; d US$111-190; P ⚔ 🖳 🐾) A progressive recycling strategy, a solar-energy system and

Rufous-tailed hummingbird

SHANNON NACE

a huge solar-powered – but nice and hot – Jacuzzi are among this nonsmoking hotel's noteworthy environmentally sound practices. Large rooms with full bathrooms and wraparound picture windows have garden or forest views. The grounds are attractively landscaped with a variety of native plants, emphasizing ferns, bromeliads and mosses, and a short trail leads to a bluff with an observation platform.

Hidden Canopy Treehouses (☎ 2645-5447; www.hiddencanopy.com; d garden rooms US$186, tree houses US$242-322, all incl breakfast & afternoon tea; P ✗) One of the most unique accommodations in Costa Rica, this new boutique hotel lets guests live out their wildest childhood tree-house fantasies, but in a grown up, blissfully luxurious setting. Hidden within 13 acres of private rainforest are four standalone, wood-and-glass tree houses, each with a unique floor plan, decor and name. All feature a treetop balcony, luxurious bedding, private bathroom, waterfall shower, custom-made furniture, and paintings by local artists.

EATING

Stella's Bakery (☎ 2645-5560; mains ₡800-3200; ☺ 6am-10pm) Order your choice of sandwich on delicious homemade breads with a convenient order form (one side is in English), and don't skimp on the veggies, many of which are locally grown (and organic). You can also get soups, salads, quiches and lots of tempting sweet pastries.

Café Caburé (☎ 2645-5020; mains ₡2300-5000; ☺ 8am-8pm Mon-Sat; ☺) Looking for something different? Argentine owner Susana Salas has created one of the most eclectic menus around, including Mexican chicken *mole,* chipotle-rubbed steak, sweet-and-sour chicken wraps, curries and mouth-watering, homemade chocolates and other desserts.

Chimera (☎ 2645-6081; tapas ₡1700-5000; ☺ 11:30am-9:30pm) Latin-infused tapas are complemented by an excellent wine list featuring robust reds like Chilean syrah-cabernets and crisp whites like pinot grigio. Dine alfresco at the trellis patio or the big-windowed dining room with beautiful jungle views.

Musashi (☎ 2645-7160; sushi ₡2500-4000, rolls & mains ₡2500-9000; ☺ 11am-11pm Tue-Sun) Who ever thought you'd find good sushi in the middle of the rainforest? But look no further than this tiny restaurant in the heart of Santa Elena. Venezuelan owner Jesus is a classically trained sushi chef with an eye for perfection.

La Pizzería de Johnny (☎ 2645-5066; www.pizzeriadejohnny.com; mains ₡2200-8300; ☺ 11:30am-10pm) Wood-fired, thin-crust pizzas will warm you right up after a long hike through the cloud forests (or up the hill from Santa Elena). The warm atmosphere and lovely dining area make it feel as though you are having a nice dinner out without paying the price.

Sabor Español (☎ 2645-5387; sabor espanola@hotmail.com; mains ₡3000-7500; ☺ noon-9pm) She's from Barcelona. He's from Ibiza. And together, Heri and Montse have created one of the most authentic and lovely Spanish restaurants in Costa Rica. The couple specializes in paella, fresh fish, meats and chicken.

Tree House Restaurant & Café (☎ 2645-5751; www.canopydining.com; mains ₡4000-9000; ☺ 6am-10pm; ☺) Built around a half-century-old *higuerón* (fig) tree, this hip cafe serves up your favorite Mexican dishes from burritos to *huevos rancheros* (eggs served with tortillas and a tomato sauce), but also has a healthy selection of salads and sandwiches.

Trio (☎ 2645-7254; mains ₡5000-7000; ☺ lunch & dinner) From the same folks who brought us Chimera and Sofia comes this amazing new fusion restaurant. We were in heaven after savoring the *camarones mojitos* – grilled shrimp drenched in a garlic, cumin, onion, rum and orange juice sauce, served on a bed of potatoes, veggies and avocado. Follow up the flavor explosions with to-die-for desserts like the mango split sorbet.

Sofia (☎ 2645-7017; mains ₡6800-9000; ⏱ 11:30am-9:30pm) Sofia has established itself on the Monteverde restaurant scene as one of the best places in town with its Nuevo Latino cuisine – a modern fusion of traditional Latin American cooking styles. The ambience is flawless – soft lighting, hip music, picture windows, romantic candle settings, sloping wooden ceilings, pastel paintwork and potent cocktails to lighten the mood.

DRINKING & ENTERTAINMENT

A cathedral of music built by the Hotel El Sapo Dorado, **La Guarida del Sapo** (☎ 2645-7010; ⏱ 6pm-midnight Mon-Thu, to 2am Fri & Sat) resembles an old church – right down to the ornate stained-glass windows with Costa Rican nature scenes. Friday is the most lively night when the place is transformed into a discotheque. There's live music on most Monday and Saturday nights. The international restaurant (mains ₡6000 to ₡12,000) serves everything from filet mignon to escargot. A small cover charge applies for special events.

Housed in Santa Elena's original tavern, **Matáe Caña** (☎ 2645-4883; ⏱ noon-late Tue-Sun) is a chic new lounge that fills the void once felt in the Monteverde bar scene. A waterfall graces one entire wall of the bar and there are numerous padded nooks and crannies where you can sip a drink with your date. During warm weather, guests can lounge on beds in the outdoor patio.

SHOPPING

Art House (Casa de Arte; ☎ 2645-5275; www. monteverdearthouse.com; ⏱ 9am-6:30pm) Several rooms stuffed with colorful Costa Rican artistry is what you'll find at the Art House. There's jewelry, ceramic work,

ANNELIES MERTENS

Colorful plants guarantee a visual feast in the Reserva Biológica Bosque Nuboso Monteverde (p143)

Boruca textiles and paintings. Though styles here differ quite a bit, it's more along the crafty end of the artsy-craftsy spectrum. It's a great place to find a unique local souvenir.

Atmosphera (☎ 2645-6555; complejo atmosphera@yahoo.com.mx; ⌚ 9am-6pm) An upscale Cerro Plano gallery that specializes in wood sculpture created by artists from all over Costa Rica. Several are from the Monteverde area, and the pieces run the gamut of style and function. They're also priced accordingly, from about US$25 to US$5000.

Luna Azul (☎ 2645-6638; lunaazulmon teverde@gmail.com; ⌚ 9am-6:30pm) This funky boutique is decked out in celestial murals, and it's a relaxing spot to do a little souvenir shopping for your friends…or yourself. There's a great variety of clothing, handmade jewelry and local art up for grabs, as well as various aromatherapy products.

Río Shanti (☎ 2645-6121; www.rioshanti. com; ⌚ 10am-5pm Mon-Sat, noon-5pm Sun; ♿) The real reason to come here is for a spa treatment, massage or yoga class for adults and children (be sure to call ahead for an appointment or schedule), but this calming space on the road into Monteverde also has a gallery of local art for sale.

Artes Stulio (☎ 2645-5567; artestulio@ yahoo.com; ⌚ 11am-5pm Mon-Sat) A working studio where you can browse the gallery and also roam upstairs to watch the artists at work. The art here is a bit more experimental and an intriguing look into the contemporary scene fostered by the magical Monteverde atmosphere.

Alquimia Artes (☎ 2645-5847; www. alquimiaartes.com; ⌚ 10am-5pm) This place has work that is a tad more affordable than at some other places (check out the jewelry by Tarsicio Castillo from the Ecuadorian Andes), but this doesn't mean its collection of wood sculpture, paintings and prints by Costa Rican artists isn't astounding.

Casem (Cooperativa de Artesanía Santa Elena Monteverde; ☎ 2645-5190; www.casemcoop.org; ⌚ 8am-5pm Mon-Sat, 10am-4pm Sun high season) Begun in 1982 as a women's cooperative representing eight female artists, today Casem has expanded to include almost 150 local artisans, eight of whom are men. Embroidered and hand-painted clothing, polished wooden tableware, handmade cards and other work, some priced even for budget souvenir shoppers, make for an eclectic selection.

Bromelias Books (☎ 2645-6272; www. bromeliasmusicgarden.com; ⌚ 10am-5:30pm) Don cute felt shoes before entering this bookstore, with its polished-wood Cerro Plano expanse of local arts and crafts, including some intricate batik. There are also books about the region, in particular natural history, in English and Spanish, plus lots of excellent Costa Rican and Central American music.

Hummingbird Gallery (☎ 2645-5030; ⌚ 8:30am-5pm) This gallery just outside Monteverde reserve has beautiful photos, watercolors, art by the indigenous Chorotega and Boruca people and, best of all, feeders that constantly attract several species of hummingbird. Great photo ops include potential hot shots of the violet sabrewing (Costa Rica's largest hummer) and the coppery-headed emerald, one of only three mainland birds endemic to Costa Rica.

GETTING THERE & AWAY
BUS

Puntarenas ₡1235; three hours; departs from the front of Banco Nacional at 6am.

Reserva Monteverde ₡600; 30 minutes; departs from the front of Banco Nacional at 6:15am, 7:20am, 1:20pm and

3pm, and returns at 6:45am, 11:30am, 2pm and 4pm.

Reserva Santa Elena ₡1200; 30 minutes; departs from the front of Banco Nacional at 6:30am, 8:30am, 10:30am, 12:30pm, 1pm and 3pm, and returns at 11am, 1pm and 4pm.

San José (TransMonteverde) ₡2500; 4½ hours; departs from the Santa Elena bus station at 6:30am and 2:30pm.

Tilarán ₡1800; seven hours; departs from the bus station at 6am.

HORSEBACK

Several tour companies offer horseback-riding trips between La Fortuna and Monteverde. The trip (a combination of horse, taxi or boat) takes about five to seven hours and costs about US$85, including separate transport of your luggage. One highly recommended company is Desafío Adventure Company (p137).

JEEP-BOAT-JEEP

The fastest route between Monteverde-Santa Elena and La Fortuna is a jeep-boat-jeep combo (around US$25 to US$30, three hours), which can be arranged through almost any hotel or tour operator in either town. A 4WD jeep taxi takes you to Río Chiquito, meeting a boat that crosses Laguna de Arenal, where a taxi on the other side continues to La Fortuna. This is increasingly becoming the primary transportation between La Fortuna and Monteverde as it's incredibly scenic, reasonably priced and saves half a day of rough travel.

RESERVA BIOLÓGICA BOSQUE NUBOSO MONTEVERDE

When Quaker settlers first arrived in the area, they agreed to preserve about a third of their property in order to protect the watershed above Monteverde. By 1972, however, encroaching squatters began to threaten the region. The community joined forces with environmental organizations such as the Nature Conservancy and the World Wildlife Fund to purchase 328 hectares adjacent to the

NORTHERN COSTA RICA

RESERVA BIOLÓGICA BOSQUE NUBOSO MONTEVERDE

KARL LEHMANN

Giant grasshopper

already preserved area. This was called the Reserva Biológica Bosque Nuboso Monteverde (Monteverde Cloud Forest Biological Reserve), which the Centro Científico Tropical (Tropical Science Center) began administrating in 1975. In 1986 the Monteverde Conservation League (MCL) was formed to buy land to expand the reserve. Two years later it launched the International Children's Rainforest project, which encouraged children and school groups from all over the world to raise money to buy and save tropical rainforest adjacent to the reserve.

INFORMATION

The **visitors center** (☎ 2645-5122; www.cct. or.cr; park admission adult/student & child/child under 6yr US$17/9/free; ☽ 7am-4pm) is adjacent to the reserve gift shop, where you can get information and buy trail guides, bird and mammal lists, and maps.

The annual rainfall here is about 3000mm, though parts of the reserve reportedly get twice as much. It's usually cool, with high temperatures around 18°C (65°F), so wear appropriate clothing.

ACTIVITIES

There are 13km of marked and maintained trails – a free map is provided with your entrance fee. The most popular of the nine trails, suitable for day hikes, make a rough triangle (El Triángulo) to the east of the reserve entrance. The triangle's sides are made up of the popular **Sendero Bosque Nuboso** (1.9km), an interpretive walk (booklet ₡400 at gate) through the cloud forest that begins at the ranger station, paralleled by the more open, 2km **El Camino**, a favorite for bird-watchers. The **Sendero Pantanoso** (1.6km) forms the far side of El Triángulo, traversing swamps, pine forests and the continental divide. Returning to the entrance, **Sendero Río** (2km) follows the Quebrada Cuecha past a few photogenic waterfalls.

Bisecting the triangle, the gorgeous **Chomogo Trail** (1.8km) lifts hikers 150m to 1680m, the highest point in the triangle, and other little trails crisscross the region, including the worthwhile **Sendero Brillante** (300m), with bird's-eye views of a miniature forest. There's also a 100m suspension bridge about 1km from the ranger station. However, keep in mind that despite valiant efforts to contain crowd sizes, these shorter trails are among the most trafficked in the country, and wildlife learned long ago that the region is worth avoiding unless they want a good look at hominids.

GETTING THERE & AWAY

Public buses (₡600, 30 minutes) depart the Banco Nacional in Santa Elena at 6:15am, 7:20am, 1:20pm and 3pm. Buses return from the reserve at 6:45am, 11:30am, 2pm and 4pm. You can flag down the buses from anywhere on the road between Santa Elena and the reserve – inquire at your hotel about what time they will pass by. Taxis are also available for around ₡2800.

The 6km walk from Santa Elena is uphill, but lovely – look for paths that run parallel to the road. There are views all along the way, and many visitors remark that some of the best bird-watching is on the final 2km of the road.

RESERVA SANTA ELENA

Though Monteverde gets all the attention, this exquisitely misty reserve has plenty to recommend it. You can veritably hear the canopy, draped with epiphytes, breathing in humid exhales as water drops onto the leaf litter and mud underfoot. The odd call of the three-wattled bellbird or low crescendo of a howler monkey punctuates the higher-pitched bird chatter and chirps. Though about 10% of species here won't be found in Monteverde, you can see quetzal here too, as well as Volcán Arenal exploding in the distance.

This cloud-forest reserve was created in 1989 and opened to the public in March 1992. It was one of the first community-managed conservation projects in the country, and is now managed by the Santa Elena high-school board. You can visit the **reserve office** (☎ 2645-5693; ⏲ 8am-4pm Wed-Fri) at the high school.

More than 12km of **trails** are open (8am to 4pm Wednesday through Friday) for hiking, featuring four circular trails offering walks of varying difficulty and length, from 45 minutes to 3½ hours (1.4km to 4.8km) along a stable (though not 'concrete-blocked') trail system. Rubber boots (₡600) can be rented at the entrance.

A daily shuttle (₡1200, 30 minutes) between the village of Santa Elena and the reserve departs from the Banco Nacional in town at 6:30am, 8:30am, 10:30am, 12:30pm, 1pm and 3pm, and returns at 11am, 1pm and 4pm. A taxi from Santa Elena costs ₡5000.

LIBERIA

pop 45,000

Well, the secret's out. These days, though, travelers are getting their first glimpse of *pura vida* Costa Rica at Liberia's own Aeropuerto Internacional Daniel Oduber Quirós. And why not? Liberia is a great base for exploring the attractions in the north and the beaches of the Península de Nicoya. As such, the government is looking to expand the airport, with an eye to accommodating as much traffic, or more, as Juan Santamaría airport in San José. And, though most of the historic buildings in the city center are a little rough around the edges and in desperate need of a paint job, the 'white city' is a pleasant one, with a good range of accommodations and services for travelers on all budgets.

SIGHTS & ACTIVITIES

Near the entrance to town, a **statue** of a steely-eyed *sabanero,* complete with

Living at a crossroads, Liberia

IMAGEBROKER/SIEPMANN

LUKE HUNTER

Green lilies, Parque Nacional Palo Verde

↘ IF YOU LIKE...

If you like the **Reserva Santa Elena** (p144), we think you'll like these other protected areas in northern Costa Rica:

- **Parque Nacional Guanacaste** At one of the least visited parks in Costa Rica, the land transitions from dry tropical forest to humid cloud forest.
- **Refugio Nacional de Vida Silvestre Caño Negro** The lagoons of Caño Negro attract a wide variety of birds year-round.
- **Parque Nacional Palo Verde** More than 300 bird species have been recorded in this wildlife-rich wetland.
- **Refugio Nacional de Vida Silvestre Bahía Junquillal** Another small, peaceful protected site, this refuge has a beach backed by mangrove swamp and tropical dry forest.

an evocative poem by Rodolfo Salazar Solórzano, stands watch over Av 25 de Julio, the main street into town. The blocks around the intersection of Av Central and Calle Central contain several of the town's oldest houses, many dating back about 150 years.

The pleasant Parque Central frames a modern church, **Iglesia Inmaculada**

Concepción de María. The park is also the seasonal hangout of the Nicaraguan grackle, a tone-deaf bird that enjoys eating parrot eggs and annoying passersby with its grating calls.

Walking six blocks northeast of the park along Av Central brings you to the oldest church in town, popularly called **La Agonía** (although maps show it with the name of La Iglesia de la Ermita de la Resurección). Strolling to La Agonía and around the surrounding blocks makes a fine walk.

About 9km south of Liberia, **Africa Mía** (☎ 2666-1111; www.africamia.net; self-guided walking tour adult/child US$16/11, guided van tour adult/child US$27/22; ☻ 9am-5pm) is a private wildlife reserve with free-roaming elephants, zebras, giraffes, ostriches and other animals. Splurge for the deluxe African Safari Wildlife Tour (adult/child US$65/55) in an open-top Hummer with a stop at a waterfall.

SLEEPING

Hostal Ciudad Blanca (☎ 2666-3962; Av 4 btwn Calles 1 & 3; s/d with fan US$30/40, s/d with air-con US$35/45; ℗ ✗) One of Liberia's most attractive hotels is in a historic colonial mansion that has been completely refurbished. Tree-shaded rooms have air-con, fan, cable TV, nice furnishings and private hot-water bathroom. The charming little restaurant-bar downstairs is perfect for a nightcap – or a game of pinball.

Hotel La Siesta (☎ 2666-0678; lasiesta liberia@hotmail.com; Calle 4 btwn Avs 4 & 6; s/d incl breakfast US$40/50; ℗ ✗ ⬜ ⬚) Spotless, standard rooms with cable TV and private cold showers are arranged around a pretty poolside garden. Rooms upstairs are slightly larger, but all are very quiet and the place has a relaxed feel. There's also an attached restaurant (meals ₡2500 to ₡4000, breakfast and lunch), which is regarded by locals as having the best *casado* in town.

Hotel El Bramadero (☎ 2666-0371; www. hotelelbramadero.com; cnr Interamericana & Hwy 21; s/d US$40/58; P ❄ ☐ ♨) El Bramadero is a comfortable, midrange hotel that has well-appointed rooms with air-con, hot showers and cable TV. It has a *sabanero* theme, so it follows that the restaurant (meals ₡3500 to ₡7900, lunch and dinner) has some of the thickest and juiciest steaks you've ever feasted on.

Hotel Boyeros (☎ 2666-0722, 2666-0809; www.hotelboyeros.com; cnr Interamericana & Av 2; s/d/tr US$56/65/76; P ✖ ❄ ♈ ♨) The largest hotel in Liberia feels like a cross between a dude ranch and the Holiday Inn. Immaculate rooms all have comfortable furnishings, air-con and cable TV, and the upstairs rooms have private balconies. There's also a 24-hour restaurant, free wi-fi, pool with waterslide, kiddie pool and a shaded sitting area. Look for the sculpture of the *boyero* (oxcart driver) out front.

Bed & Breakfast El Punto (☎ 2665-2986; www.elpuntohotel.com; cnr Interamericana & Av

4; s/d US$60/97; P ❄ ☐ ♨) This converted elementary school is now a chic hotel, and would definitely feel more at home in trendy Miami than in humble Guanacaste. The saturated tropical colors of the loft apartments manage to be understated and minimalist. All rooms have beautifully tiled bathrooms, kitchenettes, hammocks, free wi-fi and colorful modern art. The common area features low outdoor sofas and even crayons for the kids, and the bilingual architect-owner Mariana is charm personified.

Hilton Garden Inn Liberia Airport (☎ 2690-8888; www.hilton.com; d US$80-160; P ✖ ❄ ☐ ♨ ♈) Liberia's newest hotel is also the fanciest, with all the usual 4-star amenities including pool, gym and tennis courts. All rooms have fridge, microwave, flat-screen TV, and free internet and wi-fi access. It's directly across from Liberia airport, perfect if you have an early morning flight.

EATING

Panadería Alemania (☎ 2665-2061; Calle 25 de Junio btwn Calles 10 & 8; mains ₡500-3000;

The vibrant colors of Liberia (p145)

IMAGEBROKER/SIEPMANN

breakfast, lunch & dinner) A German bakery with beautifully flaky croissants, a respectably authentic sushi counter doing what it can with the local rice and an international kitchen turning out Euro-style numbers can all be found at this local hangout.

Café Liberia (☎ 2665-1660; www.cafe liberia.com; Calle 8 btwn Avs 25 de Julio & 2; items ₡600-3500; ☺ 8:30am-6pm Mon-Fri, 10am-6pm Sat; ☒ ▢ ☏ ⓥ) Run by a sweet Tica named Radha, this hip spot is a dream: serving organic juices, Costa Rican coffee, fresh sandwiches, salads and crepes, pastries, wines and lots of vegetarian items.

Pizza Pronto (☎ 2666-2098; cnr Av 4 & Calle 1; mains ₡2800-5000; ☺ lunch & dinner) Situated in a handsome 19th-century house, this romantic pizzeria is in a class of its own. You can choose from a long list of toppings for your wood-fired pizza, including fresh, local seafood or pineapple; the pastas are just as tasty.

La Toscana (☎ 2665-0653; Plaza Santa Rosa; mains ₡2200-8000; ☺ noon-11pm; ☒) Satisfy those pangs for gnocchi or spaghetti carbonara at one of the most authentically Italian restaurants in the region. Tuscan wine, tablecloths and tiramisu await.

LIBERIA

INFORMATION
BAC San José **1** A4
Banco de Costa Rica.............**2** C3
Banco Nacional......................**3** B3
Banco Popular........................**4** B4
Citibank....................................**5** B4
HSBC...**6** C3

SIGHTS & ACTIVITIES
Iglesia Inmaculada
Concepción de María **7** C3
La Agonía..................................**8** D2
Sabanero Statue....................**9** B4

SLEEPING
Bed & Breakfast El
Punto....................................**10** B4
Hostal Ciudad Blanca........**11** D3
Hotel Boyeros.......................**12** B4
Hotel El Bramadero.............**13** A4
Hotel La Siesta.....................**14** C4

EATING
Café Liberia............................**15** B4
Casa Verde..............................**16** B4
El Zaguán................................**17** C3
La Toscana ....(see 1)

Panadería Alemania............**18** B4
Pizza Pronto..........................**19** C3

DRINKING
Las Tinajas.............................**20** C3
Liberia Supremacy...............**21** D3

ENTERTAINMENT
LIB...**22** A4

TRANSPORT
Liberia Travel........................**23** B3
Terminal Liberia...................**24** A3
Terminal Pulmitan **25** B3

El Zaguán (☎ 2666-2456; cnr Av Central & Calle 1; mains ₡3300-8500; ☺ 11:30am-10pm; ♿) Located in a beautiful colonial building, this family-friendly restaurant has an extensive international menu specializing in meat including New York Strip, filet mignon and burgers. You'll also find fish, pasta and rice dishes. The outdoor balcony is a great people-watching spot.

Casa Verde (☎ 2665-5037; Interamericana; mains ₡4000-10,000; ☺ 11am-11pm Tue-Sun; ☎) California-Asian chic comes to Liberia. The sophisticated and stylish Casa Verde is one of our favorite dining experiences in northwest Costa Rica. Located near the Bed & Breakfast El Punto, the restaurant's contemporary decor includes a slate bar, black leather couches, candlelit tables, an outdoor patio lit by tiki torches, and chill ambient music, with live music on Friday evenings. The fusion menu specializes in fish and meat dishes and has an extensive wine list.

DRINKING & ENTERTAINMENT

Las Tinajas (Calle 2 btwn Avs Central & 1; ☺ lunch & dinner) Sip a cold beer and nosh on some greasy fries at this parkside pub, an ideal place to people-watch in Parque Central.

Liberia Supremacy (Av 1 btwn Calles 5 & 7; ☺ 4pm-late Tue-Sun) A bit of Jamaica comes to Liberia at this popular reggae bar decorated with posters of Bob Marley and Che. There's a friendly vibe, cheap beer, an extensive Mexican *bocas* menu, as well as the most uncomfortable bar stools ever made.

LIB (Plaza Santa Rosa; ☺ 5pm-2am Mon-Sat) The best nightspot in town, this open-air disco bathed in neon is on the 2nd floor of Plaza Santa Rosa, blaring salsa and rock music onto the masses below. There's a good *bocas* menu to help soak up the alcohol.

GETTING THERE & AWAY
AIR

Since 1993, Aeropuerto Internacional Daniel Oduber Quirós (LIR), 12km west of Liberia, has served as the country's second international airport, providing easy access to all those beautiful beaches without the hassle of dealing with the lines and bustle of San José. It's a tiny airport, jam-packed with increasing traffic. A new US$35 million airport terminal is currently under construction.

There are no car-rental desks at the airport; make reservations in advance, and your company will meet you at the airport with a car. You'll find a money-exchange counter, cafe and gift shop. Taxis to Liberia cost ₡6000. Downtown-based **Liberia Travel** (☎ 2666-4383; cnr Av 25 de Julio & Calle

Green iguana
LUKE HUNTER

NORTHERN COSTA RICA

LIBERIA

Aeropuerto Internacional Daniel Oduber Quirós (p149), Liberia

RH PRODUCTIONS/PHOTOLIBRARY

6; ☽ 8am-6pm Mon-Fri, to noon Sat) can help book flights worldwide.

The majority of international flights are through the USA, though some airlines fly directly between Liberia and the USA, including American Airlines, Continental, Delta, United and US Airways. Charter airlines now fly seasonally from Canada, Belgium and the UK. Domestic airline destinations include the following:

NatureAir (☎ 2220-3054; www.natureair. com) Flights to/from San José, Quepos, La Fortuna, Tambor and Playa Tamarindo.

Sansa (☎ 2668-1047; www.flysansa.com) Flights to/from San José and Playa Tamarindo.

BUS

Buses arrive and depart from **Terminal Liberia** (Av 7 btwn Calles 12 & 14) and **Terminal Pulmitan** (Av 5 btwn Calles 10 & 12). Routes, fares, journey times and departures are as follows:

Nicoya, via Santa Cruz ₡1000; 1½ hours; departs from Terminal Liberia every 30 minutes from 4:30am to 9pm.

Playa Brasilito ₡1000; 1½ hours; departs from Terminal Liberia at 4:30am, 6:10am, 11:10am and 6pm.

Playa del Coco ₡580; one hour; departs from Pulmitan hourly from 5am to 11am, then at 12:30pm, 2:30pm and 6:30pm.

Playa Tamarindo ₡1180; 1½ to two hours; departs from Terminal Liberia hourly from 3:50am to 6pm. Some buses take a longer route via Playa Flamingo.

Puntarenas ₡1400; three hours; eight buses from 5am to 3:30pm. It's quicker to jump off the San José–bound bus in Puntarenas.

San José ₡2700; four hours; 11 departures from Pulmitan from 4am to 8pm.

CAR

There are at least 30 rental-car agencies in Liberia (none of which have desks at the airport), all charging about the same rates. Most can arrange pick-up in Liberia and drop-off in San José, though they'll try to charge you extra. Rental agencies are on Hwy 21 between Liberia and the airport, but should be able to drop off your car in town. Some recommended car-rental agencies:

Adobe (☎ 2667-0608; www.adobecar.com)

Avis (☎ 2668-1196; www.avis.co.cr)

Budget (☎ 2668-1024; www.budget.com)

Europcar (☎ 2668-1023; www.europcar.co.cr)

Hola (☎ 2667-4040; www.hola.net)

Mapache (☎ 2665-4444; www.mapache.com)

Toyota Rent a Car (☎ 2666-8190; www. carrental-toyota-costarica.com)

VOLCÁN MIRAVALLES AREA

Volcán Miravalles (2028m) is the highest volcano in the Cordillera de Guanacaste, and although the main crater is dormant, the geothermal activity beneath the ground has led to the rapid development of the area as a hot-springs destination. As more travelers land in Liberia, they're starting to discover this nearby refuge from the ubiquitous cold shower.

SIGHTS & ACTIVITIES

All the listed hot springs are north of the tiny village of Fortuna de Bagaces (not to be confused with La Fortuna de Arenal).

Thermo Manía (☎ 2673-0233; www.thermo mania.net; adult/child US$10/8; ☷ 8am-10pm; ☎) is the biggest complex in the area, with seven thermal pools that are connected by waterslides, heated rivers, waterfalls and faux-stone bridges. There's also a full spa, playground, museum, zoo, soccer field and picnic tables. The busy restaurant-bar (mains US$4 to US$10) is housed in a 170-year-old colonial cabin furnished with museum-worthy period pieces. Guests who stay in the 26 log-cabin rooms (per person adult/child US$22/11) have free access to the pools during their stay, with TV and cold-water bathrooms (neatly counter-balancing the lack of cold-water pools).

El Guayacán (☎ 2673-0349; www.termales elguayacan.com; adult/child US$5/3), whose hissing vents and mud pots (absolutely stay on the trail!) are on the family *finca*, lie just behind Thermo Manía. With its five thermal pools and one cold pool in front of its simple, cold-water *cabinas* (adult/child US$22/11), this unpretentious place has a mellow, family vibe to it. There's an onsite restaurant (mains ₡1000 to ₡3000).

Nearby **Yökö Hot Springs** (☎ 2673-0410; www.yokotermales.com; adult/child US$8/6; ☷ 7am-11pm; ☎) has four hot springs with a small waterslide and waterfall, set in an attractive meadow at the foot of Miravalles. The 12 elegant *cabinas* (single/double with breakfast US$40/75) have huge bathrooms and gleaming wood floors. Extra amenities include a Jacuzzi, sauna and a relaxed restaurant (mains ₡1000 to ₡5000) serving everything from burgers to filet mignon.

For some local flavor, **Termales Miravalles** (☎ 8357-8820, 8305-4072; adult/child US$4/3) has two pools and a waterslide, and lies along a thermal stream. The owners have set up a small restaurant and offer camping (per person US$6) on the property. It's usually open on weekends year-round, and daily during high season. The access road is directly across from Yökö Hot Springs.

On the southern slopes of Miravalles, **Las Hornillas** (☎ 8839-9769; www.las hornillas.com; admission US$20; ☷ 9am-5pm) is the center of volcanic activity in the area. The entrance fee includes an informative tour around the small crater (again, stay on the trail, kids) and allows you to soak in the thermal pools. This wonderfully isolated, family-run spot also offers hiking and tractor tours (US$40) via hanging bridges to a waterfall, including lunch and access to the mud and pools.

Just north of Fortuna de Bagaces is the lovely new **Ailanto Bed & Breakfast**

(☎ 8353-7386; www.ailantocostarica.com; d/ ste incl breakfast US$75/125; P ☒ ☐ ☎ ☒). Judith and David have created this little bit of paradise at the foot of Miravalles on 33 acres of primary and secondary forest. The Tuscan-styled villa has four rooms with comfy furnishings; some have shared bathrooms. Property amenities include a shared kitchen, TV lounge, terrace with views, a thermal pool and hiking trails.

Near the base of the volcano is **Centro de Aventuras** (☎ 2673-0469; www.volcano adventuretour.com; campsite US$5, d US$30; ☒), which has a number of offerings including a canopy tour (with/without lunch US$28/20) and horseback riding (US$25 to US$50). The clean, brightly painted *cabinas* have private hot-water bathrooms and are centered on a pool that's fed by mountain springwater.

GETTING THERE & AWAY
Buses (₡500, one hour) from Liberia to Guayabo or Aguas Claras (via Fortuna) depart at 6am, 9am, 11am and 2pm and pass by all the hot spring entrances. Return buses to Liberia (via Guayabo) pass by the hot springs at about 2:30pm, 3:30pm and 4:30pm.

PARQUE NACIONAL RINCÓN DE LA VIEJA
Given its proximity to Liberia – really just a hop, skip and a few bumps away – this 141-sq-km **national park** (☎ 2661-8139; www.acguanacaste.ac.cr; admission US$10; ☼ 7am-5pm, no entry after 3pm, closed Mon) feels refreshingly uncrowded and remote. Named after the active Volcán Rincón de la Vieja (1895m), the steamy main attraction, the park also covers several other peaks in the same volcanic range, including the highest, Volcán Santa María (1916m). The park breathes geothermal energy, which you can see for yourself in its multihued

fumaroles, hot springs, lively *pailas* (mud pots) bubbling and blooping clumps of ashy gray mud, and a young and feisty *volcancito* (small volcano).

ACTIVITIES
HIKING
A circular trail east of Las Pailas (about 3km in total) takes you past the boiling mud pools, sulfurous fumaroles and a *volcancito* (which may subside at any time). About 700m west of the ranger station along the **Sendero Cangreja** is a swimming hole, which is prescribed for lowering your body temperature after too much time in the hot springs. Further away along the same trail are several waterfalls – the largest, **Catarata La Cangreja**, 5km west, is a classic, dropping straight from a cliff into a small lagoon where you can swim. Dissolved copper salts give the falls a deep-blue color. This trail winds through forest, then onto open grassland on the volcano's flanks, where you can enjoy views as far as the Golfo de Nicoya. The slightly smaller **Cataratas Escondidas** (Hidden Waterfalls) are 4.3km west on a different trail.

The longest and most adventurous hike in the area is the 16km round-trip trek to the summit of Rincón de la Vieja and to nearby **Laguna de Jilgueros**, which is reportedly where you may see tapirs – or more likely their footprints, if you are observant. The majority of this hike follows a ridge trail, and is known for being extremely windy and cloudy – come prepared for the weather. It's also advised that you hire a guide from the ranger station.

SIMBIOSIS SPA
Affiliated with Hacienda Guachipelín, this **spa** (☎ 2666-8075; www.simbiosis-spa.com; admission US$15; ☼ 9am-5:30pm) is also open to the public. With spring-fed hot pools, vol-

canic mud, a sauna, showers and lounge chairs, all in a natural outdoor setting, this is a lovely place to unwind. You can also arrange massages and spa treatments (US$35 to US$75) on the spot, though it recommends reserving ahead.

SLEEPING & EATING

Hacienda Guachipelín (☎ 2666-8075; www. guachipelin.com; s with/without air-con US$85/70, d with/without air-con US$100/89, all incl breakfast; P ✗ ⬚ ⬚ ⬚) This 19th-century working cattle ranch is on 12 sq km of primary and secondary forest, and has over 100 attractively designed, spacious rooms and suites with private hot-water bathrooms and porches.

Borinquen Mountain Resort & Spa (☎ 2690-1900; www.borinquenresort. com; s incl breakfast US$188-329, d US$210-365; P ✗ ✗ ⬚ ⬚) If you want to splurge, wallow here. The most luxurious resort in the area features plush, fully air-conditioned bungalows with private deck, minibar and satellite TV. The onsite hot springs, mud baths and natural saunas are beautifully

laid out and surrounded by greenery, but a treatment at the unbelievable Anáhuac Spa (treatments US$35 to US$100, open from 10am to 6pm), suspended over the river and jungle, is the icing on this decadent mud pie.

GETTING THERE & AWAY

There's no public transportation, but any of the lodges can arrange transfers from Liberia for around US$20 per person each way (two or three people minimum). Alternatively, you can hire a 4WD taxi from Liberia for about US$25 to Las Pailas, or US$45 to Santa María, each way.

PARQUE NACIONAL VOLCÁN TENORIO

They say when God finished painting the sky blue, he washed his paintbrushes in the Río Celeste. The heavenly blue-colored river, waterfalls and ponds of Parque Nacional Volcán Tenorio are one of the most spectacular natural phenomena in Costa Rica. Established in 1976, this magical 184-sq-km national park

CRAIGE BEVIL/ALAMY

Catarata de Río Celeste (p154), Parque Nacional Volcán Tenorio

remains one of the most secluded and least-visited park in the country due to the dearth of public transportation and park infrastructure. As a result, it remains a blissfully pristine rainforest abundant with wildlife. Soaring 1916m above the cloud rainforest is the park's namesake, Volcán Tenorio, which is actually comprised of three peaked craters: Montezuma, Tenorio I (the tallest) and Tenorio II.

INFORMATION

Your first stop will be the **Puesto El Pilón ranger station** (☎ 2200-0135; www.sinac. go.cr/acat_volcantenorio.php, in Spanish; admission US$10; ☺ 8am-4pm), which houses a small exhibit of photographs and dead animals. Pick up a free English or Spanish hiking map.

SIGHTS & ACTIVITIES

The well-signed trail begins at the ranger station parking lot and winds 1.5km through the rainforest until you reach an intersection. Turn left and climb down a very steep and slippery staircase to the **Catarata de Río Celeste**, a milky-blue waterfall that cascades 30m down the rocks, like heavy cream being poured out of a jug and into a fantastically aquamarine pool.

Climb back up to the main trail and continue 700m further until you reach the technicolored **Pozo Azul** (Blue Lagoon). The trail loops around the lagoon 400m until you arrive at the confluence of rivers known as **Los Teñidores** (The Stainers). Here, two small rivers – one whitish-blue and one brownish yellow – mix together to create the blueberry milk of Río Celeste.

For the final reward, continue 300m to the **Aguas Termales** (hot springs) to soak your weary muscles. This is the only place in the park where you're permitted to enter the water; bring your own towel and swimsuit. Plans for a circuit trail are afoot, but for now the trail ends here. Retrace your steps to return to the ranger station. Hiking to the volcano crater is strictly prohibited.

Allow three to four hours to complete the entire hike. It's only about 7km round-trip, but parts of the trail are steep and rocky. And because this is a rainforest, the trail can be wet and muddy almost year-round. Good hiking shoes or boots are a must. After your hike, you'll find an area to wash your footwear near the trailhead.

SLEEPING & EATING

Tenorio Lodge (☎ 2466-8282; www. tenoriolodge.com; s/q/tr/q incl breakfast US$90/95/120/135; P ⚟) Located on a lush hilltop with amazing views of Volcán Tenorio, Tenorio Lodge has some of the most romantic and private accommodations around. There are eight roomy bungalows, each containing two orthopedic beds (one king and one queen), private bathroom with solar-heated water, and panoramic windows and balcony with volcano views. The gorgeous lodge has a lovely restaurant featuring a dinner menu that changes daily.

La Carolina Lodge (☎ 8380-1656; www. lacarolinalodge.com; s/d incl 3 meals & horseback rides from US$75/130; P ⚟) This isolated lodge run by a gracious American named Bill is on a working cattle ranch on the slopes of the volcano, and is highly recommended for anyone looking for a beautiful escape from the rigors of modern life. The remote location means there's limited electricity – but candlelight only adds to the ambience. Amazing meals (organic beans, rice, fruits, cheeses, chicken and pork from the farm), cooked over an outdoor wood-burning stove, are a treat, as is soaking in the wood-fired hot tub.

Celeste Mountain Lodge (☎ 2278-6628; www.celestemountainlodge.com; s/d/tr incl all meals US$130/160/190, child US$25; Ⓟ) One of the most innovative and sustainable hotels we've ever seen, Celeste Mountain Lodge is proof that one can be ecofriendly without giving up comfort or style. The French owned, Belgian-designed contemporary hotel is absolutely stunning, an open-air hilltop lodge in the shadow of Volcán Tenorio. It was built in 2007 using ecofriendly materials like recycled wood, plastic, 1000 old truck tires and coconut fiber as seat cushions. Lamps, sculptures and other decorative items are made of scrap metal. Hot water comes from solar power, and cooking gas is partially produced by kitchen waste. There's even an ingenious hot tub heated by burning salvaged wood.

GETTING THERE & AWAY

There are no direct buses to the national park, though if you don't have your own car, most lodges can arrange transfer from Liberia.

PARQUE NACIONAL SANTA ROSA

Among the oldest (established in 1971) and largest national parks in Costa Rica, Santa Rosa's sprawling 386 sq km on the Península Santa Elena protects the largest remaining stand of tropical dry forest in Central America, and some of the most important nesting sites of several species of sea turtle. However, a good number of travelers are here for one reason – the chance to surf the near-perfect beach break at Playa Naranjo, which is created by the legendary offshore monolith known as Witch's Rock (also known locally as Roca Bruja).

HISTORY

Santa Rosa is famous among Ticos as a symbol of historical pride. A foreign army has only invaded Costa Rica three times, and each time the attackers were defeated in Santa Rosa. The best known of these events was the Battle of Santa Rosa, which took place on March 20, 1856, when the soon-to-be-self-declared president of

LUKE HUNTER

The greenery of Parque Nacional Santa Rosa

Nicaragua, an American named William Walker, invaded Costa Rica. Walker was the head of a group of foreign pirates and adventurers known as the 'Filibusters' that had already seized Baja and southwest Nicaragua, and were attempting to gain control over all of Central America. In a brilliant display of military prowess, Costa Rican President Juan Rafael Mora Porras guessed Walker's intentions, and managed to assemble a ragtag group of fighters that proceeded to surround Walker's army in the main building of the old Hacienda Santa Rosa, known as La Casona. The battle was over in just 14 minutes, and Walker was forever driven from Costa Rican soil.

ORIENTATION & INFORMATION

From the **Santa Rosa Sector park entrance** (☎ 2666-5051; admission US$10, campsite per person US$2; ☽ 8am-4pm), a very rough track leads down to the coast to Playa Naranjo, 12km away. Even during the dry season, this road is only passable to high-clearance 4WDs, and you must sign a waiver at the park entrance stating that you willingly assume all liability for driving this road. If you want to surf here, it's infinitely easier to gain access to the beach by hiring a boat from Playa del Coco or Playa Tamarindo, further south.

SIGHTS

The historic **La Casona**, the main building of the old Hacienda Santa Rosa, is near the park headquarters in the Santa Rosa sector. Unfortunately, the original building was burnt to the ground by arsonists in May 2001, but was rebuilt in 2002 using historic photos and local timber. The battle of 1856 was fought around this building, and the military action, as well as the region's natural history, is described with the help of documents, paintings, maps and other displays (mostly in Spanish). If you

remember your dictionary, this will be an inspiring (and perhaps humbling) history lesson in how not to invade a country.

ACTIVITIES
SURFING

The surfing at Playa Naranjo is truly world-renowned, especially near **Witch's Rock**, a break famous for its fast, hollow 3m rights. The surfing is equally legendary at **Ollie's Point** off Playa Portero Grande, which has the best right in all of Costa Rica with a nice, long ride, especially with a south swell.

Ollie's Point was immortalized in the film *Endless Summer II,* and is named after US Marine Lieutenant Colonel Oliver North. North is most famous for illegally selling weapons to Iran during the Reagan era, and using the profits to fund the Contras in Nicaragua – Ollie's Point refers to a nearby troop staging area that everyone but the US Congress knew about.

WILDLIFE-WATCHING

The olive ridley sea turtle is the most numerous, and during the July to December nesting season tens of thousands of turtles make their nests on Santa Rosa's beaches. The most popular beach is Playa Nancite, where, during September and October especially, it is possible to see as many as 8000 of these 40kg turtles on the beach at the same time. The turtles are disturbed by light, so flash photography and flashlights are not permitted. Avoid the nights around a full moon – they're too bright and turtles are less likely to show up. Playa Nancite is strictly protected and entry restricted, but permission may be obtained from park headquarters to observe this spectacle; call ahead.

HIKING

Near Hacienda Santa Rosa is **El Sendero Indio Desnudo**, a 1km trail with signs interpreting the ecological relationships among the animals, plants and weather patterns of Santa Rosa.

Behind La Casona a short trail leads up to the **Monumento a Los Héroes** and a lookout platform. There are also longer trails through the dry forest, including a gentle 4km hike to the Mirador, with spectacular views of Playa Naranjo, which is accessible to hikers willing to go another 9km along the deeply rutted road to the sea. The main road is lined with short trails to small waterfalls and other photogenic natural wonders.

From the southern end of Playa Naranjo, there are two hiking trails – **Sendero Carbonal** is a 20km trail that swings inland and then terminates on the beach at Cerros Carbonal, while **Sendero Aceituno** parallels Playa Naranjo for 13km and terminates near the estuary across from Witch's Rock.

SLEEPING & EATING

Make reservations in advance to stay at the **research station** (☎ 2666-5051; dm US$15); eight-bed bunkrooms have cold showers and electricity. Good meals (₡1700 to ₡4000) are available, but you must make arrangements the day before.

GETTING THERE & AWAY

Santa Rosa is best accessed by either private vehicle or boat.

LA VIRGEN

Welcome to one of the premier kayaking and rafting destinations in Costa Rica. Surprisingly, most travelers have never even heard about La Virgen, and those who have would be hard-pressed to find it on a map. But, to the dedicated groups of hard-core rafters and kayakers that spend days running the Río Sarapiquí, La Virgen is a relatively off-the-beaten-path paradise.

SIGHTS & ACTIVITIES
WHITE-WATER RAFTING

The Río Sarapiquí isn't as wild as the white water on the Río Pacuare near Turrialba, though it will still get your heart racing, and the dense jungle that hugs the

JOHN COLETTI/THE IMAGE BANK/GETTY IMAGES

Rafting down the Río Sarapiquí, La Virgen

riverbank is lush and primitive. You can run the Sarapiquí year-round, but July through December are considered peak months. Although it's possible to get a rafting trip on short notice, it's far better to make reservations at least two days in advance. Several tour operators in La Fortuna and San José organize trips. You can also call directly to the companies listed in this section.

There are three basic runs offered by several companies, and all have a minimum age of nine or 10; prices and times vary a bit, but the following are average. The Class I-II Chilamate put-in (US$60 per person, three hours) is a gentle float more suited to younger kids and wildlife-watching. The Class III-IV Lower Sarapiquí (US$75, three hours) puts in close to La Virgen and is a scenic and challenging trip that's a good choice for healthy people without white-water experience. The Class IV-V Upper Sarapiquí (US$85, five hours) is 11km of serious white water – perfect for thrill-seekers.

In addition to offering rafting trips from La Virgen, San José and La Fortuna, **Aguas Bravas** (☎ 2292-2072; www.aguas-bravas.co.cr) is a safety-oriented, Tico-run outfit that can also arrange horseback rides and bike tours.

Aventuras del Sarapiquí (☎ 2766-6768; www.sarapiqui.com) near Chilamate, and **Hacienda Pozo Azul Adventures** (☎ 2438-2616, in USA & Canada 877-810-6903; www.haciendapozoazul.com) are also reputable local professionals who organize rafting trips.

KAYAKING

If you're a kayaker, several accommodations in town are directly on the river, which means that you can roll out of bed, brush your teeth and have a quick paddle before breakfast. **Rancho Leona** (☎ 2761-1019; www.rancholeona.com) is something of a meeting spot for kayakers, which isn't surprising as its prime riverside location allows for easy launches and free kayak storage. Staff can provide information regarding launches in the area before you set out on the river.

OTHER ACTIVITIES

Hacienda Pozo Azul Adventures (☎ 2438-2616, in USA & Canada 877-810-6903;

THE SARAPIQUÍ VALLEY

This flat, steaming stretch of *finca*-dotted lowlands was once part of the United Fruit Company's cash-cow of banana holdings. Harvests were carried from the plantations to Puerto Viejo de Sarapiquí where they were packaged and shipped down the river on boats destined for the lucrative North American market. However, with the advent of the railway in 1880 that connected most of the country to the new shipping port in Puerto Limón, Puerto Viejo de Sarapiquí became a sleepy backwater.

Banana harvesting continued in the area through most of the 20th century, though in recent years farmers have switched to a more lucrative cash crop – sugarcane. Although Puerto Viejo de Sarapiquí never managed to recover its faded glory, the valley has since emerged as the premier destinations in Costa Rica for kayakers. There are also a number of stellar ecolodges in the region that are open to nonguests, and feature everything from rainforest hiking and suspension bridges to pre-Columbian ruins and chocolate tours.

www.haciendapozoazul.com) specializes in adventure activities, including horseback-riding tours starting from two-hour jaunts (US$40) to multiday treks. It also runs a canopy tour (US$50) over the lush jungle and river, can take you rappelling (US$31), and leads mountain-bike tours (half-day US$50, full-day US$70) and guided hikes (US$18).

SERPENTARIO

A great, locally run attraction is La Virgen's famous **snake garden** (☎ 2761-1059; adult/student & child US$7/6; ☺ 9am-5pm), where you can get face-to-face with more than 60 different species of reptiles and amphibians, including poison-dart frogs, anacondas and the star attraction, an 80kg Burmese python. The owner of the *serpentario*, Lydia, gives impromptu tours and takes certain snakes out of their cages for big hugs and memorable photo ops.

SLEEPING & EATING

Rancho Leona (☎ 2761-1019; www.rancholeona.com; r without bathroom per person US$12; P ▢) This shady, riverside spot is a gem – kayakers congregate here to swap tales of white-water adventure, bird-watchers linger over huge breakfasts (₡3500) as the local color of avian life flits by, and artistically minded travelers admire the lodge's incredible stained glass, which was handmade by the owners. The handful of simple, spotless rooms in the wood-plank lodge share hot-water bathrooms, and there's a small bathing pool for taking a cool dip; spa services are also available. The superfriendly staff sometimes prepare family-style dinners in the evenings, and they can take you out on inflatable 'ducky' or kayak trips, as well as arrange rafting tours for you.

  Hacienda Pozo Azul Adventures (☎ 2438-2616, in USA & Canada 877-810-6903;

CRAIGE BEVIL/ALAMY

Surfing the break at Witch's Rock (p156)

www.haciendapozoazul.com; s/d/tr luxury tents US$80/92/115; P ▢ 🛜 ⛲) If you've ever dreamed of camping in the rainforest, this is your chance to do it in style. Located near the south end of La Virgen, Pozo Azul features luxurious, recently remodelled 'tent suites' scattered on the edge of the treeline, all on raised, polished-wood platforms and outfitted with luxurious bedding, private bathroom and mosquito nets. The onsite adventure activities include canopy tours, horseback riding, white-water rafting, hiking and rappelling.

GETTING THERE & AWAY

Buses running between San José and Puerto Viejo de Sarapiquí make regular stops in La Virgen.

LA VIRGEN TO PUERTO VIEJO DE SARAPIQUÍ

The three luxurious lodges east of La Virgen feature a number of interesting attractions including museums, private trails and a Maleku archaeological site, so there's plenty to do in the area even on a rest day. Public transportation along this stretch of Hwy 126 is limited, which means it's best to have your own wheels.

CENTRO NEOTRÓPICO SARAPIQUÍS

Approximately 2km north of La Virgen is **Centro Neotrópico Sarapiquís** (☎ 2761-1004; www.sarapiquis.org; d/tr US$105/130; P ☒ ☒ ☐), a unique ecolodge that aims to foster sustainable tourism by educating its guests about environmental conservation and pre-Columbian history and culture. The entire complex consists of *palenque*-style, thatched-roof buildings modeled after a 15th-century pre-Columbian village, and contains a clutch of luxuriously appointed hardwood rooms, which each have huge, solar-heated bathrooms and private terraces. However, the main reason guests rave about this ecolodge is the variety of exhibits and attractions located on the grounds.

Even if you're not staying at the lodge, it's worth stopping by just to visit its real claims to fame, namely the **Alma Ata Archaeological Park**, **Rainforest Museum of Indigenous Cultures** and **Sarapiquís Gardens** (adult/child under 8yr US$15/free; ☯ 9am-5pm). The admission price includes entry to all three places, though alternatively, you can purchase tickets for the individual attractions. The archaeological site is estimated to be around 600 years old, and is attributed to the Maleku. Currently, about 70 small stone sculptures marking a burial field are being excavated by Costa Rican archaeologists who have revealed a number of petroglyphs and pieces of pottery.

The museum chronicles the history of the rainforest (and of human interactions with it) through a mixture of displays and videos, and also displays hundreds of Costa Rican indigenous artifacts including some superbly crafted musical instruments. The gardens boast the largest scientific collection of medicinal plants in Costa Rica. Finally, an onsite **restaurant** (mains ₡4000-12,000; ☯ breakfast, lunch & dinner) serves meals incorporating fruits, vegetables, spices and edible flowers used in indigenous cuisine, many of which are grown on the premises.

TIRIMBINA RAINFOREST CENTER

A working environmental research and education center, **Tirimbina Rainforest Center** (☎ 2761-0055/333; www.tirimbina.org; r incl breakfast US$60) also provides tours and accommodations for visitors. The 350-hectare private reserve of Tirimbina and the nearby Centro Neotrópico Sarapiquís are connected by two suspension bridges, 267m and 117m long, that span the Río Sarapiquí. Halfway across, a spiral staircase drops down to a large island in the river.

Tirimbina reserve has more than 9km of trails with suspension bridges; some of the trails are paved or wood-blocked. There are also several different guided tours on offer (US$17 to US$27) including bird-watching, frog and bat tours, night walks and a recommended guided chocolate tour, which allows you to explore a working cacao plantation and learn about the harvesting, fermenting and drying processes. Child and student discounts are available.

Tirimbina is about 2km north of La Virgen, next door to Centro Neotrópico Sarapiquís.

LA QUINTA DE SARAPIQUÍ LODGE

Approximately 5km north of La Virgen, this pleasant family-run **lodge** (☎ 2761-1052; www.laquintasarapiqui.com; s/d/tr/ste US$110/110/125/140; P ⚇ ⚑ ⚒) is on the banks of the Río Sardinal, which branches off from the Sarapiquí in the north and runs to the west of it. The lodge has covered paths through the landscaped garden connecting thatched-roof, hammock-strung rooms. All rooms have a terrace, ceiling fan and private hot-water shower. You can also get meals in the open-air restaurant (mains ₡4640 to ₡7540).

On the hotel grounds, **La Galería** (admission US$6, lodge guests free) features an eclectic collection of regional ephemera, including an extensive collection of insect specimens such as the *machaca* (also known as the lantern bug), a bizarre-looking insect about 7.5cm long. Even more interesting are the unusual exhibits on Costa Rican history. Indigenous artifacts, including some worthwhile copies of the area's more important archaeological finds, are a treat. The collection of Spanish-colonial relics is even more impressive, featuring not only antiques collected by the owners, but interesting family heirlooms as well.

COLLIN STREET BAKERY PINEAPPLE PLANTATION

You won't find any bread at Collin Street Bakery (its name reflects the ownership). Instead, you'll discover the sweetest, most delicious pineapples, grown right here at the world's largest organic pineapple plantation. Collin Street offers **tours** (☎ 2551-5804; www.collinstreet.com/pages/finca_corsicana; tour adult/child US$31/27; ⏱ 8am, 10am & 2pm Mon-Fri) through its 12 sq km of pineapple fields plus the processing and packing plant that ships 38 million pineapples a year. The interesting but pricey tour ends with a tasting of fresh pineapple, washed down with a piña colada. Yum! The plantation is located 2km north of La Quinta and is well signed from the highway.

SELVA VERDE LODGE

In Chilamate, about 7km west of Puerto Viejo, this former *finca* is now an elegant **lodge** (☎ 2766-6800, in USA & Canada 800-451-7111; www.selvaverde.com; s/d incl breakfast US$107/125, incl all meals US$137/184; P ⚇ ⚑) that protects over 200 hectares of rainforest. Guests can choose to stay at the river lodge, which is elevated above the rainforest floor on wooden platforms, or in a private bungalow, quietly tucked away in the nearby rainforest. Wood-floored

HEMIS/ALAMY
Luxurious lodges dot this part of northern Costa Rica

rooms have private hot-water shower, screened windows, in-room safe and, of course, your very own hammock.

There are several kilometers of walking trails through the grounds and into the premontane tropical wet forest; you can either get a trail map or hire a bilingual guide from the lodge (US$17 per person, three hours). There's also a garden of medicinal plants, as well as a **butterfly garden** (admission US$6, lodge guests free). Various boat tours on the Río Sarapiquí are also available, from rafting trips to guided canoe tours; locally guided horseback rides (US$29 for two to three hours) can also be arranged.

CHILAMATE RAINFOREST ECO RETREAT

Founded in 2009 by Sarapiquí native Davis Azofeifa and his Irish-Canadian wife Meghan Casey, **Chilamate** (☎ 2766-6949, 8842-1171; www.chilamaterainforest.com; dm US$17, s/d incl breakfast US$35/65; P ✖ 🛜 ♿ 🏊) is the most exciting new ecolodge project in the area. The young couple have spent three years building their little piece of paradise on 20 hectares of prime virgin rainforest.

The four large cabins built by Davis and friends are basic but full of character, with comfortable hand-crafted furniture, private bathroom, fan and traditional architectural style that provides natural air-cooling. Out back, the bunkhouse has 12 dorm beds with shared bathroom and kitchen, perfect for groups or those on a tight budget. Other resort amenities include a small bar, restaurant and laundry facilities. Davis and Meghan have two young children, so the resort is naturally quite kid-friendly. Covered, flat walkways allow you to move between buildings in the complex without ever getting wet (after all, this is the rainforest!).

Behind the cabins, 6km of paths wind through the jungle, where you might spot sloths, monkeys, toucans, frogs, snakes and more. The resort provides rubber boots for sloshing through the rainforest. Davis is a wealth of local information and can help arrange excursions in the area. For those who want a true ecolodge experience without the high ecotourism prices, we highly recommend Chilamate.

PUERTO VIEJO DE SARAPIQUÍ & AROUND

At the scenic confluence of Ríos Puerto Viejo and Sarapiquí, Puerto Viejo de Sarapiquí was once the most important port in Costa Rica. Boats laden with bananas, coffee and other commercial exports plied the Sarapiquí as far as the Nicaraguan border, then turned east on the Río San Juan to the sea. Today, Puerto Viejo (the full name distinguishes it from Puerto Viejo de Talamanca on the Caribbean coast) is simply a jungle border town – slightly seedy in a film-noir sort of way. There are, however, numerous opportunities in the surrounding area for bird-watching, rafting, boating and jungle exploration.

ACTIVITIES

Grassroots environmental activity is strong in this area. Local guide Alex Martínez (owner of the Posada Andrea Cristina B&B – see opposite), who speaks excellent English, maintains an **ecotourism center** (☎ 2766-6265; ⏰ 8am-3pm), which focuses on conservation activities and wilderness tours – **bird-watching** trips in particular. You can also arrange transportation and make other reservations here, as well as learn about worthwhile volunteer opportunities in the region.

If you're looking to organize a rafting or kayaking trip, a branch of **Aguas Bravas** (☎ 2292-2072; www.aguas-bravas.co.cr) is across the road from the bank. You can also try **Costa Rica Fun Adventures** (☎ 2290-6015; www.crfunadventures.com), which is 2km north of town and offers a good variety of guided hiking and horseback-riding trips.

SLEEPING & EATING

Posada Andrea Cristina B&B (☎ 2766-6265; www.andreacristina.com; s/d incl breakfast US$28/48, tree-house d US$55, extra person US$15; P) About 1km west of the center, this recommended B&B has eight quiet, immaculate cabins in its garden, each with fan, private hot-water bathroom, hammock and outdoor table and chairs. It's also situated on the edge of the rainforest, so there are plenty of opportunities for bird-watching while you sit outside and eat breakfast. The owner, Alex Martínez, is an excellent, amiable guide as well as a passionate frontline conservationist.

Hotel Ara Ambigua (☎ 2766-7101; www.hotelaraambigua.com; s/d/tr incl breakfast from US$65/75/82; P X ⬚ ⬚) About 1km west of Puerto Viejo near La Guaíra, this countryside retreat offers cozy rooms that are well equipped with private hot-water shower and cable TV. The superior rooms feature log-style furniture and flagstone floors. The real draw is the varied opportunities for wildlife-watching – you can see poison-dart frogs in the *ranario* (frog pond), caimans in the small lake, and the birds that come to feed near the onsite Restaurante La Casona (meals ₡2320 to ₡5800; open for breakfast, lunch & dinner), which is particularly recommended for its oven-baked pizza and typical homemade cuisine.

GETTING THERE & AWAY

Local buses run frequently between La Virgen and Puerto Viejo de Sarapiquí. The 30-minute trip costs ₡350.

San José (Autotransportes Sarapiquí) ₡1650; two hours; departs at 6:30am, 7:30am, 10am, 11:30am, 1:30pm, 2:30pm, 3:30pm, 4:30pm and 6pm.

Coffee-plantation worker carts a load of beans

CHRISTER FREDRIKSSON

NORTHERN COSTA RICA

PUERTO VIEJO DE SARAPIQUÍ & AROUND

SOUTH OF PUERTO VIEJO DE SARAPIQUÍ

SUEÑO AZUL RESORT

Yoga-retreat groups make up the majority of guests at Sueño Azul (☎ 2764-1000; www.suenoazulresort.com; s/d/ste US$100/122/174; P 🏊 🐎), a top-end resort upon a hill. Independent travelers interested in honing their yoga practice will appreciate the appeal of this peaceful place, especially at the secluded bamboo yoga platform if no groups have scheduled a stay. Spacious, airy rooms have a hot-water shower and bamboo furnishings, and are nestled on the grounds of this private jungle reserve. Hiking trails offer jungle walks to waterfalls, and the reserve can also be explored on horseback.

HELICONIA ISLAND

This self-proclaimed 'oasis of serenity' is arguably the most beautiful garden in all of Costa Rica. Heliconia Island (☎ 2764-5220; www.heliconiaisland.com; s/d incl breakfast US$55/72, d with air-con US$85; P 🏊) is a masterpiece of landscape architecture that was started in 1992 by New York City native Tim Ryan, a former professor of art and design. Today, this 2.3-hectare island is owned by Dutch couple Henk and Carolien, and is home to more than 80 varieties of heliconias, tropical flowers, plants and trees. The grounds are a refuge for 228 species of birds (hummingbirds are the sole pollinators of heliconias). There are also resident howler monkeys, river otters and a few friendly dogs that will greet you upon arrival.

Henk and Carolien will guide you through the property, showing off a number of memorable plants including the Madagascar traveling palm, rare hybrids of heliconia found only on the island, and the *Phenakospermum guyannense* (Phenomenal sperm), a unique flowering plant native to Guyana. The admission fee (self-guided/guided tours US$11/17) is waived for overnight guests. You can stay in this oasis in immaculate raised cabins, which have stone floors, hot-water showers and breezy balconies.

Heliconia Island is about 5km north of Horquetas, and there are signs along the highway pointing to the entrance. When you arrive at the entrance, park your car, walk across the metal bridge and turn left on the island to reach the gardens.

PENÍNSULA DE NICOYA

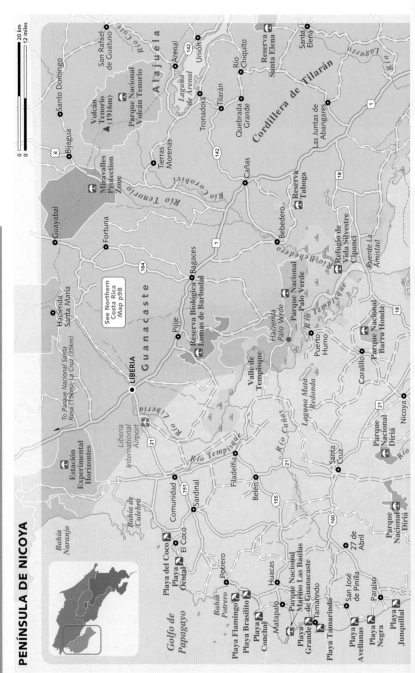

San Rafael de Guatuso

Santo Domingo

Bijagua

Volcán Tenorio (1916m)

Parque Nacional Volcán Tenorio

Alajuela

Río Coto

Arenal

Unión

Laguna de Arenal

142

Río Chiquito

Reserva Santa Elena

Santa Elena

Laguna

Tilarán

Tronadora

Quebrada Grande

Cordillera de Tilarán

Las Juntas de Abangares

1

142

Tierras Morenas

Cañas

Reserva Taboga

18

Río Corobicí

Miravalles Protection Zone

Río Tenorio

Bebedero

Refugio de Vida Silvestre Cipanci

Puente La Amistad

Guayabal

Fortuna

164

Bagaces

See Northern Costa Rica Map p98

Reserva Biológica Lomas de Barbudal

Parque Nacional Palo Verde

Río Bebedero

Hacienda Santa María

Guanacaste

Pijije

1

Hacienda Palo Verde

Parque Nacional Palo Verde

Río Tempisque

Puerto Humo

Parque Nacional Barra Honda

18

To Parque Nacional Santa Rosa (15km); La Cruz (35km)

LIBERIA

Río Liberia

Valle de Tempisque

Laguna Mata Redonda

Corralillo

21

Nicoya

Liberia International Airport

21

Estación Experimental Horizontes

Río Tempisque

Río Cañas

Santa Cruz

Parque Nacional Diriá

Río

Bahía de Culebra

Comunidad

Filadelfia

Belén

155

21

Parque Nacional Diriá

Sardinal

151

Bahía Naranjo

Golfo de Papagayo

Playa del Coco

Playa Ocotal

El Coco

Potrero

Huacas

160

27 de Abril

Bahía Potrero

Playa Flamingo

Playa Brasilito

Matapalo

Parque Nacional Marino Las Baulas de Guanacaste

San José de Pinilla

Paraíso

Playa Conchal

Playa Grande

Tamarindo

Playa Tamarindo

Playa Avellanas

Playa Negra

Playa Junquillal

0   20 km
0   12 miles

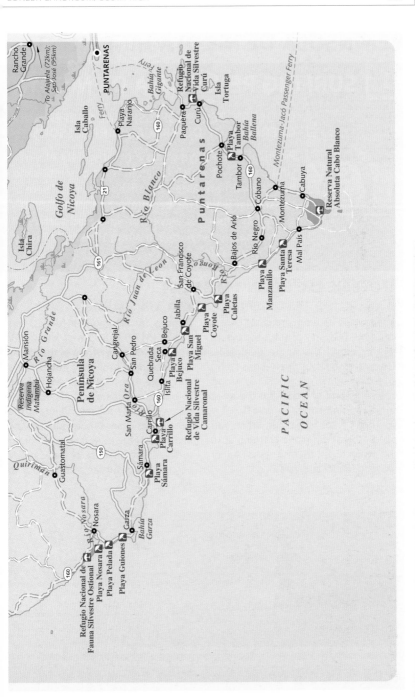

Rancho Grande

To Alajuela (72km);
San José (95km)

PUNTARENAS

PUNTARENAS

Bahía Gigante

Refugio Nacional de Vida Silvestre Curú

Isla Tortuga

Isla Caballo

Playa Naranjo

160

Paquera

Curú

P u n t a r e n a s

Pochote

Playa Tambor

Bahía Ballena

Golfo de Nicoya

21

Río Blanco

Tambor

Cóbano

160

Reserva Natural Absoluta Cabo Blanco

Isla Chira

161

Río Juan de Leon

Bajos de Arió

Río Negro

Montezuma

Cabuya

Mal País

Playa Santa Teresa

Río Grande

Mansión

Reserva Indígena Matambú

Hojancha

Península de Nicoya

Cangrejal

San Pedro

Río Nosara

Quebrada Seca

Bejuco

Jabilla

San Francisco de Coyote

Playa Manzanillo

Playa Caletas

Río Ora

Isita Playa Bejuco

Playa San Miguel

Playa Coyote

160

San Marta

Quirimán

Guastomatal

150

Sámara

Carrillo

Playa Carrillo

Refugio Nacional de Vida Silvestre Camaronal

P A C I F I C

O C E A N

Playa Sámara

Río Nosara

Nosara

Garza

Bahía Garza

160

Refugio Nacional de Fauna Silvestre Ostional

Playa Nosara

Playa Pelada

Playa Guiones

Ferry

Bahía Gigante

Montezuma-Jacó Passenger Ferry

PENÍNSULA DE NICOYA HIGHLIGHTS

1 SURFING PENÍNSULA DE NICOYA

BY DEBBIE ZEC, PROFESSIONAL SURFER AND OPERATOR OF DOMINICAL SURF LESSONS

Península de Nicoya offers a great variety of surf spots, many of which break in front of white-sand beaches and are aided by offshore winds. There are special waves for beginners and intermediates, as well as plenty of waves for advanced surfers. In fact, nearly every beach along the north Pacific coast is surfable.

🔖 DEBBIE ZEC'S DON'T MISS LIST

❶ MAL PAÍS & SANTA TERESA

This long, sweeping stretch of coastline (p195) is one of the best places to surf along the entire peninsula. The waves here are very consistent, and they have great shape during both high and low tide. But there are some random rocks, so watch out – you don't want to get cut! When you need a break from the crashing surf, the beach towns themselves are full of hip restaurants and cafes.

❷ PLAYA GRANDE

Famous for nesting sea turtles, this beach (p179) is also well known for the sheer number of waves that break along nearly 7km of coast. Tubes, tubes and more tubes are easy to find here, so bring your board and get ready for some seriously hollow riding. In the evening, you can venture out onto the beach with the park rangers in order to witness the miracle of life as newly hatched baby turtles scamper out to sea.

Clockwise from top: Checking out the waves at Playa Santa Teresa (p195); Heading out to catch some waves, Mal País (p195)

CLOCKWISE FROM TOP: CHRISTIAN ASLUND; CHRISTIAN ASLUND

❸ PLAYA TAMARINDO

The number-one party destination in the Nicoya is this tourist town (p180), which has a well-developed infrastructure of resort hotels, sophisticated dining options and plenty of bars and dance clubs. The waves here are fairly tame, but they're great for beginners who need some time to practice standing up, maintaining balance and riding into shore. This is also a great place to shop for used boards, or to fix up any existing dings and scratches.

❹ NOSARA AREA

Attracting both intermediate and advanced surfers, this collection of great wilderness beaches (p186) has simply amazing waves that are renowned for their beautiful shape and regular consistency. With so many different breaks to choose from, you could easily spend several days exploring the Nosara area without ever having to surf the same place twice.

↘ THINGS YOU NEED TO KNOW

Access Mal País and Tamarindo are well served by bus; Playa Grande and Nosara are best reached by car More information Find surf reports at Costa Rica Surf (www.crsurf.com) See our author's surfing coverage, p181 and p195

PENÍNSULA DE NICOYA HIGHLIGHTS

⬐ MONTEZUMA

One of Costa Rica's classic beach destinations, Montezuma (p190) is tucked away at Nicoya's southeastern end. Improved transportation links mean it's much easier to get here than it used to be, but that doesn't mean it's easy to leave. On the contrary, abandoned stretches of winding coastline invite long bouts of beachcombing, while calm Pacific waters provide refreshing respite from the tropical heat.

⬐ PLAYA SÁMARA

This up-and-coming beach destination (p187) really does seem to have it all. Families with little ones in tow positively rave about the spotless beach and tranquil town, while hipsters delight in the surprisingly sophisticated restaurants, cafes and bars. Given that it's far less high-profile than Costa Rica's brasher beaches, you can't help but feel you're in on a secret that few other travelers know about.

4

🢃 RESERVA NATURAL ABSOLUTA CABO BLANCO

An off-the-beaten-path nature reserve (p194) that's definitely worth seeking out, Cabo Blanco is Costa Rica's first protected space. Literally at the extreme tip of the peninsula, it encompasses coastal wilderness in addition to offshore islands that are home to nesting colonies of seabirds.

5

🢃 PLAYA DEL COCO

This beach town (p176) has the deserved reputation of being one of Nicoya's biggest party destinations (though it generally takes second place to Tamarindo). Even if you're not a big boozer, you still might want to stop by as the waters offshore from Playa del Coco are home to some of the country's best scuba diving.

6

🢃 PLAYAS AVELLANAS & NEGRA

Appearing in the silver-screen surf classic *Endless Summer II*, these adjacent beaches (p183) are thrashed on a daily basis by huge waves that are primarily the domain of intermediate and advanced surfers. If the gentle waves at Tamarindo start to grow boring, consider these breaks just a bit further down the coast.

2 MARK NEWMAN; 3 IMAGEBROKER/SIEPMANN; 4 ADRIAN HEPWORTH/HEPWORTHIMAGES; 5 JOHNNY HAGLUND; 6 AARON MCCOY

2 Montezuma (p190); 3 Playa Sámara (p187); 4 Reserva Natural Absoluta Cabo Blanco (p194); 5 Schools of fish make their home along the Costa Rican coast; 6 Playa Avellanas (p183)

PENÍNSULA DE NICOYA'S BEST...

⚓ SECRET SPOTS

- **Playa Conchal** (p179) A secret beach of crushed seashells that is best accessed by foot.
- **Reserva Natural Absoluta Cabo Blanco** (p194) The country's first protected space helped give rise to the modern eco-boom.
- **Nicoya** (p185) A true Tico town with a few hidden lashings of colonial charm.

⚓ THRILLS

- **Festivals** (p185) The provincial town of Santa Cruz offers plenty of excitement during festival season.
- **Off-Road Driving** (p174) If you've got a 4WD and a spare tire, consider going off-road.
- **Surfing** (p168) Península de Nicoya is Costa Rica's surfing mecca.

⚓ SPLURGES

- **Florblanca** (p197) Sets the standard for luxury in Mal País and Santa Teresa.
- **Ylang-Ylang Beach Resort** (p192) A holistic resort where you can work on your tan while searching for Zen.
- **Sueño del Mar B&B** (p183) A secluded upmarket retreat that serves as a tranquil escape from nearby Tamarindo.

⚓ EATS

- **La Guinguette** (p178) A Tico-French fusion joint that brings the bistro to the beach.
- **Seasons by Shlomy** (p183) This Israeli-Mediterranean gem is in its own class.
- **Playa de los Artistas** (p193) A romantic beachside eatery with local ingredients and artistic flourishes.

IMAGEBROKER/HANS ZAGLITSCH

Seashell-encrusted sand of Playa Conchal (p179)

THINGS YOU NEED TO KNOW

⤹ VITAL STATISTICS

- **Population** Nicoya 13,000; Santa Cruz 12,000
- **Best time to visit** December to March is bone-dry.

⤹ BEACHES IN A NUTSHELL

- **Mal País & Santa Teresa** (p195) Wilderness beaches with famous surf.
- **Montezuma** (p190) The quintessential Península de Nicoya beach destination.
- **Playa Tamarindo** (p180) This party beach has well-developed tourist infrastructure.
- **Playa Sámara** (p187) Relaxed, easygoing and a great place for kids.

⤹ ADVANCE PLANNING

- **Surfing school** Península de Nicoya is home to some serious surf, which means that you might want to practice elsewhere before showing up with board in hand.

⤹ RESOURCES

- **Costa Rica Tourism Board** (www.visitcostarica.com)
- **Tico Times** (www.ticotimes.net)

⤹ EMERGENCY NUMBERS

- **Emergency** (☎ 911)
- **Fire** (☎ 118)
- **Police** (☎ 117)

⤹ GETTING AROUND

- **Boat** Jacó, located along the central Pacific coast, is a quick boat ride away from Montezuma.
- **Bus** Intercity buses are frequent and cheap, which makes moving around a cinch.
- **Car** Península de Nicoya is one region in particular where a 4WD vehicle can come in handy.
- **Walk** From Playa Brasilito, you can easily walk to Playa Conchal.

⤹ BE FOREWARNED

- **Roads** If you're driving on unpaved roads during the rainy season, make sure you have a 4WD with high clearance, as well as a comprehensive insurance policy. Many roads will be impassable – always ask locally about conditions before setting out.
- **Riptides** Currents can get ferocious, even in shallow waters, so pay attention to local advisories. If you find yourself caught in a riptide, immediately call for help. It's important to relax, conserve your energy and not fight the current.

PENÍNSULA DE NICOYA

THINGS YOU NEED TO KNOW

PENÍNSULA DE NICOYA ITINERARIES

TAMARINDO & AROUND Three Days

If you can only spare a few days to explore the Nicoya, it's probably best to focus on the town that first put the peninsula on the tourist map, namely Tamarindo. Beach bums can sprawl out on the hot sand and splash about in the cool sea, while revelers can start the night out with signature cuisine, and then unwind in the bars and clubs until the wee hours of the morning.

The best arrival and departure point for Nicoya-focused travelers is the international gateway city of **(1) Liberia** (p145). From here, it's just over an hour or so by paved highway to the famed beach getaway of **(2) Tamarindo** (p180). You'll have no problem keeping busy in this cosmopolitan tourist enclave, though there are a few nearby diversions if you want a change of scene. Nature buffs can watch sea turtles nest on **(3) Playa Grande** (p179), while surfers with a bit of experience under their belt can cut loose at **(4) Playas Avellanas & Negra** (p183).

THE FAR SOUTH Five Days

The southern tip of Península de Nicoya has a reputation for remoteness, but improved transportation connections have made it possible to venture here and back in under a week. Of course, once you set your eyes on the stunning wilderness beaches and overall lack of civilization, you might have second thoughts about heading anywhere else.

Your jumping-off point is the central Pacific coastal town of **(1) Jacó** (p211). From here, you can catch a speedboat across the gulf to **(2) Montezuma** (p190), which saves you several long days of overland travel. With all this extra time added to your itinerary, you shouldn't feel guilty about winding down to slow crawl. Of course, if you can manage to sum up enough energy to leave the beach, there is some excellent hiking to be had just around the corner in the **(3) Reserva Natural Absoluta Cabo Blanco** (p194). And, if you happen to have any extra steam you'd like to burn off, grab a board and hit the monumental surf at **(4) Mal País & Santa Teresa** (p195).

COASTAL CRUISING One Week

The coastal stretches of the Nicoya peninsula are perfectly suited for exploration by private vehicle. If you stick to the highways, a normal car should get you where you want to go, though a 4WD with high clearance will allow you to tackle scenic byways and rural backroads – not to mention a few river crossings! If you've got what it takes to push the pedal to the metal, this extended itinerary is most definitely for you.

Starting in the north, your first stop is (1) Playa del Coco (p176), a modest beach town that happens to front some of the country's best scuba-diving sites. Heading south, you can pay a visit to (2) Tamarindo (p180) and stock up on food, snacks and other goodies before pressing on. The coastal road from here on is slow-going and a bit hair-raising, but your reward awaits in stunningly picturesque (3) Playa Sámara (p187). Surfing aficionados might want to make another detour to (4) Nosara (p186), though be sure to save time for your final destination, the chilled-out paradise that is (5) Montezuma (p190).

DISCOVER THE PENÍNSULA DE NICOYA

The allure of the Península de Nicoya needs no explanation. Archetypical tropical beaches edge this jungle-trimmed rich coast, whose shores have been imprinted on the memories of the millions of marine turtles who return to their birthplaces to nest. The travelers, too, descend on these beaches, seeking to witness such magical patterns of nature for themselves. And who can be blamed for wanting to play, beckoned by waves that never seem to close out, tropical forests teeming with wild things, the slow, sane pace of *la vida costarricense* (Costa Rican life) and what lies beyond that next turn down a potholed dirt road?

Humans, however, make more of an environmental impact than the leatherbacks do. Development is the name of the game at the moment, and Nicoya is the high-stakes playing field. The next moves will require a sustained effort to maintain the peninsula's intrinsic wildness, but we are betting on the Ticos and local expats to rise to the occasion.

PLAYA DEL COCO

Connected by good roads to San José, Playa del Coco is the most easily accessible of the peninsula's beaches. Its beaches are a grayish-brown color, and the sand that lies between its two rocky headlands can appear, well, dirty. While nearby Tamarindo has become the enclave of moneyed foreigners, Playa del Coco is more the party destination for young Ticos on weekends, the playground of divers during the week.

COREY WISE

Idyllic location for walks on the beach: Playa del Coco

PLAYA DEL COCO

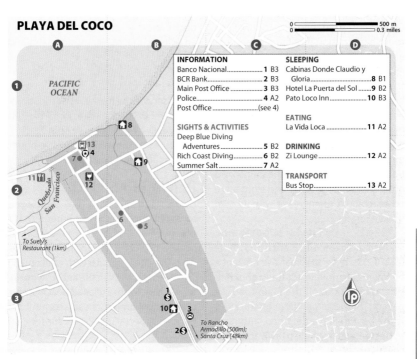

0 — 500 m
0 — 0.3 miles

INFORMATION	
Banco Nacional.....................**1** B3	
BCR Bank............................**2** B3	
Main Post Office **3** B3	
Police.................................**4** A2	
Post Office ....(see 4)	

SIGHTS & ACTIVITIES	
Deep Blue Diving	
Adventures **5** B2	
Rich Coast Diving.................**6** B2	
Summer Salt **7** A2	

SLEEPING	
Cabinas Donde Claudio y	
Gloria................................**8** B1	
Hotel La Puerta del Sol **9** B2	
Pato Loco Inn......................**10** B3	

EATING	
La Vida Loca **11** A2	

DRINKING	
Zi Lounge **12** A2	

TRANSPORT	
Bus Stop.................................**13** A2	

PENÍNSULA DE NICOYA

PLAYA DEL COCO

ACTIVITIES

The northern area of the peninsula is one of the best and most easily accessible sites in the country for diving. The following agencies are thoroughly recommended.

Deep Blue Diving Adventures (☎ 2670-1004; www.deepblue-diving.com) Inside the Coco Bay Hotel & Casino, this outfitter runs two-tank boat dives for US$80.

Rich Coast Diving (☎ 2670-0176, in USA & Canada 800-434-8464; www.richcoastdiving.com) On the main street, this Dutch-owned dive shop has a trimaran for overnight diving trips. A two-tank dive costs US$80, plus US$20 for equipment rental.

Summer Salt (☎ 2670-0308; www.summer -salt.com) This friendly little Swiss-run dive shop has professional, bilingual staff who are as interested in showing you a good time as they are in your safety. Two-tank

dive trips are US$100 with snacks included.

FESTIVALS & EVENTS

The biggest festival in Coco is the **Fiesta de la Virgen del Mar**, celebrated in mid-July with a vivid religious-themed boat procession in the harbor and a horse pageant.

SLEEPING

Cabinas Donde Claudio y Gloria (☎ 2670-1514; d/tr/q US$35/45/45; P 🌐) Located smack-dab on the beach, these clean *cabinas* are a fantastic deal. All rooms have air-con, TV, two double beds, private bathroom, and patio with ocean views.

Pato Loco Inn (☎ 2670-0145; www. costa-rica-beach-hotel-patoloco.com; d US$40-60; P 🌐 🖥 🛜 🔊) This small inn is one of

Coco's most pleasant places to stay. Each room has a design motif and a range of amenities depending on your budget, and the bar in front is a welcoming spot to hang out with a beer and shoot the breeze with the other guests.

Hotel La Puerta del Sol (☎ 2670-0195; lapuertadelsolcostarica@hotmail.com; s/d/tr/ste incl breakfast US$70/90/120/120; P 🞮 🖳) A five-minute walk from town, this unpretentiously luxurious Mediterranean-inspired hotel has two large suites and eight huge pastel-colored rooms, each with its own private terrace.

Rancho Armadillo (☎ 2670-0108; www.ranchoarmadillo.com; d incl breakfast US$170, ste US$170-232; P 🞮 🖳) Near the entrance to town, this private estate is on a hillside about 600m off the main road (all paved). The view from the common areas is the best in Playa del Coco, and it's a perfect retreat from the heavily touristed coastline.

EATING & DRINKING

La Vida Loca (☎ 2670-0181; mains ₡1200-4000; 🕙 11am-2pm) Across a creaky wooden footbridge on the south end of the beach is where you'll find the most popular gringo hangout in town. Opened in 1999 by Oregonian 'Jimbo' Jensen, the beachfront bar specializes in American comfort food.

Suely's Restaurant (☎ 2670-1696; sti-costarica@hotmail.com; mains ₡4000-8000; 🕙 6-10:30pm Mon-Sat) This much-welcomed gourmet addition to Coco's dining scene is the brainchild of French chef Sebastien and his Brazilian-Belgian wife Thais. The passionate daily changing menu focuses on fresh fish and seafood, like the divine tempura jumbo shrimp in Thai sauce.

Zi Lounge (☎ 2670-1978; 🕙 4pm-2:30am) If you're looking for a stylish venue, head here where you can relax on big sofas

under large white tents while DJs spin an eclectic mix of electronica, salsa and hip-hop.

GETTING THERE & AWAY

Buses service the following destinations:

Liberia ₡700; one hour; departs eight times daily from 5:30am to 6pm.

San José (Pulmitan) ₡3200; five hours; departs at 4am, 8am and 2pm.

PLAYA BRASILITO

Underrated Brasilito has managed to avoid the overdevelopment that's plagued much of northern Nicoya. This is still very much a working fishing village. Playa Brasilito is popular with weekending Ticos and travelers 'in the know,' who are drawn here for the relaxed beach scene, pleasant swimming, cheap accommodations and spectacular Pacific sunsets.

SLEEPING & EATING

Hotel Brasilito (☎ 2654-4237; www.brasilito.com; r with/without air-con US$46/39; P 🞮 🛜) On the beach side of the plaza, this recommended hotel is the perfect place to slow down and chill out for a few days.

Conchal Hotel (☎ 2654-9125; www.conchalcr.com; d incl breakfast US$85; P 🞮 🖳 🛜 🖳) Rooms at this recommended hotel are simply stunning – whitewashed walls are offset by exposed wooden beams, ceramic tiling and elegant bathroom.

La Guinguette (mains ₡2000-9000; 🕙 lunch & dinner) He's Tico. She's French. And when Yohann and Geraldine combined their talents, the result was this fabulously imaginative fusion restaurant that's part Costa Rican *soda*, part French gastropub and 100 percent pure passion.

GETTING THERE & AWAY

Buses between Liberia and Playa Flamingo travel through Brasilito.

PLAYA CONCHAL

Just 1km south of Brasilito is Playa Conchal, which is widely regarded as the most beautiful beach in all of Costa Rica. The name comes from the billions of *conchas* (shells) that wash up on the beach, which are gradually crushed into coarse sand. The ocean water is an intense turquoise blue, which is indeed a rarity on the Pacific coast. If you have snorkeling gear, this is the place to bust it out.

With 285 hectares of property, including an over-the-top free-form pool and a championship golf course, the **Paradisus Playa Conchal Beach & Resort** (☎ 2654-4123; www.paradisus-playa-conchal.com; d from US$478; P ⊠ 🖳 🛜 🐾) has got it all.

The easiest way to reach Conchal is to simply walk 15 minutes down the beach from Playa Brasilito.

PLAYA GRANDE

From Huacas, the southwesterly road leads to Playa Grande, a beach famous among conservationists and surfers alike. By day, the offshore winds create steep and powerful waves, especially at high tide and in front of the Hotel Las Tortugas. By night, an ancient cycle continues to unfurl as leatherback sea turtles bearing clutches of eggs follow the ocean currents back to their birthplace. Since 1991 Playa Grande has been part of the Parque Nacional Marino Las Baulas de Guanacaste, which bars beachfront development to ensure that one of the most important leatherback nesting areas in the world is preserved for future generations.

Surfing is most people's motivation for coming to Playa Grande, aside from the turtles, of course.

SLEEPING & EATING

La Marejada Hotel (☎ 2653-0594, in USA & Canada 800-559-3415; www.lamarejada.com; r incl breakfast US$70; ⊠ 🛜 🐾) Hidden behind a bamboo fence, this stylish boutique hotel is the friendliest, most relaxing hotel in Playa Grande.

Hotel Las Tortugas (☎ 2653-0423; www.lastortugashotel.com; d/ste US$95/135, apt US$35-100; P ⊠ 🖳 🐾) The owner of this hotel,

CHRISTIAN ASLUND
Costa Rica lays claim to some of Central America's best surf beaches

Louis Wilson, is a local hero as he was instrumental in helping to designate Playa Grande as a national park. Although his hotel is near the beach, it was carefully designed to keep ambient light away from the nesting area, and to block light from development to the north.

Una Ola (☎ 2653-2682, in USA & Canada 888-958-7873; www.unaola.com; r US$100; ✸ ⚧ ⚐) This intimate resort has eight white-washed rooms in minimalist design, some with king-sized bed. Resort amenities include a communal kitchen with honor bar, large pool and a high-tech media entertainment room.

Kike's Place (☎ 2653-0834; www.kikesplace. com; ⚐ breakfast, lunch & dinner) On the road into town, take note of Kike's (pronounced 'kee-kays'), the friendly local bar and restaurant where you can shoot some pool, eat some *ceviche* (marinated seafood) and let your hair down.

GETTING THERE & AWAY

There are no buses to Playa Grande. You can drive to Huacas and then take the paved road to Matapalo, followed by a rough dirt road to Playa Grande.

Alternatively, you can catch a dinghy across the estuary from Tamarindo to the southern end of Playa Grande (around ₡650 per person).

PARQUE NACIONAL MARINO LAS BAULAS DE GUANACASTE

This **national park** (☎ 2653-0470; admission US$10, with guided tour US$25; ⚐ 8am-noon & 1-5pm) is considered one of the most important nesting sites in the entire world for the *baula* (leatherback turtle). Despite increased conservation efforts, however, fewer and fewer leatherbacks are nesting on Playa Grande each year. In 2004 an all-time low of 46 leatherbacks visited the beach, which was a vast departure from the estimated 1000 turtles that nested here in the 1990s. While it's easy to point fingers at developers in Tamarindo, park rangers attribute the decline in nesting turtles to longline commercial fishing.

Reservations for turtle-watching can be made up to seven days in advance, and they're highly recommended as there is a limited number of places each evening. If you phone ahead, you will be promised a spot within a week, though there is usually a vacancy within a day or two. You can also show up in the evening as there are frequent no-shows, though this is less likely on weekends and during the busy winter holiday season.

The show kicks off anytime from 9pm to as late as 2am, though there is no guarantee that you will see a turtle. This also means that you might only have to wait for 10 minutes before a turtle shows up, or you could be there for five hours. A small stand at the exhibit sells snacks and sodas, but bring a (thick) book or a deck of cards for entertainment. It could be a very long night – but well worth it.

As a group, you will be accompanied by a guide to a designated viewing area, though photography, filming or lights of any kind are *not* allowed. Over the span of one to two hours, you can watch as the turtle digs its nest, lays about 150 silver shiny eggs and then buries them in the sand (while grunting and groaning the whole time).

PLAYA TAMARINDO

Well, they don't call it Tamagringo for nothing. Call it what you will, but Tamarindo's long status as Costa Rica's top surf and party destination has made it the first and last stop for many tourists and expats. This is the most developed beach on the peninsula with no shortage of hotels, bars, restaurants, strip malls and pricey condos. After years of unchecked development, the pace is finally slowing down, partly because of the Great Recession and partly thanks to the work of concerned residents. Tamarindo is slowly recapturing its Tico roots.

ACTIVITIES

MOUNTAIN BIKING

The local expert on mountain biking, distance cycling, bike tours and repairs is Blue Trailz (☎ 2653-0221; www.bluetrailz.com; ⏰ 7am-7pm Mon-Sat). And if mountain biking ain't your thing, you can also rent a beach cruiser (two hours US$10, all day US$20).

SAILING

For sunset and daylong sailing excursions, book in advance by phone or online with Blue Dolphin Sailing

(☎ 2653-0867, 8842-3204; www.sailblue dolphin.com). Reader-recommended trips on Captain Jeff's catamaran include a 4½ hour snorkel and sunset sail (US$75/38 per adult/child under 12) with gear, open bar and snacks.

SURFING

The most popular wave in Tamarindo is a medium-sized right that breaks directly in front of the Tamarindo Diria hotel. The waters here are full of virgin surfers learning to pop up, most of whom can't help but play aquatic bumper cars. There is also a good left that's fed by the river mouth, though be advised that crocodiles are occasionally sighted here, particularly when the tide is rising (which is, coincidentally, the best time to surf).

A number of surf schools and surf tour operators line the main stretch of road in

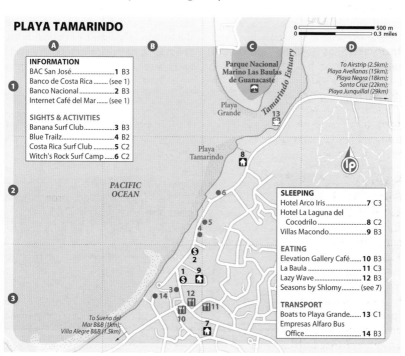

PLAYA TAMARINDO

0 — 500 m
0 — 0.3 miles

INFORMATION
BAC San José........................**1** B3
Banco de Costa Rica ....(see 1)
Banco Nacional **2** B3
Internet Café del Mar ....(see 1)

SIGHTS & ACTIVITIES
Banana Surf Club.................**3** B3
Blue Trailz............................**4** B2
Costa Rica Surf Club **5** C2
Witch's Rock Surf Camp **6** C2

SLEEPING
Hotel Arco Iris **7** C3
Hotel La Laguna del
    Cocodrilo.........................**8** C2
Villas Macondo.....................**9** B3

EATING
Elevation Gallery Café.......**10** B3
La Baula **11** C3
Lazy Wave...........................**12** B3
Seasons by Shlomy...........(see 7)

TRANSPORT
Boats to Playa Grande.......**13** C1
Empresas Alfaro Bus
    Office...............................**14** B3

Parque Nacional Marino Las Baulas de Guanacaste

Playa Grande

Tamarindo Estuary

To Airstrip (2.5km); Playa Avellanas (15km); Playa Negra (18km); Santa Cruz (22km); Playa Junquillal (29km)

Playa Tamarindo

PACIFIC OCEAN

To Sueño del Mar B&B (1km); Villa Alegre B&B (1.5km)

PENÍNSULA DE NICOYA

PLAYA TAMARINDO

Tamarindo. Surf lessons hover at around US$40 for 1½ to two hours, and most operators will let you keep the board for a few hours beyond that to practice. All outfits can organize daylong and multiday excursions to popular breaks, rent equipment and give surf lessons.

Banana Surf Club (☎ 2653-0130/2463; www.bananasurfclub.com; ☺ 8am-6pm) This outfit has fair prices on new and used boards.

Blue Trailz (☎ 2653-0114; rasurfshop@yahoo.com; ☺ 7am-7pm) One of the largest and best shops in town; offers lessons, trips and rents surfboards, body boards and skim boards.

Costa Rica Surf Club (☎ 2653-1270; www.costaricasurfclub.com; ☺ 8am-8pm Mon-Sat, 9am-7pm Sun) Two locations in town offering rentals, lessons, repairs and sales.

Witch's Rock Surf Camp (☎ 2653-0239; www.witchsrocksurfcamp.com; ☺ 8am-8pm) Board rentals, surf camps, lessons and regular excursions to Witch's Rock and Ollie's Point are available, but they're pricey.

SLEEPING

Villas Macondo (☎ 2653-0812; www.villasmacondo.com; s/d/tr US$35/40/50, with air-con US$60/65/75, 2-/4-person apt US$105/145, extra person US$10; P ✶ ☐ ☞ ☎) Although it's only 200m from the beach, this German-run establishment is an oasis of serenity in an otherwise frenzied town – it's also one of the best deals around.

Hotel La Laguna del Cocodrilo (☎ 2653-0255; www.lalagunadelcocodrilo.com; d US$68-79, ste US$130; P ✶ ☞) A beachfront location blesses this charming French-owned hotel, with luxurious, well-kept rooms overlooking either the shady grounds or the ocean and estuary. Adjacent to a crocodile-filled lagoon (hence the name), the hotel has a private trail leading to the beach.

Hotel Arco Iris (☎ 2653-0330; www.hotelarcoiris.com; d standard/deluxe incl breakfast US$99/109; P ✶ ☐ ☞) A cluster of garden bungalows and deluxe rooms makes up this wonderfully reclusive boutique hotel. The rooms have a contemporary style, and feature wonderful touches, such as

CHRISTER FREDRIKSSON

Sun, surf and sea: Costa Rica's blissful holy trinity

bamboo ceilings, and bathrooms with slate walls.

Villa Alegre B&B (☎ 2653-0270; www.villaalegrecostarica.com; r US$170-185, villas US$230, all incl breakfast; P ❄ ▣ ⚑ ⚙) This beachside B&B in nearby Playa Langosta has five rooms of various sizes, each decorated with memorabilia from the owners' world travels (you can choose between the Caribbean, USA, California, Guatemala or Mexico rooms). Or stay in the Japan or Russia villas, which are equipped with a full kitchen.

Sueño del Mar B&B (☎ 2653-0284; www.sueno-del-mar.com; d US$195-295, ste US$220-240; P ❄ ▣ ⚑) This stunning Spanish-style *posada* (country-style inn) in nearby Playa Langosta is run by lovely innkeepers Ashton and Tui, and decorated with handcrafted rocking chairs, hammocks and a cozy living room that's perfect for relaxing with the other guests.

EATING & DRINKING

Elevation Gallery Café (☎ 8302-3590; mains ₡2500-6100; ☽ 8am-3pm Wed-Sun; ☜) Readers rave about the breakfast and lunch menu at this stylish coffee house. Co-owner Lane Patrick is a former Four Seasons chef.

Lazy Wave (☎ 2653-0737; meals ₡2700-13,200; ☽ 6-10pm Sat-Thu) Dine at a table if you must, but the best place to enjoy your Asian- and Euro-influenced *bocas* and glass of wine is on the covered pavilion, where you can curl up amid pillows in cushy lounge chairs

La Baula (☎ 2653-1450; mains ₡4400-6300; ☽ 5:30-11pm; ⚑) By far the best pizza in Tamarindo – this casual open-air restaurant has real wood-fired pizza, pasta and other Italian fare. It's also one of the most family-friendly restaurants in town, with a nice playground to keep the kids entertained.

Seasons by Shlomy (☎ 8368-6983; www.hotelarcoiris.com; mains ₡6600-8500, fixed-price menu ₡14,000; ☽ 6-10pm Mon-Sat) Don't leave town without eating here – it may be the best meal you have in Costa Rica. Israeli chef Shlomy serves innovative dishes with Mediterranean accents that change daily depending on the availability of local ingredients.

In Tamarindo, all you really have to do is follow the party scene wherever it happens to be on that night. On weekends especially, cruising the main drag has the festive feel of a mini Mardi Gras or spring break.

GETTING THERE & AWAY

Buses go to these destinations:

Liberia ₡1200; 2½ hours; departs 13 times per day from 4:30am to 6:30pm.

San José ₡4860; six hours; departs at 3:30am and 5:30am. Alternatively, take a bus to Liberia and change for frequent buses to the capital.

Santa Cruz ₡300; 1½ hours; departs at 6am, 9am, noon, 2pm, 3pm and 4pm.

PLAYAS AVELLANAS & NEGRA

These popular surfing beaches have some of the best, most consistent waves in the area, made famous in the surf classic *Endless Summer II*. Playa Avellanas is a long stretch of white sand backed by mangroves, and Playa Negra, a few kilometers further south, is a darker, caramel-color beach broken up by rocky outcrops.

ACTIVITIES

At Avellanas, **Little Hawaii** is a powerful and open-faced right at medium tide, while **Beach Break** barrels at low tide (though the surfing is good any time of day). Playa Negra has a world-class right that barrels, especially with a moderate offshore wind.

PENÍNSULA DE NICOYA

PLAYAS AVELLANAS & NEGRA

SLEEPING & EATING
PLAYA AVELLANAS

Las Avellanas Villas (☎ 2652-9212; www.las avellanasvillas.com; d/tr/q US$65/75/85; P ⊚) Stunningly designed by Costa Rican architect Victor Cañas, these four *casitas* (cottages) are covetable as permanent residences. With an aesthetic balancing of the interior environment with the exterior, they have sunken stone floors crossed by wooden bridges, open-air showers, and large windows looking out on front and back terraces.

Mauna Loa Surf Resort (☎ 2652-9012; www.hotelmaunaloa.com; d US$70; P ⊠ 🖵) This pleasant Italian-run spot is a great place for families, with a secure location that's a straight shot to the beach. Paths lead from the pool area through a well-tended garden, and the cute bungalows have orthopedic beds and hammocks hanging on the terraces.

Lola's on the Beach (☎ 2652-9097; meals ₡5500-11,000; ☽ lunch & dinner Tue-Sun) Lola's is the place to hang out, in low-slung plank chairs on a palm-fringed stretch of Avellanas sand, if the water is looking a bit glassy. Try the amazing *poke* (Hawaiian raw-fish salad) or green papaya salad with a beer.

PLAYA NEGRA

Mono Congo Surf Lodge (☎ 2652-9261; www.monocongolodge.com; r/ste from US$60/95; P ⊠ 🖵 ⊚) This large, open-air, Polynesian-style tree-house lodge is surrounded by howler-filled trees and is the pinnacle of tropical luxury in Playa Negra. High-ceilinged, polished-wood rooms are exquisite.

Hotel Playa Negra (☎ 2652-9134; www. playanegra.com; s/d/tr/q US$81/93/105/116; P ⊚ 🖭) This charming hotel, right on the beach at Playa Negra's reef break, is a collection of 10 spacious, circular bungalows with thatched roofs, bright tropical colors and traditional indigenous-style tapestries and linens.

Pablo Picasso (☎ 2652-9158; mains ₡1250-4000; ☽ 6am-9pm; ⊚) The house specialty at this American-owned restaurant is the 'burger as big as your head.'

ADRIAN HEPWORTH/HEPWORTHIMAGES

Olive ridley turtle

GETTING THERE & AWAY

Buses to Santa Cruz depart at 5:30am and 1:30pm. Note that there are no afternoon buses on Sunday.

SANTA CRUZ

pop 12,000

A stop in Santa Cruz, a *sabanero* (cowboy) town typical of inland Nicoya, provides some of the local flavor missing from foreign-dominated beach towns. Unfortunately, there aren't any attention-worthy sights in town, so most travelers' experience in Santa Cruz consists of changing buses and perhaps buying a mango or two.

FESTIVALS & EVENTS

There is a rodeo during the Fiesta de Santa Cruz in the second week in January, and on July 25 for Día de Guanacaste. At these events, you can check out the *sabaneros,* admire prize bulls and drink plenty of beer while listening to eardrum-bursting music.

GETTING THERE & AWAY

Some buses depart from Terminal Tralapa, which is located on the northern side of Plaza de Los Mangos.

Liberia (La Pampa) ₡770; 1½ hours; departs every 30 minutes from 4:10am to 8:40pm.

Nicoya (La Pampa) ₡310; one hour; departs every 30 minutes from 4:50am to 9:20pm.

San José ₡4690; 4½ hours; seven buses from 4:30am to 5pm (Tralapa); eight buses from 3am to 4:30pm (Empresas Alfaro).

Other local buses leave from Terminal Diria 400m east of the plaza.

Playa Avellanas ₡800; 1½ hours; departs at 11:30am and 6pm.

Playa Negra ₡800; 1½ hours; departs at 8am.

Playa Tamarindo ₡400; 1½ hours; departs at 4:20am, 5:30am, 9am, 10:30am, 1pm, 3:30pm and 5pm. The last bus does not operate on Sunday.

NICOYA

pop 13,000

Nicoya is one of the most pleasant cities in the region, and the bright buildings and bustling streets contribute to the welcoming atmosphere – for travelers, Nicoya primarily serves as a transportation hub.

SIGHTS

In Parque Central, a major town landmark, is the attractive white colonial Iglesia de San Blas, which dates back to the mid-17th century. It has a small collection of colonial religious artifacts, or have a look at the wooden Jesus with articulated joints and bleeding stigmata.

FESTIVALS & EVENTS

The town goes crazy for Día de Guanacaste, on July 25, so expect plenty of food, music and beer in the plaza to celebrate the province's annexation from Nicaragua.

GETTING THERE & AWAY

Take a bus to these destinations:

Liberia ₡1000; 2½ hours; departs every 30 minutes from 3:30am to 8pm.

Playa Naranjo, for ferry to Puntarenas ₡1300; three hours; departs at 5am, 9am, 1pm and 5pm.

Playa Nosara ₡1050; 2½ hours; departs at 5am, 10am, noon, 3pm and 5:30pm.

Sámara ₡850; two hours; 13 buses per day from 5am to 9pm.

San José (Empresas Alfaro) ₡3750; five hours; departs five times daily.

NOSARA AREA

A pocket of luxuriant vegetation backs the attractive beaches near the small Tico village of Nosara. The entire area is a magical destination as you can sometimes see parrots, toucans, armadillos and monkeys just a few meters away from the beaches.

ORIENTATION

The Nosara area is spread out along the coast and a little inland (making a car a bit of a necessity). Log on to Nosara Travel's website (www.nosaratravel.com/map. html) for a handy map.

North of the river is **Playa Nosara**, which is difficult to access and primarily used by fisherfolk. Further south is **Playa Pelada**, a small crescent-shaped beach with an impressive blowhole that sends water shooting through the air at high tide. The southernmost beach is **Playa Guiones**, a 7km stretch of sand that's one of the best surf spots on the central peninsula.

ACTIVITIES

CANOPY TOURS

Miss Sky (☎ 2682-0969; www.missskycanopy tour.com; adult/child US$60/30; ☷ 7am-5pm) has brought a canopy tour to Nosara. It's the longest one in the world – at least for now – with a total length of 11,000m above a pristine, private reserve. The zip lines don't go from platform to platform, but from mountainside to mountainside, and have double cables for added safety. The last of 21 zip lines whisks you directly into the top floor of the onsite disco-bar!

HIKING

The **Reserva Biológica Nosara** (☎ 2682-0573; www.lagarta.com) behind the Lagarta Lodge has private trails leading through a mangrove wetland down to the river (five minutes) and beach (10 minutes). This is a great spot for bird-watching, and there's a good chance you'll see some reptiles as well (look up in the trees as there are occasionally boa constrictors here). Nonguests can visit the reserve for US$6.

JIMMY CHIN/AURORA PHOTOS

Playa Nosara at sunset

SURFING

Check out Playa Guiones for the best beach break in the central peninsula, especially when there is an offshore wind. Although the beach is usually full of surfers, there are plenty of take-off points.

YOGA

In the hills near Playa Guiones is the famous Nosara Yoga Institute (☎ 2682-0071, toll-free 866-439-4704; www.nosarayoga. com). The institute offers regular classes, open to the public, as well as workshops, retreats and instructor-training courses.

SLEEPING & EATING

PLAYA GUIONES

Casa Romántica (☎ 2682-0272; www. casa-romantica.net; d incl breakfast from US$90; P ⛄ ⛄ ⛄ ⛄) Right next to Playa Guiones is this recommended Spanish colonial mansion with several rooms with private bathrooms. They all have views of the manicured gardens surrounding the pool.

Harbor Reef Lodge (☎ 2682-0059; www. harborreef.com; d US$95-149, ste US$129-239, casas per week from US$1495; P ⛄ ⛄ ⛄ ⛄) These cool, tiled rooms with private hot-water bathroom, air-con and fridge have wood detailing and attractive Latin American textiles.

L'Acqua Viva Hotel & Spa (☎ 2682-1087; www.lacquaviva.com; r US$232, ste US$350-385, villas US$593-831; P ⛄ ⛄ ⛄) A bit of Bali in Nosara, L'Acqua Viva is one of the most luxurious hotels on the central peninsula. Inside and out, the property is simply stunning, with water, wood and bamboo features throughout.

Beach Dog Café (items ₡1000-3500; ⛄ 7am-7:30pm; ⛄) Just steps from the beach, our favorite new cafe in Nosara has the best breakfast in town. The delicious lunch menu includes organic salads, sandwiches, wraps, pasta and more.

PLAYA PELADA

Lagarta Lodge (☎ 2682-0035; www.lagarta. com; s/d/tr US$75/81/87; P ⛄ ⛄) Further north, a road dead-ends at this six-room hotel, a recommended choice high on a steep hill above the private 50-hectare Reserva Biológica Nosara. Bird-watching and wildlife-spotting are good here – and you can watch from the comfort of the hotel balcony or see many more species if you go on a hike.

Villa Mango B&B (☎ 2682-0130; www.villa mangocr.com; s/d incl breakfast US$78/89; P ⛄) You can't help but relax at this tiny B&B in the trees, with ocean views and hosts who enjoy chatting with their guests.

La Luna (☎ 2682-0122; dishes ₡3000-10,000; ⛄ lunch & dinner) On the beach, to the right of the Hotel Playas de Nosara, you'll find this impressive stone building that houses a trendy restaurant-bar and art gallery. The eclectic menu has Asian and Mediterranean flourishes.

GETTING THERE & AWAY

Traroc buses depart for Nicoya (₡800, two hours) at 5am, 7am, noon and 3pm. Empresas Alfaro buses going to San José (₡4500, five to six hours) depart from the pharmacy by the soccer field at 12:30pm.

To get to Sámara, take any bus out of Nosara and ask the driver to drop you off at *la bomba de Sámara* (Sámara gas station). From there, catch one of the buses traveling from Nicoya to Sámara.

PLAYA SÁMARA

The crescent-shaped strip of pale-gray sand at Sámara is one of the most beloved beaches in Costa Rica – it's safe, tranquil, reasonably developed and easily accessible by public transportation. Not surprisingly, it's popular with vacationing Tico families, backpackers, wealthy tourists, snorkelers and surfers alike (even Oscar Arias, the

Playa Sámara (p187)

IMAGEBROKER/SIEPMANN

↘ IF YOU LIKE...

If you like **Playa Sámara** (p187), we think you'll like these other beaches on the Península de Nicoya:

- **Playa Ocotal** This small but attractive gray-sand beach has tidal pools on both ends.
- **Playa Flamingo** The white-sand shoreline itself is a blue-flag beach, making it a lovely place to while away the time.
- **Playas San Miguel & Coyote** This pair of wilderness beaches, separated by the mouth of the Río Jabillo, has fine, silver-gray sand.

ex-president, has a vacation house near here). In recent years the village has undergone a bit of a transformation. Sámara is becoming increasingly more sophisticated.

ACTIVITIES
CANOPY TOURS
The local zip-line operator is **Wing Nuts** (☎ 2656-0153; adult/child US$55/35), on the eastern outskirts of town off the main paved road.

FISHING
The French-owned **Sámara Fishing Trip** (☎ 2656-1033; www.samarafishingtrip.com; US$450-550) offers a variety of inshore and offshore sportfishing trips.

FLIGHTS
Several kilometers to the west, in Playa Buenavista, the **Flying Crocodile** (☎ 2656-8048; www.flying-crocodile.com) offers ultra-light flights (20-minute tour US$75). It also offers flight lessons (US$170 per hour).

DIVING & SNORKELING
The highly recommended **Pura Vida Dive Center** (☎ 2656-0643, 8313-3518; www.pura vidadive.com; 2-tank dive incl equipment US$95) arranges diving, snorkeling, fishing and dolphin- and whale-watching tours.

SURFING
Experienced surfers will probably be bored with Sámara's inconsistent waves, though beginners can have a blast here.

SLEEPING
Tico Adventure Lodge (☎ 2656-0628; www. ticoadventurelodge.com; s/d/apt US$34/68/130; P ✂ 🛜 🐾) The American owners are proud of the fact that they built this lodge without cutting down a single tree, and they have every reason to be – it's stunning. Lush vegetation and old-growth trees surround nine double rooms with private bathroom and wood accents.

Entre Dos Aguas B&B (☎ 2656-0998; www.hoteldosaguas.com; s/d/tr/q incl breakfast US$47/52/60/70; P 💻 🐾) Seven brightly colored rooms have a private stone shower, vibrant woven linens and homey little touches like incense and candles. A well-manicured garden surrounds the pool, and the common courtyard is invitingly strung with hammocks and set with heavy tables.

Sámara Pacific Lodge (☎ 2656-1033; www.samara-pacific-lodge.com; d/tr/q US$85/96/107; P ✂ 🛜 🐾 🏊) Located 1.4km west of downtown, this quiet, colonial-style hotel has been returned to its previous glory by the new French owners. Spacious, whitewashed, individually decorated rooms have a high ceiling and private bathroom and terrace, some with king-sized beds.

El Pequeño Gecko Verde (☎ 2656-1176; www.gecko-verde.com; 2-3 person bungalow US$145, 4-5 person bungalow US$185; P X ☎ ☐) Five contemporary and beautifully decorated bungalows are surrounded by a tropical garden of Eden. Onsite amenities include a salt-water swimming pool with waterfall and a fabulous open-air restaurant and bar. Behind the property, a 400m jungle trail leads to a stunning cove beach backed by high cliffs with amazing sunset views.

EATING & DRINKING

Shake Joe's (☎ 2656-0252; mains ₡2800-8500; ☺ 11am-late) This hip beachside spot is awash with chilled-out electronica and cool, calm travelers lounging on the huge wooden outdoor couches. You can grab a burger here after your surf session, but the ambience is tops when the sun goes down and the drinks start to flow.

Al Manglar (☎ 2656-0096; mains ₡3000-5000; ☺ 5-10pm) Consistently the best restaurant in town, this thatched-roof, open-air restaurant serves some of the best Italian food in town at reasonable prices. The pasta dishes, such as gnocchi and ravioli, are real winners.

El Lagarto (☎ 2656-0750; ww.ellagartobbq.com; mains ₡9000-16,000; ☺ 11am-11pm; ☎) Grilled meats are the big draw at this beachfront alfresco restaurant draped by old trees. Watching the chefs work their magic on the giant wood-fired oven is part of the fun.

SHOPPING

Koss Art Gallery (☎ 2656-0284) Visit Jaime at his outdoor studio on the beach, where he frequently displays his richly hued works in the high season. Call ahead for a viewing.

Galería Dragonfly (☎ 2656-0964; www.samaraarte.com) You'll see Leonardo Palacios' mural as you walk the main street; the gallery inside houses uniquely wrought jewelry in all sorts of media like

PENÍNSULA DE NICOYA

PLAYA SÁMARA

CARVERMOSTARDI/ALAMY

Sportfishing has its rewards in Costa Rica, including hauling species such as blue marlin

leather and seashells, along with sculpture, paintings and decorative pieces in a very organic style.

GETTING THERE & AWAY

Empresas Alfaro has a bus to San José (₡3600, five hours) that departs at 4:30am, 8:30am and 1pm Monday to Saturday. On Sunday there is only one bus at 9am. Traroc buses to Nicoya (₡900, two hours) depart 11 times daily from the *pulpería* (corner store) by the soccer field.

PLAYA NARANJO

This tiny village next to the ferry terminal caters to travelers either waiting for the ferry or arriving from Puntarenas. There really isn't any reason to hang around, though thankfully you won't have to as the ferries tend to run reasonably on time.

GETTING THERE & AWAY
BOAT
The Coonatramar ferry (☎ 2661-1069; www.coonatramar.com; adult/child/car ₡860/515/1850) to Puntarenas departs daily at 8am, 12:30pm, 5:30pm and 9pm, and can accommodate both cars and passengers. The trip takes 1½ hours. If traveling by car, get out and buy a ticket at the window, get back in your car and then drive on to the ferry.

BUS
Buses meet the ferry and take passengers to Nicoya (₡1000, three hours). Departures are at approximately 7am, 10:50pm, 2:50pm and 7pm.

PAQUERA

Paquera is more of a population center than Playa Naranjo, though again, there's little reason to stay here longer than it takes to embark or disembark the ferry.

GETTING THERE & AWAY
BOAT
Ferry Naviera Tambor (☎ 2641-2084; www.navieratambor.com; adult/child/car ₡810/485/1900) departs daily at 6am, 9am, 11am, 1pm, 3pm, 5pm, 7pm and 9pm (the last ferry doesn't run in low season). The trip takes about an hour. Buy a ticket at the window, get back into your car and then drive onto the ferry.

BUS
Buses from the terminal head directly to Montezuma (₡1400, two hours).

TAXI
Getting several travelers together to share a taxi is a good option since the ride will take half as long as the bus. The ride to Montezuma costs about ₡5000 per person, and to Mal País it's about ₡7000.

MONTEZUMA

Montezuma was one of the original 'destinations' in Costa Rica, and its remote location and proximity to Costa Rica's first nature reserve, Cabo Blanco, attracted hippies, artists and dreamers alike. You had to work to get here, and no one had plans to leave quickly. Montezuma is still a charming village, and foreign travelers continue to be drawn here by the laid-back atmosphere, cheap hotels and sprawling beaches. And while nothing ever stays the same, Montezuma has managed to hang on to its tranquil appeal.

SIGHTS & ACTIVITIES
BEACHES
Picture-perfect white-sand beaches are strung out along the coast, separated by small rocky headlands and offering great beachcombing and tide-pool studying.

Unfortunately, there are strong rips along the entire coastline, so inquire locally before going for a swim and take care.

The beaches in front of the town are nice enough, but the further northeast you walk, the more isolated and pristine they become. During low tide, the best **snorkeling** is in the tide pools, and at Playa Las Manchas, 1km west of downtown. There's great **surf** if you're willing to walk the 7km up the coastline to Playa Grande, or if you head south about 3km to Playa Cedros.

BUTTERFLY GARDEN

The **Montezuma Gardens** (☎ 8888-4200; www.montezumagardens.com; admission US$8; ⏱ 8am-4pm) are about 1km up the hill toward Cóbano, alongside the waterfall trail. You can take a tour through this lush *mariposario* (butterfly garden) and nursery where the mysterious metamorphoses occur.

CANOPY TOURS

After you've flown down nine zip lines, the **Montezuma Waterfall Canopy Tour** (☎ 2642-0808; www.montezumatraveladventures.

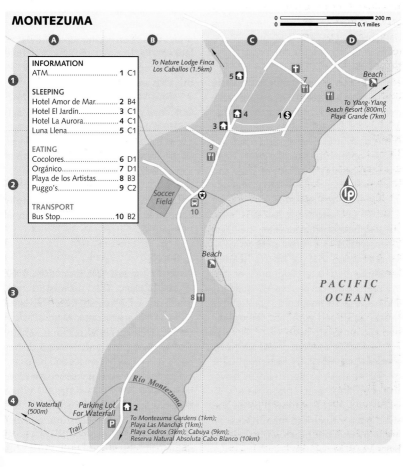

MONTEZUMA

INFORMATION	
ATM	**1** C1

SLEEPING	
Hotel Amor de Mar	**2** B4
Hotel El Jardín	**3** C1
Hotel La Aurora	**4** C1
Luna Llena	**5** C1

EATING	
Cocolores	**6** D1
Orgánico	**7** D1
Playa de los Artistas	**8** B3
Puggo's	**9** C2

TRANSPORT	
Bus Stop	**10** B2

To Nature Lodge Finca Los Caballos (1.5km)

Beach

To Ylang-Ylang Beach Resort (800m); Playa Grande (7km)

Soccer Field

Beach

PACIFIC OCEAN

To Waterfall (500m)

Parking Lot For Waterfall

Trail

Río Montezuma

To Montezuma Gardens (1km); Playa Las Manchas (1km); Playa Cedros (3km); Cabuya (9km); Reserva Natural Absoluta Cabo Blanco (10km)

0   200 m
0   0.1 miles

com; US$45) winds up with a hike down – rather than up – to the waterfalls; bring your swimsuit.

FESTIVALS & EVENTS

Festival de Arte Chunches de Mar (www.chunchesdemar.com) This arts festival brings together artists and musicians to camp on the beach for one month and create art together from found objects – dates change every year, but it is usually during high season.

Montezuma International Film Festival (www.montezumafilmfestival.com) Usually held in November, this is a great excuse to celebrate the arts in Montezuma before high season kicks in.

SLEEPING

Luna Llena (☎ 2642-0390; www.lunallenahotel.com; s without bathroom US$25, d without bathroom US$35-50; P) On the northern edge of town on a hilltop overlooking the bay is this delightful German-American–run budget option that's terrific value. There are 12 rooms in a variety of sizes and prices, all with mosquito net, fan and safe large enough to fit a laptop.

Hotel La Aurora (☎ 2642-0051; www.playamontezuma.net/aurora.htm; s without bathroom US$25-45, d without bathroom US$30-50, extra person US$5; P ⊠ ⊜) Reader-recommended Hotel La Aurora is ocated in a pretty, vine-covered yellow building, and has an assortment of 15 comfortable rooms equipped with fan, orthopedic bed and mosquito net.

Hotel Amor de Mar (☎ 2642-0262; www.amordemar.com; d US$58-124, houses from US$210; P ⊜) At the southern end of town, this charming, serene place has a well-manicured lawn strewn with palms and strung with luxurious hammocks, all fronting a beautiful beach with a tide pool big enough to swim in.

Hotel El Jardín (☎ 2642-0548; www.hoteleljardin.com; d US$85-95, 4-person villas US$135; P ⊠ ⊜ ⊛) This hillside hotel has 15 luxurious stained-wood *cabinas* of various sizes and amenities (some have a stone bathroom and ocean views). The grounds are landscaped with tropical flowers and lush palms, and there's a pool and Jacuzzi for soaking your cares away.

Nature Lodge Finca Los Caballos (☎ 2642-0124; www.naturelodge.net; d incl breakfast US$97-165, extra person US$20; P ⊛) North of Montezuma on the road to Cóbano, this 16-hectare ranch has a variety of rooms around the property with either jungle or ocean views. The Canadian owner prides herself on having some of the best looked-after horses in the area, and there are great opportunities here for riding on the trails around the reserve.

Ylang-Ylang Beach Resort (☎ 2642-0636; www.ylangylangresort.com; luxury tents US$160, d/ste US$195/235, standard/deluxe bungalows US$265/295, all incl breakfast & dinner; ⊠ ⊛) About a 15-minute walk north of town along the beach is this resort catering to holistic holiday-seekers. Here you'll find a collection of beautifully appointed rooms, suites and polygonal bungalows.

EATING

Puggo's (☎ 2642-0308; mains ₡4000-7000; ⊙ 8am-10:30pm) This promising new Israeli-owned restaurant decorated like a Bedouin tent specializes in Middle Eastern cuisine including falafel, hummus, kebabs, and aromatic fish and seafood dishes cooked in imported spices and herbs.

Orgánico (www.organicomontezuma.com; mains ₡4400-5500; ⊙ 8am-late; Ⓥ) When they say 'pure food made with love,' they mean it – this healthy cafe turns out vegetarian or vegan treats you can feel good about.

MARK NEWMAN

A sprinkling of cascades in the Montezuma area

↘ THE MONTEZUMA WATERFALL

A 20-minute stroll south of town takes you to a set of three scenic waterfalls. The main attraction here is to climb the second set of falls and jump in. Though countless people do this every day, be aware that even despite a warning sign about half a dozen people have died attempting this. A lot of travelers enjoy the thrill, but as with anything of this nature, you undertake it at your own risk.

The first waterfall has a good swimming hole, but it's shallow and rocky and not suitable for diving. From here, if you continue on the well-marked trail that leads around and up, you will come to a second set of falls. These are the ones that offer a good clean leap (from 10m up) into the deep water below. To reach the jumping point, continue to take the trail up the side of the hill until you reach the diving area. Do *not* attempt to scale the falls. The rocks are slippery and this is how most jumpers have met their deaths. From this point, the trail continues up the hill to the third and last set of falls. Once again, these aren't that safe for jumping. However, there is a rope swing that will drop you right over the deeper part of the swimming hole (just be sure to let go on the out-swing!).

Things you need to know: To get there, follow the main Montezuma road south out of town, then take the trail to the right after Hotel La Cascada, past the bridge. You'll see a clearly marked parking area for visitors (₡1000 per car) and the beginning of the trail that leads up.

Cocolores (☎ 2642-0348; mains ₡4000-11,000; 🕒 5-10pm Tue-Sun) One of the best restaurants in Montezuma, beachside Cocolores has a pleasant, thatched-roof patio that's perfect for candlelit dinners. The menu focuses on French-influenced cuisine and also offers some Tico-fusion standards.

Playa de los Artistas (☎ 2642-0920; www.playamontezuma.net/playadelosartistas.htm; mains ₡5000-10,000; 🕒 lunch & dinner Thu-Sat, lunch only Mon-Wed, closed Sun) This artfully decorated beachside spot is the most adored and romantic restaurant in town. The international menu, heavy with Mediterranean influences, changes daily depending on locally available ingredients.

GETTING THERE & AWAY
BOAT
Travelers are increasingly taking advantage of the jet-boat transfer service that connects Jacó to Montezuma (US$37).

BUS
Cabo Blanco ₡600; 45 minutes; departs at 8:15am, 10:15am, 2:15pm and 6:15pm.

Paquera ₡1300; 1½ hours; departs at 5:30am, 8am, 10am, noon, 2:15pm and 4pm.

San José ₡5800; six hours; departs at 6:15am and 2:30pm.

RESERVA NATURAL ABSOLUTA CABO BLANCO
Just 11km south of Montezuma is Costa Rica's oldest protected wilderness area

(☎ 2642-0093; admission US$10; ⏱ 8am-4pm Wed-Sun). In fact, Cabo Blanco is called an 'absolute nature reserve' because prior to the late 1980s, visitors were not permitted. The moist microclimate present on the tip of the peninsula fosters the growth of evergreen forests, which are unique when compared with the dry tropical forests typical of the Nicoya. The park also encompasses a number of pristine white-sand beaches and offshore islands that are favored nesting areas for various bird species.

From the ranger station, the Swedish Trail and Danish Trail lead 4.5km down to a wilderness beach at the tip of the peninsula. Monkeys, squirrels, sloths, deer, agoutis and raccoons are usually present, and armadillos, coatis, peccaries and anteaters are occasionally sighted. The coastal area is known as an important nesting site for the brown booby, mostly found 1.6km south of the mainland on Isla Cabo Blanco (White Cape Island).

Buses (₡600, 45 minutes) depart from the park entrance for Montezuma at

Fishing boats docked along the coast

RICHARD CUMMINS

7am, 9am, 1pm and 4pm. A taxi from Montezuma to the park costs about ₡7000.

MAL PAÍS & SANTA TERESA

The legendary waves at Mal País have been attracting surfers since the 1970s, so it's not surprising that many of them grew up and decided to stay. In the last several years, this once isolated corner of the peninsula has become something of the backpackers' version of Nosara – surf session in the morning, yoga in the afternoon and cruising at night. Widespread development is rapidly carving up the beachfront but the town still retains its old fishing-village roots. The coastal dust road remains unpaved and there are few transportation links to the outside world.

ORIENTATION

Mal País (Bad Country) refers to the southwestern corner of Península de Nicoya that's famous among surfers for its consistent waves. The area lies more or less north to south along the coastline, with Santa Teresa being the largest village in the area. Further south is the smaller village of Playa El Carmen, and more southerly still is Mal País, the village. *¿Comprende?* Don't worry if it doesn't make sense at first; the villages have pretty much merged into one surf community lining the coast, and are collectively known as Mal País.

ACTIVITIES

SURFING

About 8km north of the intersection, Playa Manzanillo is a combination of sand and rock that's best surfed when the tide is rising and there's an offshore wind.

The most famous break in the Mal País area is at Playa Santa Teresa, and is char-

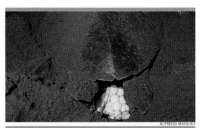
ALFREDO MAIQUEZ
Olive ridley turtle laying eggs

⟩ IF YOU LIKE...

If you like **Reseva Natural Absoluta Cabo Blanco** (opposite), we think you'll like these other parks and reserves on the Península de Nicoya:

- **Parque Nacional Barra Honda** Best in the dry season, you can go spelunking in the limestone caves of this underground wonderland.
- **Refugio Nacional de Vida Silvestre Curú** The small area of this privately owned reserve is an unexpected oasis of diverse landscapes.
- **Refugio Nacional de Fauna Silvestre Ostional** Olive ridleys nest and sometimes have *arribadas* (mass nestings) at Ostional.

acterized as being fast and powerful. This beach can be surfed virtually any time of day, though be cautious as there are scattered rocks.

Playa El Carmen, which is at the end of the road leading down from the main intersection, is a good beach break that can also be surfed anytime.

YOGA

Horizon Yoga Hotel (☎ 2640-0524; www.horizon-yogahotel.com) offers three classes daily, in a serene environment overlooking the ocean.

SLEEPING & EATING
SANTA TERESA

Don Jon's (☎ 2640-0700; grupodonjons@gmail. com; dm/d/apt from US$12/35/60; P ✂ 🛜) This friendly spot run by Colombian brothers Jon and Jeison offers several rustic teak bungalows and modern apartments plus dorm accommodations. The two-bedroom apartment has a full kitchen and is roomy enough for four. The on-site restaurant serves burritos, tacos and sandwiches.

Casa Zen (☎ 2640-0523; www.zencostarica. com; dm US$12, d without bathroom US$24-45, apt from US$55; P) This recommended Asian-inspired guesthouse is decked out in Zen art, celestial murals and enough happy Buddha sculptures to satisfy all your belly-rubbing needs. The owner, Kelly, is committed to helping guests 'chill and recreate on their own time.' She also runs an eclectic restaurant (mains ₡2000 to ₡4400) that has everything from veggie sandwiches and burgers to fresh sushi and Thai curries.

Funky Monkey Lodge (☎ 2640-0272; www.funky-monkey-lodge.com; r/bungalows/ste/ apt US$50/80/85/120; P ✂ 🛜) This funky lodge is situated at the top of a natural-rock hill, and has sweet, rustic-style bungalows built out of bamboo. Each one has an open-air shower, and the larger ones have a fully equipped kitchen. A popular bar-restaurant (sushi rolls ₡2200 to ₡4500) packs in the crowds with good international food and excellent sunsets.

Trópico Latino Lodge (☎ 2640-0062; www.hoteltropicolatino.com; d US$120, bunga-lows US$160-180; P ✂ 🛜) Beautifully decorated with dark wood and deep, saturated colors, the roomy bungalows here are peppered around a tropical gar-den and along the beach, and feature air-con, king-sized bed, hammock-strung patio and private hot-water bathroom (one bungalow also has a full kitchen). There's a dreamy pool fringed with palms and heliconia, and a surfside restaurant (dishes ₡2100 to ₡4200) that specializes in Italian food.

JOHNNY HAGLUND

Fish are abundant in the waters around the Península de Nicoya

Playa El Carmen, Mal País (p195)

CHRISTIAN ASLUND

Milarepa (☎ 2640-0023; www.milarepa hotel.com; bungalows from US$198; P ⎌ 🛋) This self-proclaimed 'small hotel of luxurious simplicity' has Asian-inspired bungalows constructed of bamboo and Indonesian teak. Each is furnished with four-poster beds draped in voluminous mosquito nets, and comes complete with a shower open to the sky.

Florblanca (☎ 2640-0232; www.flor blanca.com; villas incl breakfast US$552-989; P 🍽 🖥 🛋) The most sumptuous hotel in Santa Teresa is truly in a class of its own – 10 romantic villas are scattered around three hectares of land next to a pristine white-sand beach. Each villa is lit in warm hues, with indoor-outdoor spaces such as open-air sunken bathtub and living area.

MAL PAÍS

The Place (☎ 2640-0101; www.theplacemalpais. com; d incl breakfast US$68-136, bungalows US$224; P 🍽 ⎌ 🛋) Cheaper rooms in this Swiss-run guesthouse are air-conditioned and have a private hot-water bathroom, but it's absolutely worth it to splurge on the

more expensive bungalows – each one is creatively decorated according to a different theme (check the website for pictures). Rooms ring a small pool amid the somewhat random landscaping. The owners can arrange surfing lessons and tours, and the small restaurant serves Mediterranean-style seafood by candle-light in the evenings.

Star Mountain Eco Resort (☎ 2640-0101; www.starmountaineco.com; s/d/tr incl breakfast US$50/70/90, casitas US$130; P 🍽 🖥 ⎌ 🛋) This intimate and secluded lodge was built without cutting down a single tree, and today the grounds of the resort abound with wildlife. There are four hill-side rooms, each simply and thoughtfully decorated in muted tropical colors.

Beija Flor (☎ 2640-1007; www.beijaflor resort.com; r US$96-135, ste/villas US$153/210; P ⎌ 🛋) One of the loveliest new properties in Mal País, Beija Flor is a luxurious, Balinese-styled boutique hotel. The clean and spacious rooms are decorated in min-imalist stone and wood interiors and have outdoor showers.

Umi Sushi (☎ 2640-0968; sushi ₡1800-5000; ☺ noon-10pm) In the courtyard of the Centro Comercial Playa El Carmen, this sushi bar has a pleasant dining room and tables outside. If you're lucky, it will have a surf movie projected on the outside wall while you savor your Mal País roll.

Soda Piedra Mar (☎ 2640-0069; mains ₡1800-8500; ☺ breakfast, lunch & dinner) This is one of the best local places to eat in Mal País, with generous portions of fresh seafood and, as the name suggests, a rocky location right by one of the most beautiful blue beaches on the entire peninsula.

Mary's Restaurant (☎ 2640-0153; mains ₡3000-7000; ☺ 5:30-10pm Thu-Tue) Hidden in a jungly garden on the south end of town, this charming restaurant is locally known for the scrumptious wood-fired pizzas, plus fish tacos, burritos, quesadillas and other yummies.

GETTING THERE & AWAY

A new direct bus from Mal País to San José via the Paquera ferry departs at 6am and 2pm (₡6800, six hours). Local buses to Cóbano depart at 7am, 11:30am, 2pm and 6:30pm (₡800, 45 minutes).

Montezuma Expeditions (☎ 2642-0919; www.montezumaexpeditions.com; Centro Comercial Playa El Carmen) offers shuttle-van transfers to San José, Tamarindo or Sámara (US$40), plus La Fortuna and Monteverde (US$45).

CENTRAL PACIFIC COAST

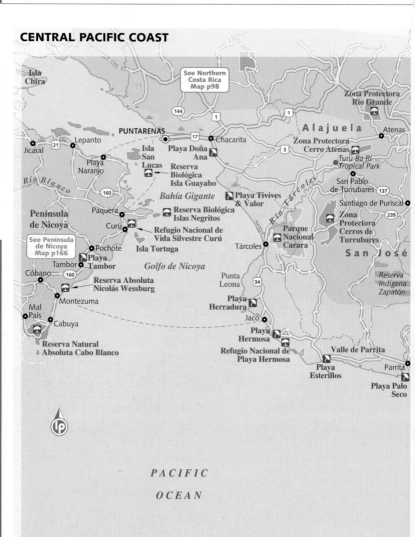

See Northern Costa Rica Map p98

Isla Chira

Zona Protectora Río Grande

144

1

1

Alajuela

Atenas

Lepanto

PUNTARENAS

17

Chacarita

Zona Protectora Cerro Atenas

3

Jicaral

21

Playa Doña Ana

Turu Ba-Ri Tropical Park

Playa Naranjo

Isla San Lucas

Reserva Biológica Isla Guayabo

San Pablo de Turrubares

137

Río Blanco

160

Bahía Gigante

Playa Tivives & Valor

Santiago de Puriscal

239

Península de Nicoya

Páquera

Reserva Biológica Islas Negritos

Zona Protectora Cerros de Turrubares

San José

Curú

See Península de Nicoya Map p166

Pochote

Refugio Nacional de Vida Silvestre Curú

Isla Tortuga

Parque Nacional Carara

Reserva Indígena Zapatón

Tambor

Playa Tambor

Tárcoles

Cóbano

160

Golfo de Nicoya

Reserva Absoluta Nicolás Wessburg

Punta Leona

34

Mal País

Montezuma

Playa Herradura

Cabuya

Jacó

Reserva Natural Absoluta Cabo Blanco

Playa Hermosa

Refugio Nacional de Playa Hermosa

Valle de Parrita

Playa Esterillos

Parrita

Playa Palo Seco

PACIFIC

OCEAN

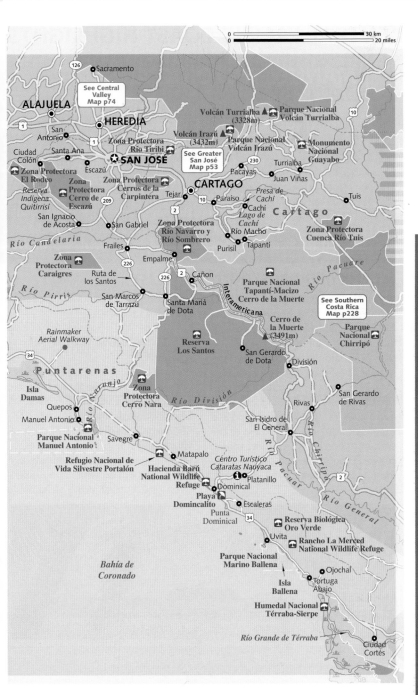

CENTRAL PACIFIC COAST HIGHLIGHTS

1   MANUEL ANTONIO AREA

BY DENNYS QUIROS, ASSISTANT MANAGER OF THE HOTEL SÍ COMO NO

Manuel Antonio is Costa Rica's smallest national park, but also its most visited one. The pristine beaches, luscious rainforests and incredible variety of flora and fauna make it the complete nature experience. Where the jungle meets the ocean, you can follow well-designed trails in search of wildlife, lie on golden sands and swim in crystal-clear waters.

↘ DENNYS QUIROS' DON'T MISS LIST

❶ MANUEL ANTONIO BEACHES

The national park is home to a huge variety of wilderness beaches (p222) that start at the information center and stretch out along the coast of the peninsula. They're accessed by a network of trails that wrap around forests and hug the shoreline, providing ample opportunities for sunning, swimming and snorkeling. The beaches closest to the park entrance see the largest tourist crowds, though you can easily escape the masses by hiking a bit deeper in, and seeking out your own abandoned stretch of sand.

❷ SANTA JUANA MOUNTAIN VILLAGE

If you're looking for an off-the-beaten-path experience in the Manuel Antonio area, consider a visit to the inland village of Santa Juana (p220) in the Fila Chonta mountain range. Here, the local villagers are embracing the concept of community-based ecotourism, and are experimenting with various initiatives aimed at achieving sustainable

Clockwise from top: Collared aracari toucan; beach in Parque Nacional Manuel Antonio (p222)

development through conservation. Independent excursions are possible if you have your own 4WD, though you can also book transportation and a bilingual guide through the Hotel Sí Como No.

❸ FINCAS NATURALES

This private **wildlife refuge** (p219) features 1500m of trails, designed for all ages. The refuge is researching and developing ways to help protect and reproduce locally endangered species including orchids, bromeliads and amphibians. It is also home to Butterfly Botanical Gardens, an Aquatic Garden and the new Crocodile Lagoon exhibit. In-house naturalists regularly conduct guided tours in both Spanish and English.

❹ WHITE-WATER RAFTING

For some memorable thrills and spills, consider taking a **white-water rafting trip** (p220) on the nearby Río Naranjo. Even if you're traveling as a family, there are a multitude of runs catering to all ages and skill levels.

❯ THINGS YOU NEED TO KNOW

Access Visitors to Manuel Antonio can bed down either in Quepos (p217) or along the road connecting Quepos to Manuel Antonio (p219) **Wildlife-watching checklist** The national park is home to iguanas, sloths, capuchins, and howler and squirrel monkeys **See our author's coverage, p222**

CENTRAL PACIFIC COAST HIGHLIGHTS

2

↘ PARQUE NACIONAL CARARA

Don't let the small size of this **national park** (p211) detract you from the enormous biodiversity on display here. Lying at the intersection of Costa Rica's northern dry forests and southern rainforests, Carara exists as a unique transition zone. The species count here soars, though the undeniable star of the show is the scarlet macaw, a flaming-red bird with visually striking blue and yellow accents.

3

↘ JACÓ

The big city of the central Pacific coast, **Jacó** (p211) is unapologetically loud and proud. Home to resident expats from around the world, Jacó serves up the region's most cosmopolitan mix of restaurants alongside boutique hotels and a couple of large resorts. The beach is shaped by decent novice-friendly surf, and there is a laundry list of activities on offer here for anyone who can't sit still.

4

➘ PLAYA HERMOSA

Something of a younger brother to Jacó, **Playa Hermosa** (p215) may lack size and sophistication, but it certainly holds its own when it comes to surf. For intermediate and experienced riders, Playa Hermosa offers some of the sickest waves in the Pacific, particularly in August when the annual surf competition is held.

5

➘ DOMINICAL

Another legendary surf town, **Dominical** (p222) has been drawing in legions of boarders for decades. Even if you happen to be a self-professed newbie, Dominical still warrants a visit as the incredibly laid-back ambience of the beach is positively infectious. Don't be surprised if you get stuck here for much longer than you intended.

6

➘ PARQUE NACIONAL MARINO BALLENA

This off-the-beaten-path **marine park** (p226) lies at the extreme southern end of the central Pacific coast, though the remote location shouldn't deter you from coming. On the contrary, Marino Ballena is a stunning slice of sea that harbors astonishing marine life including pods of dolphins and migrating whales.

2 Scarlet macaws are plentiful at the Parque Nacional Carara (p211); 3 Jacó (p211); 4 Playa Hermosa (p215); 5 Pacific sunset near Dominical (p222); 6 Parque Nacional Marino Ballena (p226)

THE CENTRAL PACIFIC COAST'S BEST...

⭘ WILDLIFE

- **Scarlet Macaws** (p211) Catch a glimpse of red birds amid green trees in Parque Nacional Carara.
- **Squirrel Monkeys** (p222) Adorable little fur balls in Parque Nacional Manuel Antonio.
- **Humpback Whales** (p226) Migrating pods swim through Parque Nacional Marino Ballena.

⭘ ACTIVITIES

- **Hang Gliding** (p213) Scope out the Pacific from high above.
- **Surfing** (p212) Grab your short board and go thrash some swells.
- **Canopy Tours** (p213) Zip-line your way through the lofty treetops.

⭘ SPLURGES

- **Hotel Sí Como No** (p221) A family-friendly hotel that has garnered the government's highest rating for ecofriendliness.

- **Arenas del Mar** (p221) Another award-winning ecohotel, this luxury resort offers unmatched intimacy.
- **Docelunas** (p213) A teak-accented mountain retreat surrounded by virgin rainforest and bountiful wildlife.

⭘ EATS & DRINKS

- **Pacific Bistro** (p214) Mouth-watering Pan-Asian cuisine highlights the bounty of the Pacific Ocean.
- **Kapi Kapi Restaurant** (p221) An eclectic eatery with international leanings and romantic table settings.
- **El Avión** (p221) Savor an ice-cold beer in the shadow of a 1954 Fairchild C-123.

SHANNON NACE

White-faced capuchin monkey, Parque Nacional Manuel Antonio (p222)

THINGS YOU NEED TO KNOW

⬆ VITAL STATISTICS

- **Population** Puntarenas 10,400
- **Best time to visit** Rains fall heavily during the months between April and November, while December to March is comparatively dry.

⬆ BEACHES IN A NUTSHELL

- **Jacó** (p211) The most developed beach town along the central Pacific coast.
- **Playa Hermosa** (p215) There's less development here, but it's home to some seriously strong surf that attracts veterans.
- **Dominical** (p222) Long-favored by the backpacking set, this beach town is chilled out.
- **Parque Nacional Manuel Antonio** (p222) This national park is home to stunning wilderness beaches.
- **Parque Nacional Marino Ballena** (p226) A marine park that protects shallows seas and remote strips of sand.

⬆ ADVANCE PLANNING

- **Surfing school** The Pacific coast is home to some serious surf, which means that you might want to practice elsewhere before showing up with board in hand.

⬆ RESOURCES

- **Costa Rica Tourism Board** (www. visitcostarica.com)
- **Tico Times** (www.ticotimes.net)

⬆ EMERGENCY NUMBERS

- **Emergency** (☎ 911)
- **Fire** (☎ 118)
- **Police** (☎ 117)

⬆ GETTING AROUND

- **Boat** The beach town of Montezuma on the tip of the Península de Nicoya is a quick boat ride away from Jacó.
- **Bus** Intercity buses are frequent and cheap, which makes moving around a cinch.
- **Car** The smoothly paved and well-signed coastal highway is conducive to self-drivers.
- **Walk** Parque Nacional Manuel Antonio has a range of hikes catering to both novices and seasoned trekkers.

⬆ BE FOREWARNED

- **Prostitution** Jacó has a seedy underbelly at night, so be mindful of your surroundings and use discretion.
- **Riptides** Currents can get ferocious, even in shallow waters, so pay attention to local advisories. If you find yourself caught in a riptide, immediately call for help. It's important to relax, conserve your energy and not fight the current.

CENTRAL PACIFIC COAST ITINERARIES

QUEPOS & MANUEL ANTONIO Three Days

It takes time to traverse the full length of the coast, though fortunately this itinerary will give you a quick but fulfilling taste of Pacific wonderment. Relying entirely on public transportation, you can take in both tropical seas and forest-covered mountains, and then leave the coast behind en route to another corner of the country.

Your first destination is none other than the authentic Tico town of **(1) Quepos** (p216). While the friendly locals and inviting restaurants are certainly appealing, be sure to save plenty of time for nearby **(2) Parque Nacional Manuel Antonio** (p222). One of the country's top national parks, Manuel Antonio can be summed up with three words: beaches, rainforests and monkeys. If you have a bit of extra time, you should also pay a brief visit to the **(3) Rainmaker Aerial Walkway** (p220), which lets you explore the canopy by walking across a series of elevated platforms.

SURFER'S PARADISE Five Days

If you're looking to burn off some adrenaline, the central Pacific is home to a string of spectacular beach towns with fairly consistent year-round surf. Even if you're not an expert nor in possession of your own board, surf rental shops are abundant, as are surf schools plying their trade. Surf's up – and even when it's not, there is still plenty of sun, sea and sand to enjoy.

With modest waves and a gentle beach break, **(1) Jacó** (p211) is a great place to practice standing up and balancing your weight. Even if you don't succeed, you'll still enjoy your evenings in the unofficial party capital of the Pacific coast. If you're ready to test your skills, head a bit further south down the coast to **(2) Playa Hermosa** (p215), where sharper curls and faster swells present a mighty challenge. In roughly the same league is **(3) Dominical** (p222), a true surfer's paradise chock-full of budget-friendly lodgings and eateries, not to mention the obligatory crashing surf and setting sun.

PACIFIC ROAD TRIP One Week

The Pacific presents plenty of opportunities for carefree road-tripping, especially given the excellent network of highways and roads. By foregoing public transportation, you can independently cruise the coast at your own speed. Plus, there is nothing more magical than driving down country roads with the deep-blue ocean on one side, and soaring mountains of bright green on the other.

(1) Jacó (p211) is inevitably where you should start your Pacific road trip, but make a point to save some time to tackle the trails at

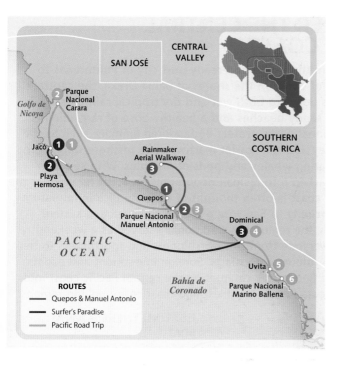

(2) Parque Nacional Carara (p211), where you can feast your eyes on swooping scarlet macaws. The undisputed highlight of the region is (3) Parque Nacional Manuel Antonio (p222), though if you want to survey the surf scene, (4) Dominical (p222) makes for a great stop. However, one of the benefits of having your own wheels is being able to access further-flung destinations. The attractive Tico town of (5) Uvita (p225) warrants a stop, especially since it's the jumping-off point for the beautiful but rarely visited (6) Parque Nacional Marino Ballena (p226).

DISCOVER THE CENTRAL PACIFIC COAST

Stretching from the rough and ready port city of Puntarenas to the tiny town of Uvita on the shores of Bahía Drake, the central Pacific coast is home to both wet and dry tropical rainforests, sun-drenched sandy beaches and a healthy dose of rare wildlife. On shore, national parks protect endangered animals, such as the squirrel monkey and the scarlet macaw, while offshore waters are home to migrating whales and pods of dolphins. With so much biodiversity packed into a small geographic area, it's no wonder the central Pacific coast is often thought of as Costa Rica in miniature.

Given its proximity to San José and its well-developed system of paved roads, the region has traditionally served as a weekend getaway for everyone from sun-worshippers and sportfishers to tree-huggers and outdoors enthusiasts. Foreign investment and expats alike have also flooded in, catapulting the central Pacific coast into the ranks of Costa Rica's wealthiest and most cosmopolitan regions.

PUNTARENAS

pop 10,400

The city's ferry terminal will continue to serve as a convenient way to access the more pristine beaches further south in southern Península de Nicoya. While few travelers are keen to spend any more of their time here than it takes to get on and off the boat, stopping through here is something of a necessary evil en route to greener pastures and bluer seas.

SIGHTS

The **Puntarenas Marine Park** (☎ 2661-5272; www.parquemarino.org; adult/child under 12yr US$7/4; ⏰ 9am-5pm Tue-Sun), on the site of the old train station, has an aquarium that showcases manta rays and other creatures from the Pacific.

You can stroll along the beach or the aptly named **Paseo de los Turistas** (Tourists' Stroll), a pedestrian boulevard stretching along the southern edge of town, with a variety of souvenir stalls and *sodas* (informal lunch counters).

GETTING THERE & AWAY

BOAT

Schedules are completely variable, change seasonally (or even at whim), and can be affected by inclement weather. Check with the ferry office by the dock for any changes.

To Playa Naranjo (for transfer to Nicoya and points west), **Coonatramar** (☎ 2661-1069; northwestern dock) has several daily departures (adult/child/car ₡860/515/1850, two hours).

To Paquera (for transfer to Montezuma and Mal País), **Ferry Peninsular** (☎ 2641-0118; northwestern dock) also has several daily departures (adult/child/car ₡810/485/1900, two hours).

BUS

Jacó ₡800; 1½ hours; departs at 5am, 11am, 2:30pm and 4:30pm.

Quepos ₡2100; 3½ hours; departs at 5am, 11am, 2:30pm and 4:30pm.

San José ₡1500; 2½ hours; departs every hour from 4am to 9pm.

Santa Elena & Monteverde ₡1500; 2½ hours; departs at 1:15pm and 2:15pm.

PARQUE NACIONAL CARARA

Straddling the transition between the dry forests of Costa Rica's northwest and the sodden rainforests of the southern Pacific lowlands, this **national park** (admission US$10; ☻ 7:30am-4pm) is a biological melting pot of the two. Acacias intermingle with strangler figs, and cacti with deciduous kapok trees, creating heterogeneity of habitats with a blend of wildlife to match. The significance of this national park cannot be understated – surrounded by a sea of cultivation and livestock, it is one of the few areas in the transition zone where wildlife finds sanctuary.

Carara is also the famed home to one of Costa Rica's most charismatic bird species, namely the scarlet macaw. This is one of the most visually arresting birds in the neotropical rainforest. Flamboyantly colored with bright-red body, blue-and-yellow wings, long red tail and white face, these macaws make their presence known with signature squeaks and squawks that echo for kilometers across the forest canopy. With life spans reaching up to 75 years, they have an undeniable air of both beauty and wisdom.

While catching a glimpse of this tropical wonder is a rare proposition in most of the country, macaw sightings are virtually guaranteed at Carara. And, of course, there are more than 400 other avian species flitting around the canopy, as well as Costa Rica's largest crocodiles in the waterways – best to leave your swimming trunks at home!

There are no buses to Carara, but any bus between Puntarenas and Jacó can leave you at the entrance. If you're driving, the entrance to Carara is right on the Costanera and is clearly marked.

JACÓ

Like all cases concerning the delicate balance between conservation and development, Jacó is steeped in its fair share

Beaches at Jacó are great for both swimming and surfing

RUSSELL KORD/MINNOWIMAGES.COM/AURORA

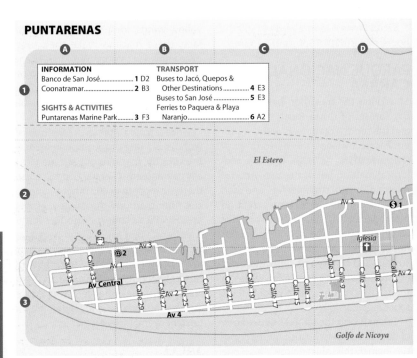

PUNTARENAS

INFORMATION		TRANSPORT	
Banco de San José	**1** D2	Buses to Jacó, Quepos &	
Coonatramar	**2** B3	Other Destinations	**4** E3
		Buses to San José	**5** E3
SIGHTS & ACTIVITIES		Ferries to Paquera & Playa	
Puntarenas Marine Park	**3** F3	Naranjo	**6** A2

of controversy. However, it's probably best to ignore the hype and the stereotypes alike, and make your own decisions about the place. Although the American-style cityscape of shopping malls and gated communities may be off-putting to some, it's impossible to deny the beauty of the beach and the surrounding hillsides, and the consistent surf that first put the beach on the map is still as good as it ever was.

ACTIVITIES
SURFING
Although the rainy season is considered best for Pacific coast surfing, Jacó is blessed with consistent year-round breaks. Even though more advanced surfers head further south to Playa Hermosa, the waves at Jacó are strong, steady and a lot of fun.

Looking for a quick surf lesson? **Dominical Surf Lessons** (www.dominical surflessons.com) operates in the Jacó area; see also p168.

HORSEBACK RIDING
Discovery Horseback Tours (☎ 8838-7550; www.horseridecostarica.com; from US$60) is run by an English couple and offers an extremely high level of service and professionalism.

KAYAKING
Kayak Jacó Costa Rica Outriggers (☎ 2643-1233; www.kayakjaco.com) offers a wide variety of customized day and multiday kayaking and sea canoeing trips, plus snorkeling trips to tropical islands. This outfit does not have an office in Jacó, so it's best to either phone them, or have your accommodations do so for you.

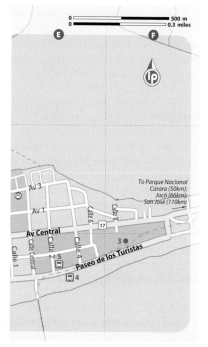

of the central Pacific coast. Therefore, you'll find that your own children are very well cared for in Jacó, and there is enough on offer to keep even those with the shortest attention spans amused for days on end.

SLEEPING

AparHotel Vista Pacífico (☎ 2643-3261; www.vistapacifico.com; d incl breakfast from US$68; Ⓟ Ⓧ ▯ Ⓡ) Located on the crest of a hill just outside Jacó, this Canadian-run hotel is an absolute gem that is worth seeking out. The views of the coastline from here are phenomenal, particularly at sunset.

Hotel Mar de Luz (☎ 2643-3259; www.mardeluz.com; Av Pastor Díaz btwn Calles Las Palmeras & Las Olas; d/tr/q incl breakfast US$78/98/118; Ⓟ ▯ Ⓡ) This adorable little hotel with Dutch-inspired murals of windmills and tulips has tidy and attractive air-con rooms that are perfect for a little family fun in the sun.

Villa Gecko (☎ 2643-1314; www.villagecko. net; Calle Hidalgo; 2-3 person studios US$80, 3-5 person ste US$150; Ⓟ ▯ Ⓡ) By far the most charming accommodations on the beach, Villa Gecko is managed by a French artist whose touch can be seen throughout the property – from stenciled drawings on the walls to mosaic murals in the bathrooms.

Hotel Tangerí (☎ 2643-3001; www.hotel tangeri.com; Av Pastor Díaz btwn Calles Las Palmeras & Las Olas; r from US$115, villas from US$190; Ⓟ ▯ ♟ Ⓡ) This low-key resort complex is smack-dab in the middle of it all, and the tropical-infused grounds are extremely well manicured, and home to no fewer than three pools where you can soak up the rays while floating the daylight away.

Docelunas (☎ 2643-2277; www.doce lunas.com; Costanera Sur; d/junior ste incl breakfast US$140/160; Ⓟ Ⓧ ▯ ♟ Ⓡ) Situated in the foothills across the highway, 'Twelve

HANG GLIDING

HangGlide Costa Rica (☎ 2643-4200; www. hangglidecr.com; from $100) will pick you up in Jacó and shuttle you to an airstrip south of Playa Hermosa where you can tandem-ride in a hang glider or fly in a three-seat ultralight plane. There's no office in town.

CANOPY TOURS

In Jacó there are two competing companies offering similar products: **Canopy Adventure Jacó** (☎ 2643-3271; www.adven turecanopy.com; tours adult/child US$60/45) and **Waterfalls Canopy Tour** (☎ 2632-3322; www.waterfallscanopy.com; tours adult/child US$60/45). There are no offices in town.

JACÓ FOR CHILDREN

Jacó has long been on the radar screens of Tico families looking to swap the congestion of San José for the ocean breezes

Moons' is a heavenly mountain retreat consisting of 20 rooms sheltered in a pristine landscape of tropical rainforest. Each teak-accented room is intimately decorated with original artwork.

EATING

Taco Bar (mains ₡3000-6000) A one-stop shop for Mexican, seafood, salads and smoothies. Get your drink with the gargantuan 1L sizes, or your greens at the salad bar featuring more than 20 different kinds of exotic and leafy combinations.

KEVIN SCHAFER/GETTY IMAGES
Catarata Manantial de Agua Viva

⬎ IF YOU LIKE...

If you like **Parque Nacional Carara** (p211), we think you'll like these other reserves along the central Pacific coast:

- **Hacienda Barú National Wildlife Refuge** Near Dominical, this reserve encompasses a range of tropical habitats and is part of a major biological corridor.
- **Catarata Manantial de Agua Viva** Outside Jacó, this 200m-high waterfall is reportedly the highest in the country.
- **Rancho La Merced National Wildlife Refuge** In the Uvita area, this former cattle ranch has primary and secondary forests and mangroves lining the Río Morete.

Tsunami Sushi (Av Pastor Díaz, north of Calle Cocal; sushi ₡3500-6500) If you've got a hankering for raw fish, don't miss Tsunami, a modern and lively restaurant that serves up an exquisite assortment of sushi, sashimi and Californian rolls.

Rioasis (cnr Calle Cocal & Av Pastor Díaz; pizzas ₡4500-8000) There's pizza, and then there's *pizza* – this much loved pizzeria definitely falls into the latter category, especially considering that there are more than 30 different kinds of pies on the menu.

Pacific Bistro (Av Pastor Díaz, south of Calle Las Palmeras; meals ₡10,000-16,000) Whether you're partial to Indonesian-style noodles or more refined fish fillets topped with exotic Chinese sauces, one thing is for certain: this gem of a restaurant really hits the spot if you're craving Pan-Asian cuisine.

DRINKING & ENTERTAINMENT

Le Loft (Av Pastor Díaz) A highly touted addition to Jacó's nightlife offering, the Loft aims to balance out the mix of beach clubs and girly bars with some much needed urban sophistication.

Tabacon (Av Pastor Díaz) Definitely one of the more modest night spots in town, Tabacon is a casually elegant lounge that occasionally hosts live music.

GETTING THERE & AWAY

AIR

NatureAir (www.natureair.com) and **Alfa Romeo Aero Taxi** (www.alfaromeoair.com) offer charter flights.

BOAT

Travelers are increasingly taking advantage of the jet-boat transfer service that connects Jacó to Montezuma (US$37).

BUS

Puntarenas ₡800; 1½ hours; departs at 6am, 9am, noon and 4:30pm.

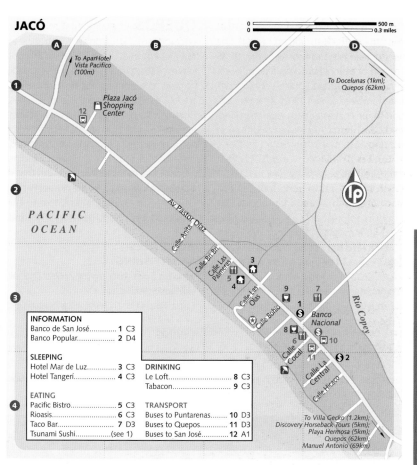

JACÓ

0 500 m
0 0.3 miles

To AparHotel
Vista Pacífico
(100m)

Plaza Jacó
Shopping
Center

To Docelunas (1km);
Quepos (62km)

PACIFIC
OCEAN

Av Pastor Díaz

Calle Anita

Calle Bri Bri

Calle Las
Palmeras

Calle Las
Olas

Calle Bohío

Calle Cocal

Calle La
Central

Calle Hicaco

Río Copey

Banco
Nacional

To Villa Gecko (1.2km);
Discovery Horseback Tours (5km);
Playa Hermosa (5km);
Quepos (62km);
Manuel Antonio (69km)

INFORMATION	
Banco de San José	1 C3
Banco Popular	2 D4

SLEEPING	
Hotel Mar de Luz	3 C3
Hotel Tangerí	4 C3

EATING	
Pacific Bistro	5 C3
Rioasis	6 C3
Taco Bar	7 D3
Tsunami Sushi	(see 1)

DRINKING	
Le Loft	8 C3
Tabacon	9 C3

TRANSPORT	
Buses to Puntarenas	10 D3
Buses to Quepos	11 D3
Buses to San José	12 A1

Quepos ₡800; 1½ hours; departs at 6am, noon, 4:30pm and 6pm.

San José ₡2000; three hours; departs at 5am, 7:30am, 11am, 3pm and 5pm.

PLAYA HERMOSA

While newbies struggle to stand up on their boards in Jacó, a few kilometers south in Playa Hermosa seasoned veterans are thrashing their way across the faces of some truly monster waves. Regarded as one of the most consistent and powerful breaks in the whole country, Hermosa serves up serious surf that commands the utmost respect. Most of the adrenaline-soaked action takes place at the northern reaches, where there are no less than half a dozen clearly defined beach breaks.

FESTIVALS & EVENTS

Even if you can't hack it with the aspiring pros, consider stopping by in August when local and international pro surfers descend on Playa Hermosa for the annual **surf competition**. Dates vary, though the event is heavily advertised around the country, especially in neighboring Jacó.

SLEEPING & EATING

Costanera Bed & Breakfast (☎ 2643-1942; www.costaneraplayahermosa.com; r from US$55; P ✗) For a bit of European flair, this well-priced Italian-run B&B has a very sophisticated ambience. Five rooms of various sizes and shapes have vaulted wooden ceilings and beachfront terraces, each offering a fair degree of privacy and intimacy.

Terraza del Pacífico (☎ 2643-3222; www. terrazadelpacifico.com; r/ste from US$115/175; P ✗ ▢ 🛜 🏊) The granddaddy of top-end hotels is this standout property with Spanish colonial accents and luxurious tiled-floor rooms throughout.

Backyard Bar (☎ 2643-7011; meals ₡2500-7000; ☽ noon-late) This is where you should head for an expansive menu that reaches beyond the usual surfer fare. As the town's de facto nightspot, the Backyard Bar occasionally hosts live music.

GETTING THERE & AWAY

Located only 5km south of Jacó, Playa Hermosa can be accessed by any bus heading south from Jacó.

QUEPOS

Located just 7km from the entrance to Manuel Antonio, the tiny town of Quepos serves as the gateway to the national park, as well as a convenient port of call for travelers in need of goods and services. Although the Manuel Antonio area was rapidly and irreversibly transformed following the ecotourism boom, Quepos has largely remained an authentic Tico town. Exuding a traditional Latin American charm that is absent from so much of the central Pacific, Quepos is a low-key alternative to the tourist-packed gringo trail not far beyond.

ACTIVITIES

SPORTFISHING

Bluefin Sportfishing (☎ 2777-2222; www. bluefinsportfishing.com)

Luna Tours (☎ 2777-0725; www.lunatours.net)

DIVING

Manuel Antonio Divers (☎ 2777-3483; www.manuelantoniodivers.com)

Oceans Unlimited (☎ 2777-3171; www. oceansunlimitedcr.com)

Some sort of natural shelter is never far from Costa Rican beaches

IMAGEBROKER/OLIVER GERHARD

RAFTING

Ríos Tropicales (☎ 2777-4092; www.rios tropicales.com)

QUEPOS FOR CHILDREN

The entire Quepos and Manuel Antonio area is one of Costa Rica's leading family-friendly destinations. With beaches and rainforest in proximity – not to mention a healthy dose of charismatic wildlife – the region can enchant young minds regardless of their attention spans.

SLEEPING

Hotel Sirena (☎ 2777-0572; www.lasirenahotel. com; s/d/tr US$60/75/85; P ☻) An unexpectedly Zen-inducing hotel, the Sirena has whitewashed walls with soft pastel trims that are subtly lit by blue Tiffany lamps.

Hotel Villa Romántica (☎ 2777-0037; www.villaromantica.com; s/d from US$65/85; P ☒ ☐ ☻ ⚒) A short walk southeast from the town center brings you to this peaceful garden oasis, which is overflowing with verdant greens and tropical flowers.

Best Western Hotel Kamuk (☎ 2777-0379; www.kamuk.co.cr; r from US$95; P ☒ ☐ ☻ ⚒) This upmarket Quepos stalwart provides excellent value, and is housed in a surprisingly refreshing historic building. The core of the hotel is a winding wooden staircase that fans out to breezy hallways adorned with colonial flourishes.

Rancho Casa Grande (☎ 2777-3130; www.ranchocasagrande.com; ste/bungalows/villas from US$118/146/280; P ☒ ☐ ☻ ⚒) This resort hotel, located out on the road to the Quepos airport, benefits from an expansive concession that is crisscrossed by hiking and horseback-riding trails.

EATING & DRINKING

Café Milagro (dishes ₡1000-3000; ☺ 6am-10pm Mon-Fri) Serving some of the country's best

Playa Matapalo
IMAGEBROKER/HANS ZAGLITSCH

➘ IF YOU LIKE...

If you like **Playa Hermosa** (p215), we think you'll like these other beach towns along the central Pacific coast:

- **Playa Esterillos** South of Jacó you'll find a beautiful stretch of pale gray sand with a few great surf spots.
- **Playa Tortuga** South of Uvita, this wilderness beach is largely undiscovered and virtually undeveloped.
- **Playa Matapalo** North of Dominical, the river mouth at this palm-fringed beach generates some wicked waves.

cappuccinos and espressos, this is a great place to perk up in the morning.

Monchados (dishes ₡4000-7500; ☺ 5pm-midnight) Something of a Quepos institution, this long-standing Mex-Carib spot is always bustling with dinner-goers who line up to try traditional Limón-style dishes and Mexican standards. There's fairly regular live music.

El Patio (meals ₡5500-12,000; ☺ 6am-10pm) The unspoken rule at this Nuevo Latino spot is fresh and local, which means that meat, seafood and produce are always of the highest quality, and always prepared in a way that highlights their natural flavor.

GETTING THERE & AWAY
AIR
Both **NatureAir** (www.natureair.com) and **Sansa** (www.sansa.com) service Quepos, the base town for accessing Manuel Antonio. The airport is located 5km out of town, and taxis make the trip for around ₡3000, depending on traffic.

BUS
Jacó ₡800; 1½ hours; departs at 4:30am, 7:30am, 10:30am and 3pm.

Puntarenas ₡2100; 3½ hours; departs at 8am, 10:30am and 3:30pm.

San Isidro, via Dominical ₡2000; three hours; departs at 5am and 1:30pm.

San José (**Transportes Morales**) ₡3500 to ₡3700; four hours; departs at 5am, 8am, 10am, noon, 2pm, 4pm and 7:30pm.

Uvita, via Dominical ₡4000; 4½ hours; departs at 10am and 7pm.

GETTING AROUND
BUS
Buses between Quepos and Manuel Antonio (₡200) depart roughly every 30 minutes from the main terminal between 6am and 7:30pm, and less frequently after

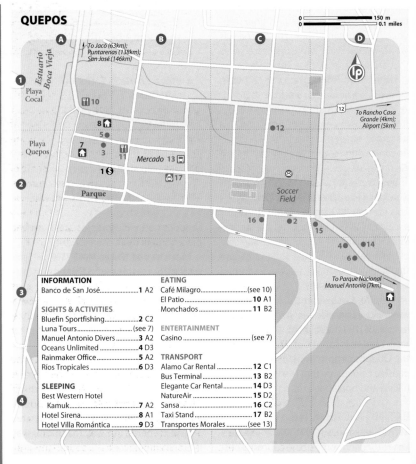

QUEPOS

0 — 150 m
0 — 0.1 miles

To Jacó (63km);
Puntarenas (138km);
San José (146km)

Estuario Boca Vieja

Playa Cocal

Playa Quepos

Mercado

Parque

Soccer Field

To Rancho Casa Grande (4km);
Airport (5km)

To Parque Nacional
Manuel Antonio (7km)

INFORMATION	
Banco de San José	**1** A2

SIGHTS & ACTIVITIES	
Bluefin Sportfishing	**2** C2
Luna Tours	(see 7)
Manuel Antonio Divers	**3** A2
Oceans Unlimited	**4** D3
Rainmaker Office	**5** A2
Ríos Tropicales	**6** D3

SLEEPING	
Best Western Hotel Kamuk	**7** A2
Hotel Sirena	**8** A1
Hotel Villa Romántica	**9** D3

EATING	
Café Milagro	(see 10)
El Patio	**10** A1
Monchados	**11** B2

ENTERTAINMENT	
Casino	(see 7)

TRANSPORT	
Alamo Car Rental	**12** C1
Bus Terminal	**13** B2
Elegante Car Rental	**14** D3
NatureAir	**15** D2
Sansa	**16** C2
Taxi Stand	**17** B2
Transportes Morales	(see 13)

IMAGEBROKER/MICHAEL ZEGERS

Public bus, Quepos (p216)

7:30pm. The last bus departs Manuel Antonio at 10:25pm. There are more frequent buses in the dry season.

CAR
The following rental companies operate in Quepos; reserve ahead and reconfirm to guarantee availability.

Alamo (☎ 2777-3344; 7:30am-noon & 1:30-5:30pm)

Elegante (☎ 2777-0115; 7:30am-5pm Mon-Fri)

TAXI
Colectivo taxis between Quepos and Manuel Antonio will usually pick up extra passengers for a few hundred colones. A private taxi will cost a few thousand colones. Call **Quepos Taxi** (☎ 2777-0425/734) or catch one at the taxi stand south of the market.

QUEPOS TO MANUEL ANTONIO

From the port of Quepos, the road swings inland for 7km before reaching the beaches of Manuel Antonio village and the entrance to the national park. This serpentine route passes over a number of hills awash with picturesque views of forested slopes leading down to the palm-fringed coastline. Although this area is anything but cheap, it is home to some of Costa Rica's finest hotels and restaurants. While budget travelers are somewhat catered for, this is one part of the country where those with deep pockets can bed down and dine out in the lap of luxury.

SIGHTS & ACTIVITIES
You can relax after a day's activities at the **Serenity Spa** (☎ 2777-0777, ext 220; Hotel Sí Como No), a good place for couple's massages, sunburn-relief treatments, coconut body scrubs and tasty coffee.

Also belonging to the Hotel Sí Como No and situated just across the street is **Fincas Naturales** (☎ 2777-0850; www.wild liferefugecr.com; adult/child US$15/8), a private rainforest preserve and butterfly garden. About three dozen species of butterfly are bred here. There is a sound-and-light

RALPH HOPKINS

Scarlet macaws: one of Costa Rica's most striking bird species

⬃ RAINMAKER AERIAL WALKWAY

Rainmaker was the first aerial walkway through the forest canopy in Central America, though it is still regarded as one of the region's best. From its tree-to-tree platforms there are spectacular panoramic views of the surrounding primary and secondary rainforest, as well as occasional vistas out to the Pacific Ocean. The reserve is also home to the full complement of tropical wildlife, which means that there are myriad opportunities here for great bird-watching as well as the occasional monkey sighting. Standard tours cost US$70 and include a light breakfast and lunch, and there are also bird-watching (US$90) and night tours (US$60) available.

Things you need to know: Map p218; ☎ in Quepos 2777-3565; www.rainmakercostarica.org

show at night (US$35 per person), and the garden is surrounded by nature trails.

Amigos del Río (☎ 2777-1084; www.adventuremanuelantonio.com) runs whitewater rafting trips for all skill levels on the Ríos Savegre and Naranjo.

TOURS

The Hotel Sí Como No can arrange **tours** (☎ 2777-0777; www.sicomono.com/tours/santa_juana.php; adult/child US$95/50) to the village of Santa Juana in the Fila Chonta mountain range. Here you'll get the opportunity to swim in waterfalls, try your hand at tilapia fishing, learn about citrus growing and coffee production, and even participate in

a tree-planting initiative. This tour is not only a wonderful example of how tourism can empower local communities, but also a nice day out for you and your friends or family!

SLEEPING

Hotel Mono Azul (☎ 2777-2572; www.monoazul.com; r US$40-65, child under 12yr free; P ⚒ 🖳 🛜 🐾 👶) This is a great family option, as the entire hotel is decorated with animal murals and rainforest paraphernalia, not to mention the three pools and games room.

Hotel Costa Verde (☎ 2777-0584; www.costaverde.com; efficiency/studios from

US$115/149, Boeing 727 fuselage home US$500; **P** ❌ 🖥 🛜 🚻) This collection of rooms, studios and – believe it or not – a fully converted Boeing 727 fuselage occupies a lush, tropical setting that is frequented by regular troops of primate visitors.

Hotel Sí Como No (☎ 2777-0777; www.sicomono.com; r US$210-265, ste US$305-340, child under 6yr free; **P** ❌ 🖥 🛜 🚻 👶) This flawlessly designed hotel is an example of how to build a resort while maintaining environmental sensibility. No surprise here that the Sí Como No is one of only four hotels in the entire country to have been awarded five out of five leaves by the government-run Certified Sustainable Tourism campaign.

Arenas del Mar (☎ 2777-2777; www.arenasdelmar.com; r US$330-550; **P** ❌ 🖥 🛜 🚻) There are no more than 40 rooms on the premises, which ensures an unmatched level of personal service and attention. Arenas del Mar, which has won numerous ecotourism awards since its inception, was designed to incorporate the beauty of the natural landscape.

EATING

El Avión (☎ 2777-3378; dishes ₡3000-6500) This unforgettable airplane bar-restaurant was constructed from the body of a 1954 Fairchild C-123. It now sits on the side of the main road, where it looks as if it had crash-landed into the side of the hill. It's a great spot for a beer, guacamole and a Pacific sunset, and in the dry season there is regular live music in the evenings.

Ronny's Place (☎ 2777-5120; mains ₡3000-6500; ⏲ 7:30am-10pm) The bilingual Tico owner has worked hard to make his rest stop a favorite of locals and travelers alike. Feast on some fresh seafood while enjoying views of two pristine bays and 360° of primitive jungle.

Kapi Kapi Restaurant (☎ 2777-5049; dishes ₡7500-20,000) Kapi Kapi, named after a traditional greeting of the indigenous Maleku people, welcomes diners with soft lights, flush earthy tones and soothing natural decor. The menu is no less ambitious, spanning the globe from America to Asia, and making several pivotal stops along the way.

CHRISTER FREDRIKSSON

Rainforest meets the beach at the Parque Nacional Manuel Antonio (p222)

GETTING THERE & AWAY

This area is accessed either by rented car or buses running between Quepos and Manuel Antonio (see p218).

PARQUE NACIONAL MANUEL ANTONIO

One of Costa Rica's top tourist destinations, this **national park** (☎ 2777-0644; admission US$10; ☺ 7am-4pm Tue-Sun) is absolutely stunning, and on a good day, at the right time, it's easy to convince yourself that you've died and gone to a coconut-filled paradise. The park's clearly marked trail system winds through rainforest-backed tropical beaches and rocky headlands, and the views across the bay to the pristine outer islands are unforgettable. As if this wasn't enough of a hard sell, add to the mix iguanas, howlers, capuchins, sloths and squirrel monkeys, which may be the gosh-darn cutest little fur balls you've ever seen.

SIGHTS & ACTIVITIES

After the park entrance, it's about a 30-minute hike to **Playa Espadilla Sur**, where you'll find the park ranger station and information center; watch out for birds and monkeys as you walk. A trail leads around the peninsula to **Punta Catedral**, from where there are good views of the Pacific Ocean and various rocky islets that are bird reserves and form part of the national park. You can continue around the peninsula to **Playa Manuel Antonio** where the trail divides. The lower trail is steep and slippery during the wet months and leads to the quiet **Playa Puerto Escondido**. The upper trail climbs to a **lookout** on a bluff overlooking Puerto Escondido and Punta Serrucho beyond – a stunning vista.

You'll probably hear mantled howler monkeys soon after sunrise and, like capuchins, they can be seen virtually anywhere inside the park and even along the road to Quepos. Agoutis and coatis can be seen darting across various paths, and both three-toed and two-toed sloths are also common in the park. Guides are extremely helpful in spotting sloths as they tend not to move around all that much. However, the movements of the park's star animal and Central America's rarest primate, namely the Central American squirrel monkey, are far less predictable. These adorable monkeys are more retiring than capuchins, and though they are occasionally seen near the park entrance in the early morning, they usually melt into the forest well before opening time.

GETTING THERE & AWAY

This area is accessed either by rented car or buses running between Quepos and Manuel Antonio (see p218).

DOMINICAL

With monster waves, chilled-out vibes and a freewheelin' reputation for reefer madness, Dominical is the kind of place where travelers get stuck for longer than they intended – so long as the surf's up and the spliff isn't out. As proud residents are quick to point out, Dominical recalls the mythical 'old Costa Rica,' namely a time when the legions of international jet-setters had yet to jump onto the ecotourism bandwagon. And in part, they've got a valid point, as evidenced by the town's motley crew of surfers, backpackers and do-nothings.

SIGHTS & ACTIVITIES

Centro Turístico Cataratas Nauyaca (☎ 2787-0198, 2771-3187; www.cataratasnauyaca.com) is a Costa Rican family–owned and operated tourist center and home to

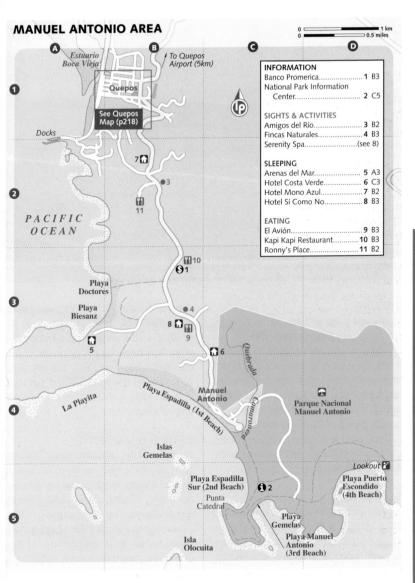

MANUEL ANTONIO AREA

0 — 1 km
0 — 0.5 miles

INFORMATION		
Banco Promerica	**1**	B3
National Park Information Center	**2**	C5

SIGHTS & ACTIVITIES		
Amigos del Río	**3**	B2
Fincas Naturales	**4**	B3
Serenity Spa	(see 8)	

SLEEPING		
Arenas del Mar	**5**	A3
Hotel Costa Verde	**6**	C3
Hotel Mono Azul	**7**	B2
Hotel Sí Como No	**8**	B3

EATING		
El Avión	**9**	B3
Kapi Kapi Restaurant	**10**	B3
Ronny's Place	**11**	B2

a series of wonderful waterfalls that cascade through a protected reserve of both primary and secondary forest.

If you're traveling with kids who love slick and slimy reptiles, **Parque Reptilandia** (☎ 2787-8007; www.crreptiles. com; adult/child US$10/1; ☑ 9am-4:30pm), 10km outside of Dominical in the town of Platanillo, offers the chance to get face to face with some of Costa Rica's most famous creatures. For an added bonus, stop by on Friday for feeding time.

World in shades of green and blue: Parque Nacional Manuel Antonio (p222)

ANNELIES MERTENS

SURFING

Dominical owes its fame to its seriously sick point and beach breaks, though surf conditions here are variable. In general, however, it pays to have a bit of board experience, as you can really get thrashed out here if you don't know what you're doing. If you're just getting started, the nearby beach of **Domincalito** is tamer.

If you want to arrange local surf classes, contact **Dominical Surf Lessons** (www. dominicalsurflessons.com); see also p168.

SLEEPING

Domilocos (☎ 2787-0244; www.domilocos.net; r US$50; P ✖ 🖥 🐾) This Italian-owned property is a solid option, with Mediterranean-inspired grounds, an attractive swimming pool lined with potted plants and one of the town's best restaurants.

Hotel y Restaurante Roca Verde (☎ 2787-0036; www.rocaverde.net; r US$85; P ✖ 🖥 🛜 🐾 ♿) Overlooking the beach about 1km south of town, this chic and stylish hotel is decorated with hardwoods, tile mosaics, festive murals and rock inlays.

Hotel DiuWak (☎ 2787-0087; www.diuwak. com; r US$75-120, ste US$140-160; P 🖥 📶 🛜 🐾 ♿) This proper resort complex offers low-key luxury as opposed to unchecked hedonism. Still, the grounds surrounding the waterfall-fed pool are palm-fringed, which makes for relaxing days of idle laziness.

EATING & DRINKING

Maracutú (dishes ₡3000-5500, drinks ₡1000-2000) The self-proclaimed 'world-music beach bar and Italian kitchen' serves up an eclectic culinary offering that is highlighted by some delicious vegetarian and vegan fare.

ConFusione (meals ₡5500-12,000) Italian-Latin fusion gets top billing at the Domilocos main dining room, which has a warm candlelit Mediterranean ambience and a nice selection of Chianti.

GETTING THERE & AWAY

Catch a bus to these destinations:

Quepos ₡3200; three hours; departs at 7:30am, 8am, 10:30am, 1:45pm, 4pm and 5pm.

Uvita ₡800; one hour; departs at 4:30am, 10:30am, noon and 6:15pm.

UVITA

This little hamlet is really nothing more than a loose straggle of farms, houses and tiny shops, though it should give you a good idea of what the central Pacific coast looked like before the tourist boom. Uvita does, however, serve as the base for visits to Parque Nacional Marino Ballena, a pristine marine reserve famous for its migrating pods of humpback whales.

SIGHTS & ACTIVITIES

Surfers passing through the area tend to push on to more extreme destinations further south, though there are occasionally some swells at **Playa Hermosa** to the north and **Playa Colonia** to the south.

SLEEPING & EATING

Cabinas Los Laureles (☎ 2743-8235; www. cabinasloslaureles.com; campsites US$10, s/d from US$20/25; P) This locally run spot has eight clean, polished-wood cabins that are set in a beautiful grove of laurels. If you're looking for a bit of local flavor and authentic Costa Rican hospitality, this is a good choice.

Cascada Verde (☎ 2743-8191; www. cascadaverde.org; dm US$12, shared lofts per person US$12, s/d from US$16/25; P) About 2km inland and uphill from Uvita, this organic permaculture farm and holistic retreat attracts legions of dedicated alternative lifestylers, who typically spend weeks here searching for peace of mind and sound body.

Las Terrazas de Ballena (☎ 2743-8034; www.terrazasdeballena.com; ste US$150-170; P 🖳 🏊) Located about 1.5km up in the hills about Uvita, this secluded Balinese-style boutique hotel quickly transports you to the other end of the Earth. Three luxury suites are given life through exposed stone and thatch, and they open up to expansive views of the marine national park below. Even if you're not staying here, stop by for some Pan-Asian fusion that combines freshly caught seafood and flavorful spices from the Orient.

ADRIAN HEPWORTH/HEPWORTHIMAGES

Eyelash viper – one of the dangers of tropical habitats

GETTING THERE & AWAY

Most buses depart from the two sheltered bus stops on the Costanera in the main village.

San Isidro de El General ₡800; 1½ hours; departs at 6am and 2pm.

San José ₡2500; seven hours; departs at 5am, 6am and 2pm.

PARQUE NACIONAL MARINO BALLENA

This stunner of a **marine park** (☎ 2743-8236; admission US$6; ☼ dawn-dusk) protects coral and rock reefs surrounding Isla Ballena. Despite its small size, the importance of this area cannot be overstated, especially since it protects migrating humpback whales, pods of dolphins and nesting sea turtles, not to mention colonies of sea birds and several terrestrial reptiles. Although Ballena is essentially off the radar for most coastal travelers, this can be an extremely rewarding destination for beach-lovers and wildlife-watchers alike.

The beaches at Parque Nacional Marino Ballena are a stunning combination of golden sand and polished rock. All are virtually deserted and perfect for peaceful swimming and sunbathing. Although the park gets few human visitors, the beaches are frequently visited by a number of different animal species, including nesting seabirds, bottle-nosed dolphins and a variety of lizards. The star attraction are the pods of humpback whales that pass through the national park from August through October and December through April.

Parque Nacional Marino Ballena is best accessed from Uvita, either by private vehicle or a quick taxi ride – inquire at your accommodations for the latter.

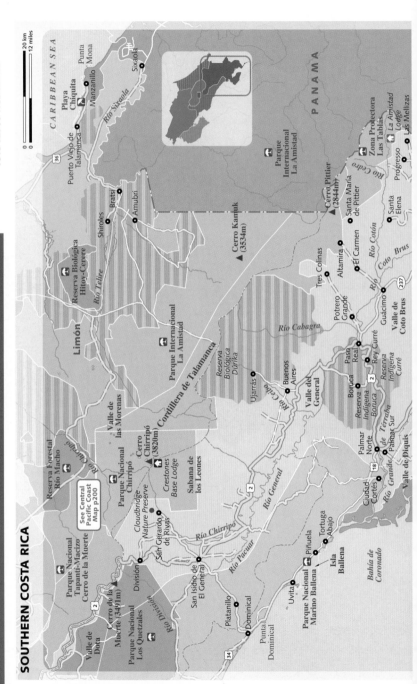

SOUTHERN COSTA RICA

0   20 km
0   12 miles

CARIBBEAN SEA

PANAMA

Punta Mona
Sixaola
Playa Chiquita
Manzanillo
Puerto Viejo de Talamanca
Río Sixaola
Bratsi
Amubri
Shiroles
Reserva Biológica Hitoy-Cerere
Río Telire
Limón

Parque Internacional La Amistad

Cerro Kamuk (3534m)

Cordillera de Talamanca

Parque Internacional La Amistad

Cerro Pittier (2844m)
Zona Protectora Las Tablas
La Amistad Lodge
Las Mellizas
Progresso
Río Cedro
Santa María de Pittier
Santa Elena
El Carmen
Río Cotón
Altamira
Tres Colinas
Río Coto Brus
Valle de Coto Brus
Guácimo
Potrero Grande
Río Cabagra
Reserva Biológica Dúrika
Rey Curré
Paso Real
Reserva Indígena Curré
Buenos Aires
Ujarrás
Río Ceibo
Valle del General
Boruca
Reserva Indígena Boruca
Reserva Forestal Río Macho
Río Macho
Valle de las Morenas
Parque Nacional Chirripó
Cerro Chirripó (3820m)
Crestones Base Lodge
Sabana de los Leones
Cloudbridge Nature Preserve
San Gerardo de Rivas
Río Chirripó

See Central Pacific Coast Map p200

Palmar Norte
de Térraba
Palmar Sur
Ciudad Cortés
Río Grande
Valle de Diquís

Parque Nacional Tapantí–Macizo Cerro de la Muerte
Cerro de la Muerte (3491m)
División
Río División
Valle de Dota
Parque Nacional Los Quetzales

San Isidro de El General
Río Pacuar
Río General

Platanillo
Dominical
Punta Dominical
Uvita
Piñuela
Tortuga Abajo
Isla Ballena
Parque Nacional Marino Ballena
Bahía de Coronado

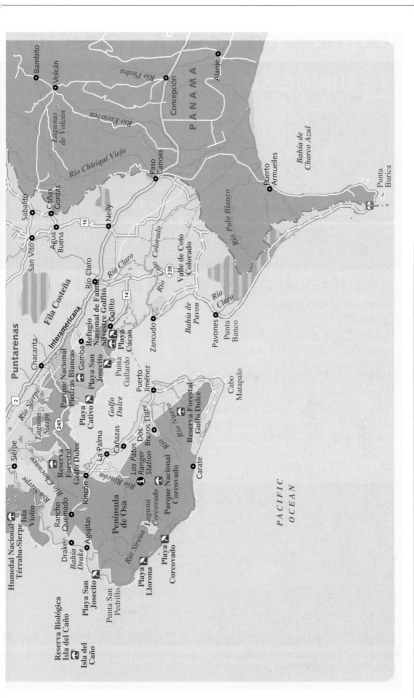

SOUTHERN COSTA RICA HIGHLIGHTS

1 HIKING SOUTHERN COSTA RICA

BY WALTER ODIO VICTORY, OWNER OF COSTA RICA TREKKING

Waking up in southern Costa Rica, either atop Cerro Chirripó or in the rainforests of Corcovado, allows you to journey beneath the first rays of the sun, when the morning dew is still clinging to vegetation. Trekking along remote trails through the wilds of nature is an experience loaded with adventure and intensity.

↘ WALTER ODIO VICTORY'S DON'T MISS LIST

❶ PARQUE NACIONAL CHIRRIPÓ

Scaling Costa Rica's **highest peak** (p263) isn't exactly a walk in the park. A minimum of two days is needed to climb from the ranger station in San Gerardo de Rivas to the summit and back. You'll walk away with a few blisters and bruises, but the memories will last long after your wounds have healed.

❷ BACKCOUNTRY CHIRRIPÓ

For hard-core adventurers, an alternative route is to take a guided three- or four-day loop trek starting in Herradura with a day or two traversing the cloud forest and *páramo* (highland habitat) on the slopes of Fila Urán. Hikers ascend Cerro Urán (3600m) before the final ascent of Chirripó, then descend through **San Gerardo de Rivas** (p261).

Clockwise from top: Green iguana, Parque Nacional Corcovado (p251); Hiking through a forest of mountain oak, Parque Nacional Chirripó (p262)

❸ SIRENA TO LA LEONA

In **Parque Nacional Corcovado** (p251), the 16km hike from Sirena to La Leona follows the shoreline through coastal forest and along deserted beaches. The journey between Sirena and La Leona takes six or seven hours. You can camp at La Leona; otherwise, it takes an hour to hike the additional 3.5km to Carate, where you can stay in a local lodge or catch a *colectivo* taxi to Puerto Jiménez.

❹ SIRENA TO SAN PEDRILLO

At 23km, this is the longest trail in **Corcovado** (p251), and most definitely not for the faint of heart. The majority of this hike is along the beach, which means loose sand and little shade – grueling, especially with a heavy pack.

This trail is only open from December to April, since heavy rains can make the Río Sirena impassable.

❺ SIRENA TO LOS PATOS

The expert-only route to Los Patos goes 18km through the heart of **Corcovado** (p251), affording the opportunity to pass through plenty of primary and secondary forest. The trail is relatively flat for the first 12km, but you must wade through two river tributaries before reaching the Laguna Corcovado. From this point, the route undulates steeply, mostly uphill.

⬐ THINGS YOU NEED TO KNOW

Access Book in advance for dorm-style lodging in Chirripó (p264) and Corcovado (p254) national parks **Hiking tip** Hikes may be undertaken solo, but a local guide provides an extra measure of safety, and can help you identify flora and fauna **See our author's hiking coverage, p253 and p263**

SOUTHERN COSTA RICA HIGHLIGHTS

2 | BAHÍA DRAKE

BY SHAWN LARKIN, CO-OWNER/MANAGER OF COSTA CETACEA

Before lamenting about having missed wild Costa Rica back in the day, put your boots on and hoof it from Bahía Drake along the coast to Corcovado. You will find the country's wildest beaches, trails, lodges and campsites tucked away among thickly forested rocky points and much wildlife. There really are more monkeys, dolphins and waterfalls than people here.

↘ SHAWN LARKIN'S DON'T MISS LIST

❶ RÍO AGUJITAS

This **river** (p242) feeds into Bahía Drake, and provides a rich habitat for a large number of charismatic creatures. With a reliable kayak, you can travel through various biomes at a relaxing pace, stopping occasionally to search for signs of surrounding life. If the waves in the bay are picking up – and you're feeling particularly adventurous – you can even kayak-surf a few crashing beach breaks.

❷ DOLPHIN-WATCHING

In Costa Rica it's illegal to get closer than 100m to **dolphins** (p243) in the wild, but, with a knowledgeable guide, you can still enjoy watching frolicking pods from a safe distance. In the blue-water ecosystem of Bahía Drake, you'll find enormous pods of spinner dolphins, some of which number in the thousands. Dolphins are some of the most intelligent animals on the planet, and the opportunity to responsibly interact with them should not be missed.

Clockwise from top: Scuba diving off Isla del Caño (p244); Golfo Dulce, Parque Nacional Corcovado (p251)

❸ HIKING

Hiking along the coastline of **Bahía Drake** (p244) between Agujitas and Corcovado is akin to stepping into a time machine and heading back to the Costa Rica of yesteryear. Here you'll find enormous stretches of virgin wilderness and abandoned beaches, not to mention heaving concentrations of wildlife. While hard-core trekkers can press on as far as Parque Nacional Corcovado, more casual hikers can break up their journey with long bouts of swimming and sunbathing.

❹ SCUBA DIVING

Isla del Caño (p244) is a tiny island in the middle of the bay that happens to be home to a protected biological reserve. Of course, most of the action here takes place under the surface of the sea, particularly at the rock pinnacle of Bajo del Diablo. If you've donned scuba gear, you can descend into the blue depths where enormous schools of fish thrive.

❑ THINGS YOU NEED TO KNOW

Access Arrange boat transfers between Sierpe and Bahía Drake through your accommodations (see p243 and p245) **More information** Find out more about Shawn's work with the dolphins at Costa Cetacea's website (www.costacetacea.com) **See our author's coverage of the area, p241**

SOUTHERN COSTA RICA HIGHLIGHTS

3

↘ PAVONES

You'll need to sacrifice a good chunk of your schedule to access this far-flung **beach** (p257). But trust us – it's worth the time and effort, especially if you want to take a crack at what is reportedly the longest left-hand surf break known to humankind. Even if you're not a hard-core surfer, this comparatively undeveloped corner of the country recalls a quieter, less touristed time in Costa Rica's history.

4

↘ PARQUE INTERNACIONAL LA AMISTAD

Even Corcovado bows its head in respect when it comes to this rough and rugged **binational park** (p267), which straddles the Costa Rica–Panama border. Much of the 'Friendship' park is completely inaccessible, but outdoors enthusiasts can hire a local guide and embark on a serious wilderness adventure. If you're looking for wildlife and a complete absence of tourist crowds, this is the destination for you.

⬎ CABO MATAPALO

Located at the extreme tip of the Península de Osa, **Cabo Matapalo** (p249) is regarded as a remote corner of an already remote region. But the attraction here is the fact that you hike in relative isolation, far from maddening crowds, all the while soaking up some of the most beautiful landscapes and seascapes that the country has on offer.

⬎ PUERTO JIMÉNEZ

The closest town of any real size to Parque Nacional Corcovado, so-called **Port Jim** (p246) is a great place to stock up on supplies and organize logistics before embarking on a trekking expedition. The town itself is also loaded with character, with frequent wildlife encounters in proximity to diverse accommodations and eating options.

⬎ ZANCUDO

A low-key **beach town** (p255) that caters to do-it-yourself travelers, this is the sort of place where you can explore things independently and at your own pace. Pacific waters gently lap attractive beaches, while nearby mangrove swamps are much more intimidating, offering close encounters with crocs and caimans.

3 Pavones boasts a mammoth left-hand surf break; 4 Gray-tailed mountain-gem, Parque Internacional La Amistad (p267); 5 Cabo Matapalo (p249); 6 Scarlet macaws, Puerto Jiménez (p246); 7 Crocodiles, Zancudo (p255)

SOUTHERN COSTA RICA'S BEST...

⬐ WILDLIFE

- **Dolphins & Whales** (p243) The waters of Bahía Drake are incredibly rich in marine life.
- **Tapirs** (p251) The largest land mammal in Costa Rica is found throughout Parque Nacional Corcovado.
- **Sloths & Crocs** (p256) The mangrove swamps near Zancudo harbor all manner of creatures.

⬐ SPLURGES

- **Drake Bay Rainforest Chalet** (p243) A jungle getaway in the middle of pristine rainforest that fronts Bahía Drake.
- **Casa Corcovado Jungle Lodge** (p246) Private bungalows with a dash of class hug an undeveloped coastline.
- **Iguana Lodge** (p247) This luxury getaway uses natural stone and bamboo flourishes to set the mood.

⬐ SECRET SPOTS

- **Reserva Indígena Boruca** (p265) The indigenous reserve for the Boruca population welcomes visitors to watch their unique festivals.
- **Parque Nacional Isla del Cocos** (p258) This island chain in the Pacific is a true Lost World.
- **Palmar** (p240) Hidden around Palmar are pre-Columbian granite spheres.

⬐ ECOHOTELS

- **Lapa Ríos** (p250) A living classroom where sustainability meets eco-luxury.
- **Tiskita Jungle Lodge** (p257) Set amid virgin forest and a huge orchard.
- **Ranchos Almendros** (p250) A reforestation project that plants almond trees to attract scarlet macaws.

TOM BOYDEN

The Baird's tapir inhabits the most remote wilderness areas

THINGS YOU NEED TO KNOW

⤷ VITAL STATISTICS

- **Population** San Isidro de El General 45,000
- **Best time to visit** During the rainy season (from mid-April through mid-December) the amount of precipitation is astounding. Even in the dry season (mid-December through mid-April) you can expect the occasional downfall.

⤷ PARKS IN A NUTSHELL

- **Parque Nacional Corcovado** (p251) The undisputed gem in the southern zone's wide berth of wilderness offerings, Corcovado boasts unmatched wildlife-watching opportunities.
- **Parque Nacional Chirripó** (p262) Climb through the clouds as you scale Costa Rica's highest peak, Cerro Chirripó (3820m).
- **Parque Internacional La Amistad** (p267) Catering primarily to experienced trekkers, La Amistad is as untamed as it gets in these parts.

⤷ ADVANCE PLANNING

- **Reservations** It's best to plan in advance if you want to sleep in Bahiá Drake, trek across Parque Nacional Corcovado, explore Parque Internacional La Amistad or make the ascent of Cerro Chirripó.
- **Gear** Last-minute supplies are available in Puerto Jimenéz, but highly personalized items such as hiking boots are best brought from home.

⤷ RESOURCES

- **Costa Rica Tourism Board** (www.visitcostarica.com)
- **Tico Times** (www.ticotimes.net)

⤷ EMERGENCY NUMBERS

- **Emergency** (☎ 911)
- **Fire** (☎ 118)
- **Police** (☎ 117)

⤷ GETTING AROUND

- **Air** Small planes and charters to Puerto Jiménez can save you lots of time-consuming overland travel.
- **Boat** Lodges in Bahiá Drake are accessed by boat from Sierpe.
- **Bus** Large cities in southern Costa Rica are surprisingly well-served by public buses.
- **Walk** Bring your hiking boots as the region is best explored on foot.

⤷ BE FOREWARNED

- **Climate** Bring adequate clothing if you're planning to climb Cerro Chirripó – it's cold and wet at high altitudes.

SOUTHERN COSTA RICA ITINERARIES

BAHÍA DRAKE & AROUND Three Days

Southern Costa Rica is far from the main tourist circuit, but it is possible to dip in and out with just a few days to spare. If this sounds like your cup of shade-grown coffee, consider setting your sights on any of the myriad hotels and resorts lining Bahiá Drake. For the most part, accommodation options in this part of the country are fairly expensive, but bedding down in eco-paradise is certainly worth the splurge.

From (1) Sierpe (p241) a boat will take you on a scenic ride through the sparkling-clear waters of (2) Bahía Drake (p241). Upon arriving at your destination, expect to spend your entire stay swimming, hiking, boating and searching for all manner of wildlife. If you want to head a bit further down the coast, there are other excellent options spanning the stretch from (3) Bahía Drake to Corcovado (p244).

CLIMBING CHIRRIPÓ Four Days

One of the quintessential Costa Rican experiences is an ascent of Cerro Chirripó, the country's highest peak. From these lofty heights, you can enjoy panoramic views of both the Caribbean Sea and the Pacific Ocean – assuming, of course, that the weather holds. On that note, bring extra clothing as the weather up here is cold and wet, but the unpleasant climate is part of the challenge.

(1) San Isidro de El General (p259), the largest city in the southern zone, is the jumping-off point for this high-altitude adventure. From here it's a quick skip and a jump (and a bus ride) away to the tiny town of (2) San Gerardo de Rivas (p261), where you can finalize your reservations for the mountaintop hostel, carbo-load on *gallo pinto* (blended rice and beans) and get an all-important good night's rest. Finally, grab a bus up to the ranger station at the entrance to (3) Parque Nacional Chirripó (p262), and get ready for the climb of your life.

TREKKING IN CORCOVADO One Week or More

You will need to devote a good chunk of time to this itinerary, but the trek across Parque Nacional Corcovado is a once-in-a-lifetime chance to have an up-close-and-personal encounter with rare and endangered animals. Here you stand a very good chance of eyeing a tapir and a jaguar – well, at least their prints and poo – as well as the more common monkeys, sloths, peccaries and tropical birds.

Things start off in the frontier town of (1) Puerto Jiménez (p246), where you should go through your predeparture checklist. Assuming everything is in order, catch the bus to the village of (2) Carate (p251), which lies at the doorstep of Parque Nacional Corcovado. From the entrance at (3) La Leona Ranger Station (p253), your destination is

the (4) Sirena Ranger Station (p253), where wildlife reaches astounding concentrations, though you're going to have to first tackle virgin jungles, roaring rivers and plenty of creepy-crawlies. If your return flight is rapidly approaching, you can hop a quick domestic flight back to San José. If you have more time to spare, you can head overland back to Puerto Jiménez, or consider taking the longer, more difficult trek up the coastline to the (5) San Pedrillo Ranger Station (p253).

DISCOVER SOUTHERN COSTA RICA

In southern Costa Rica, the Cordillera de Talamanca descends dramatically into agricultural lowlands carpeted with sprawling plantations of coffee beans, bananas and African palms. Here, *campesinos* (farmers) work their familial lands, maintaining agricultural traditions that have been passed down through the generations. While the rest of Costa Rica embraces globalization, life in the southern zone remains constant, much as it has for decades, and in some places centuries on end. In a country where little pre-Columbian influence remains, southern Costa Rica is where you'll find the most pronounced indigenous presence.

And then there is the Península de Osa, which captivates travelers with its abandoned wilderness beaches, world-class surf and endless opportunities for rugged exploration. Simply put, it's a place for travelers with youthful hearts, intrepid spirits and a yearning for something truly wild. If you've been growing old in a concrete jungle, come spend some time in this verdant one.

PALMAR

At the intersection of the country's two major highways, the unremarkable village of Palmar is a transportation hub that serves as a gateway to the Península de Osa and Golfo Dulce.

SIGHTS

Lack of charm aside, Palmar is one of the best sites in the country to see the **granite spheres**, or *esferas de piedra,* a legacy of pre-Columbian cultures – some of which exceed 2m in diameter. They are scattered all over town, including at the airstrip – some of the largest and most impressive are in front of the peach-colored *el colegio* (school) on the Interamericana.

SLEEPING

Brunka Lodge (☎ 2786-7489; www.brunka lodge.com; s/f from US$35/45; ❄ ▯ ☎ ☎) The Brunka Lodge is undoubtedly the most inviting option in Palmar Norte. Sun-filled, clean-swept bungalows are clustered around a swimming pool and a popular, pleasant open-air restaurant, and all rooms have hot-water bathrooms, cable TV and high-speed internet connections.

GETTING THERE & AWAY

AIR

Departing from San José, **NatureAir** (www.natureair.com) and **Sansa** (www.sansa. com) have daily flights to the Palmar airstrip.

Taxis meet incoming flights and charge up to ₡2500 to Palmar Norte and between ₡7500 and ₡12,500 to Sierpe.

BUS

San Isidro de El General (Tracopa) ₡2000; three hours; departs at 8:30am, 11:30am, 2:30pm and 4:30pm.

San José (Tracopa) ₡2800; five hours; departs at 5:25am, 6:15am, 7:45am, 10am, 1pm, 3pm and 4:45pm.

Sierpe ₡650; one hour; departs at 4:30am, 7am, 9:30am, 11:30am, 2:30pm and 5:30pm.

SIERPE

This sleepy village on the Río Sierpe is the gateway to Bahía Drake, and if you've made a reservation with any of the jungle lodges further down the coast, you will be picked up here by boat.

GETTING THERE & AWAY
BOAT
If you are heading to Bahía Drake, your lodge will make arrangements for the boat transfer.

BUS
Buses to Palmar Norte (₡650, one hour) depart at 5:30am, 8:30am, 10:30am, 12:30pm, 3:30pm and 6pm.

BAHÍA DRAKE

Parque Nacional Corcovado aside, the jungle-fringed crystalline waters of Bahía Drake are arguably Península de Osa at its best. As one of the peninsula's (and the country's) most isolated destinations, Bahía Drake is a veritable Lost World of tropical landscapes and abundant wildlife. In the rainforest canopy, howlers greet the rising sun with their haunting bellows, while pairs of macaws soar between the treetops, filling the air with their cacophonous squawking. Offshore in the bay itself, pods of migrating dolphins flit through turquoise waters.

ORIENTATION
The shores of Bahía Drake are home to two settlements: Agujitas, a tiny town of 300 residents spread out along the southern shore of the bay, and Drake, a few kilometers to the north, which is little more than a few houses alongside the airstrip.

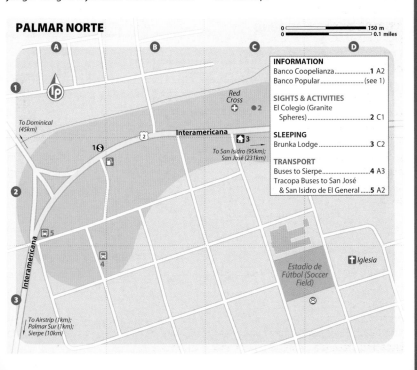

PALMAR NORTE

INFORMATION
Banco Coopelianza.....................**1** A2
Banco Popular.........................(see 1)

SIGHTS & ACTIVITIES
El Colegio (Granite
    Spheres)...........................**2** C1

SLEEPING
Brunka Lodge..........................**3** C2

TRANSPORT
Buses to Sierpe.......................**4** A3
Tracopa Buses to San José
    & San Isidro de El General.....**5** A2

To Dominical (45km)

Red Cross

Interamericana
To San Isidro (95km); San José (231km)

Estadio de Fútbol (Soccer Field)

Iglesia

To Airstrip (1km); Palmar Sur (1km); Sierpe (10km)

SOUTHERN COSTA RICA

BAHÍA DRAKE

ACTIVITIES
SWIMMING & SNORKELING
Beyond Isla del Caño, there are opportunities for snorkeling on the coast between Agujitas and Corcovado. **Playa San Josecito** attracts scores of colorful species, which hide out among the coral reef and rocks. Another recommended spot is **Playa Las Caletas**, and **Playa Cocalito**, a small, pretty beach near Agujitas that is pleasant for swimming and sunbathing.

HIKING
All of the lodges offer tours to Parque Nacional Corcovado, usually a full-day trip to San Pedrillo ranger station (from US$75 to US$150 per person), including boat transportation, lunch and guided hikes.

In addition to Corcovado, other popular day trips include nearby **Playa San Josecito**, a stunningly remote beach where you can slow down and soak up the beauty of the bay. If you want to head inland, you can also explore the **Punta Río Claro Wildlife Refuge**, which can be accessed from Playa San Josecito.

KAYAKING
A fantastic way to explore the region's biodiversity is to paddle through it. The idyllic **Río Agujitas** attracts a huge variety of birdlife and lots of scaly reptiles. The river conveniently empties out into the bay, which is surrounded by hidden coves and sandy beaches ideal for exploring in a sea kayak.

HORSEBACK RIDING
The **coastal trail** running between Agujitas and Corcovado is perfect for horseback riding, especially if you relish the idea of galloping wildly across deserted beaches

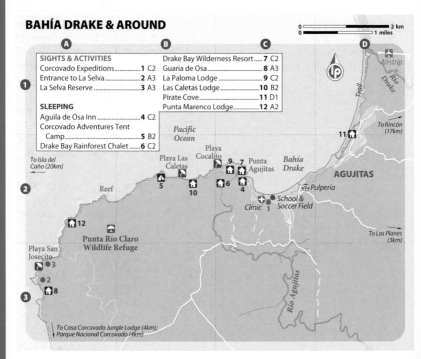

BAHÍA DRAKE & AROUND

0 ——————— 2 km
0 ——————— 1 miles

SIGHTS & ACTIVITIES	
Corcovado Expeditions.................1 C2	Drake Bay Wilderness Resort.....7 C2
Entrance to La Selva......................2 A3	Guaria de Osa................................8 A3
La Selva Reserve 3 A3	La Paloma Lodge 9 C2
	Las Caletas Lodge......................10 B2
SLEEPING	Pirate Cove...................................11 D1
Aguila de Osa Inn 4 C2	Punta Marenco Lodge...............12 A2
Corcovado Adventures Tent	
Camp...5 B2	
Drake Bay Rainforest Chalet 6 C2	

Airstrip

Río Drake

Trail

To Rincón (17km)

To Isla del Caño (20km)

Pacific Ocean

Playa Las Caletas

Playa Cocalito

Punta Agujitas

Bahía Drake

AGUJITAS

Pulperia

Reef

School & Soccer Field

Clinic

To Los Planes (3km)

Punta Río Claro Wildlife Refuge

Playa San Josecito

Río Agujitas

To Casa Corcovado Jungle Lodge (4km);
Parque Nacional Corcovado (4km)

while the waves crash below you. **Los Planes** is another popular destination for horseback riders, with ample opportunities for wildlife-watching along the way. Again, most of the upscale lodges in the area offer guided rides from US$75.

SPORTFISHING

Bahía Drake claims more than 40 fishing records, including sailfish, marlin, yellowfin tuna, wahoo, cubera snapper, mackerel and roosterfish. Fishing is excellent year-round, although the catch may vary according to the season. Many lodges can arrange fishing excursions, but you need to be prepared to pay heavily – half-/full-day excursions cost around US$600/1000.

DOLPHIN- & WHALE-WATCHING

Bahía Drake is rife with marine life, including more than 25 species of dolphins and whales that pass through on their migrations throughout the year. Humpbacks can be spotted in Bahía Drake year-round (except May), but the best months to see whales are late July through early November.

Marine biologist Shawn Larkin has an infectious enthusiasm about marine mammals. He spends his time researching and filming dolphins and whales for his educational organization, **Costa Cetacea** (www.costacetacea.com).

SLEEPING & EATING

High-season rates are quoted; prices are per person, including three meals.

Pirate Cove (☎ 2234-6154; www.piratecovecostarica.com; r per person from US$90; 👶) Breezy, tentlike bungalows and spacious hardwood cabins both offer an element of laid-back luxury. With private terraces that are strung with hammocks, most guests seem content to just swing the day away.

Drake Bay Wilderness Resort (☎ 2770-8012; www.drakebay.com; 4-day package per person from US$770; 👶) Sitting pretty on Punta Agujitas, this relaxed resort occupies the optimal piece of real estate in all of Bahía Drake. Naturalists will be won over by the lovely landscaping, from flowering trees to the ocean-fed pool. Accommodations are in comfortable cabins, which have mural-painted walls and private patios with ocean views.

Aguila de Osa Inn (☎ 2296-2190; www.aguiladeosa.com; s/d 2-night package US$623/1048) This swanky lodge consists of roomy quarters with shining wood floors, cathedral ceilings and private decks overlooking the ocean. The vast centerpiece of the lodge, however, is the comfortable yet elegant open-air *rancho* (small houselike building).

La Paloma Lodge (☎ 2239-7502; www.lapalomalodge.com; 3-/4-/5-day package from US$1100/1245/1390; 👶) Perched on a lush hillside, this exquisite lodge provides guests with an incredible panorama of ocean and forest, all from the comfort of the sumptuous, stylish quarters. Rooms have shiny hardwood floors and queen-sized orthopedic beds.

Drake Bay Rainforest Chalet (☎ 8382-1619; www.drakebayholiday.com; 3-/4-/5-/6-/7-day package from US$1150/1275/1400/1525/1650) Set on 18 hectares of pristine rainforest, this jungle getaway is a remote, romantic adventure. Huge French windows provide a panoramic view of the surrounding jungle, enjoyed from almost every room in the house.

GETTING THERE & AWAY
AIR

Departing from San José, **NatureAir** (www.natureair.com) and **Sansa** (www.sansa.com) have daily flights to the Drake airstrip, which is 2km north of Agujitas. **Alfa Romeo Aero Taxi** (☎ 2735-5353;

ERNEST MANEWAL

Marine life abounds around the Isla del Caño

↘ ISLA DEL CAÑO

About 20km west of Agujitas, this tiny island in Bahía Drake is one of Costa Rica's top spots for diving, with attractions including intricate rock and coral formations and an amazing array of underwater life, teeming with colorful reef fish and incredible coral formations. Divers report that the schools of fish swimming overhead are often so dense that they block the sunlight from filtering down. Common sightings include jacks, snappers, barracudas, puffers, parrotfish, moray eels and even the occasional shark or two.

Things you need to know: A two-tank dive runs from US$100 to US$150 depending on the spot. Most of the upscale lodges in the area either have onsite dive centers or can arrange trips and courses through a neighboring lodge.

ww.alfaromeoair.com) offers charter flights connecting Drake to Puerto Jiménez, Golfito, Carate and Sirena.

BOAT
All of the hotels offer boat transfers between Sierpe and Bahía Drake with prior arrangements.

BAHÍA DRAKE TO CORCOVADO

This craggy stretch of coastline is home to sandy inlets that disappear at high tide, leaving only the rocky outposts and luxuriant rainforest. Virtually uninhabited and undeveloped beyond a few tourist lodges, the setting here is magnificent and wild.

SIGHTS & ACTIVITIES
Scenic little inlets punctuate this entire route, each with a wild, windswept beach. Just west of Punta Agujitas, a short detour off the main trail leads to the picturesque **Playa Cocalito**, a secluded cove perfect for sunning, swimming and body surfing. With no lodges in the immediate vicinity, it's often deserted. **Playa Las Caletas**, in front of the Corcovado Adventures Tent Camp, is excellent for snorkeling.

Further south, the Río Claro empties out into the ocean. Water can be waist-deep or higher, and the current swift, so take care when wading across. This is also the start of the Río Claro trail, which leads inland into the 400-hectare **Punta Río Claro Wildlife Refuge** and passes a picturesque waterfall along the way.

South of Río Claro, the **Playa San Josecito** is the longest stretch of white-sand beach on this side of the Península de Osa. From here you can access another private reserve, **La Selva**. A short, steep climb leads from the beach to a lookout point, offering a spectacular view over the treetops and out to the ocean. A network of trails continues inland, and eventually connects La Selva to the Río Claro reserve.

The border of Parque Nacional Corcovado is about 5km south of here (it takes three to four hours to hike the entire distance from Agujitas to Corcovado). The trail is more overgrown as it gets closer to the park, but it's a well-traveled route.

SLEEPING & EATING

High-season rates are quoted; prices are per person, including three meals.

Las Caletas Lodge (☎ 8381-4052, 8326-1460; www.caletas.co.cr; r per person from US$70; 🖥 🛜 👣) This adorable little hotel is set on the picturesque beach of the same name and consists of five cozy wooden cabins that are awash with sweeping views. The Swiss-Tico owners are passionate about environmental sustainability, which means that solar and hydroelectric power provides electricity around the clock.

Corcovado Adventures Tent Camp (☎ 8384-1679; www.corcovado.com; r per person from US$80, 3-/4-day package per person US$400/535; 👣) Less than an hour's walk from Drake brings you to this fun, family-run spot. It's like camping, but comfy: spacious, walk-in tents are set up on covered platforms and fully equipped with sturdy wood furniture. Twenty hectares of rainforest offer plenty of opportunity for exploration, and the beachfront setting is excellent for water sports.

Punta Marenco Lodge (☎ 2234-1308, 2234-1227; www.puntamarenco.com; 3-day package per person US$339; 👣) This intimate family-run lodge shares access to the Punta Río

Punta Agujitas, Bahía Drake (p241)

TRAVELIB PRIME/ALAMY

Claro Wildlife Refuge, providing excellent opportunities for independent hiking and wildlife-watching. Accommodations are in thatch-roof *cabañas* (cabins) in the style of the Boruca indigenous peoples.

Guaria de Osa (☎ 2235-4313, in USA 510-235-4313; www.guariadeosa.com; 3-day package per person US$395) Cultivating a new-age ambience, this Asian-style retreat center offers yoga, tai chi and all kinds of massage, along with the more typical rainforest activities. The lovely grounds include an ethnobotanical garden, which features exotic local species used for medicinal and other purposes.

Casa Corcovado Jungle Lodge (☎ 2256-3181, in USA 888-896-6097; www.casacorcovado.com; 3-day package per person from US$955; ☒) A spine-tingling boat ride takes you to this luxurious lodge on 175 hectares of rainforest bordering the national park. Each bungalow is tucked away in its own private tropical garden, and artistic details including antique Mexican tiles and handmade stained-glass windows make the Casa Corcovado one of this area's classiest accommodation options.

GETTING THERE & AROUND
BOAT
All of the hotels offer boat transfers between Sierpe and Bahía Drake with prior arrangements.

HIKING
The only way to get around the area is by boat or by foot, which means that travelers are more or less dependent on their lodges.

PUERTO JIMÉNEZ
As the preferred jumping-off point for travelers heading to the famed Sirena ranger station, the town is a great place to organize an expedition, stock up on

supplies, eat a hot meal and get a good night's rest before hitting the trails. Puerto Jiménez is something of a natural wonder in itself. Sliced in half by the swampy, overgrown Quebrada Cacao, and flanked on one side by the emerald waters of the Golfo Dulce, this untamed environment is shared equally by local residents and wildlife.

INFORMATION
Oficina de Área de Conservación Osa (Osa Conservation Area Headquarters; ☎ 2735-5580; ⏱ 8am-noon & 1-4pm Mon-Fri) has information about Corcovado, Isla del Caño, Parque Nacional Marino Ballena and Golfito parks and reserves. Make reservations here to camp in Corcovado.

SIGHTS & ACTIVITIES
About 5km east of town, the secluded – and often deserted – **Playa Platanares** is excellent for swimming, sunning and recovering from too much adventure. The nearby mangroves of Río Platanares are a paradise for kayaking and bird-watching.

On the east side of the airstrip, **Herrera Gardens & Conservation Project** (☎ 2735-5267; admission US$5, 2hr guided tour US$15; ⏱ 6am-5pm) is a 100-hectare reserve with beautiful botanical gardens. This innovative, long-term reforestation project offers an ecologically and economically sustainable alternative to cattle-grazing.

SLEEPING
Cabinas Eilyn (☎ 2735-5465; d with/without air-con US$40/35; ℗ ☒ ♿) Hospitality is a family affair at these quiet quarters on the edge of town. High ceilings, tile floors and a comfy porch enhance the decor of the four cozy *cabinas* that are attached to the Tico owners' home.

La Choza del Manglar (☎ 2735-5002; www.manglares.com; r US$40-99; ℗ ☒ ▯ ⏃ ♿)

Wildlife sightings are de rigueur on these beautifully landscaped grounds – from crocodiles to kinkajous, monkeys to macaws. Bright and airy rooms have hand-carved furniture and mural-painted walls, as well as large windows overlooking the lush surroundings.

Playa Preci-Osa Lodge (☎ 8818-2959; www.playa-preciosa-lodge.de; Playa Platanares; s/d from US$45/70; Ⓟ) All of the options at this romantic beach lodge on nearby Playa Platanares offer excellent value: four spacious thatch-roof bungalows have a sleeping loft and plenty of living space

(great for families), while eight screened platform tents are set in the secluded garden.

Black Turtle Lodge (☎ 2735-5005; www.blackturtlelodge.com; Playa Platanares; s/d from US$85/140; Ⓟ) A peaceful yoga retreat along Playa Platanares, this ecolodge offers the choice of two-story *cabinas*, which have magnificent views over the treetops to the Golfo Dulce, and the less-spacious *cabinettas* (small cabins) nestled into the tropical garden below.

Iguana Lodge (☎ 2735-5205; www.iguanalodge.com; Playa Platanares; casitas per

SOUTHERN COSTA RICA

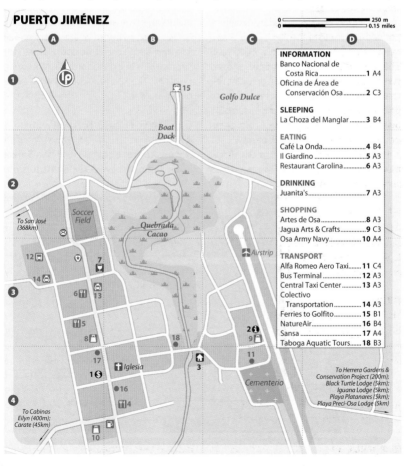

PUERTO JIMÉNEZ

PUERTO JIMÉNEZ

0 — 250 m
0 — 0.15 miles

INFORMATION	
Banco Nacional de Costa Rica	1 A4
Oficina de Área de Conservación Osa	2 C3
SLEEPING	
La Choza del Manglar	3 B4
EATING	
Café La Onda	4 B4
Il Giardino	5 A3
Restaurant Carolina	6 A3
DRINKING	
Juanita's	7 A3
SHOPPING	
Artes de Osa	8 A3
Jagua Arts & Crafts	9 C3
Osa Army Navy	10 A4
TRANSPORT	
Alfa Romeo Aero Taxi	11 C4
Bus Terminal	12 A3
Central Taxi Center	13 A3
Colectivo Transportation	14 A3
Ferries to Golfito	15 B1
NatureAir	16 B4
Sansa	17 A4
Taboga Aquatic Tours	18 B3

Golfo Dulce

Boat Dock

Soccer Field

To San José (368km)

Quebrada Cacao

Airstrip

To Cabinas Eilyn (400m); Carate (45km)

Iglesia

Cementerio

To Herrera Gardens & Conservation Project (200m); Black Turtle Lodge (5km); Iguana Lodge (5km); Playa Platanares (5km); Playa Preci-Osa Lodge (5km)

person US$155, villas US$450, all incl full board; ⓟ 🐾 ♿) This luxurious lodge fronting Playa Platanares has the most architecturally alluring cabins in the area: four two-story bungalows have huge breezy decks, bamboo furniture, orthopedic beds draped in mosquito netting and lovely stone bathrooms with garden showers.

EATING & DRINKING

Café La Onda (light meals ₡1000-3500) A funky and eclectic travelers' cafe that's equally suited for chilling out or chatting up, La Onda sets the stage with homemade pastries accompanied by excellent coffees and fruit smoothies.

Restaurant Carolina (dishes ₡1500-4000) This is *the* hub in Puerto Jiménez. Expats, nature guides, tourists and locals all gather here for food, drinks and plenty of carousing. The food is famous locally and the fresh-fruit drinks and cold beers go down pretty easily on a hot day.

Il Giardino (☎ 2735-5129; meals ₡3500-6000; ⏱ 10am-2pm & 5-10pm) The specialties

of the house at Il Giardino are homemade pasta and fresh seafood.

You can get decent Mexican food at **Juanita's** (⏱ 5pm-2am), but it's more popular for the margaritas.

SHOPPING

Artes de Osa (☎ 2735-5429; ⏱ 8am-5pm) This cutesy souvenir shop has the usual tourist knick-knacks in addition to some attractive handcrafted furniture and hand-painted pottery.

Jagua Arts & Crafts (☎ 2735-5267; ⏱ 8am-5pm) A great collection of art and jewelry by local and expat craftspeople, including some amazing painted masks.

Osa Army Navy (⏱ 8am-7pm Mon-Sat, 9am-4pm Sun) Your one-stop shop for sportswear, boogie boards, fishing gear, bug nets, knives, backpacks and other outdoor gear.

GETTING THERE & AWAY
AIR

NatureAir (www.natureair.com) and **Sansa** (www.sansa.com) have daily flights to/from

Trucking it around Puerto Jiménez (p246)

IMAGEBROKER/JAN KRIMMER

San José. **Alfa Romeo Aero Taxi** (☎ 2775-5353; www.alfaromeoair.com) has light aircraft (three and five passengers) for charter flights to Golfito, Carate, Drake, Sirena, Palmar Sur, Quepos and Limón.

BOAT
Two passenger ferries travel to Golfito (₡3000, 1½ hours), departing at 6am and 10am daily. Note that these times are subject to change; in this part of the country, schedules often fall prey to the whims of the captain.

Taboga Aquatic Tours (☎ 2735-5265) runs water taxis to Zancudo for ₡25,000.

BUS
San Isidro ₡3000; five hours; departs at 1pm.

San José (Autotransportes Blanco Lobo) ₡5900; eight hours; departs at 5am and 11am.

TAXI
Colectivo Transportation (☎ 8837-3120, 8832-8680; Soda Deya) runs a jeep-taxi service to Cabo Matapalo (₡2000) and Carate (₡3500) on the southern tip of the national park. Departures are from the Soda Deya at 6am and 1:30pm, returning at 8:30am and 4pm.

Otherwise, you can hire a 4WD taxi from **Taxi 348** (☎ 8849-5228; taxicorcovado@racsa.co.cr) or from the **Central Taxi Center** (☎ 2735-5481). Taxis usually charge up to ₡37,500 for the ride to Carate, up to ₡15,000 for the ride to Matapalo, and more than ₡50,000 for the overland trek to Drake.

CABO MATAPALO
The tip of the Península de Osa and the entrance to Golfo Dulce lies just 17km south of Puerto Jiménez, but this heavily forested and beach-fringed cape is a

B. VON HOFFMANN/ROBERTSTOCK/AURORA
Scarlet macaw, Parque Nacional Corcovado (p251)

↘ IF YOU LIKE...
If you like **Parque Nacional Corcovado** (p251), we think you'll like these other national parks in Península de Osa:

- **Humedal Nacional Térraba-Sierpe** Approximately 330 sq km of protected mangrove wetlands that harbor numerous species of aquatic birds.
- **Refugio Nacional de Fauna Silvestre Golfito** This tiny 28-sq-km reserve surrounding the town of Golfito is home to rare cycads or living plant fossils.
- **Reserva Forestal Golfo Dulce** On the northern shore of Golfo Dulce, this is an important biological corridor for migrating wildlife.

vastly different world. A network of trails traverses the foothills, which are uninhabited except for migrating wildlife from the Reserva Forestal Golfo Dulce. Along the coastline, miles upon miles of beaches of pristine wilderness are virtually abandoned, except for handfuls of surfers in the know.

SIGHTS & ACTIVITIES
A fantastic and easy hiking destination is **King Louis**, a magnificent, 28m-tall waterfall that can be accessed by trail from

Playa Matapalo. For ocean adventures, most of the lodges also offer **kayaks**, and the wild, beautiful beach – surrounding on three sides – is never more than a short walk away.

These pristine beaches around Cabo Matapalo offer three breaks that are putting this little peninsula on the surfing map. **Playa Pan Dulce** is a double point break, while **Backwash Bay** offers a nice beach break at low tide. **Playa Matapalo** also has an A-plus right break, with the biggest and best waves in the area. Conditions are usually good with a west swell; surfing season coincides with the rainy season, which lasts from April through October.

SLEEPING & EATING

Ojo del Mar (☎ 2735-5531; www.ojodelmar. com; s/d from US$65/110; Ⓟ) Tucked in amid the windswept beach and the lush jungle, this is a little plot of paradise. The four beautifully handcrafted bamboo bungalows are entirely open-air, allowing for all the natural sounds and scents to seep in (thatched roofs and mosquito nets provide protection from the elements).

Ranchos Almendros (Kapu's Place; ☎ 2735-5531; http://home.earthlink.net/~kapu/; Cabo Matapalo; r per person from US$75; Ⓟ) The property includes three cozy *cabañas* that are equipped with solar power, large screened windows, full kitchens and garden showers. As per the name, 'Almond Tree Ranch' is part of an ongoing project dedicated to the reforestation of almond trees to create habitat for the endangered scarlet macaw.

Lapa Ríos (☎ 2735-5130; www.laparios. com; road to Carate, 17km; s/d incl full board US$495/610; Ⓟ Ⓡ) Scattered over the site are 16 spacious, thatched bungalows, all decked out with queen-sized bed, bamboo furniture, garden shower and private deck with panoramic views. An extensive trail system allows exploration of the 400-hectare reserve, while swimming, snorkeling and surfing are at your doorstep. As one of the select few hotels in Costa Rica to earn five leaves in the government-run Certified Sustainable

IMAGEBROKER/BELE OLMEZ

Parque Nacional Corcovado (p251)

Tourism program, Lapa Ríos also serves as a living classroom.

GETTING THERE & AWAY

A *colectivo* will drop you here; it passes by at about 6:30am and 2pm heading to Carate, and 10am and 5:30pm heading back to Jiménez. A taxi will come here from Puerto Jiménez for about ₡15,000.

CARATE

About 45km south of Puerto Jiménez, the dirt road that rounds the peninsula comes to an abrupt dead end in the village of Carate, which is literally nothing more than an airstrip and a *pulpería* (corner grocery store). Carate may not rate high on the list of Osa's top tourist destinations, but it does serve as the southwestern gateway for anyone hiking into Sirena ranger station.

SLEEPING

La Leona Eco-Lodge (☎ 2735-5704; www.laleonaecolodge.com; s/d from US$95/160; Ⓟ Ⓡ) On the edge of Parque Nacional Corcovado 2km west of the *pulpería,* this friendly lodge offers all of the thrills of camping, without the hassles. Sixteen comfy forest-green tents are nestled between the palm trees, with decks facing the beach. All are fully screened and comfortably furnished; solar power provides electricity in the restaurant.

Lookout Inn (☎ 2735-5431; www.lookout -inn.com; r per person from US$115; Ⓟ ▯ Ⓡ) A deep wilderness retreat, the Lookout has comfortable quarters with mural-painted walls, hardwood floors, beautifully carved doors and – you guessed it – unbeatable views. Accommodations are in 'tiki huts,' which are open-air, A-frame huts accessible only by a wooden walkway winding through the giant joba trees (prime bird-watching territory).

GETTING THERE & AWAY
AIR
NatureAir (www.natureair.com) and **Alfa Romeo Aero Taxi** www.alfaromeoair.com) offer charter flights.

TAXI
Transportation Colectivo (₡3000, 2½ hours) departs Puerto Jiménez for Carate at 6am and 1:30pm, returning at 8:30am and 4pm. Alternatively, catch a taxi from Puerto Jiménez (₡30,000).

PARQUE NACIONAL CORCOVADO

Famously labeled by *National Geographic* as 'the most biologically intense place on earth,' this **national park** (☎ 2735-5580; park fee per person per day US$10; ◷ 8am-noon & 1-4pm) is the last great original tract of tropical rainforest in Pacific Central America. The bastion of biological diversity has long attracted a devoted stream of visitors who descend from Bahía Drake and Puerto Jiménez to explore the remote location and spy on a wide array of rare wildlife.

INFORMATION

Information and maps are available at the **Oficina de Área de Conservación Osa** (p246) in Puerto Jiménez. Contact this office to make reservations for lodging and meals at all of the ranger stations and to pay your park fee.

ACTIVITIES
WILDLIFE-WATCHING
The best wildlife-watching in Corcovado is at Sirena, but the coastal trails have two advantages: they are more open, and the constant crashing of waves covers the sound of noisy walkers. White-faced capuchins, red-tailed squirrels, collared peccaries, white-nosed coatis and northern tamanduas are regularly seen on both

HIKING IN PARQUE NACIONAL CORCOVADO

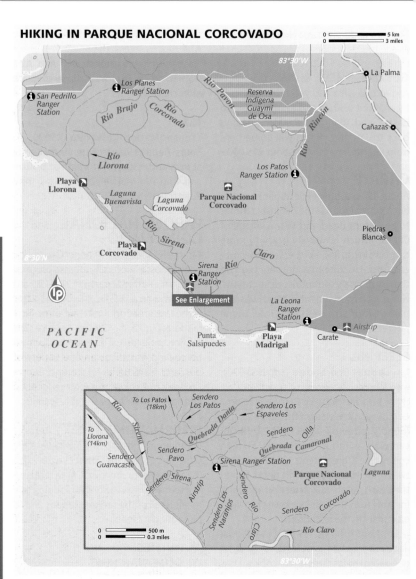

of the following trails. On the less-traveled San Pedrillo–Sirena trail, Playa Llorona is a popular nesting spot for marine turtles, including leatherback, olive ridley and green turtles. Both coastal trails produce an endless pageant of birds.

For wildlife-watchers frustrated by the difficulty of seeing rainforest mammals, a stay at Sirena ranger station is a must. Topping the list, Baird's tapirs are practically assured – that is a statement that can be made at few other places in the world. Sirena is excellent for other herbivores, both species of peccary, agoutis and tayras. Corcovado is the only national park in Costa Rica with all four of the country's primate species.

HIKING

The most popular route traverses the park from Los Patos to Sirena, then exits the park at La Leona (or vice versa). This allows hikers to begin and end their journey in or near Puerto Jiménez, offering easy access to La Leona and Los Patos. The trek between Sirena and San Pedrillo is more difficult, both physically and logistically. Hiking is best in the dry season (from December to April), when there is still regular rain but all of the trails are open. It's still muddy, but you won't sink quite as deep.

TOURS

The main routes across Parque Nacional Corcovado are well marked and well traveled, making the journey easy enough to complete independently. However, hiring a guide can greatly enhance this experience, not only because you will not have to worry about taking a wrong turn. Besides their intimate knowledge of the trail, local guides are amazingly knowledgeable about flora and fauna, including the best places to spot various species.

Guides are most often hired through the park office in Puerto Jiménez, at any of the ranger stations heading into the park, or near the airstrip in either Carate or Sirena. As you'd imagine, prices vary considerably depending on the season, availability, the size of your party and the type of expedition you want to arrange. In all cases, you want to negotiate a price that is inclusive of park fees, meals and transportation to the park.

Corcovado Expeditions (Map p242; ☎ 8818-9962; www.corcovadoexpeditions. net) is a recommended company that offers competitively priced tours to Corcovado as well as a wide variety of specialty hikes including unique excursions to look for rare tropical birds and poison-dart frogs.

TOM BOYDEN

Collared peccaries roam throughout Costa Rica's national parks

SLEEPING & EATING

Camping costs US$4 per person per day at any station; facilities include potable water and latrines. Sirena ranger station has a covered platform, but other stations have no such luxuries. Remember to bring a flashlight or a kerosene lamp, as the campsites are pitch black at night. Camping is not permitted in areas other than the ranger stations.

Simple dormitory lodging (US$12) and meals are available at Sirena station only. Food and cooking fuel have to be packed in, so reserve at least 15 to 30 days in advance through the **Oficina de Área de Conservación Osa** (p246) in Puerto Jiménez. Scientists and researchers working at the Sirena biological station get preference over travelers for accommodations and meals, but if you secure a reservation, you will be taken care of.

Otherwise, campers must bring all their own food. Note that ranger stations face a challenge with trash disposal, so all visitors are required to pack out all of their trash.

GETTING THERE & AWAY
AIR
Alfa Romeo Aero Taxi (☎ 2735-5353; www. alfaromeoair.com) offers charter flights connecting Puerto Jiménez, Drake and Golfito to Carate and Sirena.

BUS
In the southeast, the closest point of access is Carate, from where La Leona station is a one-hour, 3.5km hike west along the beach.

HIKING
From Bahía Drake, you can walk the coastal trail that leads to San Pedrillo station (about four hours from Agujitas), or any lodge can drop you here as a part of their regular tours to Corcovado. Alternatively, you can consider heading inland to the Los Planes station, though this is a longer, more heavily forested route.

GOLFITO

As the largest town in Golfo Dulce, Golfito is a major transportation hub for hikers heading to Corcovado, surfers heading to Pavones and sportfishers docking for the night. Although it's unlikely that you'll want to stick around for any longer than you have to, there is a certain charm to this historic banana port slowly fading into obscurity.

SLEEPING
La Purruja Lodge (☎ 2775-1054; www. purruja.com; 4.5km south of Golfito; s/d/tr incl breakfast US$30/40/50; P 🖳 🛜 🐾) A delightful Swiss-Tica couple runs this secluded lodge, which is home to five simple but sparkling cabins that have all the necessary comforts. The tranquil and tree-filled grounds are renowned for bird sightings, and the personable owners can organize tours throughout the area.

Las Gaviotas Hotel (☎ 2775-0062; s/d/tr US$65/75/85; P 🞬 🖳 🛜 🐾) This decidedly low-key resort hotel comprises a clutch of stucco cabins set amid a lovely tropical garden. Here, you can pass the time in Golfito proper by sipping rum on your private porch or doing a few laps in the inviting pool.

GETTING THERE & AWAY
AIR
The airport is 4km north of the town center near the duty-free zone. **NatureAir** (www.natureair.com) and **Sansa** (www.sansa. com) have daily flights to/from San José.

BOAT
Two passenger ferries travel to Puerto Jiménez from the Muellecito (₡3000, 1½ hours), departing at 6am and 10am daily.

The boat taxi for Zancudo (₡2500, 45 minutes) departs from the dock at Samoa del Sur hotel at noon, Monday through Saturday. The return trip is at 7:30am the next day (except Sunday).

If you're staying at any of the coastal lodges north of Golfito and you've made prior arrangements for transportation, the lodge will send a boat to pick you up at the docks.

BUS

Pavones ₡2500; three hours; departs at 10am and 3pm. This service may be af-fected by road and weather conditions, especially in the rainy season.

San José, via San Isidro (Tracopa) ₡4700; seven hours; departs from the terminal near Muelle Bananero at 5am and 1:30pm.

Zancudo ₡2500; three hours; departs at 1:30pm.

ZANCUDO

Occupying a slender finger of land that juts into the Golfo Dulce, the tiny village of Zancudo is about as laid-back a beach destination as you'll find in Costa Rica. On the west side of town, gentle, warm

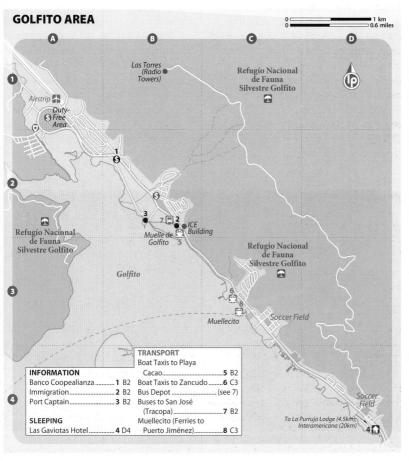

GOLFITO AREA

0 — 1 km
0 — 0.6 miles

Las Torres (Radio Towers)

Refugio Nacional de Fauna Silvestre Golfito

Airstrip

Duty-Free Area

Refugio Nacional de Fauna Silvestre Golfito

Golfito

Muelle de Golfito

ICE Building

Refugio Nacional de Fauna Silvestre Golfito

Muellecito

Soccer Field

To La Purruja Lodge (4.5km); Interamericana (20km)

Soccer Field

INFORMATION
Banco Coopealianza **1** B2
Immigration **2** B2
Port Captain **3** B2

SLEEPING
Las Gaviotas Hotel **4** D4

TRANSPORT
Boat Taxis to Playa
Cacao **5** B2
Boat Taxis to Zancudo **6** C3
Bus Depot .... (see **7**)
Buses to San José
(Tracopa) **7** B2
Muellecito (Ferries to
Puerto Jiménez) **8** C3

Pacific waters lap onto black sands. On the east side, a tangle of mangrove swamps attracts birds, crocodiles and plenty of fish. Unlike nearby Pavones, an emerging surf destination, Zancudo is content to remain a far-flung village in a far-flung corner of Costa Rica.

ACTIVITIES

The main activities at Zancudo are undoubtedly swinging on hammocks, strolling on the beach and **swimming** in the aqua-blue waters of the Golfo Dulce. Here, the surf is gentle, and at night the water sometimes sparkles with bioluminescence – tiny phosphorescent marine plants and plankton that light up if you sweep a hand through the water. The effect is like underwater fireflies.

The **mangrove swamps** offer plenty of opportunities for exploration: birdlife is prolific, while other animals such as crocodiles, caimans, monkeys and sloths are also frequently spotted. The boat ride from Golfito gives a glimpse of these waters, but you can also paddle them

yourself: rent kayaks from any of the accommodations listings following.

SLEEPING & EATING

Cabinas Los Cocos (☎ 2776-0012; www. loscocos.com; cabins US$60; P) This unique beachfront lodge is home to two historic cabins that used to be banana company homes in Palmar but were transported to Zancudo, reassembled and completely refurbished. The other two more-spacious cabins are also charming, with loft sleeping areas under palm-frond roofs.

Oceano (☎ 2776-0921; http://bestcostarica-vacations.com; r US$79; P) With its back to the beach, this friendly little Canadian-run inn has just two rooms, both spacious and airy with wood-beamed ceiling, tiled bathroom and quaint details like throw pillows and folk art. The open-air restaurant is also inviting for dinner or drinks, especially if the sea has been kind to the local fishermen.

Playa Zancudo Bed & Breakfast (☎ 2776-0006; www.playazancudobedand breakfast.com; r from US$80; P ✖ ☐) This

Parque Nacional Chirripó (p262)

ADRIAN HEPWORTH/HEPWORTHIMAGES

American-run B&B also has just two rooms in a vaulted plantation-style house adorned with rich hardwoods and accentuated by sweeping verandas. Another highly personable option; guests receive intimate service and attention throughout their stay.

GETTING THERE & AWAY
BOAT
A water taxi to Golfito (₡2500, 45 minutes) departs from the dock at 7am, returning at noon, Monday through Saturday.

BUS
The bus for Golfito (₡2500) leaves at 5am for the three-hour trip, with a ferry transfer at the Río Coto Colorado.

PAVONES
Home to what is reportedly the longest left-hand surf break on the planet, Pavones is a legendary destination for surfers the world over. As this is Costa Rica's southernmost point, you'll need to work hard to get down here. However, the journey is an adventure in its own right. And although the village is off the beaten path, both foreigners and Ticos are transforming Pavones from a relative backwater into a hip and happening hot spot.

SIGHTS
Set on a verdant hillside between Pavones and Punta Banco, the **Tiskita Jungle Lodge** (☎ in San José 2296-8125; www.tiskita-lodge.co.cr; guided hike US$15) consists of 100 hectares of virgin forest and a huge orchard, which produces more than 100 varieties of tropical fruit from all over the world. Fourteen trails wind through surrounding rainforest, which contains waterfalls and freshwater pools suitable for swimming.

ACTIVITIES
SURFING
Pavones has become legendary among surfers for its wicked long left. Some claim it is among the world's longest, offering a two- or three-minute ride on a good day. Conditions are best with a southern swell, usually between April and October.

YOGA
Yoga Farm (www.yogafarmcostarica.org; dm/r per night US$35/40, per week US$175/240) This yoga retreat center and working farm is a unique and welcome addition to Pavones. The price includes accommodations in simple and clean rooms with wood bunk beds; three vegetarian meals, prepared primarily with ingredients from the organic garden; and daily yoga classes, which take place in a fabulous open-air studio overlooking the ocean. This place is a 15-minute walk from Rancho Burica in Punta Banco: take the road going up the hill to the left, go through the first gate on the left and keep walking up the hill. Inquire about volunteer opportunities.

SLEEPING & EATING
Riviera Riverside Villas (☎ 8823-5874; www.pavonesriviera.com; s/d US$85/90; P 🐾) This clutch of villas in Pavones proper offers fully equipped kitchens, cool tile floors and attractive hardwood ceilings. Big shady porches overlook the landscaped gardens, which offer a degree of intimacy and privacy found at few other places in town.

Casa Siempre Domingo (☎ 8820-4709; www.casa-domingo.com; d/tr US$100/150; P) The most unbelievable views of Golfo Dulce are from this luxurious B&B, perched high in the hills above Pavones. Lodgings at the 'Always Sunday House' are elegant and glorious, with soaring cathedral ceilings and an overwhelming sense of openness.

Tiskita Jungle Lodge (☎ in San José 2296-8125; www.tiskita-lodge.co.cr; s/d from US$155/275; P ▯ ▯ ▯ ▯ ▯) Set amid extensive gardens and orchards, this lodge is arguably the most beautiful and intimate in all of Golfo Dulce. Accommodations are in a clutch of stunning wooden cabins accented by stone garden showers that allow you to freshen up while you go bird-watching. Daily rates include fresh home-cooked meals and guided walks.

Esquina del Mar Cantina (dishes ₡1500-2500) A Pavones institution that has great views of the left break, this is where you should grab a drink after your last ride.

GETTING THERE & AWAY

AIR
NatureAir (www.natureair.com) and **Alfa Romeo Aero Taxi** (www.alfaromeoair.com) offer charter flights.

BUS
Two daily buses go to Golfito (₡2500, three hours) at 5:30am and 12:30pm.

TAXI
A 4WD taxi will charge about US$50 from Golfito.

PARQUE NACIONAL ISLA DEL COCOS

In the opening minutes of the classic film *Jurassic Park,* a small helicopter swoops over and around Isla Nublar, a lushly forested island with dramatic tropical peaks descending straight into clear blue waters. The inspiration for this silver-screen island was none other than Isla del Cocos, and that single scene turned Costa Rica's most remote national park into much more than a figment of our collective imagination.

ORIENTATION
Isla del Cocos is around 500km southwest of the mainland in the middle of the eastern Pacific, and is often referred to as the 'Costa Rican Galápagos' due to both its total isolation and unique ecosystem. As it's the most far-flung corner of Costa Rica, you will have to join up with an organized tour, though few other destinations in the country are as wildly exotic and visually arresting.

SIGHTS & ACTIVITIES
The famous oceanographer and diving guru Jacques Cousteau famously dubbed Cocos 'the most beautiful island in the world.' Rugged, heavily forested and punctuated by cascading waterfalls, Cocos is ringed and transected by an elaborate network of trails. The highest point is at **Cerro Iglesias** (634m), where you can soak up spectacular views of the lush, verdant island and the deep-blue Pacific.

Named by PADI (Professional Association of Diving Instructors) as one of the world's top 10 dive spots, the surrounding waters of Isla del Cocos harbor abundant pelagics including one of the largest known schools of hammerhead sharks in the world.

TOURS
Two liveaboard dive operators, both of which dock their vessels in Puntarenas (p210), offer guided excursions to the island. Diving and food are included in the tour prices listed below.

Okeanos Aggressor (☎ in USA 866-653-2667; www.aggressor.com/subpage10.php) Offers eight-/10-day land and sea expeditions with room for 22 from US$3335/3735 per person.

Undersea Hunter (☎ 2228-6613, in USA 800-203-2120; www.underseahunter.com) Offers

10-/12-day land and sea expeditions with room for 14/18 people from US$4750/5150 per person.

GETTING THERE & AWAY

With advance reservations, the tour companies listed will arrange your transfers from San José or Liberia through to Puntarenas.

SAN ISIDRO DE EL GENERAL

pop 45,000

Considering that most settlements in the southern zone are mere mountain villages, it doesn't take much in these parts to be called a 'big city.' Indeed, 'El General' is the region's largest population center and major transportation hub, so it's likely that you'll pass through here at some point in your travels.

INFORMATION

Ciprotur (☎ 2770-9393; www.ecotourism.co.cr; Calle 4 btwn Avs 1 & 3; ☺ 7:30am-5pm Mon-Fri, 8am-noon Sat) Tourist office with information about the southern region.

Minae park service office (Sinac; ☎ 2771-3155; aclap@sinac.go.cr; Calle 2 btwn Avs 2 & 4; ☺ 8am-noon & 1-4pm Mon-Fri) Dispenses very basic information about Parque Nacional Chirripó. Make reservations here for the mountaintop hostel at Chirripó; see p263 for details.

SLEEPING & EATING

Hotel Los Crestones (☎ 2770-1200, 2770-1500; www.hotelloscrestones.com/es/index.php; Calle Central at Av 14; s/d from US$36/48; P ⊠) This sharp motor court is decked with blooming flowerboxes and climbing vines outside, which is indeed a welcome sight to the road-weary traveler. Inside, functional rooms feature modern

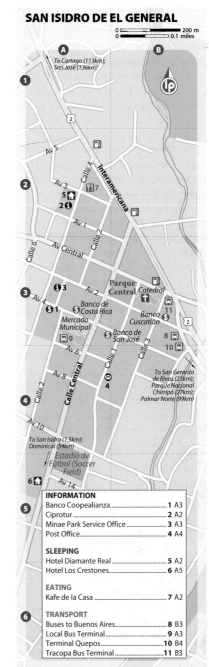

SAN ISIDRO DE EL GENERAL

INFORMATION	
Banco Coopealianza	**1** A3
Ciprotur	**2** A2
Minae Park Service Office	**3** A3
Post Office	**4** A4

SLEEPING	
Hotel Diamante Real	**5** A2
Hotel Los Crestones	**6** A5

EATING	
Kafe de la Casa	**7** A2

TRANSPORT	
Buses to Buenos Aires	**8** B3
Local Bus Terminal	**9** A3
Terminal Quepos	**10** B4
Tracopa Bus Terminal	**11** B3

furnishings and fixtures, which are made all the better by the attentive staff that keep this place running efficiently.

Hotel Diamante Real (☎ 2770-6230; www.hoteldiamantereal.com; cnr Av 3 & Calle 4; standard/luxury r US$40/60; P ⊠ ▯ ⊚ ﴾) 'Executive Elegance' is the boast of this upscale business hotel, which is surprisingly swish for fairly understated San Isidro. The classy quarters are painted bright yellow and fitted with shiny black-lacquer furniture to complete the executive package.

Kafe de la Casa (Av 3 btwn Calles 2 & 4; meals ₡3000-6500; ☽ 7am-8pm) Set in an old Tico house, this bohemian cafe features brightly painted rooms decorated with eclectic artwork, an open kitchen and shady garden seating. With a menu featuring excellent breakfasts, light lunches, gourmet dinners and plenty of coffee drinks, this funky place receives a stream of regulars.

GETTING THERE & AWAY
BUS
FROM TRACOPA TERMINAL

Palmar Norte ₡2000; three hours; departs at 4:45am, 7:30am, 12:30pm and 3pm.

San José ₡2100; three hours; departs at 7:30am, 8am, 9:30am, 10:30am, 11am, 1:30pm, 4pm, 5:45pm and 7:30pm.

San Vito ₡2100; three hours; departs at 5:30am and 2pm.

FROM TERMINAL QUEPOS

Dominical ₡1800; 2½ hours; departs at 7am, 8am, 1:30pm and 4pm.

Palmar Norte ₡2000; three hours; departs at 6:30am and 3pm.

Puerto Jiménez ₡3000; five hours; departs at 6:30am and 3pm.

Quepos ₡2000; three hours; departs at 7am and 1:30pm.

Uvita ₡800; 1½ hours; departs at 8:30am and 4pm.

Shoal of bigeye trevally, Isla del Cocos (p258)

NPR/IMAGEBROKER

SOUTHERN COSTA RICA

Tiskita Jungle Lodge, Pavones (p257)

VARIO IMAGES GMBH & CO.KG/ALAMY

SAN GERARDO DE RIVAS

FROM OTHER BUS STOPS
The following buses originate in San Isidro:

Buenos Aires (Gafeso) ₡650; one hour; departs hourly from 5am to 5pm from north of Terminal Quepos.

San Gerardo de Rivas, for Parque Nacional Chirripó ₡1800; 2½ hours; departs from Parque Central at 5am and from the local terminal on Av 6 at 2pm.

TAXI
A 4WD taxi to San Gerardo de Rivas will cost between ₡10,000 and ₡15,000. To arrange one, it's best to inquire through your accommodations.

SAN GERARDO DE RIVAS
If you have plans to climb to the summit of Chirripó, then you're in the right place – the tiny but tranquil town of San Gerardo de Rivas marks the entrance to the national park. Here, you can make reservations for accommodations within the park, pick up a few last-minutes supplies and – perhaps most important of all –

get a good night's rest, a decent meal and a hot shower before embarking on the trek.

INFORMATION
The **Chirripó ranger station** (Sinac; ☎ 2200-5348; ☽ 6:30am-noon & 1-4:30pm) is located about 1km below the soccer field on the road from San Isidro. Stop by here (the earlier the better) to check for space and availability at Crestones Base Lodge (p264), and to confirm and pay your fee before setting out.

SLEEPING & EATING
Casa Mariposa (☎ 2742-5037; www.hotel casamariposa.net; dm US$13, s/d US$17/30; P ⬚) This warm and welcoming backpacker hostel offers an excellent communal atmosphere that is conducive to picking up a few travel companions for the Chirripó trek. Carved out of the side of the mountain, the close but cozy quarters have stone walls and plenty of character.

Albergue de Montaña El Pelicano (☎ 8382-3000; r/cabins from US$20/40; P ⬚)

About 300m below the ranger station, this simple but functional budget lodge has a collection of spartan but spotless rooms that overlook the river valley. The highlight of the property is the gallery of the owner, a late-blooming artist who sculpts whimsical wood pieces.

Talamanca Reserve (☎ 2772-1715; www. talamancareserve.com; r/ste US$70/80; P 🖳) This sprawling 16-sq-km private reserve is dotted with Talamanca indigenous sculptures that pose ominously among the stone cabins. Spacious interiors are furnished with lacquered wood and highlighted by picture windows, which open up to an impressive network of hiking trails.

Río Chirripó Retreat (☎ 2742-5109; www. riochirripo.com; Canaán; r per person incl 3 meals from US$80; P 🖳 📶 📺) About 1.5km below the ranger station, in Canaán, this upscale lodge is centered on both a beautiful yoga studio overlooking the river, and a vast open-air, Santa Fe–style communal area. You can hear the rush of the river from eight secluded cabins,

where woven blankets and stenciled walls evoke the southwest USA.

GETTING THERE & AWAY
Buses to San Isidro depart from the soccer field at 7am and 4pm (₡1800, 2½ hours). The ranger station for Chirripó is about 18km up this road from the Interamericana – any of the accommodations listed above can arrange onward private transportation.

PARQUE NACIONAL CHIRRIPÓ
Parque Nacional Chirripó offers a respite from the heat and humidity of the rainforest. Cerro Chirripó, at 3820m above sea level, is the highest and most famous summit in Costa Rica. The only way up to Chirripó is by foot, and you will have to be prepared for the cold and wet slog to the top. Although the trekking routes are long and challenging, watching the sunrise over the Caribbean from such lofty heights is an undeniable highlight of traveling in Costa Rica.

Three-toed sloth with baby, Parque Nacional Chirripó

ORIENTATION

The dry season (from late December to April) is the most popular time to visit Chirripó. February and March are the driest months, though it may still rain. On weekends, and especially during holidays, the park is crowded with Tico hiking groups, and the mountaintop hostel is often full. The park is closed in May, but the early months of the rainy season are still good for climbing as it usually doesn't rain in the morning.

INFORMATION

It is essential that you stop at the **Chirripó ranger station (Sinac; ☎ 2200-5348; ☺ 6:30am-noon & 1-4:30pm)** at least one day before you intend to climb Chirripó so that you can check availability at the mountaintop hostel and pay your park entry fee (US$15 for two days, plus US$10 for each additional day). Space at the hostel is limited, so it's best to arrive early – first thing in the morning – to inquire about space on the following day. Even if you have a reservation, you must stop here the day before to confirm (bring your reservation and payment confirmation). You can also make arrangements here to hire a porter (about US$30 to US$50 for up to15kg) or to store your luggage while you hike.

CLIMBING CHIRRIPÓ

The park entrance is at San Gerardo de Rivas, which lies 1350m above sea level; from here the summit is 2.5km straight up! An easy-to-follow 16km trail leads all the way to the top and no technical climbing is required.

Allow seven to 14 hours to cover the 10km from the trailhead to the hostel, depending on how fit you are: the recommended departure time is 5am or 6am. The trailhead lies 50m beyond Albergue Urán in San Gerardo de Rivas (about 4km from the ranger station). The main gate is open from 4am to 10am to allow climbers to enter; no one is allowed to begin the ascent after 10am. Inside the park the trail is clearly signed at every kilometer.

The open-sided hut at **Llano Bonito**, halfway up, is a good place for a lunch break. There is shelter and water, but it is intended for emergency use, not overnight stays.

About 6km from the trailhead, the **Monte Sin Fe** (which translates as 'Mountain Without Faith'; this climb is not for the faint of heart) is a preliminary crest that reaches 3200m. You then enjoy 2km with gravity in your favor, before making the 2km ascent to the Crestones Base Lodge at 3400m.

Reaching the hostel is the hardest part. From there the hike to the summit is about 6km on relatively flatter terrain (although the last 100m is very steep): allow at least two hours if you are fit, but carry a warm jacket, rain gear, water, snacks and a flashlight just in case. From the summit on a clear day, the vista stretches to both the Caribbean Sea and the Pacific Ocean. The deep-blue lakes and the plush-green hills carpet the Valle de las Morenas in the foreground. Readers recommend leaving the base camp at 3am to arrive in time to watch the sunrise from the summit.

TOURS

Some travelers prefer to access the park either independently or by hiring a local guide, though **Costa Rica Trekking** (☎ 2771-4582; www.chirripo.com) is highly recommended if you prefer organized adventure. This well-established company offers several different guided excursions around Chirripó, ranging from a one-day trek to Llano Bonito to a four-day trek around the Urán loop. Note that prices are variable, and ultimately dependant on the size of the party and the time of year.

SLEEPING & EATING

The only accommodations in Parque Nacional Chirripó are at **Crestones Base Lodge** (Centro Ambientalista el Parámo; dm US$10), housing up to 60 people in dorm-style bunks. The basic stone building has a solar panel that provides electric light from 6pm to 8pm and sporadic heat for showers. The lodge rents a variety of gear including sleeping bags, blankets, cooking equipment and gas canisters for a few dollars per day.

Reservations are absolutely necessary at Crestones Base Lodge. Your tour company will likely make reservations for you; but for those traveling independently, it is virtually impossible to make reservations before your arrival in Costa Rica. Once in Costa Rica, however, it is necessary to contact the **Minae office** (☎ 2771-3155; fax 2771-3297; aclap@sinac.go.cr) in San Isidro. If space is available, you will be required to pay by credit card in order to confirm the reservation. You must present your reservation and payment confirmation at the ranger station in San Gerardo de Rivas on the day before you set out.

Fortunately, the lodge reserves 10 spaces per night for travelers who show up in San Gerardo and are ready to hike on the following day. This is the more practical option for most travelers, although there is no guarantee that there will be space available on the days you wish to hike. Space is at a premium during holiday periods and on weekends during the dry season. The ranger station opens at 6:30am – the earlier you arrive, the more likely you will be able to hike the following day.

Crestones Base Lodge provides drinking water, but no food. Hikers must bring all of their own provisions.

GETTING THERE & AWAY

See information under San Gerardo de Rivas for directions on how to get here (p262).

Parque Nacional Chirripó (p262)

RESERVA INDÍGENA BORUCA

The picturesque valley of the Río Grande de Térraba is the setting for the various towns that comprise the indigenous reserve of Boruca (Brunka) peoples. At first glance it is difficult to differentiate these towns from a typical Tico village, aside from a few artisans selling their handiwork. In fact, these towns hardly cater to the tourist trade, which is one of the main reasons why traditional Boruca life is continuing on without much distraction.

HISTORY

Historians believe that the present-day Boruca have evolved out of several different indigenous groups, including the Coto, Quepos, Turrucaca, Burucac and Abubaes, whose territories stretched all the way to the Península de Osa in pre-Columbian times. Today, however, the entire Boruca population is largely confined to the small villages of Rey Curré, which is bisected by the Carretera Interamericana, and Boruca, 8km north.

SIGHTS

Rey Curré (usually just 'Curré' on maps) is about 30km south of Buenos Aires, right on the Interamericana. Drivers can stop to visit a small **cooperative** (9am-5pm Mon-Fri, 2-5pm Sat) that sells handicrafts. In Boruca, local artisans post signs outside their homes advertising their handmade balsa masks and woven bags. Exhibits are sometimes on display in the informal **museum** (hours vary), a thatched-roof *rancho* 100m west of the *pulpería* (corner grocery store).

FESTIVALS & EVENTS

The **Fiesta de los Diablitos** is a three-day Boruca event that symbolizes the

Resplendent quetzal

MSI/IMAGEBROKER

⇖ IF YOU LIKE...

If you like **Parque Nacional Chirripó** (p262), we think you'll like these other national parks in the southern zone:

- **Cloudbridge Nature Preserve** A tiny private reserve on the slopes of Cerro Chirripó that is operated by two New Yorkers, and is the site of an ongoing reforestation project.
- **Parque Nacional Los Quetzales** Costa Rica's newest national park is extremely rich in birdlife and offers a good chance of spotting the quetzal in all its resplendent glory.
- **Reserva Biológica Dúrika** This private reserve within Parque Internacional La Amistad is home to an independent, sustainable community committed to conservation.

struggle between the Spanish and the indigenous population. Sometimes called the Danza de los Diablitos, or 'dance of the little devils,' the culmination of the festival is a choreographed battle between the opposing sides. Villagers wearing wooden devil masks and burlap costumes play the role of the natives in their fight against the Spanish conquerors. The Spaniards, represented

BETH WALD/AURORA PHOTOS

Playing soccer in the rainforest, Península de Osa

by a man in a bull costume, lose the battle. This festival is held in Boruca from December 31 to January 2 and in Curré from February 5 to 8.

The lesser-known **Fiesta de los Negritos**, held during the second week of December, celebrates the Virgin of the Immaculate Conception. Traditional indigenous music (mainly drumming and bamboo flutes) accompanies dancing and costumes.

SLEEPING & EATING

The only regular place to stay in the area is at the Tico-owned **Bar Restaurante Boruca** (☎ 2730-2454; d from US$10) in Boruca, which consists of five basic rooms with cold-water bathroom.

However, for a more in-depth understanding of the Boruca culture and lifestyle, it's recommended that you arrange a homestay through **Pedro Rojas Morales** (☎ 506-362-2545; saribu@yahoo.com). A soft-spoken Boruca artist who is certainly a local expert, Señor Morales can help you arrange a wide range of activities on the reservation. Prices are negotiable.

SHOPPING

The Boruca are celebrated craftspeople and their traditional art plays a leading role in the survival of their culture. While most people make their living from agriculture, some indigenous people have begun producing fine handicrafts for tourists. The tribe is most famous for its ornate masks, carved from balsa or cedar, and sometimes colored with natural dyes and acrylics. Boruca women also use pre-Columbian backstrap looms to weave colorful, natural cotton bags, placemats and other textiles.

GETTING THERE & AWAY

You will need private transportation to access the indigenous reserve – a 4WD road leaves the Interamericana about 3km south of Curré (look for the sign), and it's another 5km to the village of Boruca. A taxi from Buenos Aires to Boruca is about ₡10,000.

SAN VITO

Founded by Italian immigrants in the 1950s, San Vito is home to their descendants, who have retained their language and culture (not to mention their cuisine!). Of course, this is no small feat considering that this remote mountain town is located on the edge of Parque Internacional La Amistad, one of Central America's last great frontier areas. As such, the town serves as a base for travelers in need of a hot meal and a good night's sleep before descending into the deep wilderness.

INFORMATION

If you're planning on heading to La Amistad, San Vito is home to the **Minae parks office** (☎ 2773-3955; 9am-4pm), which can help you get your bearings before heading to the national park.

SIGHTS

About 3km south of town, **Finca Cántaros** (☎ 2773-3760; admission US$1, campsites per person US$6; 9:30am-5pm Tue-Sun;) is a recreation center, campground and reforestation project. The 10 hectares of grounds – which used to be coffee plantations and pastureland – are now a lovely park with garden trails, picnic areas and a dramatic lookout over the city. The reception is housed in a cabin that contains a small selection of local and national crafts.

SLEEPING & EATING

Hotel El Ceibo (☎ 2773-3025; s/d from US$35/45;) The best option in town – though fairly subdued by any account – is El Ceibo, conveniently located about 100m west of the main intersection. Here, you can sleep easy in simple but functional rooms (some with forest views) and dig into some truly authentic Italian pastas and wines.

Pizzería Restaurante Lilliana (pizza ₡2000-4500; 10:30am-10pm) This great spot for Italian fare proudly offers more than a dozen different kinds of pizza, all of which are made from scratch. The mountain views and old-world environs make this a pleasant place to spend an afternoon.

GETTING THERE & AWAY

AIR

Alfa Romeo Aero Taxi (www.alfaromeoair.com) offers charter flights to San Vito from Puerto Jiménez and Golfito.

BUS

San Isidro ₡2100; three hours; departs at 6:45am and 1:30pm.

San José ₡4200; seven hours; departs at 5am, 7:30am, 10am and 3pm.

PARQUE INTERNACIONAL LA AMISTAD

This 4070-sq-km international park was established jointly in 1988 by Panama and Costa Rica – hence its Spanish name, La Amistad (Friendship). It is by far the largest protected area in Costa Rica, and stands as a testament to the possibilities of international cooperation in the name of environmental conservation. In 1990 La Amistad was declared a Unesco World Heritage Site, and later became part of the greater Mesoamerican Biological corridor, which protects a great variety of endangered habitats. Although most of the park's area is high up in the Talamanca, and remains virtually inaccessible, there is no shortage of hiking and camping opportunities available for intrepid travelers at lower altitudes.

La Amistad Lodge (☎ 2200-5037, in San José 2289-7667; www.laamistad.com; s/d US$100/175;) is about 3km by poor dirt road from the village of Las Mellizas, and sits on 100 sq km of wilderness and organic farmland. Since 1940, the congenial Montero family has worked the land, and balanced the needs of development with the protection of the environment. The main lodge has tropical hardwood cabins with hot water and electricity provided by a low-impact hydroelectric plant. Four additional jungle camps have been built at different altitudes and habitats, allowing visitors to do a multiday trek around the area without leaving the comforts of a solid bed and good cooking. The extensive network of trails (40km) is excellent for bird-watching and horseback riding. Guests are also invited to participate in the harvesting and processing (and drinking) of the homegrown coffee. Check its website for detailed directions on accessing the lodge by 4WD.

CARIBBEAN COAST

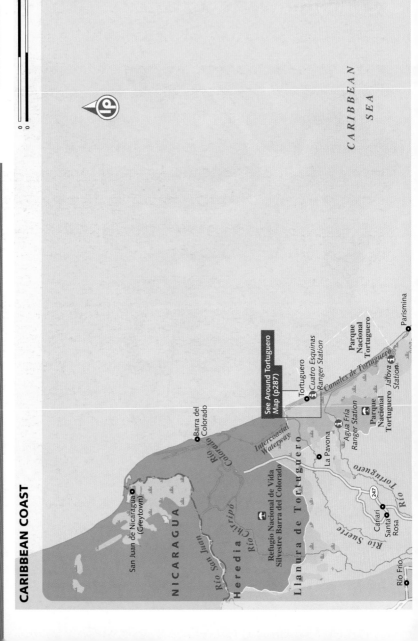

30 km
20 miles

0
0

CARIBBEAN SEA

San Juan de Nicaragua
(Greytown)

Barra del
Colorado

NICARAGUA

Río San Juan

Río Colorado

Heredia

Río Chirripó

Refugio Nacional de Vida
Silvestre Barra del Colorado

Intercoastal
Waterway

Llanura de Tortuguero

See Around Tortuguero
Map (p287)

Tortuguero

Cuatro Esquinas
Ranger Station

Canales de Tortuguero

Parque
Nacional
Tortuguero

Agua Fría
Ranger Station

La Pavona

Parque
Nacional
Tortuguero Jalova
Station

Parismina

247

Cariari

Santa
Rosa

Río Tortuguero

Río Suerte

Río Frío

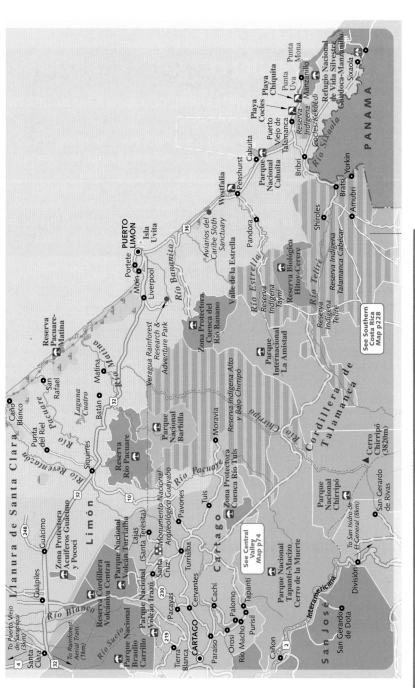

CARIBBEAN COAST HIGHLIGHTS

1 MANZANILLO

BY SHAWN LARKIN, CO-OWNER/MANAGER OF COSTA CETACEA

This town has the most positive vibe of any place I know. Roots, reef and rainforest round out one little community. Here grows a beautiful tolerance – no matter where you're from, you can make friends immediately. Everything's within walking, swimming or paddling distance. The town lives up to its slogan: in Manzanillo the least you can get is the best.

⤴ SHAWN LARKIN'S DON'T MISS LIST

❶ JOURNEY TO PUNTA MONA

One of the best adventures you can have in the Manzanillo area involves following the coastal trail to **Punta Mona** (p298) in the Refugio Nacional de Vida Silvestre Gandoca-Manzanillo. On land, you'll traverse an incredible range of biomes as you put your calf muscles to the test. Or, instead of hiking, you can rent an ocean kayak and follow the winding coastline with paddle in hand.

❷ DOLPHIN-WATCHING

There are several species of **dolphin** (p298) that call the Caribbean Sea home, though the most widely known species is the Atlantic bottlenose. Their playful and dramatic antics are truly memorable, and easily one of the highlights of the shallow seas near Manzanillo. With a knowledgeable guide, you can watch these amazing creatures from a safe distance (as it's illegal in Costa Rica to get closer than 100m to dolphins in the wild).

Clockwise from top: Spiny lobsters; beach at Manzanillo (p296)

CLOCKWISE FROM TOP: MARK WEBSTER; IMAGEBROKER/SIEPMANN

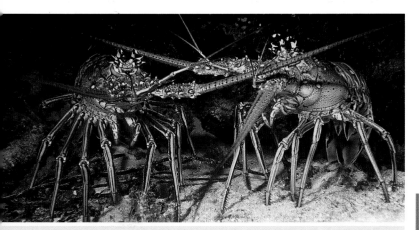

❸ CORAL REEFS

Directly in front of town you'll find a number of unique coral reef formations, called Sugar, Bloody, Jimmy and Wash a Woman. The easiest way to explore the underwater world is to don a mask, fins and snorkel, and spend an hour or so cruising above the reef and occasionally diving down for a closer look. Alternatively, try your hand at either surfing or kayaking, and see if you can catch a reef break as it sweeps across the shoreline.

❹ SCUBA DIVING

The best way to explore the ocean depths is to rent scuba gear, and bring along an experienced divemaster for the plunge. In addition to the nearby outlying reefs, there are some further-flung dive spots that harbor astonishing varieties of marine life. From spiny lobsters hiding in the rock beds to enormous pelagics such as pilot whales, the Caribbean Sea is a never-ending showcase of some of the planet's weirdest and most wonderful wildlife.

↘ THINGS YOU NEED TO KNOW

Access You can bed down in Manzanillo (p296) or visit on a day trip from nearby Puerto Viejo de Talamanca (p292) **Sea-creature checklist** Tucuxi, spinner and bottlenose dolphins; leatherback, green, hawksbill and loggerhead turtles; spiny lobsters; pilot whales **See our author's coverage, p296**

CARIBBEAN COAST HIGHLIGHTS

2

↰ PARQUE NACIONAL TORTUGUERO

Shattering stereotypes of idyllic Caribbean landscapes, this **national park** (p287) is rugged and untamed. Navigation through Tortuguero's largely impenetrable jungles and expansive marshlands consists of canoeing down narrow waterways. Your reward? Phenomenal wildlife-watching, with nesting sea turtles, bounding troops of monkeys, and a few more dangling serpents than you'd care to spot.

3

↰ PUERTO VIEJO DE TALAMANCA

This is without a doubt the cultural heart of the Caribbean coast. A loud and proud bastion of Rastafarianism, **Puerto Viejo** (p292) lures in countless visitors with the promise of Jamaican-influenced music and munchies. When you're not either jamming to reggae beats or stuffing your face full of jerk chicken, you can simply kick back on a blissful stretch of sand while sipping fresh coconut milk.

⤴ CAHUITA

This Afro-Caribbean **beach town** (p289) isn't nearly as developed as Puerto Viejo de Talamanca, though that's exactly the way the local residents like it. Indeed, Cahuita offers a measure of authenticity that is missing from its brasher neighbor, not to mention that it's also the jumping-off point for a stunning national park of the same name.

⤴ RAINFOREST AERIAL TRAM

If you truly want to appreciate the scale of the rainforests lining the Caribbean coast, there is no better place than the **Rainforest Aerial Tram** (p283). Something of a glorified ski lift – minus the snow, of course – this tram carries you up into the canopy in search of lofty vegetation and high-flying avians.

⤴ SALSA BRAVA

This truly legendary **wave** (p293) has been chewing up and spitting out surfers for generations. A gnarly break just off the coast of Puerto Viejo de Talamanca, Salsa Brava is named for the heaped helping of 'spicy sauce' it serves up on the sharp, shallow reef, continually collecting its debt of fun in broken skin, boards and bones.

2 CHRISTER FREDRIKSSON; 3 CHRISTER FREDRIKSSON; 4 CHRISTER FREDRIKSSON; 5 MSI/IMAGEBROKER; 6 CHRISTIAN ASLUND

2 Parque Nacional Tortuguero (p287); 3 Puerto Viejo de Talamanca (p292); 4 Chestnut-mandibled toucan, Parque Nacional Cahuita (p289); 5 Rainforest Aerial Tram (p283); 6 Salsa Brava (p293), Puerto Viejo de Talamanca

THE CARIBBEAN COAST'S BEST...

⬎ JOURNEYS

- **Parque Nacional Tortuguero** (p287) Boating through remote backwaters is arguably the best journey in the Caribbean.
- **Puerto Viejo de Talamanca** (p292) Departing Puerto Viejo and cycling down the coast lets you slow down the pace and enjoy the journey.
- **Rainforest Aerial Tram** (p283) A true journey up into the clouds.

⬎ SPLURGES

- **Tortuga Lodge & Gardens** (p286) Take a break from the paddling by exploring acres of private gardens.
- **Cashew Hill Jungle Cottages** (p295) A secluded spot set far back from the Puerto Viejo scene.
- **Congo Bongo** (p297) Bed down in the middle of a reclaimed cacao plantation.

⬎ VISTAS

- **Parque Nacional Tortuguero** (p287) Panoramic views of incredible nature surround your tiny canoe.
- **Parque Nacional Cahuita** (p291) Watching the sunrise over Caribbean shores is a spiritual moment.
- **Salsa Brava** (p293) Even if you don't have the experience to ride this wave, watching others tackle the 'spicy sauce' is memorable.

⬎ EATS

- **Miss Miriam's** (p286) A popular locals' spot with authentic Caribbean cuisine.
- **El Loco Natural** (p295) This fusion bistro has some of the best eats in the entire country.
- **Maxi's Restaurant** (p297) Seafood specialists at the end of the coastal road.

CHRISTER FREDRIKSSON

Idyllic scenery of the Parque Nacional Cahuita (p291)

THINGS YOU NEED TO KNOW

⋙ VITAL STATISTICS

- **Population** Puerto Limón 27,000
- **Best time to visit** It rains throughout the year, though precipitation tends to be lighter in February and March, as well as in September and October.

⋙ BEACHES IN A NUTSHELL

- **Cahuita** (p289) Home to Playa Negra, a black-sand beach, and Playa Blanca, which has gray sand.
- **Parque Nacional Cahuita** (p291) Eight kilometers of coastal trails lead to all manner of stunning wilderness beaches.
- **Puerto Viejo de Talamanca** (p292) The region's most famous surf beach is best tackled with a short board, especially when the swells are high.
- **Refugio Nacional de Vida Silvestre Gandoca-Manzanillo** (p298) A stretch of white-sand beach is the focus of this nature reserve.

⋙ ADVANCE PLANNING

- **Surfing school** The Caribbean coast is home to some serious surf, which means you might want to practice elsewhere before showing up with board in hand.

⋙ RESOURCES

- **Costa Rica Tourism Board** (www.visitcostarica.com)
- **Tico Times** (www.ticotimes.net)

⋙ EMERGENCY NUMBERS

- **Emergency** (☎ 911)
- **Fire** (☎ 118)
- **Police** (☎ 117)

⋙ GETTING AROUND

- **Bicycle** From Puerto Viejo de Talamanca to Manzanillo, this is the best way to travel.
- **Boat** The only way to access Parque Nacional Tortuguero – other than flying in, of course.
- **Bus** The Caribbean coast is well serviced by buses, alleviating the need for a rental car.
- **Walk** Any of the region's beaches invite long sessions of beachcombing.

⋙ BE FOREWARNED

- **Crime** Puerto Limón has a few rough corners, so keep your wits about if you're transiting this gritty city.
- **Riptides** Currents can get ferocious, even in shallow waters, so pay attention to local advisories. If you find yourself caught in a riptide, immediately call for help. It's important to relax, conserve your energy and not fight the current.

CARIBBEAN COAST

THINGS YOU NEED TO KNOW

CARIBBEAN COAST ITINERARIES

PUERTO VIEJO & AROUND Three Days

If you can only spare a few days on the Caribbean coast, your port of call should be none other than Puerto Viejo de Talamanca. The region's most developed beach town will not only give you a good taste of Afro-Caribbean culture, but it also serves as a convenient jumping-off point for a few nearby attractions.

From **(1) San José** (p51), direct buses connect the capital to **(2) Puerto Viejo de Talamanca** (p292) in just a few hours of travel time. After arriving, stow your belongings at the accommodations of your choice, and make straight for the beach. Serious surfers should consider testing their mettle at the infamous Salsa Brava, while less-experienced riders can head next door to Playa Cocles. In the evenings, dine on some of the country's best cuisine and relax to the rhythm of the reggae beats. If you have extra energy to burn off, rent a bike and head along the 13km road past gorgeous palm-lined beaches to the idyllic community of **(3) Manzanillo** (p296), for some snorkeling, diving or kayaking.

EXPLORING TORTUGUERO Four Days

If you've got a bit more time – and a serious adventurous streak – you might want to consider forgoing Caribbean comforts and tackling the region's wildest national park. From spying on sea turtles to canoeing past caimans and crocodiles, Tortuguero is rightfully regarded as the Amazon in miniature.

After a brief stop in **(1) Puerto Limón** (p280), where you can take in the sights of the Caribbean's largest city, head to the docks in nearby **(2) Moín** (p282) for the real start of your journey. By boat, you'll travel the canal-lined coast to the remote village of **(3) Tortuguero** (p284). Although it's a destination in its own right, your journey continues into the jungles and mangroves of the surrounding **(4) Parque Nacional Tortuguero** (p287), a true wilderness area that is a world away from the airbrushed beach towns further down the coast.

CARIBBEAN BEACHCOMBER One Week

One week may seem like a lot of time to devote to such a small region, but this itinerary is perfect for anyone who is looking for utter relaxation without the need to travel too far. Once you've arrived on the coast, you can meander from beach to beach at your own pace, pausing frequently to soak up the Caribbean sun in its full tropical glory.

Your first port of call should be **(1) Cahuita** (p289), a terminally laid-back village that is home to a lovely pair of beaches, namely Playa Negra and Playa Blanca. But the main attraction is the adja-

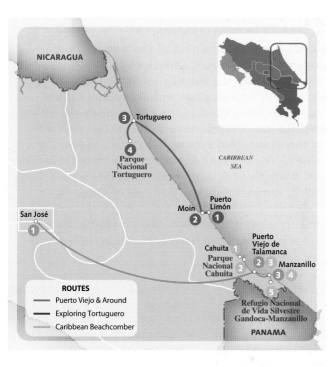

cent (2) Parque Nacional Cahuita (p291), which has a further 8km of beachfront to explore at your will. Heading south, your next stop is (3) Puerto Viejo de Talamanca (p292) and nearby Playa Cocles. These two beaches cater largely to the wave-thrashing surf set, though more tranquil waters are just a quick bike ride away. Your final destination is (4) Manzanillo (p296), a stunning beach in its own right, though the Caribbean's ultimate wave-lapped shores are part of the (5) Refugio Nacional de Vida Silvestre Gandoca-Manzanillo (p298). Inside this massive nature reserve, you'll find postcard-worthy stretches of pure white sand that invite days of idle lazing.

DISCOVER THE CARIBBEAN COAST

When the Spaniards arrived in this neck of the woods in the 16th century, the country's jungle-fringed Caribbean coast was deemed too wild, too impassable and too malarial for settlement. For centuries it developed at its own pace, with its unique culture – a mix of indigenous and West Indian. In the 19th century the arrival of thousands of Jamaican railroad workers infused the area with the traditions of the islands. But even as the culture evolved, the landscape remained wild. This isn't the postcard-perfect Caribbean stereotype of salt-white beaches and gentle turquoise waters. Here, you'll find brooding, tempestuous seas and one of Costa Rica's most notorious surfing waves. Not to mention black volcanic shores and dense swamps stocked with enough nesting sea-turtles and brilliant birds to keep the *National Geographic* set occupied for a lifetime.

PUERTO LIMÓN

pop 27,000

The biggest city on Costa Rica's Caribbean coast, the birthplace of United Fruit and capital of Limón province – this hard-working port city sits at a remove from the rest of the country. A general lack of political and financial support from the federal government in San José means that Limón is not a city that has aged gracefully. It is a grid of dilapidated buildings, overgrown parks and sidewalks choked with street vendors. Crime is a problem: it's worth noting, however, that a good deal of this violence is related to organized crime and therefore does not affect travelers. Despite its shortcomings, Limón can nonetheless be a compelling destination for adventurous urban explorers.

SIGHTS & ACTIVITIES

The city's main attraction is the waterfront **Parque Vargas**, an incongruous expanse of bench-lined sidewalks beneath a lost little jungle of tall palms and tropical flow-ers, centered on an appealingly decrepit bandstand.

From here, you can head inland along Av 2, the **pedestrian mall** that caters to the cruise-ship traffic. Keep an eye out for vendors selling home-burned CDs by local bands.

From the park, it's a pleasant walk north along the **sea wall**, where views of the rocky headland are set to a steady crashing of waves against the concrete jetty.

If you are keen on getting in the water, **Playa Bonita**, 4km northwest of town, has a pleasant, sandy beach. Surfers, in the meantime, might want to hit **Isla Uvita**, the wild green rock that lies 1km offshore, and is blessed with one of the country's most powerful lefts.

FESTIVALS & EVENTS

Festival Flores de la Diáspora Africana (late August) A celebration of Afro-Caribbean culture. While it is centered on Puerto Limón, the festival sponsors events showcasing African heritage throughout the province and San José.

PUERTO LIMÓN

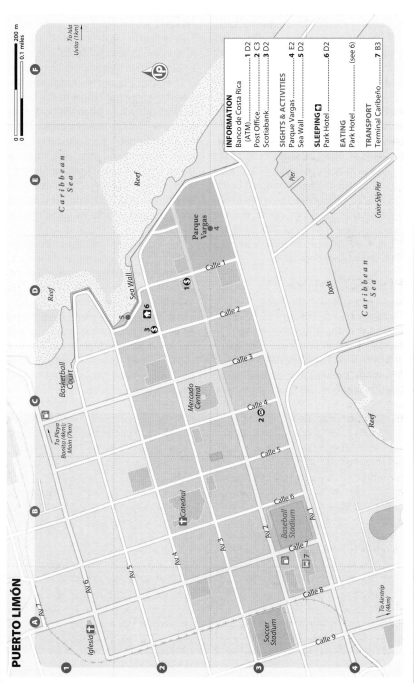

INFORMATION		
Banco de Costa Rica		
(ATM)	1	D2
Post Office	2	C3
Scotiabank	3	D2
SIGHTS & ACTIVITIES		
Parque Vargas	4	E2
Sea Wall	5	D2
SLEEPING		
Park Hotel	6	D2
EATING		
Park Hotel	(see 6)	
TRANSPORT		
Terminal Caribeño	7	B3

Día de la Raza (Columbus Day; October 12) Columbus' historic landing on Isla Uvita has traditionally inspired a small carnival, with street parades, live music and dancing.

SLEEPING & EATING

Park Hotel (☎ 2798-0555, 2758-3476; Av 3 btwn Calles 1 & 2; s/d standard US$45/59, superior US$49/69, deluxe US$53/69; P ⊠ ⊠ ⊡) Downtown Limón's most attractive hotel has 32 rooms in a peach-colored building that faces the ocean. The semi-swanky eatery inside has a long menu, but the specialty here is seafood, including fish brochettes, shrimp-studded rice and sea bass served countless ways.

GETTING THERE & AWAY

Buses go to these destinations:

Moín, for boats to Tortuguero (Tracasa; Terminal Caribeño) ₡300; 20 minutes; hourly from 5:30am to 6:30pm.

San José (Autotransportes Caribeños; Terminal Caribeño) ₡2500; three hours; departs almost hourly from 5am to 7pm.

MOÍN

This is Puerto Limón's main dock. The reason you're here, no doubt, is to catch a boat through the canals to Tortuguero.

The journey by boat to Tortuguero can take anywhere from three to five hours, depending on how often the boat stops to observe wildlife (many tours also stop for lunch). Indeed, it is worth taking your time. As you wind your way through these jungle canals, you are likely to spot howler monkeys, crocodiles, two- and three-toed sloth and an amazing array of wading birds, including roseate spoonbills.

The route is most often used by tourist boats, which means that if the canal becomes blocked by water hyacinths or logjams, the route might be closed altogether. Schedules exist in theory only and they change frequently depending on demand. If you are feeling lucky, you can just show up in Moín in the morning and try to get on one of the outgoing tour boats, but you are better off reserving in advance with a tour operator.

ANNELIES MERTENS

Paddling through the Parque Nacional Tortuguero (p287)

Enjoy your view of the canopy aboard the Rainforest Aerial Tram

⬎ RAINFOREST AERIAL TRAM

The brainchild of biologist Don Perry, a pioneer of rainforest canopy research, the Rainforest Aerial Tram is a worthwhile splurge if you want to visit the heights of the forest canopy in a gondola. The 2.6km ride takes 40 minutes each way, affording unusual plant-spotting and bird-watching opportunities. The fee includes a knowledgeable guide, and a variety of other tours are also available.

If you are staying in San José, Puerto Limón or elsewhere along the Caribbean coast, you can easily arrange a shuttle to the tram. If you are driving, look for the well-signed turnoff (it has lots of flags) just north of the Zurquí park entrance, on the east side of the road.

Things you need to know: Map p68; ☎ 2257-5961; www.rainforestrams.com; adult/student & child US$55/28, full-day tour incl lunch & guided hike US$89; ♿

Asociación de Boteros de los Canales de Tortuguero (Abacat; ☎ 8360-7325) Abacat operates regular service to Tortuguero (per person one-way US$30). Call for departure times.

Caribbean Tropical Tours (☎ 8371-2323, 2798-7027; wguerrerotuca@hotmail.com) This small, well-recommended company is run by master sloth-spotter William Guerrero and his wife, and is ideal if you want to book a leisurely ride to Tortuguero with plenty of pit-stops to see wildlife (per person one-way US$35).

Moín–Parismina–Tortuguero water taxi (☎ 2709-8005) Departs Moín at 3pm.

Reservations are essential, especially if you are requesting a stop in Parismina. A one-way trip to Tortuguero will cost US$30.

Tropical Wind (☎ 2798-6059, 8313-7164, 8327-0317) Operates almost-daily shuttles between Tortuguero and Moín (per person one-way US$30).

Viajes Bananero (☎ 8833-1066, in San José 2222-8973) Though based in Tortuguero, with an office in San José, this company makes regular (though not daily) trips between Tortuguero and Moín (per person one-way US$35). Call ahead to reserve.

Tracasa buses to Moín from Puerto Limón (₡300, 20 minutes) depart from Terminal Caribeño hourly from 5:30am to 6:30pm. Get off the bus before it goes over the bridge. If you are driving, leave your car in a guarded lot in Limón.

CARIARI

Cariari is a blue-collar, rough-around-the-edges banana town – most travelers make their way quickly through town, en route to Tortuguero.

The cheapest option is by public transportation on **Clic Clic** (☎ 2709-8155, 8844-0463) or **Coopetraca** (☎ 2767-7590), both of which charge ₡2600 per person for bus-boat service from the *estación vieja* all the way to Tortuguero. For these two options, the bus service will be the same, but the boat service will be different. Buses depart Cariari at 6am, 11:30am and 3pm.

For both of these services, buy only the bus ticket to La Pavona (₡1000). After a ride through banana plantations, you will arrive at the Río La Suerte, where a number of boat companies will be wait-ing at the dock. From this point, you will pay the remainder of your fare (₡1600) to the boatman. These companies will take you to the public boat dock in Tortuguero.

For a more expensive private service, there is **Viajes Bananero** (☎ 2709-8005), which has an office inside the San José bus terminal in Cariari. Buy your boat ticket here (per person US$10). From this same point, you will then take a bus (per person ₡600) to their proprietary boat dock. Bus departure times are at 11:30am and 2pm. If you are traveling in a group, Bananero can arrange custom pick-ups. For private service, you will need to re-serve ahead.

Buses to **San José** (₡1300, three hours) depart from Estación Nueva at 5:30am, 6:30am, 7:30am, 8:30am, 11:30am, 1pm, 3pm and 5:30pm.

TORTUGUERO VILLAGE

Accessible only by air or water, this bustling little village with strong Afro-Caribbean roots is best known for at-tracting hordes of sea turtles (the name

Banana plantation, around Puerto Limón (p280)

ADRIAN HEPWORTH/HEPWORTHIMAGES

Tortuguero means 'turtle place') – and the hordes of tourists who want to see them. While the peak turtle season is in July and August, the village has begun to attract travelers year-round. Even in October, when the turtles have pretty much returned to the sea, caravans of families and adventure travelers arrive to go on jungle hikes and to canoe the area's lush canals.

INFORMATION

A solid source of information is the town's website, www.tortuguerovillage.com, which lists local businesses and provides comprehensive directions on how to get into the area. There are no banks or ATMs in town and only a few businesses accept credit cards, so bring all the cash you'll need.

SIGHTS

About 200m north of Tortuguero village, the **Caribbean Conservation Corporation** (CCC; ☎ 2709-8091, in USA 800-678-7853; www.cccturtle.org; admission US$1; ☺ 10am-noon & 2-5pm Mon-Sat, 2-5pm Sun) operates a research station that has a small visitors center and museum. Exhibits focus on all things turtle-related, including a video about the history of local turtle conservation.

The **Canadian Organization for Tropical Education and Rainforest Conservation** (Coterc; ☎ 2709-8052, in Canada 905-831 8809; www.coterc.org; admission free) is a not-for-profit organization that operates the Estación Biológica Caño Palma, 7km north of Tortuguero village. This small biological research station houses a diminutive museum. From here, a network of trails winds through the surrounding rainforest. Coterc is surrounded on three sides by water, so you'll have to hire a boat to get there.

ACTIVITIES

Signs all over Tortuguero advertise boat tours and boats for hire – below is a list of recommended companies and guides. **Tortuguero Info Center** (☎ 2709-8055; tortuguero_info@racsa.co.cr) can provide information. Going rates are about US$20 per person for a two-hour turtle tour, and US$15 for a two-hour hiking or boat excursion.

Barbara Hartung (☎ 2709-8004; www.tinamontours.de) Offers hiking, canoe and turtle tours in German, English, French or Spanish. Also offers a unique tour about Tortuguero history, culture and medicinal plants.

Castor Hunter Thomas (☎ 8870-8634; castorhunter.blogspot.com) A local who has worked as a guide for more than 20 years leads turtle tours (in season), guided hikes and wonderful canoe tours. Ask at Soda Doña María.

Chico (☎ 2709-8033) Chico's hiking and canoe tours receive rave reviews from readers. Ask at Cabinas Miss Miriam.

Daryl Loth (☎ 8833-0827, 2709-8011; safari@racsa.co.cr) A personable Canadian-born naturalist (formerly of Coterc) offers excellent boat trips in a super-silent electric motorboat, as well as turtle tours (in season) and guided hikes.

SLEEPING
TORTUGUERO VILLAGE

Cabinas Miss Miriam (☎ 2709-8002, 8821-2037; s/d/tr US$20/25/30) Spread out over two buildings (one on the north end of the soccer field, the other south of it), this solid budget option has 16 clean tiled rooms, firm foam mattresses and electric showers.

Casa Marbella (☎ 8833-0827, 2709-8011; www.casamarbella.tripod.com; d incl breakfast US$40-60; 🖳) Owned by naturalist Daryl Loth, this charming B&B opposite the

Catholic church manages to be wonderfully serene while also being in the middle of it all. Ten simple whitewashed rooms have good lighting and ceiling fans, as well as superclean bathrooms with electric showers.

Hotel Miss Junie (☎ 2709-8029, in San José 2231-6803; www.iguanaverdetours.com; d US$40-60) At the northern end of the village, Miss Junie's place is set on wide grounds, shaded by palm trees and strewn with hammocks. Seventeen spotless rooms in a beautifully kept tropical plantation-style building are tastefully decorated with wood accents and bright bedspreads.

AROUND TORTUGUERO

Rana Roja (☎ 2709-8260; www.ranarojatortu guero.com; r per person per night US$55; 🛜 🐕) This new Tico-run midrange spot offers one of the best-value options in the area. Seventeen small, earth-colored cabins – all with private terraces and rockers – are connected by elevated walkways.

Tortuga Lodge & Gardens (☎ 2709-8034, in San José 2257-0766, 2222-0333; www. costaricaexpeditions.com; 2-night package per person from US$360; 🐕) Tortuguero's most elegant lodge, operated by Costa Rica Expeditions, is set amid 20 hectares of private gardens. Here you'll find a serene environment, as well as 27 demure rooms that channel a 19th-century safari vibe.

EATING & DRINKING

Miss Miriam's (☎ 2709-8002; mains ₡4400-11,000) This little place is bursting with flavor and character. Don't miss the well-spiced Caribbean chicken (the best we tasted on the entire coast), served with heaping sides of sautéed fresh veggies and Caribbean-style rice and beans.

Buddha Cafe (☎ 2709-8084; pizzas ₡3200-4000, dishes ₡3500-9000; 🕐 noon-8:30pm; 🅅) A riverside spot keeps a hipster vibe with ambient club music on the sound system and Buddhist 'om' symbols stenciled onto just about everything. It's a lovely spot, with excellent pizzas, rich coffee and scumptious crepes (both savory and sweet).

ANNELIES MERTENS

Heron, Parque Nacional Tortuguero (p287)

Miss Junie's (☎ 2709-8029; mains from ₡8500; ⊙ 7-9am, 11:30am-2:30pm & 6-9pm) This is Tortuguero's best-known restaurant – serving a bevy of local specialties: chicken, fish, lobster and many other dishes, all served in flavorful Caribbean sauces, with traditional rice and beans.

La Taberna (⊙ 11am-11pm) Adjacent to Tropical Lodge, overlooking the canal, this popular tavern is mellow in the afternoons, but draws the party people after dark, with cold beer and blaring reggaetón.

GETTING THERE & AWAY
AIR
The small airstrip is 4km north of Tortuguero village. **NatureAir** (☎ 2220-3054) and **Sansa** (☎ 2709-8055) both have daily flights to and from San José (the one-way flight is less than 20 minutes). Charter flights land here regularly as well.

BOAT
Tortuguero is accessible by boat from Cariari (p284) or Moín (p282).

PARQUE NACIONAL TORTUGUERO
'Humid' is the driest word that could truthfully be used to describe Tortuguero, a 311-sq-km **national park** (☎ 2709-8086; admission US$10; ⊙ 5:30am-6pm) that serves as the most important breeding ground of the green sea turtle. With an annual rainfall of up to 6000mm in the northern part of the park, it is one of the wettest areas in the country. In addition, the protected area extends into the Caribbean Sea, covering about 5200 sq km of marine habitat.

ACTIVITIES
BOATING
The famed **Canales de Tortuguero** are the introduction to this important park. A

AROUND TORTUGUERO

north–south waterway created to connect a series of lazy lagoons and meandering rivers in 1974, this engineering marvel allowed inland navigation between Limón and coastal villages in something sturdier than a dugout canoe. There are regular flights to the village of Tortuguero, but if you fly, you'll be missing half the fun.

Río Tortuguero acts as the entrance way to the aquatic network of trails. This wide, beautiful river is often covered with water lilies and frequented by aquatic birds like heron, kingfisher and anhinga. **Caño Chiquero** and **Canō Mora** are two narrower waterways with good wildlife-spotting opportunities. **Caño Harold** is actually an artificially constructed canal, but that doesn't stop the creatures – like Jesus Christ lizards and caiman – from inhabiting its tranquil waters.

HIKING

Behind the Cuatro Esquinas ranger station, **El Gavilán Land Trail** is the only public trail through the park that is on solid ground. Visitors can hike the muddy, 2km loop that traverses the tropical humid forest and follows a stretch of beach. Green parrots and several species of monkeys are commonly sighted here.

TURTLE-WATCHING

Because of the sensitive nature of the habitat and the critically endangered status of some species, turtle-watching tours are highly regulated. So as to not alarm turtles as they come to shore (a frightened turtle will return to the ocean and dump her eggs), tour groups gather in shelter sites close to the beach and a spotter relays a turtle's location via radio once she has safely crossed the high-tide mark and built her nest. At this time, visitors can then go to the beach and watch the turtle lay her eggs, cover her nest and return to the ocean. By law, tours can only take place between 8am and midnight.

Visitors should wear closed-toe shoes and rain gear. Tours cost US$20 (this is a flat rate established by the village), which includes the purchase of a US$4 sticker that pays for the patrols that help protect the turtle-nesting sites from scavengers and looters. Nesting season runs from March through October, with July and August being prime time. The next best time is April, when leatherback turtles nest in small numbers. Flashlights and cameras (of all kinds) are not allowed on the beach.

GETTING THERE & AWAY

For information on traveling to and from the area, see the Tortuguero Village section on p287.

ADRIAN HEPWORTH/HEPWORTHIMAGES

Green turtle, Parque Nacional Tortuguero (p287)

CAHUITA

Even as tourism has mushroomed on Costa Rica's southern coast, Cahuita has managed to hold onto its laid-back Caribbean vibe. The roads are made of dirt, many of the older houses rest on stilts and chatty neighbors still converse in Mekatelyu (English-based Creole spoken by Costa Ricans of West Indian origin). It's not as polished as Puerto Viejo de Talamanca to the south, which sports an air-conditioned strip mall and slick international eateries, but a graceful black-sand beach and a chilled-out demeanor hint at a not-so-distant past, when the area was little more than just a string of cocoa farms.

INFORMATION

The town's helpful new website (www.cahuita.cr) has all manner of lodging and restaurant information.

SIGHTS & ACTIVITIES

At the northwest end of Cahuita, **Playa Negra** is a long, black-sand beach flying the *bandera azul ecológica*, a flag that indicates the beach is kept to the highest ecological standards.

Playa Blanca at the entrance to the national park (see p292) is another good option for swimming.

SLEEPING

CENTER

Bungalows Aché (☎ 2755-0119; www.bungalowsache.com; bungalows US$40-60; P 🛜) In Nigeria, *Aché* means 'Amen,' and you'll likely say the same thing when you see these spotless octagonal bungalows on a peaceful property bordering the national park. The three charming, polished-wood cabins have bright red-and-white linens and come with private decks strung with hammocks.

IMAGEBROKER/SIEPMANN
Boat trip, Parque Nacional Tortuguero (p287)

CARIBBEAN COAST

CAHUITA

🡲 IF YOU LIKE...

If you like **Parque Nacional Tortuguero** (p287), we think you'll like these other parks and reserves along and near the Caribbean coast:

- **Parque Nacional Braulio Carrillo** This underexplored national park has steep hills cloaked in impossibly tall trees.
- **Aviarios del Caribe Sloth Sanctuary** About 10km northwest of Cahuita, proprietors help injured and orphaned sloths (fact: there is nothing cuter than a baby sloth!).
- **Refugio Nacional de Vida Silvestre Barra del Colorado** A remote park that draws fishing enthusiasts who come to hook species such as snook, tarpon and gar.
- **Veragua Rainforest Research & Adventure Park** In Las Brisas de Veragua, you'll find an aerial tram, a reptile vivarium, an insectarium, and hummingbird and butterfly gardens.

Cahuita National Park Hotel (☎ 2755-0244; d/tr/q US$45/55/65; apt US$130; P ✗ 🐾 🛜) This three-story building overlooks the ocean at the entrance to the national park and is equipped with 20 pleasant whitewashed rooms with wood

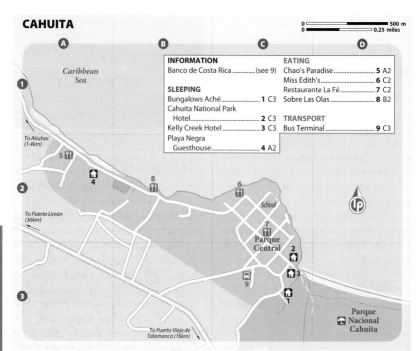

CAHUITA

0 — 500 m
0 — 0.25 miles

Caribbean
Sea

INFORMATION
Banco de Costa Rica ....(see 9)

SLEEPING
Bungalows Aché.......................**1** C3
Cahuita National Park
    Hotel.................................**2** C3
Kelly Creek Hotel **3** C3
Playa Negra
    Guesthouse.......................**4** A2

EATING
Chao's Paradise..........................**5** A2
Miss Edith's...............................**6** C2
Restaurante La Fé.......................**7** C2
Sobre Las Olas...........................**8** B2

TRANSPORT
Bus Terminal **9** C3

To Atiuhac
(1.4km)

To Puerto Limón
(36km)

School

Parque
Central

Parque
Nacional
Cahuita

To Puerto Viejo de
Talamanca (16km)

furnishings, cool tile floors and roomy bathrooms.

Kelly Creek Hotel (☎ 2755-0007; www.hotelkellycreek.com; d US$55, extra person US$10; P 🐾 🖲) This snazzy hotel on a busy stretch of beach is conveniently situated right next to the park entrance. Four graceful, tropical *cabinas* have high ceilings and are accented with cream-colored linens and mosquito nets. Public areas are decorated with paintings by local artists.

PLAYA NEGRA

Playa Negra Guesthouse (☎ 2755-0127; www.playanegra.cr; d US$60-80, 2-bedroom cottages US$120; P 🛜 🖲) This beautiful Caribbean-style plantation house, with several free-standing storybook cottages (equipped with full kitchen), is meticulously decorated and maintained. Guest rooms are

painted in sherbety colors and feature charming tropical accents – such as colorful mosaics in the bathrooms and cozy wicker lounge chairs on the private decks.

Atiuhac (☎ 8911-1347; www.atiuhac.com; d incl breakfast US$100; P) Four raw-wood bungalows surround a large *rancho* with open-air bar stocked with comfy hammock chairs. The cabins are designed to appeal to outdoorsy types: surrounded by foliage, they have roomy private decks, a living area and a shower set into the hollowed trunk of a tree.

EATING
CENTER

Restaurante La Fé (dishes ₡2500-10,000; 🕑 7am-11pm) A basic, cement eatery on the main drag is draped in swinging oropendola nests and illuminated by candlelight in the evenings. There's a laundry list of

Tico and Caribbean items on the menu, but the main reason to come here is to eat anything doused in the restaurant's delicious spicy coconut sauce.

Miss Edith's (☎ 2755-0248; mains ₡2300-12,000; ☺ 11am-10pm; **V**) This long-time local restaurant serves a whole range of Caribbean specialties, including jerk chicken, rice and beans, and potatoes stewed in garlic, in addition to a number of vegetarian options.

PLAYA NEGRA

Chao's Paradise (☎ 2755-0480; seafood mains ₡3700-7000; ☺ 11am-11pm) Follow the wafting smell of garlic and simmering sauces to this highly recommended Playa Negra outpost that serves fresh catches cooked up in spicy 'Chao' sauce. The open-air restaurant-bar has a pool table and live music some nights.

Sobre Las Olas (☎ 2755-0109; pasta ₡5500-6500, mains ₡5500-12,500; ☺ noon-10pm Wed-Mon; **V**) Cahuita's top option for waterfront dining (and an ideal spot for a date) lies only a 100m walk out of town.

It is owned by a lively Tico-Italian couple who serve a variety of Mediterranean-influenced specialties.

GETTING THERE & AWAY

Buses go to the following destinations:

Puerto Limón (Autotransportes Mepe) ₡1000; 1½ hours; departs at 6am, 9:30am, 10:45am, 1:45pm and 6:15pm.

Puerto Viejo de Talamanca/ Manzanillo ₡1000; 30 minutes to one hour; departs at 6:15am, 6:45am, 11:15am, 3:45pm and 6:45pm.

San José (Autotransportes Mepe) ₡3700; four hours; departs at 7am, 8am, 9:30am, 11:30am and 4:30pm.

PARQUE NACIONAL CAHUITA

Just 10 sq km in size, this small **national park** (☎ 2755-0302; admission US$10; ☺ 8am-4pm Mon-Fri, 7am-5pm Sat & Sun) is one of the more frequently visited national parks in Costa Rica. The reasons are simple: the nearby town of Cahuita provides attractive accommodations and easy

CHRISTER FREDRIKSSON

Howler monkeys, Parque Nacional Cahuita (p291)

access; more importantly, the white-sand beaches, coral reef and coastal rainforest are bursting with wildlife. Cahuita was declared a national park in 1978, and is typical of the entire coast (very humid), which results in dense tropical foliage.

ACTIVITIES
HIKING
An easily navigable 8km **coastal trail** leads through the jungle from Kelly Creek to Puerto Vargas. At times the trail follows the beach, at other times hikers are 100m or so away from the sand. At the end of the first beach, Playa Blanca, hikers must ford the Río Perezoso. Inquire about river conditions before you set out. The trail continues around Punta Cahuita to the long stretch of Playa Vargas. The trail ends at the southern tip of the reef,

where it meets up with a road leading to the ranger station.

SWIMMING & SNORKELING
Almost immediately upon entering the park, you'll see the 2km-long **Playa Blanca** stretching along a gently curving bay to the east. The first 500m of beach may be unsafe for swimming, but beyond that, waves are generally gentle. (Look for green flags marking safe swimming spots.) The rocky Punta Cahuita headland separates this beach from the next one, **Playa Vargas**. Offshore is one of the last living coral reefs in Costa Rica.

EATING
After the long, hot hike through the jungle, you may think you are hallucinating when you see **Boca Chica** (☎ 2755-0415; meals ₡3300-10,000; ⏱ 9am-6pm; 🍴), a small, whitewashed family recreation center, at the end of the road. It's not a mirage, just a well-placed bar and eatery, run by a charming Italian owner.

GETTING THERE & AWAY
The national park is accessible by either foot or bike from Cahuita.

PUERTO VIEJO DE TALAMANCA
This burgeoning Caribbean party town is bustling with tourist activity: street vendors ply Rasta trinkets and Bob Marley T-shirts, stylish eateries serve global fusion everything and intentionally rustic bamboo bars pump dancehall and reggaetón. The scene, in fact, can get downright hedonistic, attracting dedicated revelers who arrive to marinate in ganja and *guaro* (the local cane alcohol). Despite the reputation for revelry, Puerto Viejo nonetheless manages to hold on to an easy charm.

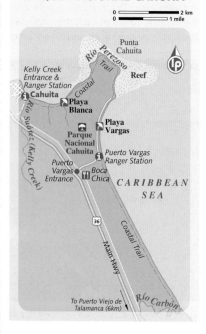

PARQUE NACIONAL CAHUITA

CHRISTER FREDRIKSSON

Puerto Viejo de Talamanca (p292)

SIGHTS

To the west of town, **Finca La Isla Botanical Garden** (☎ 2750-0046; www. costaricacaribbean.com; self-guided/guided tour US$5/10; ☺ 10am-4pm Fri-Mon) is a working tropical farm where the owners have been growing organic pepper, cacao, tropical fruits and ornamental plants for more than a decade.

ACTIVITIES
SURFING
Breaking on the reef that hugs the village, you will find the famed **Salsa Brava**, a shallow break that is also one of the country's most infamous waves. It's a tricky ride – if you lose it, the waves will plow you straight into the reef – but it's a rush (and most definitely not for beginners).

SWIMMING
The entire southern Caribbean coast – from Cahuita all the way south to Punta Mona – is lined with unbelievably beautiful beaches. Swimming conditions vary greatly, however, and the surf can get

dangerous. Inquire at your hotel or with local tour operators about conditions before setting out.

DIVING
Divers in the southern Caribbean will discover upward of 20 dive sites. The principal dive company is **Reef Runner Divers** (☎ 2750-0480; www.reefrunnerdivers.net; 1-/2-tank dive US$65/90; ☺ 8am-6pm). If you are not certified, you can use a temporary license for US$65 or spring for the full PADI certification for US$325.

SLEEPING
Hotel Pura Vida (☎ 2750-0002; www. hotel-puravida.com; s/d/tr without bathroom US$25/30/40, s/d/tr US$32/38/50; Ⓟ ☜) Though this place has budget prices, the atmosphere and amenities are solidly midrange. Ten breezy, immaculate rooms, with polished wood, bright linens and ceramic-tiled floors, make up this homey Chilean-German run inn on a quiet street.

Banana Azul (☎ 2750-2035; www.banana azul.com; d incl breakfast US$69-94, 2-person apt

PUERTO VIEJO DE TALAMANCA

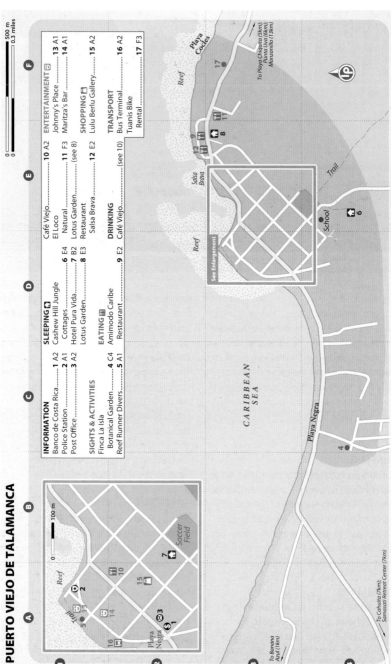

INFORMATION

Banco de Costa Rica........**1** A2
Police Station.................**2** A1
Post Office....................**3** A2

SIGHTS & ACTIVITIES

Finca La Isla
Botanical Garden..........**4** C4
Reef Runner Divers........**5** A1

SLEEPING 🏠

Cashew Hill Jungle
Cottages.....................**6** E4
Hotel Pura Vida.............**7** B2
Lotus Garden................**8** E3

EATING 🍴

Amimodo Caribe
Restaurant..................**9** E2

Café Viejo....................**10** A2
El Loco
Natural......................**11** F3
Lotus Garden..............(see 8)
Restaurant
Salsa Brava................**12** E2

DRINKING

Café Viejo..................(see 10)

ENTERTAINMENT 🎭

Johnny's Place.............**13** A1
Maritza's Bar...............**14** A1

SHOPPING 🛍

Lulu Berlu Gallery..........**15** A2

TRANSPORT

Bus Terminal................**16** A2
Tuanis Bike
Rental........................**17** F3

To Playa Chiquita (5km);
Punta Uva (6km);
Manzanillo (13km)

Playa Cocles

Reef

Salsa Brava

Reef

See Enlargement

Trail

School

CARIBBEAN SEA

Playa Negra

To Cahuita (7km);
Samasati Retreat Center (7km)

To Banana Azul (1km)

Reef

Soccer Field

Playa Negra

Trail

US$129; P 🛜 🐾) Lost in the jungle at the far end of Playa Negra this wonderfully wild hotel run sits at the edge of a blissfully tranquil black-sand beach. The 13 rooms are all done up in the finest jungle chic: shining wooden floors, white linens, mosquito nets and private decks with views.

Lotus Garden (☎ 2750-0232; http://the lotusgarden.net; d US$40, 2-person ste US$70-90; P 🍴 🛜 🐾) Channeling the Far East (by way of Puerto Viejo), the nine large, stone-lined suites at this inn come with king-sized four-poster beds, Jacuzzi tubs and gobs of Asian textiles. To complete the mood, there's the recommended Lotus Garden Restaurant.

Samasati Retreat Center (☎ 2750-0315, in USA 800-563-9643; www.samasati.com; guesthouses/bungalows per person incl 3 meals from US$85/135; P V) Set on a hillside 8km west of Puerto Viejo, this attractive yoga retreat center has sweeping views of the coast as well as nine wooden bungalows with wraparound screened windows. Meals are vegetarian, with an organic focus.

Cashew Hill Jungle Cottages (☎ 2750-0001; www.cashewhilllodge.co.cr; 1-/2-/3-bedroom cottages US$90/110/150; P 🛜 🐾 👶) Set on a lush hillside studded with pre-Columbian-style statuary, the seven cottages at this lovely, family-friendly jungle spot are bright, colorful and comfortable. The wood houses are painted in vivid shades and come with full kitchens, loft-style sleeping areas and charming rustic touches such as shell-encrusted sinks.

EATING & DRINKING

Lotus Garden (mains ₡3000-7800; 🕙 7am-11pm) Serving a mix of sushi, noodles and stir-fries, this pleasant garden restaurant is a good spot if you are in the mood for something Asian.

El Loco Natural (☎ 2750-0530; meals ₡3200-9000; 🕙 5-10pm Wed-Mon; V) This pleasant candlelit patio cafe located 200m east of town serves up creative fusion cuisine, combining elements of Caribbean, Indian, Mexican and Thai cooking. Steamed spicy mussels in red-curry sauce

Local fisherman, Puerto Viejo de Talamanca (p292)

4CORNERS/MANNAKEE TIM

Palm-lined beach, Puerto Limón (p280)

⭢ IF YOU LIKE...

If you like **Puerto Viejo de Talamanca** (p292), we think you'll like these other beaches further down the Caribbean coast:

- **Playa Cocles** Known for its great surfing and organized lifeguard system, which helps offset the danger of the frequent riptides.
- **Playa Chiquita** A broad stretch of white-sand beach that is contiguous with Playa Cocles.
- **Punta Uva** Famous for the region's most swimmable beaches, each lovelier than the next.

and tandoori chicken in coconut are just a couple of stand-outs.

Restaurant Salsa Brava (☎ 2750-0241; mains ₡4400-10,000; ☽ noon-10pm) This recommended hot spot specializes in fresh seafood and open-grill cooking. The ever-popular 'juice joint' is an oasis for thirsty beachcombers and the sangria is refreshingly good, too.

Amimodo Caribe Restaurant (☎ 2750-0257; meals ₡4700-14,500; ☽ 4-10pm Mon-Thu, noon-10pm Fri-Sun; Ⓥ) Listen to the waves crash at this local Italian favorite, where you can chow down on pizzas and homemade pasta dishes such as lobster spaghetti.

Café Viejo (☎ 2750-0817; mains ₡5000-16,000; ☽ noon-close) This pricey, sceney

Mediterranean lounge and restaurant that gets good marks for fresh pasta, tasty pizza and fancy cocktails.

ENTERTAINMENT

Maritza's Bar (☎ 2750-0003) This unfancy local spot has regular live bands and DJs that play reggae, rock and salsa, and all the funky beats in between.

Johnny's Place (☽ 1pm-3am) This place is a Puerto Viejo institution, where DJs spin reggaetón, hip-hop and salsa to a mix of locals and travelers who take up the dance floor and surround the late-night beach bonfires outside.

SHOPPING

Makeshift stalls clutter the main road, selling all manner of knick-knacks and Rasta-colored accoutrement. For finer crafts, try **Lulu Berlu Gallery** (☎ 2750-0394; ☽ 9am-9pm), which carries folk art, one-of-a-kind clothing and mosaic mirrors, among many other items.

GETTING THERE & AROUND

Buses go to the following destinations:

Cahuita & Puerto Limón ₡400; 30 minutes and 1½ hours; departs roughly every hour from 5:30am to 7:30pm.

Manzanillo ₡400; 30 minutes; departs at 7:30am, noon, 4:30pm and 7:30pm.

San José ₡4100; five hours; departs at 7:30am, 9am, 11am and 4pm.

A bicycle is a fine way to get around town, and for pedaling out to other beaches east of Puerto Viejo.

MANZANILLO

The idyllic little village of Manzanillo has long been a destination off the beaten track. Despite the fact that the paved roads arrived in 2003, this little town remains a vibrant outpost of Afro-Caribbean culture. It has also remained pristine, thanks to the 1985 establishment of the Refugio Nacional de Vida Silvestre Gandoca-Manzanillo, which includes the village and imposes strict regulations on development of the region. Activities are of a simple nature: there are fine opportunities to hike, dive, snorkel and kayak, depending on the swells.

ACTIVITIES

Aquamor Talamanca Adventures (☎ 2759-9012, 8835-6041; www.greencoast.com/aquamor.htm, www.costacetacea.com) Part of Costa Cetacea, this very reputable long-time outfit, run by marine biologist Shawn Larkin and his wife Vanessa Schot, is an excellent source of information on the refuge, the environment and the community. It also organizes scuba diving, dolphin-watching trips, kayak fishing excursions and rents snorkel gear (see also p272).

SLEEPING & EATING

Cabinas Manzanillo (☎ 2759-9033, 8839-8386; d/tr US$20/30; P) These eight *cabinas* on the western end of town are so spick-and-span, you could eat off the shining tile floors. Rooms have big beds and are painted bright pastel colors, with industrial-strength ceiling fans and spacious bathrooms.

Congo Bongo (☎ 2759-9016; www.congo-bongo.com; d/tr/q US$125/150/175, per week US$750/900/1050; P) Just outside town, on the road to Punta Uva, you'll find six charming wooden cottages set in a reclaimed cacao plantation (now dense forest).

Maxi's Restaurant (mains ₡2500-21,000, lobster from ₡9000; ☯ 6am-close; V) The most famous restaurant in Manzanillo attracts travelers from all over for large platters of tender, grilled seafood, whole red snappers, steaks and Caribbean-style lobsters.

GETTING THERE & AWAY

Buses to Manzanillo depart from Puerto Viejo (₡400, 30 minutes) at 7:30am, noon, 4:30pm and 7:30pm. They return to Puerto Viejo at 5am, 8:15am, 12:45pm and 5:15pm. All continue to Puerto Limón (₡2000, 2½ hours) for onward transfers.

CARIBBEAN COAST

MANZANILLO

PAUL KENNEDY

Playa Manzanillo, Refugio Nacional de Vida Silvestre Gandoca-Manzanillo (p298)

Playa Negra, Manzanillo (p296)

CHRISTOPHER BAKER

REFUGIO NACIONAL DE VIDA SILVESTRE GANDOCA-MANZANILLO

Called Regama for short, this little-explored **refuge** (Minae park office; ☎ 2759-9100; ⏱ 8am-noon & 1-4pm) protects nearly 70% of the southern Caribbean coast, extending from Manzanillo all the way to the Panamanian border. It encompasses 50 sq km of land plus 44 sq km of marine environment. The peaceful, pristine stretch of white sandy beach is one of the area's main attractions.

ACTIVITIES
HIKING
A coastal trail heads 5.5km east out of Manzanillo to **Punta Mona**. The first part of this path leads from Manzanillo to Tom Bay (about a 40-minute walk), and is well trammeled and clearly marked and doesn't require a guide. Once you pass Tom Bay, however, the path gets murky and it's easy to get lost – ask about conditions before you set out or hire a guide. It's a rewarding walk, with amazing scenery,

as well as excellent (and safe) swimming and snorkeling at the end.

A more difficult 9km trail leaves from just west of Manzanillo and skirts the southern edges of the Pantano Punta Mona, continuing to the small community of **Gandoca**. This trail is not commonly walked, as most people access Punta Mona and Gandoca from the park entrance at the northern edge of the refuge, on the road to Sixaola. If you want to try to hike this, be sure to hire a guide.

KAYAKING
You can explore some of the area's waterways by kayak, available from Aquamor Talamanca Adventures (per hour US$5). Paddle out to the reef, or head up the **Quebrada Home Wark**, in the west of the village, or the tiny **Simeon Creek**, at the east end of the village. These are short paddles – ideal if you've got kids.

DOLPHIN-WATCHING
In 1997 a group of local guides in Manzanillo identified tucuxi dolphins,

a little-known species previously not found in Costa Rica, and began to observe their interactions with the bottlenose dolphins. Learn more about this work through the **Talamanca Dolphin Foundation** (☎ 2759-0715/612; www.dolphin link.org), a not-for-profit dedicated to the study and preservation of local dolphin populations. Aquamor Talamanca Adventures organizes dolphin-watching excursions for US$40 per person.

TURTLE-WATCHING

Marine turtles – especially leatherback but also green, hawksbill and loggerhead – all nest on the beaches between Punta Mona and the Río Sixaola. Leatherbacks nest from March to July, with a peak in April and May. All tourists must be accompanied by a local guide to minimize the disturbance to the nesting turtles.

SLEEPING & EATING

Punta Mona (☎ 8321-8788; www.punta mona.org; dm incl 3 meals US$45, transportation US$10; Ⓥ) Five kilometers southeast of Manzanillo, this organic farm and retreat center is an experiment in permaculture design and sustainable living. Covering some 40 hectares, it grows more than 200 varieties of edible fruits and veggies, (about 85% of the huge vegetarian meals included in the daily rate). To arrange a stay and transport, email ahead.

GETTING THERE & AWAY

The reserve is best accessed from Manzanillo or Puerto Viejo de Talamanca.

ACTIVITIES

Zip through the rainforest on a Santa Elena canopy tour (p136)

PAUL KENNEDY

What truly distinguishes Costa Rica is the diversity and accessibility of the outdoors. While hard-core enthusiasts can seek out complete solitude in absolute wilderness, families and novices alike are equally well catered for. From jungle treks and beachcombing to rafting snaking rivers and surfing crashing waves – whatever you're looking for, Costa Rica has most definitely got it.

Costa Rica's lofty tally of national parks and reserves provides an incredible stage for lovers of the outdoors. Natural spaces are so entwined with Costa Rica's ecofriendly image that it's difficult to envisage the country without them. For the vast majority of travelers, Costa Rica equals rainforest, and you're certain to encounter charismatic wildlife including primates, birdlife and butterflies galore. And as you'll quickly discover, no two rainforests are created equal, providing a constantly shifting palette of nature.

CANOPY TOURS

Life in the rainforest takes place at canopy level. But with trees extending 30m to 60m in height, the average human has a hard time getting a look at what's going on up there. Indeed, it was only a matter of time before someone in Costa Rica invented the canopy tour.

Some companies have built elevated walkways through the trees that allow visitors to stroll through. **SkyTrek** (p137), in Monteverde, and **Rainmaker Aerial Walkway** (see boxed text, p220), near Quepos, are two of the most established operations in the country.

For adrenaline-seekers, consider zipping from tree to tree while harnessed into a sophisticated cable-suspension system. With a total length of 11,000m connecting no fewer than 21 platforms, **Miss Sky** (p186) is the longest canopy tour in the world, stretching from mountainside to mountainside, and finishing on the top floor of a disco-bar.

Major tourist centers, such as **Monteverde and Santa Elena** and **La Fortuna**, offer the country's largest number of canopy-tour operators. See p136 and p114, respectively, for details of operators in these towns.

You can also take a ski-lift-style ride through the treetops, such as the **Rainforest Aerial Tram** near the Caribbean coast (see boxed text, p283) or the smaller **Monteverde Trainforest** (p137) in Monteverde.

LUKE HUNTER

Parque Nacional Chirripó (p262)

COSTA RICA IN FOCUS

ACTIVITIES

HIKING & TREKKING

Whether you're interested in taking a walk in the park, or embarking on a rugged mountaineering circuit, there is no shortage of hiking opportunities around Costa Rica. At tourist-packed destinations such as Monteverde and Santa Elena, trails are clearly marked, and even lined with cement blocks in parts. This can be particularly appealing if you're traveling with little ones, or if you're lacking in navigational prowess. Sun-drenched coastlines also invite rambling walks alongside crashing waves.

Opportunities for moderate hiking are available in most parks and reserves, particularly once you leave the well-beaten tourist path. As this is Costa Rica, you can – for the most part – still rely on signs and maps for orientation, though it helps to have a bit of experience under your belt. Good hiking shoes, plenty of water, and confidence in your abilities will enable you to combine several shorter day hikes into a lengthier expedition. Tourist information centers at park entrances are great resources for planning out your intended route.

⟩THE BEST

CHRISTER FREDRIKSSON

Parque Nacional Manuel Antonio (p222)

HIKES & TREKS

- **Monteverde & Santa Elena** (p133)
- **Parque Nacional Manuel Antonio** (p222)
- **Parque Nacional Corcovado** (p253)
- **Cerro Chirripó** (p263)
- **Parque Internacional La Amistad** (p267)

COSTA RICA IN FOCUS

ACTIVITIES

THE BEST

Mal País (p195)

CHRISTIAN ASLUND

WICKED SURF

- **Parque Nacional Santa Rosa** (p156)
- **Puerto Viejo de Talamanca** (p293)
- **Mal País & Santa Teresa** (p195)
- **Dominical** (p224)
- **Playa Tamarindo** (p181)
- **Jacó** (p212)

If you're properly equipped with the various camping essentials (tent, sleeping bag, air mattress etc), the country's longer and more arduous multiday treks are at your disposal. Costa Rica's top challenges are scaling Cerro Chirripó, traversing Parque Nacional Corcovado and penetrating deep into the heart of Parque Internacional La Amistad. While all three endeavors can be undertaken either solo or with trusted companions, local guides provide an extra measure of safety, and can help in identifying flora and fauna.

SURFING

Point and beach breaks, lefts and rights, reefs and river mouths, warm water and year-round waves make Costa Rica a favorite surfing destination. For the most part, the Pacific coast has bigger swells and better waves during the latter part of the rainy season, but the Caribbean cooks from November to May. Basically, there is a wave, somewhere, waiting to be surfed at any time of the year.

For the uninitiated, lessons are available at almost all of the major surfing destinations – popular towns of note include Jacó and Tamarindo on the Pacific coast. Be mindful that surfing is a pursuit that has a steep learning curve, and can be potentially dangerous if the currents are strong. With that said, the sport is accessible to children and novices, though it's always best to inquire locally about conditions before you paddle out. Having trouble standing up? Here is a tip: long boards readily maintain their stability, even in heavy crashing surf.

Advanced surfers with plenty of experience under their belts can tackle some of the sport's most famous waves, including Salsa Brava in Puerto Viejo de Talamanca, and Ollie's Point and Witch's Rock off the coast of Parque Nacional Santa Rosa.

WHITE-WATER RAFTING & KAYAKING

Since the birth of the ecotourism-based economy in the mid-1980s, white-water rafting has emerged as one of Costa Rica's top-billed outdoor pursuits. Ranging from family-friendly Class II swells to borderline unnavigable Class V rapids, Costa Rica's rivers offer highly varied white-water experiences.

First-time runners are catered for year-round, while seasoned enthusiasts arrive en masse during the wildest months from June through October. There is also much regional variation, with gentler rivers located near Manuel Antonio along the central Pacific coast, and truly world-class runs along the Pacuare and Reventazón rivers in the Central Valley. Since all white-water rafting in Costa Rica requires the presence of

SURFER'S MAP

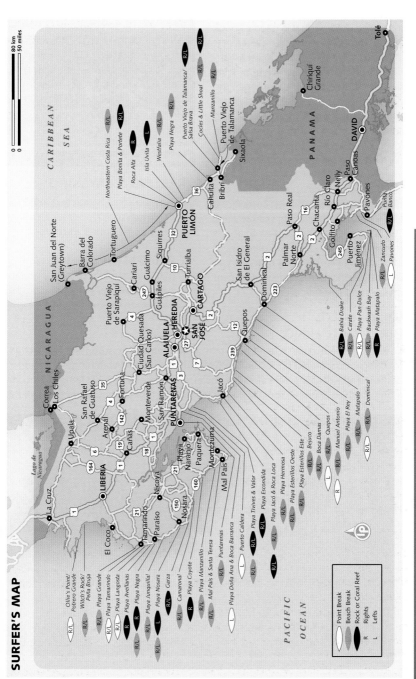

a certified guide, you will need to book all trips through a reputable tour agency.

River kayaking is not as popular as rafting, though it has its fair share of loyal fans. The tiny village of La Virgen in the northern lowlands is the unofficial kayaking capital of Costa Rica, and the best spot to hook up with other like-minded lovers of the sport. The Río Sarapiquí has an impressive variety of runs that cater to all ages and skill levels.

With 1228km of coastline, two gulfs and plentiful mangrove estuaries, Costa Rica is also an ideal destination for sea kayaking. This is a great way for paddlers to access remote areas and catch rare glimpses of birds and wildlife. Difficulty of access varies considerably, and is largely dependent on tides and currents.

⌄ THE BEST

MARESA PRYOR/DANITA DELIMONT.COM

Río Sarapiquí, La Virgen (p157)

RAFTING & KAYAKING

- **Turrialba** (see boxed text, p95)
- **La Virgen** (p157)
- **Quepos & Manuel Antonio** (p217)
- **Parque Nacional Tortuguero** (p287)
- **Bahía Drake** (p242)

WILDLIFE- & BIRD-WATCHING

Costa Rica's biodiversity is legendary, so it should come as no surprise that the country offers unparalleled opportunities for wildlife- and bird-watching. As an added bonus, people of all ages are already familiar with Costa Rica's most famous yet commonly spotted animals. You'll instantly recognize monkeys bounding through the

CHRISTER FREDRIKSSON

Reserva Biológica Bosque Nuboso Monteverde (p143)

treetops, sloths clinging to branches and toucans gliding beneath the canopy. Young children, even if they've been to the zoo dozens of times, typically enjoy the thrill of spotting creatures in the wild.

For the slightly older visitor, keeping checklists is a fun way to add an educational element to your travels. Want to move beyond the novice level? Check out your local bookstore prior to landing in Costa Rica, and be sure to pick up wildlife and bird guides – look for ones with color plates that make positive identification a cinch.

A quality pair of binoculars is highly recommended, and can really make the difference between far-off movement and a veritable face-to-face encounter. For expert bird-watchers, a spotting scope is essential, and multipark itineraries will allow you to quickly add dozens of new species to your all-time list.

◥ THE BEST

CHRISTOPHER BAKER

Parque Nacional Tortuguero (p287)

WILDLIFE-WATCHING

- **Monteverde & Santa Elena** (p128)
- **Parque Nacional Manuel Antonio** (p222)
- **Parque Nacional Corcovado** (p251)
- **Parque Nacional Tortuguero** (p287)
- **Parque Nacional Santa Rosa** (p156)

COSTA RICA IN FOCUS

ACTIVITIES

CULTURE

CHRISTER FREDRIKSSON

Chilling out beachside, Parque Nacional Cahuita (p291)

Costa Ricans – or Ticos, as they affectionately call themselves – take great pride in their country, from its ecological jewels, high standard of living and education to, above all else, the fact that it has flourished without an army for the past 60 years. They view their country as an oasis of calm in a region that has been continuously degraded by warfare. The Nobel Peace Prize that Oscar Arias Sánchez received for his work on the Central American peace accords is a point of pride and strengthens the general feeling that they are somehow different from a grosser, more violent world.

A lack of war and the presence of strong exports and heavier tourist traffic have meant that Costa Rica enjoys the highest standard of living in Central America. For the most part, Costa Ricans live fairly rich and comfortable lives, even by Western standards. Primary education is free and compulsory, contributing to the 95% literacy rate. Costa Rica also has a comprehensive socialized medical system and pension scheme that looks after the needs of the sick and elderly.

In fact, life expectancy in Costa Rica exceeds that of the United States, and most Costa Ricans are more likely to die from heart disease or cancer, as opposed to the childhood diseases that tend to claim lives in many developing nations. Universal health care and proper sanitation systems account for these positive statistics, as does a generally stress-free lifestyle, tropical climate and a balanced diet.

ECONOMY

For about 20 years, Costa Rica's economy has remained remarkably stable thanks to strong returns on tourism, agriculture and industry. Poverty levels have also been kept in check for more than 20 years by strong welfare programs. A subsistence farmer might earn as little as US$100 a year, far below the national average of US$11,500 per capita, but even in the most deprived areas, the vast majority of people have adequate facilities and clean drinking water.

In the 1940s Costa Rica was an overwhelmingly agricultural society, with most of the population employed on coffee and banana plantations. By the end of the century, the economy had shifted quite dramatically, and only one-fifth of the labor force was employed by agriculture. These days, industry employs another one-fifth, while the service sector employs more than half of the labor force. Tourism alone employs more than 10% of the labor force.

PEOPLE

More than 90% of Ticos are *mestizos,* a mix of Spanish with indigenous and/or African roots, though Ticos tend to consider themselves to be white. Although it's difficult to offer a precise explanation for this cultural phenomenon, it is partly due to the fact that Costa Rica's indigenous populations were virtually wiped out by the Spanish *conquistadores* (conquerors). As a result, most Costa Ricans prefer to trace their ancestry back to the European continent and take considerable pride in the clarity of their Spanish.

Indigenous Costa Ricans today make up only 1% of the total population. These groups include the Bribrí, Cabécar, Boruca (Brunka), Guaymí and Maleku. Blacks make up 3% of the total population, and primarily reside along the Caribbean coast. Tracing its ancestry to Jamaican immigrants who were brought to build railroads in the 19th century, this community speaks Mekatelyu, a patois of English, Spanish and Jamaican English. It identifies strongly with its counterparts in other Caribbean countries.

Chinese immigrants, who make up around 1% of the total population, also arrived in Costa Rica to build railroads in the 19th century, though there have been regular, more voluntary waves of immigration since then. In recent years North American and European immigration has greatly increased, and it is estimated that roughly 50,000 expats from these two regions presently live in Costa Rica.

More than 75% of Ticos are Catholic, and most people tend to go to church for the sacraments (baptism, first communion, confirmation, marriage and death) as well as the holidays. Roughly 14% of Costa Ricans are evangelical Christians, while the black community on the Caribbean coast is largely Protestant. There are also small Jewish populations in San José and Jacó, in addition to a sprinkling of practicing Muslims and Buddhists across the country.

LITERATURE

Few works by Costa Rican writers or novelists are available in translation and, unfortunately, much of what is written about Costa Rica and available in English (fiction or otherwise) is written by foreigners.

COSTA RICA IN FOCUS

CULTURE

◥ THE BEST

Sarchí (p86)

CULTURAL HOT SPOTS

- **Teatro Nacional** (p61)
- **Museo de Jade** (p62)
- **Museo de Arte y Diseño Contemporáneo** (p62)
- **Jazz Café** (p71)
- **Monteverde & Santa Elena** (p128)

Carlos Luis Fallas (1909–66) is widely known for *Mamita Yunai* (1940), an influential novel that took the banana companies to task for their labor practices. He remains very popular among the Latin American left.

Carmen Naranjo (1928–) is one of the few contemporary Costa Rican writers who has risen to international acclaim. She is a novelist, poet and short-story writer who also served as ambassador to India in the 1970s, and a few years later as Minister of Culture. In 1996 she was awarded the prestigious Gabriela Mistral medal from the Chilean government. Her collection of short stories, *There Never Was a Once Upon a Time,* is widely available in English. Two of her stories can also be found in *Costa Rica: A Traveler's Literary Companion.*

Tatiana Lobo (1939–) was actually born in Chile, but since 1967 she has lived in Costa Rica, where her many books are set. She received the noteworthy Premio Sor Juana Inés de la Cruz, an award for Latin American women novelists, for her novel *Asalto al paraíso* (Assault on Paradise).

Costa Rica: A Traveler's Literary Companion, edited by Barbara Ras, is a collection of short stories by modern Costa Rican writers – a glimpse of society from Ticos themselves.

Coconut milk is the drink of choice in the Parque Nacional Corcovado (p251)

GOD WAS LOOKING THE OTHER WAY

José León Sánchez (1930–) is an internationally renowned memoirist of Huetar descent. He was convicted for stealing from the famous Basílica de Nuestra Señora de los Ángeles (see boxed text, p92) in Cartago, and sentenced to serve his term at Isla San Lucas, one of Latin America's most notorious jails. Illiterate when he was incarcerated, Sánchez taught himself how to read and write, and clandestinely authored one of the continent's most poignant books, *La isla de los hombres solos* (called *God Was Looking the Other Way* in the translated version). This fictionalized account is based on the 20 years he served out of his original 45-year sentence. He later went on to produce 14 other novels and serve in several high-level public appointments.

THEATER & VISUAL ARTS

The most famous theater in the country is the Teatro Nacional in San José. The story goes that a noted European opera company was on a Latin American tour but declined to perform in Costa Rica for lack of a suitable hall. Immediately, the coffee elite put a special cultural tax on coffee exports for the construction of a world-class theater. The Teatro Nacional is now the premier venue for plays, opera, performances by the national symphony orchestra, ballet, poetry readings and other cultural events. It is also an architectural work in its own right and a landmark in any city tour of San José.

The visual arts in Costa Rica first took on a national character in the 1920s, when Teodorico Quirós, Fausto Pacheco and their contemporaries began painting landscapes that varied from traditional European styles, depicting the rolling hills and lush forest of Costa Rican countryside, often sprinkled with characteristic adobe houses.

The contemporary scene has more variety and it is difficult to define a unique Tico style. Several individual artists have garnered acclaim for their work, including the magical realism of Isidro Con Wong, the surreal paintings and primitive engravings of Francisco Amighetti, and the mystical female figures painted by Rafa Fernández. Other artists incorporate an infinite variety of themes in various media, from painting and sculpture to video and site-specific installations. The Museo de Arte y Diseño Contemporáneo in San José is the top place to see this type of work, and its permanent collection is a great primer.

MUSIC & DANCE

The mix of cultures in Costa Rica has resulted in a lively music scene, incorporating elements from North and South America and the Caribbean islands. Popular dance music includes Latin dances, such as salsa, merengue, bolero and cumbia.

One Tico salsa group that has made a significant name for itself at a regional level is Los Brillanticos, who once shared the stage with Cuban legend Celia Cruz during a tour stop she made in San José. Timbaleo is a salsa orchestra founded by Ramsés Araya, who became famous as the drummer for Panamanian salsa superstar Rubén Blades. Taboga Band is another long-standing Costa Rican group that plays jazz-influenced salsa and merengue.

BILL BACHMANN

Brightly painted *carreta* (oxcart) wheel, San José (p51)

San José features a regular line-up of domestic and international rock, folk and hip-hop artists, but you'll find that the regional sounds are equally vibrant, featuring their own special rhythms, instruments and styles. For instance, the Península de Nicoya has a rich musical history, most of it made with guitars, maracas and marimbas. The traditional sound on the Caribbean coast is calypso, which has roots in the Afro-Carib slave culture. Also check out Costa Rican–born Chavela Vargas (1919–), a folkloric singer with a hauntingly beautiful voice that has influenced generations of Latin American performers.

Guanacaste is also the birthplace of many traditional dances, most of which depict courtship rituals between country folk. The most famous dance – sometimes considered the national dance – is the *punto guanacasteco*. What keeps it lively is the *bomba,* a rhymed verse, shouted out by the male dancers during the musical interlude.

↘ ENVIRONMENT

LUKE HUNTER

La Leona Ranger Station, Parque Nacional Corcovado (p251)

Rich in natural resources, Costa Rica has gone from suffering the highest rates of deforestation in Latin America in the early 1990s, to being a global model for tropical conservation. Now in charge of an exemplary system of well-managed and accessible parks, Costa Rica is perhaps the best place in the world to experience rainforest habitats, while its stunning natural landscape is easily the top reason tourists visit this delightful country.

Despite its diminutive size, 51,000-sq-km Costa Rica is a study in contrasts and contradictions. On one coast it fronts scenic Pacific shores, while only 119km away lies the muggy Caribbean coast, with a range of active volcanoes and alpine peaks in between.

COAST TO COAST

With a length of 1016km, the Pacific coastline is infinitely varied as it twists and turns around gulfs, peninsulas and many small coves. Rugged, rocky headlands alternate with classic white- and black-sand beaches and palm trees to produce an image of a tropical paradise along some stretches. Strong tidal action creates an excellent habitat for waterbirds as well as visually dramatic crashing surf (perfect for surfers). Inland, the landscapes of the Pacific lowlands are equally dynamic, ranging from dry deciduous forests and open cattle country in the north, to lush, magnificent tropical rainforests in the south.

Monotonous in comparison, the Caribbean coastline runs a straight 212km along a low, flat plain that is inundated with brackish lagoons and waterlogged forests. A lack

COSTA RICA IN FOCUS

ENVIRONMENT

RALPH HOPKINS

The collared redstart is just one of the many birds you'll spot in Costa Rica

of strong tides allows plants to grow right over the water's edge along coastal sloughs, creating walls of green vegetation. Broad, humid plains that scarcely rise above sea level and murky waters characterize much of this region.

HIGHLANDS & VALLEYS

Running down the center of the country, the mountainous spine of Costa Rica is a land of active volcanoes, clear tumbling streams and chilled peaks clad in impenetrable cloud forests. These mountain ranges generally follow a northwest to southeast line, with the highest and most dramatic peaks in the south near the Panamanian border, culminating at the 3820m-high Cerro Chirripó (p263). The difficulties of traveling through and farming on these steep slopes have saved much of this area from development, and made it a haven for wildlife.

In the midst of the highlands is the Meseta Central – or Central Valley – which is surrounded by mountains (the Cordillera Central to the north and east and the Cordillera de Talamanca to the south). It is this fertile central plain, 1000m and 1500m above sea level with abundant rainfall and consistently mild temperatures, that contains four of Costa Rica's five largest cities and more than half of the country's population.

ANIMALS

With a total of 850 avian species recorded in Costa Rica, it's understandable that birds are one of the country's primary attractions. Even if you're not a so-called 'bird-watcher,' you will almost certainly see one of Costa Rica's four types of monkeys and two sloths. There are also an additional 230 types of mammals awaiting the patient observer, from kinkajous and porcupines to agoutis and otters.

Costa Rica's four species of sea turtles – olive ridley, leatherback, green and hawksbill – deservedly get a lot of attention. All four species are classified as endangered or critically endangered, meaning that they face an imminent threat of extinction. Fortunately, populations are increasing, thanks to various protection programs along both coasts.

Other exotic creatures include Central America's largest land mammal, the 300kg Baird's tapir, which is largely restricted to the least accessible wilderness areas. Even more gigantic is the 600kg West Indian manatee, which populates the canals of Parque Nacional Tortuguero (p287).

Costa Rica's sexiest endangered species is undoubtedly the reclusive jaguar. Jaguars require a large area to support enough prey to survive. Annually, an individual jaguar needs the equivalent of 53 white-tailed deer, 18 peccaries, 40 coatis, 25 armadillos and 55 ctenosaurs (spinytail iguanas). That is for one jaguar!

The extensive networks of protected areas are prime places to spot wildlife. But remember that these creatures do not know park boundaries, so keep your eyes peeled in the forested areas and buffer zones that often surround these sanctuaries. Early morning is the best time to see animals because many species sleep during the hottest part of the day.

PLANTS

Close to 12,000 species of vascular plants have been described in Costa Rica, and more are being added to the list every year – orchids alone account for about 1400 species. The range of habitats created when this many species mix is a wonder to behold. One day you may find yourself canoeing in a muggy mangrove swamp, and the next day squinting through bone-chilling fog to see orchids in a cloud forest.

Classic rainforest habitats are well represented in the parks of the southwest corner of Costa Rica or in mid-elevation portions of the central mountains. Here you will find

COSTA RICAN GEOLOGY

Nowhere else in the world are so many types of habitats squeezed into such a tiny area. In terms of number of species per 10,000 sq km, Costa Rica tops the list of countries at 615. This simple fact alone makes Costa Rica the premier destination for nature-lovers from all over the world.

The large number of species in Costa Rica is due to the relatively recent appearance of the country. Roughly three million years ago, Costa Rica rose from the ocean, and formed a land bridge between North and South America. As species from these two vast biological provinces started to mingle, the number of species essentially doubled in the area where Costa Rica now sits.

Costa Rica's geologic history can be traced to the impact of the Cocos Plate moving northeast and crashing into the Caribbean Plate at a rate of about 10cm every year – quite fast by geological standards. The point of impact, or subduction zone, is where the Cocos Plate forces the edge of the Caribbean Plate to break up and become uplifted. It is not a smooth process, hence Costa Rica is prone to earthquakes and ongoing volcanic activity. Volcán Arenal, in the north, is one of the world's most active volcanoes.

towering trees that block out the sky, long looping vines and many overlapping layers of vegetation. Large trees often show dramatic buttresses, wing-like ribs that extend out from their trunks for added structural support.

Along brackish stretches of both coasts, mangrove swamps are a world unto themselves. Growing stilt-like out of muddy tidal flats, five species of trees crowd together so densely that no boat and few animals can penetrate. Striking in their adaptations for dealing with salt, mangrove trees thrive where no other land plant dares tread.

Cloud forests are widespread at high elevations throughout Costa Rica, and are home to fabulous fog-drenched trees so thickly coated in mosses, ferns, bromeliads and orchids that you can hardly discern their true shapes. Be forewarned, however, that in these habitats the term 'rainy season' has little meaning because it's always dripping wet from the fog.

For a complete change of pace, try exploring the unique drier forests along the northwestern coast. During the dry season many trees drop their leaves, creating

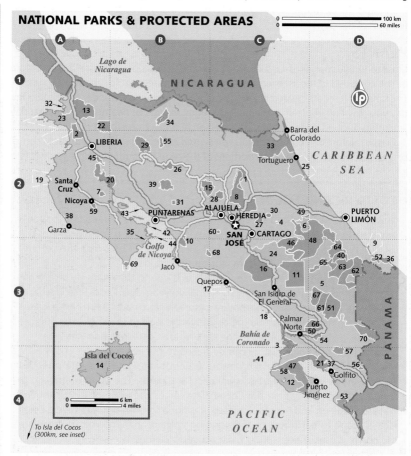

NATIONAL PARKS & PROTECTED AREAS

carpets of crackling, sun-drenched leaves and a sense of openness that is largely absent in other Costa Rican habitats. The large trees here, such as Costa Rica's national tree, the guanacaste, have broad, umbrella-like canopies.

NATIONAL PARKS

The national-park system began in the 1960s, and has since been expanded into a National Conservation Areas System with an astounding 186 protected areas, including 32 national parks, eight biological reserves, 13 forest reserves and 51 wildlife refuges. At least 10% of the land is strictly protected and another 17% is included in various multiple-use preserves.

You might also be surprised to learn that in addition to the system of national preserves, there are hundreds of small, privately owned lodges, reserves and haciendas (estates) that have been set up to protect the land, and many of these are well worth visiting.

With Costa Rican parks contributing significantly to both national and local economies through the huge influx of tourist money, there is little question that the country's healthy natural environment is important to its citizens. In general, support for land preservation remains high because it provides income and jobs to so many people, plus important opportunities for scientific investigation.

COSTA RICA IN FOCUS

ENVIRONMENT

⬎ THE BEST

RALPH HOPKINS

Parque Nacional Corcovado (p251)

ECO HOT SPOTS

- **Parque Nacional Corcovado** (p251)
- **Monteverde & Santa Elena** (p128)
- **Parque Nacional Manuel Antonio** (p222)
- **Parque Nacional Chirripó** (p262)
- **Parque Nacional Tortuguero** (p287)
- **Parque Internacional La Amistad** (p267)

SAVING THE ENVIRONMENT

No other tropical country has made such a concerted effort to protect the environment, and in 2008 Costa Rica was ranked one of the top five nations in the world for its overall environmental performance. Historically, Costa Rica lost about 80% of its forest cover before the government stepped in with a plan to protect what was left. Since then, through ambitious forest protection and reforestation, 52% of the country is once again tree-covered, a stunning accomplishment in a mere 20 years.

It is also worth noting that many private lodges and reserves are doing some of the best conservation work in the country. It's really inspiring to run across homespun efforts to protect Costa Rica's environment spearheaded by hardworking families or small organizations tucked away in some forgotten corner of the country. These include projects to boost rural economies by raising butterflies or native flowers, efforts by villagers to document their local biodiversity, or amazingly resourceful campaigns to raise funds to purchase endangered lands.

FAMILY TRAVEL

PHILIP & KAREN SMITH

Having some mud-soaked fun, Liberia (p145)

Wild animals, active volcanoes, rainforests, beaches – what kid wouldn't love Costa Rica? Parents are guaranteed a good time as well, and will definitely appreciate the country's myriad adventure possibilities as well as a culture that dotes on children. Therefore, we have authored this segment of the book with the needs of your little ones in mind.

Costa Rica is a kid-friendly country, especially since Ticos themselves tend to be extremely family-oriented, and will go out of their way to lavish attention on children. In fact, Costa Rica is arguably the most accessible family destination in Latin America, so check your worries and concerns along with the baggage, and get ready for what may be the best family vacation you've ever taken.

WHERE TO GO

Families could go just about anywhere in Costa Rica and be perfectly happy. Even San José has a few sights for children (see p62), but it's best to get out of the cities and towns and into the countryside or along the coastlines.

From plush jungle ecolodges to beachside jungle tents, you can find the type of accommodations your family needs pretty much anywhere tourists go. Most midrange and top-end hotels have reduced rates for children under 12, provided the child shares a room with parents. Top-end hotels will provide cribs and usually have activities for children. Throughout this book, we have marked particularly kid-friendly accommodations with this symbol: 👶 .

COSTA RICA IN FOCUS

FAMILY TRAVEL

WHAT TO EAT

Costa Rican cuisine is simple and hearty and somewhat bland (beans and rice and grilled chicken or steak are omnipresent), making it acceptable for even the most finicky eaters. Special kids' meals are not normally offered in restaurants, though some fancy lodges prepare them. However, most local eateries will accommodate two children splitting a meal or can produce child-size portions on request.

If you're traveling with an infant, stock up on milk formula and baby food before heading to remote areas, and always carry snacks for long drives in remote areas – sometimes there are no places to stop for a bite.

Tired of juice and water? Here are some local drinks that your kids are sure to love: *batidos* (fresh fruit shakes), either *al agua* (made with water) or *con leche* (with milk); coconut milk (sipped through a straw straight from the cracked-open coconut); and *horchata* (cinnamon-spiked rice milk).

⬎ THE BEST

PHILIP & KAREN SMITH

Boogie-boarding, Laguna de Arenal (p125)

PLACES KIDS LOVE

- **Monteverde & Santa Elena** (p128)
- **Parque Nacional Manuel Antonio** (p222)
- **Parque Nacional Tortuguero** (p287)
- **Playa Sámara** (p187)
- **Volcán Arenal** (p118)

⬎ THE NITTY GRITTY

- **Breast-feeding** OK in public
- **Change facilities** In upmarket hotels and resorts
- **Cots** In upmarket hotels and resorts (best to book in advance)
- **Health** Food-borne and infectious diseases are of very minor concern
- **Highchairs** In most tourist-friendly restaurants
- **Nappies (diapers)** Widely available
- **Strollers** Available, but best to bring your own
- **Transport** Consider private shuttles or rental car

And don't worry too much – generally speaking, tap water and ice cubes in Costa Rica are safe for foreigners to consume.

ANYTHING ELSE?

Here are some additional tips and resources:

- Children under the age of 12 get a 25% discount on internal air travel, while children under two fly free (provided they sit on an adult's lap).
- If you're traveling with an infant, bring disposable diapers, baby creams, baby aspirin and thermometer from home, or else stock up while in San José.
- For a complete resource on traveling with kids, get a copy of Lonely Planet's *Travel with Children* guide.

FOOD & DRINK

CHRISTER FREDRIKSSON

A typical Costa Rican *casado* (set meal) of chicken, beans, vegetables, plantains and rice

All it takes is a quick glance at the menu to realize that Costa Rica is firmly rooted in the tropics. Fro m exotic fruits such as mangoes, guavas and lychees and the obligatory cup of shade-grown coffee, to fillets of locally raised fish and a zesty *ceviche* (raw, well-marinated seafood) featuring the catch of the day, Costa Rica is just as much a feast for the palate as it is for the eyes.

Thatched country kitchens can be found all over Costa Rica, with local women ladling out basic but hearty home-cooked specials known as *comida típica* (literally 'typical food'). And of course, Ticos go wild for a good steak, which partially explains the abundance of cattle ranches throughout the country. If you prefer your fare a bit more upscale with a nouveau twist, the country's trendier tourist areas have seen high levels of immigration, which assures a wide selection of just about anything you might want to munch on.

BREAKFAST

Breakfast for Ticos is usually *gallo pinto* (literally 'spotted rooster'), a stir-fry of rice and beans. When combined, the beans color the rice, and the mix obtains a specked appearance. Served with eggs, cheese or *natilla* (sour cream), *gallo pinto* is generally cheap, filling and sometimes can be downright tasty.

If you are not keen on rice and beans, many hotels will provide what they refer to as a 'tropical breakfast,' which is usually freshly baked bread along with a selection of fresh fruits. North American–style breakfasts are also available for a quick fix of eggs, ham and hash browns.

LUNCH & DINNER

Most restaurants in Costa Rica offer lunch and dinner sets called a *casado* or a 'married man's meal.' This is nearly always cheap, filling and well balanced with meat, beans, rice and salad. An extremely popular *casado* is the ubiquitous *arroz con pollo*, which is chicken and rice that is usually dressed up with grains, vegetables and a good mix of mild spices. Also look out for *patacones*, which are mashed plantains that are fried and eaten like french fries (chips).

As a general rule, in Costa Rica food is not heavily spiced, unless of course you're having traditional Caribbean-style cuisine such as fiery jerk chicken. Indeed, the vast majority of Ticos have a distinct aversion to hot sauce, though most local restaurants will lay out a spicy *curtido* (a pickle of hot peppers and vegetables) or little bottles of Tabasco-style sauce for the diehards. Another popular condiment is *salsa lizano*, the Tico version of Worcestershire sauce.

Among locals, the most popular foreign food is Chinese. Nearly every town has a Chinese place, and even if it doesn't, menus will likely include *arroz cantonés* (fried rice). Italian food has also made inroads, and pizza parlors and pasta houses abound. In the tourist areas, Asian Fusion and Nuevo Latino are more recent developments that blend traditional Asian and Latin cooking styles with local and tropical ingredients.

DRINKS

Coffee is probably the most popular beverage in the country and wherever you go, someone is likely to offer you a *cafecito*. Traditionally, it is served strong and mixed with hot milk to taste, also known as *café con leche*. Most drinkers get *café negro* (black coffee) and for those who want a little milk, you can ask for *leche al lado* (milk on the side). Trendier places serve cappuccinos and espressos, and milk is nearly always pasteurized, safe to drink and delicious.

For a refresher, nothing beats *batidos* – fresh fruit drinks (like smoothies) made either *al agua* (with water) or *con leche* (with milk). The array on offer can be mind-boggling and includes mango, papaya, *piña* (pineapple), *sandía* (watermelon), *melón* (cantaloupe), *mora* (blackberry), *zanahoria* (carrot), *cebada* (barley) or *tamarindo* (fruit of the tamarind tree).

Pipas are green coconuts that have a hole macheted into the top and a straw for drinking the 'milk' – a very refreshing and filling drink. *Agua dulce* is sugarcane water,

---

NEED HELP IN THE KITCHEN?

Cocinando con Tía Florita is one of the most popular Tico cooking shows. Check out the recipes and meet Tía Florita herself at www.cocinandocontiaflorita.tv. Also keep an eye out for *Entradas: Journeys in Latin American Cuisine* by Joan Chatfield-Taylor, which has some of Costa Rica's most popular recipes – and many others. Finally, *Costa Rican Typical Foods* by Carmen de Musmani and Lupita de Weiler is out of print, but it is perhaps the only Tico-specific cookbook ever written. Need something to wash down your culinary creation? You can order gourmet Costa Rican coffee and other treats at www.cafebritt.com.

or in many cases boiled water mixed with brown sugar. *Horchata,* found mostly in the countryside, is a sweet drink made from cornmeal and flavored with cinnamon.

ALCOHOL

The most popular alcoholic drink is beer, and there are several local brands to recommend. Imperial is perhaps the most popular – either for its smooth flavor or for the ubiquitous T-shirts emblazoned with their eagle-crest logo. Pilsen, another tasty pilsner varietal, has a higher alcohol content and a stronger flavor. Bavaria produces a lager and Bavaria Negro, a delicious, full-bodied dark beer.

After beer, the poison of choice is *guaro,* which is a colorless alcohol distilled from sugarcane and usually consumed by the shot, though you can order it as a sour. It goes down mighty easily, but leaves one hell of a hangover. As in most of Central America, the local rums are inexpensive and worthwhile, especially the Ron Centenario, which recently shot to international fame.

Most Costa Rican wines are cheap, taste cheap, and will be unkindly remembered the next morning. Imported wines are fortunately available, and Chilean brands are your best bet for a palatable wine at an affordable price.

WHERE TO EAT & DRINK

The most popular eating establishment in Costa Rica is the *soda*. These are small, informal lunch counters dishing up a few daily *casados*. Other popular cheapies include the omnipresent fried- and rotisserie-chicken stands.

A regular *restaurante* is usually higher on the price scale and has slightly more atmosphere. Many *restaurantes* serve *casados,* while the fancier places refer to the set lunch as the *almuerzo ejecutivo* (literally 'executive lunch').

CHRISTOPHER BAKER

Rambutans are one of the many tropical fruits you can sample in Costa Rica

↘THE BEST

Casados (set meals) are a tasty, good-value option

PLACES TO EAT

- **Kapi Kapi Restaurant** (p221)
- **Seasons by Shlomy** (p183)
- **Pacific Bistro** (p214)
- **Machu Picchu** (p64)
- **El Loco Natural** (p295)

For something smaller, *pastelerías* and *panaderías* are shops that sell pastries and bread, while many bars serve snacks called *bocas,* which are snack-sized portions of main meals.

Lunch is usually the day's main meal and is typically served around noon. Dinner tends to be a lighter version of lunch and is eaten around 7pm.

HABITS & CUSTOMS

Costa Ricans are open and informal, and treat their guests well. If you have the good fortune to be invited into a Tico home, you can expect to be served first, receive the biggest portion and perhaps even receive a parting gift. On your part, flowers or wine are both fine gifts to bring, though the best gift you can offer is extending a future dinner invitation to your hosts.

Remember that when you sit down to eat in a restaurant, it is polite to say *buenos días* (good morning) or *buenas tardes* (good afternoon) to the waitstaff and/or any people you might be sharing a table with. It is also polite to say *buen provecho,* which is the equivalent of *bon appétit,* at the start of the meal.

HISTORY

COSTA RICA IN FOCUS

HISTORY

GER/IMAGEBROKER

Colonial architecture, San José (p51)

Humans have inhabited the coastlines and rainforests of Central America for at least 10,000 years. On the eve of European discovery some 500 years ago, an estimated 400,000 people were living in today's Costa Rica. Sadly, our knowledge about these pre-Columbian cultures is scant as natural disasters and Spanish colonization wiped away the remains of entire civilizations. However, tales of lost cities still survive in the oral histories of Costa Rica's indigenous communities, and considering that vast stretches of the country are home to inaccessible mountains and unchartered rainforests, perhaps these dreams aren't so fanciful.

On his fourth and final voyage to the New World in 1502, Christopher Columbus was forced to drop anchor near present-day Puerto Limón after a hurricane damaged his ship. While waiting for repairs, Columbus ventured into the verdant terrain, and exchanged gifts with hospitable and welcoming chieftains. He returned from this

11,000 BC	1000 BC	100 BC
The first humans occupy Costa Rica and populations flourish due to the rich land and marine resources along both coastlines.	The Huetar power base in the Central Valley is solidified around Guayabo, continuously inhabited until its mysterious abandonment in 1400.	Costa Rica becomes part of an extensive trade network for gold and other goods extending from present-day Mexico to the Andean empires.

encounter, claiming to have seen 'more gold in two days than in four years in Española.' Columbus dubbed the stretch of shoreline from Honduras to Panama as Veraguas, but it was excited descriptions of *la costa rica* or 'the rich coast' by subsequent explorers that gave the country its lasting name.

To the disappointment of his conquistador heirs, the region was not abundant with gold, and the locals were considerably less than affable. Spain's first colony in present-day Panama was abruptly abandoned when tropical disease and warring tribes decimated its ranks. Successive expeditions launched from the Caribbean coast also failed as pestilent swamps, oppressive jungles and volcanoes made Columbus' paradise seem more like a tropical hell.

NEW WORLD ORDER

It was not until the 1560s that a Spanish colony was firmly established in Costa Rica. Hoping to cultivate the rich volcanic soil of the Central Valley, the Spanish founded the village of Cartago (p90) on the banks of the Río Reventazón. Although the fledgling colony was extremely isolated, it miraculously survived under the leadership of its first governor, Juan Vásquez de Coronado. Preferring diplomacy over firearms to counter indigenous resistance, Coronado used Cartago as a base to survey the lands south to Panama and west to the Pacific, and secured deed and title over the colony.

Though Coronado was later lost at sea in a shipwreck, his legacy endured: Costa Rica was an officially recognized province of the Viceroyalty of New Spain (Virreinato de Nueva España), which was the name given to the viceroy-ruled territories of the Spanish empire in North America, Central America, the Caribbean and Asia.

For roughly three centuries, the Captaincy General of Guatemala (also known as the Kingdom of Guatemala), which extended from modern-day Texas to Panama with the exception of Belize, was a loosely administered colony in the vast Spanish empire. Since the political-military headquarters of the kingdom were in Guatemala, Costa Rica became a minor provincial outpost that had little if any strategic significance or exploitable riches.

THE FALL OF AN EMPIRE

On October 27, 1807, the Treaty of Fontainebleau, which defined the occupation of Portugal, was signed between Spain and France. Under the guise of reinforcing the Franco-Spanish army occupying Portugal, Napoleon moved tens of thousands of troops into Spain. In an act of military genius, Napoleon ordered his troops to abandon the ruse and seize key Spanish fortifications. Without firing a single shot, Napoleon's troops captured Barcelona after convincing the city to open its gates for a convoy of wounded soldiers.

AD 800	1522	1540
Indigenous production of granite spheres begins in the Diquís region, but archaeologists remain divided as to their function and significance.	Spanish settlement develops in Costa Rica, though it will be several decades before the colonists get a sturdy foothold on the land.	The Kingdom of Guatemala is established by the Spanish, and covers much of Central America, including present-day Costa Rica.

Although Napoleon's invasion by stealth was successful, the resulting Peninsular War was a horrific campaign of guerrilla combat that crippled both countries. As a result of the conflict as well as the subsequent power vacuum and internal turmoil, Spain lost nearly all of its colonial possessions in the first third of the 19th century.

In 1821 the Americas wriggled free of Spain's imperial grip following Mexico's declaration of independence for itself as well as the whole of Central America. Of course, the Central American provinces weren't too keen on having another foreign power reign over them, and subsequently declared independence from Mexico. However, all of these events hardly disturbed Costa Rica, which learned of its liberation a month after the fact.

PRE-COLUMBIAN COSTA RICA

The early inhabitants of Costa Rica were part of an extensive trading zone that extended as far south as Peru and as far north as Mexico. The region hosted roughly 20 small tribes, organized into chiefdoms, indicating a permanent leader, or *cacique,* who sat atop a hierarchical society that included shamans, warriors, toilers and slaves.

Adept at seafaring, the Carib dominated the Atlantic coastal lowlands, and served as a conduit of trade with the South American mainland. In the northwest, several tribes were connected to the great Mesoamerican cultures. Aztec religious practices and Maya jade and craftsmanship are in evidence in the Península de Nicoya, while Costa Rican quetzal feathers and golden trinkets have turned up in Mexico. In the southwest, three chiefdoms showed the influence of Andean indigenous cultures, including coca leaves, yucca and sweet potatoes.

There is also evidence that the language of the Central Valley, Huetar, was known by Costa Rica's indigenous groups, which may be an indication of their power and influence. The Central Valley is home to the only major archaeological site uncovered in Costa Rica, namely Guayabo (p95). Thought to be an ancient ceremonial center, Guayabo once featured paved streets, an aqueduct and decorative gold. Here, archaeologists uncovered exquisite gold ornaments and unusual life-size stone statues of human figures, as well as distinctive types of pottery and *metates,* stone platforms that were used for grinding corn. Today, the site consists of little more than ancient hewed rock and stone, though Guayabo continues to stand as a testament to a once-great civilization of the New World.

1562	1563	1737
Spanish conquistador Juan Vásquez de Coronado arrives in Costa Rica as governor, determined to move settlers to the more hospitable Central Valley.	The first permanent Spanish colonial settlement in Costa Rica is established by Juan Vásquez de Coronado in Cartago.	The future capital of San José is established, sparking a rivalry with neighboring Cartago that will eventually culminate in a civil war.

The newly liberated colonies pondered their fate: stay together in a United States of Central America, or go their separate national ways. At first, they came up with something in between, namely the Central American Federation (CAF), though it could neither field an army nor collect taxes. Accustomed to being at the center of things, Guatemala also attempted to dominate the CAF, alienating smaller colonies and hastening its demise.

Meanwhile, an independent Costa Rica was taking shape under Juan Mora Fernández, first head of state (1824–33). He tended toward nation-building and organized new towns, built roads, published a newspaper and coined a currency. His wife even partook in the effort by designing the country's flag.

Life returned to normal, unlike in the rest of the region where postindependence civil wars raged on. In 1824 the Nicoya-Guanacaste Province seceded from Nicaragua and joined its more easygoing southern neighbor, defining the territorial borders. In 1852 Costa Rica received its first diplomatic emissaries from the USA and Great Britain.

COFFEE RICA

In the 19th century, the riches that Costa Rica had long promised were uncovered when it was realized that the soil and climate of the Central Valley highlands were ideal for coffee cultivation. Costa Rica led Central America in introducing the caffeinated bean, which transformed the impoverished country into the wealthiest in the region.

When an export market was discovered, the government actively promoted coffee to farmers by providing free saplings. At first, Costa Rican producers exported their crop to nearby South Americans, who processed the beans and re-exported the product to Europe. By the 1840s, however, local merchants had already built up domestic capacity and learned to scope out their own overseas markets. Their big break came when they persuaded the captain of the HMS *Monarch* to transport several hundred sacks of Costa Rican coffee to London, percolating the beginning of a beautiful friendship.

The Costa Rican coffee boom was on. The drink's quick fix made it popular among working-class consumers in the industrializing north. The aroma of riches lured a wave of enterprising German immigrants to Costa Rica, enhancing the technical and financial skills in the business sector. By century's end, more than one-third of the Central Valley was dedicated to coffee cultivation, and coffee accounted for more than 90% of all exports and 80% of foreign-currency earnings.

Coffee wealth became a power resource in politics. Costa Rica's traditional aristocratic families were at the forefront of the enterprise. At midcentury, three-quarters of the coffee barons were descended from just two colonial families. The country's leading coffee exporter at this time was President Juan Rafael Mora Porras (1849–59), whose lineage went back to the colony's founder Juan Vásquez de Coronado.

1821	April 1823	December 1823
Following a unanimous declaration by Mexico on behalf of all of Central America, Costa Rica finally gains its independence from Spain.	The Costa Rican capital officially moves to the more liberal San José after intense skirmishes with the conservative residents of Cartago.	The Monroe Doctrine declares the intentions of the USA to be the dominant imperial power in the western hemisphere.

BANANA EMPIRE

The coffee trade unintentionally gave rise to Costa Rica's next export boom – bananas. Getting coffee out to world markets necessitated a rail link from the central highlands to the coast, and Limón's deep harbor made an ideal port. Inland was dense jungle and infested swamps, which prompted the government to contract the task to Minor Keith, nephew of a North American railroad tycoon.

The project was a disaster. Malaria and accidents churned through workers as Tico recruits gave way to US convicts and Chinese indentured servants, who were in turn replaced by freed Jamaican slaves. To entice Keith to continue, the government turned over 3200 sq km of land along the route and provided a 99-year lease to run the railroad. In 1890 the line was finally completed and running at a loss.

Keith had begun to grow banana plants along the tracks as a cheap food source for the workers. Desperate to recoup his investment, he shipped some bananas to New Orleans in the hope of starting a side venture. He struck gold, or rather yellow. Consumers went crazy for the elongated finger fruit. By the early 20th century, bananas surpassed coffee as Costa Rica's most lucrative export and the country became the world's leading banana exporter. Unlike in the coffee industry, however, the profits were exported along with the bananas.

CHRISTER FREDRIKSSON

Coffee *finca* (plantation), Parque Nacional Volcán Poás, Central Valley (p73)

1824	1856	1889
The Nicoya-Guanacaste region votes to secede from Nicaragua and become a part of Costa Rica.	Costa Rica puts a damper on the expansionist aims of the war hawks in the USA by defeating William Walker's army at the Battle of Santa Rosa.	Costa Rica's first democratic elections are held, though unfortunately blacks and women are prohibited by law to vote.

Costa Rica was transformed by the rise of Keith's banana empire. He joined with another North American importer to found the infamous United Fruit Company, soon to be the largest employer in Central America. To the locals, it was known as *el pulpo*, or the octopus – its tentacles stretched across the region, becoming entangled with the local economy and politics. United Fruit owned huge swaths of lush lowlands, much of the transportation and communication infrastructure and bunches of bureaucrats. The company sparked a wave of migrant laborers from Jamaica, changing the country's ethnic complexion and provoking racial tensions.

THE BEST

IMAGEBROKER/SIEPMANN

Parque Juan Santamaría, Alajuela (p84)

PLACES TO FEEL HISTORY

- **Guayabo** (p95)
- **San José** (p51)
- **Cartago** (p90)
- **Alajuela** (p84)
- **Heredia** (p88)

BIRTH OF A NATION

The inequality of the early 20th century led to the rise of José Figueres Ferrer, a self-described farmer-philosopher and the father of Costa Rica's unarmed democracy. The son of Catalan immigrant coffee planters, Figueres excelled in school and went to MIT, in Boston, to study engineering. Upon returning to Costa Rica to set up his own coffee plantation, he organized the hundreds of laborers on his farm into a utopian socialist community, and appropriately named the property La Luz Sin Fin, or 'The Struggle Without End.'

In the 1940s, Figueres became involved in national politics as an outspoken critic of President Calderón. In the midst of a radio interview in which he badmouthed the president, police broke into the studio and arrested Figueres. He was accused of having fascist sympathies and banished to Mexico. While in exile, however, he formed the Caribbean League, a collection of students and democratic agitators from all over Central America, who pledged to bring down the region's military dictators. When he returned to Costa Rica, the Caribbean League, now 700-men strong, went with him and helped protest against the powers that be.

FAST FACT

In the 1940s children in Costa Rica learned to read with a text that stated 'Coffee is good for me. I drink coffee every morning.'

1890	1900	1914
The construction of the railroad between San José and Puerto Limón is finally completed despite years of hardship and countless deaths.	The population of Costa Rica reaches 50,000 as the country prospers due to the increasingly lucrative international coffee and banana trades.	Costa Rica is given an economic boost following the opening of the Panama Canal, forged by 75,000 laborers.

When government troops descended on the farm with the intention of arresting Figueres and disarming the Caribbean League, it touched off a civil war. The moment had arrived: the diminutive farmer-philosopher now played the man on horseback. Figueres emerged victorious from the brief conflict and seized the opportunity to put into place his vision of Costa Rican social democracy. After dissolving the country's military, Figueres quoted HG Wells: 'The future of mankind cannot include the armed forces.'

As head of a temporary junta government, Figueres enacted nearly 1000 decrees. He taxed the wealthy, nationalized the banks and built a modern welfare state. His 1949 constitution granted full citizenship and voting rights to women, blacks, indigenous groups and Chinese minorities. Today, Figueres' revolutionary regime is regarded as the foundation for Costa Rica's unarmed democracy.

THE AMERICAN EMPIRE

Throughout the 1970s and '80s, the USA played the role of watchful big brother in Latin America, challenging the sovereignty of smaller nations. Big sticks, gunboats and dollar diplomacy were instruments of a Yankee policy to curtail socialist politics, especially the military oligarchies of Guatemala, El Salvador and Nicaragua.

In 1979 the rebellious Sandinistas toppled the American-backed Somoza dictatorship in Nicaragua. Alarmed by the Sandinistas' Soviet and Cuban ties, fervently

COSTA RICA IN FOCUS

HISTORY

CHRISTER FREDRIKSSON

Modern San José (p51) has accommodations to suit all travelers

1919	1940	1940s
Federico Tinoco Granados is ousted as the dictator of Costa Rica in an episode of brief violence in an otherwise peaceful political history.	Rafael Ángel Calderón Guardia is elected president and enacts minimum-wage laws as well as an eight-hour day.	José Figueres Ferrer becomes involved in national politics and opposes the ruling conservatives and President Calderón.

anticommunist President Ronald Reagan decided it was time to intervene. The Cold War arrived in the hot tropics.

The organizational details of the counterrevolution were delegated to Oliver North, an eager-to-please junior officer working out of the White House basement. North's can-do creativity helped to prop up the famed Contra rebels to incite civil war in Nicaragua. While both sides invoked the rhetoric of freedom and democracy, the war was really a turf battle between left-wing and right-wing forces.

Under intense US pressure, Costa Rica was reluctantly dragged in. The Contras set up camp in northern Costa Rica, from where they staged guerrilla raids. Not-so-clandestine CIA operatives and US military advisors were dispatched to assist the effort. Allegedly, Costa Rican authorities were bribed to keep quiet. A secret jungle airstrip was built near the border to fly in weapons and supplies. To raise cash for the rebels, North allegedly used his covert supply network to traffic illegal narcotics through the region.

The war polarized Costa Rica. From conservative quarters came a loud call to re-establish the military and join the anticommunist crusade, which was largely under-written by the US Pentagon. In May of 1984, more than 20,000 demonstrators marched through San José to give peace a chance, though the debate didn't climax until the 1986 presidential election. The victor was 44-year-old Oscar Arias Sánchez who, despite being born into coffee wealth, was an intellectual reformer in the mold of Figueres, his political patron.

Once in office, Arias affirmed his commitment to a negotiated resolution and reasserted Costa Rican national independence. He vowed to uphold his country's pledge of neutrality and to vanquish the Contras from the territory, which prompted the US ambassador to suddenly quit his post. In a public ceremony, Costa Rican school children planted trees on top of the CIA's secret airfield. Most notably, Arias became the driving force in uniting Central America around a peace plan, which ended the Nicaraguan war and earned him the Nobel Peace Prize in 1987.

In 2006 Arias once again returned to the presidential office, winning the popular election by a 1.2% margin, and subsequently ratifying the controversial Central American Free Trade Agreement (Cafta).

COSTA RICA TOMORROW

Costa Rica held free and fair presidential elections in February 2010, which were super-vised by the Organization of American States. The victor was Oscar Arias Sánchez' former Vice President Laura Chinchilla, who won just under 47% of the vote, thus retaining the political power of her center-right National Liberation Party. Chinchilla campaigned on similar economic platforms as her political mentor, namely the promotion of free trade and further increased access to US markets.

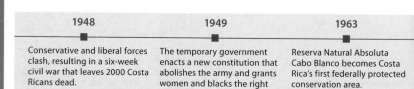

1948	1949	1963
Conservative and liberal forces clash, resulting in a six-week civil war that leaves 2000 Costa Ricans dead.	The temporary government enacts a new constitution that abolishes the army and grants women and blacks the right to vote.	Reserva Natural Absoluta Cabo Blanco becomes Costa Rica's first federally protected conservation area.

Monument donated by Anastasio Somoza, Parque Central, San José (p51)

Unlike Arias, Chinchilla is a staunch social conservative that is diametrically opposed to legalized abortion, same-sex marriage and emergency contraception. In a striking departure from her political mentor, she has pledged to fight against proposed legislation that would strip Costa Rica of its official Roman Catholic designation and establish a secular state.

Costa Rica will most likely continue its reign as the global pioneer in sustainable development, providing a model in which economic and environmental interests are complementary. Indeed, the country is one of the few in the region where environmental issues are given a proper forum for discussion as opposed to mere lip service.

1987	2000	2007
President Oscar Arias Sánchez wins the Nobel Peace Prize for his work on the Central American peace accords.	The population of Costa Rica tops four million, though the number may be far greater due to illegal settlements on the fringes of the capital.	A national referendum narrowly passes Cafta; opinion remains divided as to whether opening up trade with the USA will be beneficial in the long run.

SHOPPING

LEE FOSTER

Locally woven fabric for sale, near Parque Nacional Manuel Antonio (p222)

Costa Rica is certainly memorable in and of itself, but a few carefully selected souvenirs can go a long way in making the memories last. Fortunately, there is some excellent shopping to be had around the country, with plenty of unique items on offer ranging from shade-grown coffee and locally brewed liqueurs to artisanal woodworks and indigenous handicrafts.

The most popular purchases in Costa Rica are of the culinary variety, which means that you and your family or friends can enjoy the taste of the tropics long after you've returned to cooler climes. Woven bags of deep-roasted coffee most definitely get top billing, though variations on the caffeine fix include Café Rica liqueur and chocolate-covered espresso beans. Salsa Lizano, which is sold by the bottle nearly everywhere, will add some Latin flair to your kitchen back home.

Tico tipples are also easy to pack in a suitcase: Ron Centenario is an internationally recognized Costa Rican rum that can be enjoyed either on ice or artfully mixed with a splash of soda and lime. *Guaro,* the local firewater, may not win any awards for precision crafting, but it's guaranteed to help get the good times rolling. And of course, no trip to Costa Rica would be complete without purchasing the requisite Imperial T-shirt, a symbol of Costa Rica's most celebrated brew – a tree frog sticking to the bottle scores you extra points!

HARDWOODS

The tiny town of Sarchí in the Central Valley is famous for one thing and one thing only: *carretas,* the elaborate, colorfully painted oxcarts that are the unofficial souvenir of

Costa Rica – as well as the official symbol of the Costa Rican worker.

In Sarchí these come ready for the road (oxen sold separately) or in scaled-down versions (ready to display in gardens or used as minibars). But the town produces plenty of other curios as well: leather-and-wood furniture (including incredible rocking chairs that collapse for shipping), wood tableware and an infinite array of trinkets emblazoned with the colorful mandala design popularized by *carretas*.

Tropical-hardwood items include plates, goblets, jewelry boxes and a variety of carvings and ornaments. The most exquisite woodwork is available at Biesanz Woodworks in the San José suburb of Escazú. All of the wood here is grown on farms for the express purpose of resale, so you needn't worry about forests being chopped down for your salad bowl.

CAROL BARRINGTON - DE/AURORA

Hand-painted *carretas* (oxcarts), Sarchí (p86)

PLACES TO SHOP

- **Sarchí** (p86)
- **Monteverde & Santa Elena** (p141)
- **Mercado Central** (p66)
- **Biesanz Woodworks** (p72)
- **Galería Namu** (p65)

> THE BEST

COSTA RICA IN FOCUS

SHOPPING

ARTS & CRAFTS

Art galleries throughout Costa Rica are geared primarily toward tourists, and specialize in 'tropical art' (for lack of an official description): brightly colored, whimsical folk paintings depicting flora and fauna that evoke the work of French artist Henri Rousseau. The mountaintop getaway towns of Monteverde and Santa Elena are chock-full of cutesy, cool galleries and tourist shops where you can quickly survey the artistic scene.

Given the prominence of its pre-Columbian history, Costa Rica is home to an impressive offering of indigenous crafts, which include intricately carved and painted masks as well as handwoven bags and linens. Although they're widely available, the best place to shop for these items is at Galería Namu in San José, which cuts out the middle man and deals directly with the various indigenous craft production centers.

SUSTAINABLE TRAVEL

JAN CSERNOCH/ALAMY

Working with turtles, Punta Banco, near Pavones (p257)

As the world's most iconic ecotourism destination, Costa Rica spoils travelers with a never-ending assortment of environmentally friendly activities. However, the greatest challenge for travelers in Costa Rica is preserving the purity of this destination for future generations. The secret is out, the tourism industry is booming, and travelers are leaving behind a larger footprint on the country than ever before. As a result, travelers are increasingly looking at ways to minimize the impact of their stay in Costa Rica, and to travel in the most sustainable way possible.

One of the simplest things you can do before going to Costa Rica is to learn about the country's major conservation and environmental issues. While traveling in Costa Rica, don't be afraid to ask questions, especially since the best source of information about an area is usually a local.

An immediate benefit of tourism is a strong financial boost to the local economy. Keep this in mind if the opportunity arises to spend money at a locally run business or vendor. Enjoy the creativity of a local artisan. If you spot a piece on display that catches your eye, buy it instead of saying you'll come back later. In all cases, you'll be surprised how far your colones can stretch.

A great way of stimulating local economies in a sustainable manner is to frequent businesses that are dedicated to these aims. For a list of ecofriendly businesses in Costa Rica, see the GreenDex on p380.

PROTECT THE ENVIRONMENT

While traveling in Costa Rica, there are lots of small but substantial things that you can do to protect the environment. For example, consider filling up your bottle from a rainwater-collection system, or even purifying natural water sources while hiking. Reusing (or recycling) plastic bottles relieves pressure on crowded landfills, and reduces the chance of illegal dumping.

Speaking of garbage, don't hesitate to pick up any that you see along beaches and hiking trails – your actions might just inspire another person to do the same. And when you're out hiking, do stick to the trails as this reduces erosion and protects fragile plants and the wildlife that they support.

When in doubt, remember that common sense and awareness are always your best guides, regardless of where you are in the world.

THE BEST

Hotel Sí Como No (p221)

ECOLODGES

- **Tiskita Jungle Lodge** (p257)
- **Celeste Mountain Lodge** (p155)
- **Hotel Sí Como No** (p221)
- **Punta Mona** (p299)
- **Lapa Ríos** (p250)

COSTA RICA IN FOCUS

SUSTAINABLE TRAVEL

SAVE THE RAINFOREST

Want to do even more by helping to save the rainforest? Say no to beef. One of the main reasons for forest clearing in Central America is to make way for cattle pasture –

Olive ridley turtles, Refugio Nacional de Fauna Silvestre Ostional (p195)

La Fortuna area (p112)

CHRISTER FREDRIKSSON

mostly to feed the export market. If you can't bypass that burger, make sure you know where your cow came from. Consider indulging in grass-fed beef, which is better for your health and better for the environment.

Need caffeine? Drink organic, shade-grown coffee. Organic coffee growing avoids the use of chemical pesticides and fertilizers, minimizing their impact on flora and fauna. Shade-grown coffee is planted under shade plants that produce nitrogen, which improves the quality of both the soil and the coffee crop, and helps to ensure the survival of old-growth forests.

While traveling in Costa Rica, do your part and spread the word among fellow travelers – go green!

↘ DIRECTORY & TRANSPORTATION

DIRECTORY
ACCOMMODATIONS

The hotel situation in Costa Rica ranges from luxurious ecolodges and sparkling all-inclusive resorts to backpacker palaces and I-can't-believe-I'm-paying-for-this barnyard-style quarters. Given this astounding variety of accommodations, it's rare to arrive in a town and find nowhere to sleep.

High- or dry-season (December to April) prices are provided throughout this book, though many lodges lower their prices during the low or rainy season (May to November). Keep in mind that prices change quickly in Costa Rica, so it's best to see the prices in this book as approximations rather than facts.

Throughout this book, sleeping options are listed in order of budget, unless otherwise specified. Prices are inclusive of tax and given in US dollars, which is preferred currency for listing rates in Costa Rica. However, colones are accepted everywhere, and are usually exchanged at current rates without an additional fee.

B&BS

Almost unknown in the country prior to the ecotourism boom, the B&B phenomenon has swept through Costa Rica in the past two decades, primarily fueled by the increasing number of resident European and North American expats. Generally speaking, B&Bs in Costa Rica tend to be midrange to top-end affairs. While some B&Bs are reviewed in this guide, you can also find this type of accommodations on several websites (although they are far from exhaustive):

BedandBreakfast.com (www.bedand breakfast.com/costa-rica.html)

Costa Rica Innkeepers Association (www.costaricainnkeepers.com)

Pamela Lanier's Worldwide Bed & Breakfast Directory (www.lanierbb.com)

HOSTELS

The hostel scene has gone increasingly upmarket in recent years, and is no longer just recommended to shoestringing backpackers. In fact, hostels in Costa Rica can sometimes be surprisingly pricey affairs, though the quality of service and accommodations represents excellent value.

HOTELS

It is always advisable to ask to see a room – and a bathroom – before committing to a stay, especially in budget lodgings.

BUDGET

For the most part, you can expect a typical double to cost up to US$40 at the lower end of the scale in Costa Rica. Cheaper places generally have shared bathrooms, but it's still possible to get a double with a private bathroom for US$25 in some towns off the tourist trail. (Note that 'private' in some low-end establishments consists of a stall in the corner of your hotel room.) On the top end of the budget scale, rooms will frequently include a fan and a private bathroom that may or may not have hot water. At the cheapest ho-

---

⚓ BOOK YOUR STAY ONLINE

For more accommodations reviews and recommendations by Lonely Planet authors, check out the online booking service at www.lonely planet.com. You'll find the true, insider lowdown on the best places to stay. Reviews are thorough and independent. Best of all, you can book online.

HOSTEL & HOTEL SECURITY

Although hotels give you room keys, it is recommended that you carry a padlock for your backpack or suitcase for extra security. Furthermore, don't invite trouble by leaving valuables, cash or important documents lying around your room or in an unlocked bag. Upmarket hotels will have safes where you can keep your money and passport, so it's advised that you take advantage of them. If you're staying in a basic place, it's probably wise to take your valuables with you at all times. Theft is perhaps the number-one complaint of travelers in Costa Rica, so it can't hurt to take a few extra precautions.

tels, rooms will frequently be a stall, with walls that don't go to the ceiling.

Hot water in showers is often supplied by electric showerheads (affectionately termed the 'Costa Rican suicide shower'). Contrary to traveler folklore, they are perfectly safe – provided you don't fiddle with the showerhead while it's on. The electric showerhead will actually dispense hot water if you keep the pressure low.

MIDRANGE & TOP END

Midrange lodging options generally cost between US$40 and US$100. These rooms will be more comfortable than budget options, and usually include a private bathroom with gas-heated hot water, a choice between fan and air-con, and cable or satellite TV. The better places will offer tour services, and many will have an on-site restaurant or bar and a swimming pool or Jacuzzi. In this price range, many hotels offer kitchenettes or even full kitchens, and using them is a great way to save money if you're traveling in a large group or as a family.

Anything more than US$100 is at the higher end of the scale, and includes ecolodges, all-inclusive resorts, business and chain hotels, in addition to a strong network of more intimate boutique hotels, remote jungle camps and

upmarket B&Bs. Many such lodging options will include amenities such as hot-water bathtubs, private decks, satellite TV and air-con as well as concierge, tour and spa services.

Most midrange and top-end places charge 13% in taxes. This book has attempted to include taxes in the prices listed throughout. Note that many hotels charge per person, rather than per room – read rates carefully. For information on reserving hotels by credit card, see boxed text, p343.

CLIMATE CHARTS

For a small country, Costa Rica's got an awful lot of weather going on. The highlands are cold, the cloud forest is misty and cool, San José and the Central Valley get an 'eternal spring,' and both the Pacific and Caribbean coasts are pretty much sweltering year-round – get ready for some bad-hair days! See also the climate charts on p342.

CUSTOMS REGULATIONS

All travelers over the age of 18 are allowed to enter the country with 5L of wine or spirits and 500g of processed tobacco (400 cigarettes or 50 cigars). Camera gear, binoculars, as well as camping, snorkeling and other sporting equipment, are readily allowed into the country.

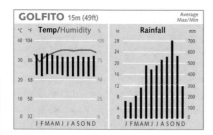

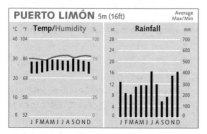

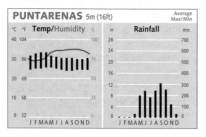

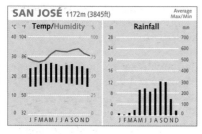

DANGERS & ANNOYANCES

For the latest official reports on travel to Costa Rica see the travel advisories on the websites of the **US State Department** (www.travel.state.gov/travel) and the **UK Foreign & Commonwealth Office** (www.fco.gov.uk).

EARTHQUAKES & VOLCANIC ERUPTIONS

Costa Rica lies on the edge of active tectonic plates, so it is decidedly prone to earthquakes. Recent major quakes occurred in 1990 (7.1 on the Richter scale) and 1991 (7.4). Smaller quakes and tremors happen quite often – particularly on the Península de Nicoya – cracking roads and knocking down telephone lines. The volcanoes in Costa Rica are not really dangerous as long as you stay on designated trails and don't try to peer into the crater of an active volcano. As a precaution, always check with park rangers before setting out in the vicinity of active volcanoes.

HIKING HAZARDS

Hikers setting out into the wilderness should be adequately prepared for their trips. Most importantly, don't bite off more than you can chew. If your daily exercise routine consists of walking from the fridge to the TV, don't start your trip with a 20km trek. There are plenty of 3km and 5km trails that are ideally suited to less-frequent hikers.

In addition, carry plenty of water, even on very short trips. The hiking is hot and dehydration sets in quickly. In Parque Nacional Corcovado, hikers have died from exhaustion on the scorching trail between San Pedrillo and Sirena ranger stations. Hikers have also been known to get lost in rainforests, so carry maps, extra food and a compass. Let someone know where you are going, so they can narrow the search area in the event of an emergency.

OCEAN HAZARDS

Approximately 200 drownings a year occur in Costa Rican waters, 90% of which are caused by riptides, which are strong currents that pull the swimmer out to sea. Many deaths in riptides are caused by panicked swimmers struggling to the point of exhaustion. If you are caught in a riptide, do not struggle. Simply float and let the tide carry you out beyond the breakers, after which the riptide will dissipate. Then swim parallel to the beach and allow the surf to carry you back in.

RIVER-RAFTING HAZARDS

River-rafting expeditions may be particularly risky during periods of heavy rain – flash floods have been known to capsize rafts. Reputable tour operators will ensure conditions are safe before setting out.

THEFTS & MUGGINGS

The biggest danger that most travelers face is theft, primarily from pickpockets. There is a lot of petty crime in Costa Rica – especially in San José – so keep your wits about you at all times and don't let your guard down.

DISCOUNT CARDS

Students with an International Student Identity Card (ISIC) or a valid ID card from a university offering four-year courses are generally entitled to discounts on museum or guided-tour fees. Cards supplied by language schools are not accepted.

EMBASSIES & CONSULATES

Mornings are the best time to go to embassies and consulates, as this is when they are at their quietest. Australia and New Zealand do not have consular representation in Costa Rica; the closest embassies are in Mexico City. For visa information see p354. All of the following are located in San José.

Canada (☎ 2242-4400; Oficentro Ejecutivo La Sabana, 3rd fl, Edificio 3, Sabana Sur) Behind La Contraloría.

France (☎ 2234-4167) On the road to Curridabat, 200m south and 50m west of the Indoor Club.

Germany (☎ 2232-5533; 8th fl, Torre La Sabana, Sabana Norte) 300m west of the ICE building.

Israel (☎ 2221-6444; 11th fl, Edificio Centro Colón, Paseo Colón btwn Calles 38 & 40)

Italy (☎ 2234-2326; cnr Av Central & Calle 41, Los Yoses)

Netherlands (☎ 2296-1490; Oficentro Ejecutivo La Sabana, 3rd fl, Edificio 3, Sabana Sur) Behind La Contraloría.

DIRECTORY

DISCOUNT CARDS

RESERVING BY CREDIT CARD

Some of the pricier hotels will require that you confirm your reservation with a credit card. Before doing so, note that some top-end hotels require a 50% to 100% payment upfront when you reserve. Unfortunately, many of them don't communicate this rule clearly.

Sometimes visitors end up 'reserving' a room only to find out that they have actually paid for it in advance. Technically, reservations can be canceled and refunded with enough advance notice. (Again, ask the hotel about its cancellation policy.) However, in Costa Rica it's a lot easier to make the reservation than to cancel it. In addition, many hotels charge a hefty service fee for credit-card use.

Have the hotel fax or email you a confirmation. Hotels often get overbooked, and if you don't have confirmation, you could be out of a room.

Spain (☎ 2222-1933; Calle 32 btwn Paseo Colón & Av 2)

Switzerland (☎ 2221-3229; 10th fl, Edificio Centro Colón, Paseo Colón btwn Calles 38 & 40)

UK (☎ 2258-2025; 11th fl, Edificio Centro Colón, Paseo Colón btwn Calles 38 & 40)

USA (☎ 2220-3939; Carretera a Pavas) Opposite Centro Commercial del Oeste.

FESTIVALS & EVENTS

See the calendar on p46 for further information.

GAY & LESBIAN TRAVELERS

Let's start with the good news. In Costa Rica, the situation facing gay and lesbian travelers is better than in most Central American countries. Homosexual acts between two consenting adults (aged 18 and over) are legal, though note that travelers may be subject to the laws of their own country in regard to sexual relations. Most Costa Ricans are tolerant of homosexuality only at a 'don't ask, don't tell' level. This is undoubtedly a side effect of the strong role of Catholicism and the persistence of traditionalism in society.

Here's the bad news. In the past decade, there has been an increasing number of outward acts of prejudice. In 1998 a gay-and-lesbian festival planned in San José was canceled following heavy opposition from Catholic clergy. The church also forced the cancellation of a gay-and-lesbian tour to Manuel Antonio, and encouraged the boycott of a coastal hotel hosting a gay group. Things took an embarrassing turn in 1999 when the tourism minister said that Costa Rica should not be a destination for sex tourism or gays. The gay community made it clear that it was against sex tourism, and that linking gay tourism with sex tourism was untrue and defamatory. The official position in Costa Rica was then modified, stating that gay tourism was neither encouraged nor prohibited.

Thankfully, Costa Rica's gays and lesbians have made some strides. In the 1990s the Supreme Court ruled against police harassment in gay nightspots and guaranteed medical treatment to people living with HIV/AIDS. And in June 2003 the first ever gay-pride festival in San José drew more than 2000 attendants. Gays and lesbians traveling in Costa Rica are unlikely to be confronted with poor treatment; nonetheless, outside of gay spots, public displays of affection are not recommended.

The undisputed gay and lesbian capital of Costa Rica is Manuel Antonio (see p219).

The monthly newspaper *Gayness* and the magazine *Gente 10* (in Spanish) are both available at gay bars in San José.

BARGAINING

A high standard of living along with a steady stream of international tourist traffic means that the Latin American tradition of haggling is fast dying out in Costa Rica. In tourist towns especially, fixed prices on hotels cannot be negotiated, and you can expect business owners to be offended if you try. Some smaller hotels in the interior regions still accept the practice. Negotiating prices at outdoor markets is acceptable, and bargaining is accepted when hiring long-distance taxis. Overall, Ticos respond well to good manners and gentle inquiries. If you demand a service for your price, chances are you won't get it.

There are a number of other resources for gay travelers:

Agua Buena Human Rights Association (☎ 2280-3548; www.aguabuena. org, in Spanish) This noteworthy nonprofit organization has campaigned steadily for fairness in medical treatment for people living with HIV/AIDS in Costa Rica.

Cipac (☎ 2280-7821; www.cipacdh.org, in Spanish) The leading gay-activist organization in Costa Rica.

International Gay & Lesbian Travel Association (IGLTA; ☎ in USA 800-448-8550, 954-776-2626; www.iglta.org) Maintains a list of hundreds of travel agents and tour operators all over the world.

Tiquicia Travel (☎ 2256-9682; www.tiquicia travel.com) Makes arrangements at gay-friendly hotels.

Toto Tours (☎ in USA 800-565-1241, 773-274-8686; www.tototours.com) Gay-travel specialists who organize regular trips to Costa Rica, among other destinations.

HEALTH

Travelers to Costa Rica need to be vigilant about food- and mosquito-borne infections. Most of these illnesses are not life-threatening, but they can certainly ruin your trip. As a general rule, it's important to use a good insect repellent and exercise care in what you eat and drink.

BEFORE YOU GO

Consult with your doctor about which vaccinations are recommended prior to embarking on a trip to Costa Rica. Since most vaccines don't produce immunity until at least two weeks after they're given, visit four to eight weeks before departure. Also ask for an International Certificate of Vaccination (otherwise known as 'the yellow booklet'), which will list all the vaccinations you've received. This is mandatory for countries that re-quire proof of yellow-fever vaccination upon entry, but it's a good idea to carry it wherever you travel.

Bring medications in their original containers, clearly labeled. A signed, dated letter from your physician describing all medical conditions and medications, including generic names, is also a good idea. If carrying syringes or needles, be sure to have a physician's letter documenting their medical necessity.

Most doctors and hospitals expect payment in cash, regardless of whether you have travel health insurance or not. If you develop a life-threatening medical problem, you'll probably want to be evacuated to a country with state-of-the-art medical care. As this may cost tens of thousands of dollars, make sure you have insurance to cover this before you leave home. A list of medical evacuation and travel insurance companies is on the website of the **US State Department** (www.travel.state.gov/medical.html).

If your health insurance does not cover you for medical expenses while you are abroad, you should consider supplemental insurance. Check the Travel Services section of the Lonely Planet website at www.lonelyplanet.com for more information. It might pay to find out in advance if your insurance plan will make payments directly to providers or if they reimburse you later for any overseas health expenditures.

There is a wealth of travel-health advice on the internet. A superb book called *International Travel and Health*, which is revised annually and is available online at no cost, is published by the **World Health Organization** (www.who.int/ith). Another website of general interest is **MD Travel Health** (www.mdtravelhealth.com), which provides complete travel-health recommendations for every country, updated daily, also at no cost.

DIRECTORY

HEALTH

For further information, see *Healthy Travel Central & South America* from Lonely Planet. If you're traveling with children, Lonely Planet's *Travel with Children* will be useful. The *ABC of Healthy Travel,* by E Walker et al, is another valuable resource.

HEALTH CARE IN COSTA RICA

Good medical care is available in most major cities, but it may be limited in rural areas. Main medical centers:

MEDICAL CHECKLIST

- acetaminophen (Tylenol) or aspirin
- adhesive or paper tape
- antibacterial ointment (eg Bactroban) for cuts and abrasions
- antibiotics
- antidiarrheal drugs (eg loperamide)
- antihistamines for hay fever and allergic reactions
- anti-inflammatory drugs (eg ibuprofen)
- bandages, gauze, gauze rolls
- insect repellent (containing DEET) for the skin
- insect spray (containing permethrin) for clothing, tents and bed nets
- iodine tablets for water purification
- oral rehydration salts
- pocket knife
- scissors, safety pins, tweezers
- steroid cream or cortisone for poison ivy and other allergic rashes
- sunblock
- syringes and sterile needles
- thermometer

CIMA San José (☎ 2208-1000; Autopista Próspero Fernández, San José) Located 500m west of the tollbooths on the highway to Santa Ana.

Clínica Bíblica (☎ 2522-1000/1030; www.clinicabiblica.com; Av 14 btwn Calles Central & 1, San José)

Hospital Nacional de Niños (☎ 2222-0122; Calle 14 & Av Central, San José) Only for children under 12 years of age.

San Juan de Dios Hospital (☎ 2257-6282; cnr Paseo Colón & Av Central, San José)

For a medical emergency, you can also call one of the following numbers:
Poison Center (☎ 2223-1028)
Red Cross Ambulance (☎ 128, 2221-5818)

For an extensive list of physicians, dentists and hospitals go to the website of the **US embassy** (usembassy.or.cr). If you're pregnant, check this site before departure to find an obstetrician, just in case.

Most pharmacies are well supplied and the pharmacists are licensed to prescribe medication. If you're taking any medication on a regular basis, make sure you know its generic (scientific) name, since many pharmaceuticals go under different names in Costa Rica. The following pharmacies in San José are open 24 hours:
Farmacia Clínica Bíblica (☎ 2522-1000; cnr Calle 1 & Av 14, San José)
Farmacia Clínica Católica (☎ 2283-6616; Guadalupe, San José)

INFECTIOUS DISEASES

DENGUE FEVER (BREAKBONE FEVER)
Dengue fever is a viral infection found throughout Central America. In Costa Rica outbreaks involving thousands of people occur every year. Dengue is transmitted by Aedes mosquitoes, which prefer to bite during the daytime and are usually found close to human habitations, often indoors.

They breed primarily in artificial water containers such as jars, barrels, cans, cisterns, metal drums, plastic containers and discarded tires. As a result, dengue is especially common in densely populated, urban environments.

Dengue usually causes flulike symptoms including fever, muscle aches, joint pains, headaches, nausea and vomiting, often followed by a rash. The body aches may be quite uncomfortable, but most cases resolve uneventfully in a few days. Severe cases usually occur in children under the age of 15 who are experiencing their second dengue infection.

Since there is no vaccine, the key to prevention is taking insect-protection measures.

HEPATITIS A

Hepatitis A is the second most common travel-related infection (after traveler's diarrhea). It's a viral infection of the liver that is usually acquired by ingestion of contaminated water, food or ice, though it may also be acquired by direct contact with infected persons. The illness occurs throughout the world, but the incidence is higher in developing nations. Symptoms may include fever, malaise, jaundice, nausea, vomiting and abdominal pain. Most cases resolve without complications, though hepatitis A occasionally causes severe liver damage. There is no treatment.

The vaccine for hepatitis A is extremely safe and highly effective. If you get a booster six to 12 months later, it lasts for at least 10 years. You should get vaccinated before you go to Costa Rica or any other developing nation. Because the safety of hepatitis A vaccine has not been established for pregnant women or children under the age of two, they should instead be given a gammaglobulin injection.

HEPATITIS B

Like hepatitis A, hepatitis B is a liver infection that occurs worldwide but is more common in developing nations. Unlike hepatitis A, the disease is usually acquired by sexual contact or by exposure to infected blood, generally through blood transfusions or contaminated needles. The vaccine is recommended for long-term travelers (on the road more than six months) who expect to live in rural areas or have close physical contact with the local population. Additionally, the vaccine is recommended for anyone who anticipates sexual contact with the local inhabitants or a possible need for medical, dental or other treatments while abroad, especially if a need for transfusions or injections is expected.

Hepatitis B vaccine is safe and highly effective. However, a total of three injections are necessary to establish full immunity. Several countries added hepatitis B vaccine to the list of routine childhood immunizations in the 1980s, so many young adults are already protected.

HIV/AIDS

The HIV/AIDS virus occurs in all Central American countries. Be sure to use condoms for all sexual encounters.

MALARIA

Malaria occurs in every country in Central America. It's transmitted by mosquito bites, usually between dusk and dawn. The main symptom is high spiking fevers, which may be accompanied by chills, sweats, headache, body aches, weakness, vomiting or diarrhea. Severe cases may involve the central nervous system and lead to seizures, confusion, coma and death.

Taking malaria pills is recommended for the provinces of Alajuela, Limón (except for Puerto Limón), Guanacaste and Heredia. The risk is greatest in the cantons of Los Chiles (Alajuela province), and Matina and Talamanca (Limón province).

For Costa Rica the first-choice malaria pill is chloroquine, taken once weekly in a dosage of 500mg, starting one to two weeks before arrival and continuing through the trip and for four weeks after departure. Chloroquine is safe, inexpensive and highly effective. Side effects are typically mild and may include nausea, abdominal discomfort, headache, dizziness, blurred vision or itching. Severe reactions are uncommon.

Protecting yourself against mosquito bites is just as important as taking malaria pills, since no pills are 100% effective.

If you may not have access to medical care while traveling, you should bring along additional pills for emergency self-treatment, which you should take if you can't reach a doctor and you develop symptoms that suggest malaria, such as high spiking fevers. One option is to take four tablets of Malarone once daily for three days. If you start self-medication, you should try to see a doctor at the earliest possible opportunity.

If you develop a fever after returning home, see a physician as malaria symptoms may not occur for months.

ENVIRONMENTAL HAZARDS
INSECT BITES

No matter how much you safeguard, getting bitten by mosquitoes is part of every traveler's experience in the country. While there are occasional outbreaks of dengue in Costa Rica, for the most part the great-

PRACTICALITIES

- **Electricity** Electrical current is 110V AC at 60Hz; plugs are two flat prongs (same as in the USA).
- **Emergency** The local tourism board, Instituto Costarricense de Turismo (ICT; www.visitcostarica.com), is located in San José and distributes a helpful brochure with up-to-date emergency numbers for every region.
- **Magazines** The Spanish-language *Esta Semana* is the best local weekly news magazine.
- **Newspapers** The most widely distributed newspaper is *La Nación* (www. nacion.co.cr), followed by *Al Día* (a tabloid), *La República* (www.larepublica. net) and *La Prensa Libre* (www.prensalibre.co.cr). *Tico Times* (www.ticotimes. net), the English-language weekly newspaper, hits the streets every Friday afternoon.
- **Radio** The English-language radio station on 107.5FM plays current hits and provides a regular BBC news feed.
- **TV** Cable and satellite TV are widely available for a fix of CNN, French videos or Japanese news, and local TV stations have a mix of news, variety shows and *telenovelas* (Spanish-language soap operas).
- **Video Systems** Videos on sale use the NTSC image registration system (same as in the USA). DVDs in Costa Rica are region 4.
- **Weights & Measures** Costa Ricans use the metric system for weights, distances and measures.

est worry you will have with bites is the general discomfort that comes with them, namely itching.

The best prevention is to stay covered up – wearing long pants, long sleeves, a hat and shoes (rather than sandals). Unfortunately, Costa Rica's sweltering temperatures might make this a bit difficult. Therefore, the best measure you can take is to invest in a good insect repellent, preferably one containing DEET. (These insect repellents can also be found in Costa Rica.) This should be applied to exposed skin and clothing (but not to eyes, mouth, cuts, wounds or irritated skin).

In general, adults and children over 12 can use preparations containing 25% to 35% DEET, which usually lasts about six hours. Children between two and 12 years of age should use preparations containing no more than 10% DEET, applied sparingly, which will usually last about three hours. Neurologic toxicity has been reported from DEET, especially in children, but appears to be extremely uncommon and generally related to overuse. Compounds containing DEET should not be used on children under the age of two.

Insect repellents containing certain botanical products, including eucalyptus and soybean oil, are effective but last only 1½ to two hours.

A particularly good item for every traveler to take is a bug net to hang over beds (along with a few thumbtacks or nails with which to hang it). Many hotels in Costa Rica don't have windows (or screens) and a cheap little net will save you plenty of nighttime aggravation. The mesh size should be less than 1.5mm.

Dusk is the worst time for mosquitoes, so it's best to take extra precautions once the sun starts to set.

SNAKE BITES

Costa Rica is home to all manner of venomous snakes and any foray into forested areas will put you at (a very slight) risk of snake bite. The best prevention is to wear closed, heavy shoes or boots and to keep a watchful eye on the trail. Snakes like to come out to cleared paths for a nap, so watch where you step. In the event of a bite from a venomous snake, place the victim at rest, keep the bitten area immobilized and move the victim immediately to the nearest medical facility. Avoid tourniquets, which are no longer recommended.

WATER

It's generally safe to drink tap water everywhere in Costa Rica, other than in the most rural and undeveloped parts of the country. However, if you prefer to be cautious, buying bottled water is your best bet. If you have the means, vigorous boiling for one minute is the most effective way of water purification. At altitudes greater than 2000m, boil for three minutes. Another option is to disinfect water with iodine pills: add 2% tincture of iodine to 1L of water (five drops to clear water, 10 drops to cloudy water) and let stand for 30 minutes. If the water is cold, longer times may be required.

TRAVELING WITH CHILDREN

In general, it's safe for children and pregnant women to go to Costa Rica. However, because some of the vaccines listed previously are not approved for use by children or during pregnancy, these travelers should be particularly careful not to drink tap water or consume any questionable food or beverage. Also, when traveling with children, make sure they're up-to-date on all routine immunizations. It's sometimes appropriate to give children

WHAT'S THAT ADDRESS?

Though some larger cities have streets that have been dutifully named, signage is rare in Costa Rica and finding a Tico who knows what street they are standing on is even rarer. Everybody uses landmarks when providing directions; an address may be given as 200m south and 150m east of a church. A city block is *cien metros* – literally 100m – so *250 metros al sur* means '2½ blocks south,' regardless of the distance. Churches, parks, office buildings, fast-food joints and car dealerships are the most common landmarks used – but these are often meaningless to the foreign traveler who will have no idea where the Subaru dealership is to begin with.

some of their vaccines a little early before visiting a developing nation. You should discuss this with your pediatrician. Lastly, if pregnant, bear in mind that should a complication such as premature labor develop while you're abroad, the quality of medical care may not be comparable to that in your home country.

HOLIDAYS

Días feriados (national holidays) are taken seriously in Costa Rica. Banks, public offices and many stores close. During these times, public transportation is tight and hotels are heavily booked. Many festivals (see p46) coincide with public holidays.

INSURANCE

No matter where you travel to in the world, getting a comprehensive travel-insurance policy is a good idea. For travel to Costa Rica, a basic theft/loss and medical policy is recommended. Read the fine print carefully as some companies exclude dangerous activities from their coverage, which can include scuba diving, motorcycling and even trekking. You may prefer a policy that pays doctors or hospitals directly rather than you having to pay on the spot and make a claim later. See also p360 for details on car insurance, and p345 for more on health insurance.

INTERNET ACCESS

Internet cafes abound in Costa Rica, and you don't have to look very far to find cheap and speedy internet access. The normal access rate in San José and tourist towns is US$1 to US$2 per hour, though you can expect to pay upwards of US$5 per hour in the hard-to-reach places.

Wi-fi access is on the rise in Costa Rica. If you keep your eyes open (and computer on), you'll find wireless hot spots in San José, Alajuela, Jacó, Monteverde and Santa Elena, La Fortuna, Tamarindo, Puerto Jiménez and Puerto Viejo de Talamanca. Furthermore, the majority of top-end hotels and backpacker hostels offer secure wireless networks to their customers.

LEGAL MATTERS

If you get into legal trouble and are jailed in Costa Rica, your embassy can offer limited assistance. This may include an occasional visit from an embassy staff member to make sure your human rights have not been violated, letting your family know where you are and putting you in contact with a Costa Rican lawyer, who you must pay yourself. Embassy officials will not bail you out and you are subject to Costa Rican laws, not the laws of your own country.

In Costa Rica the legal age for driving, voting and having heterosexual sex is 18 years, and you can get married when you are 15 years old. There is no specific legal age for homosexual sex, but sex with anyone under 18 is not advisable. Keep in mind that travelers may be subject to the laws of their own country in regard to sexual relations.

DRIVERS & DRIVING ACCIDENTS

Drivers should carry their passport and driver's license at all times. If you have an accident, call the police immediately to make a report (required for insurance purposes) or attend to any injured parties. Leave the vehicles in place until the report has been made and do not make any statements except to members of law-enforcement agencies. The injured should only be moved by medical professionals.

Keep your eye on your vehicle until the police arrive and then call the car-rental company to find out where you should take the vehicle for repairs (do not have it fixed yourself). If the accident results in injury or death, you could be jailed or prevented from leaving the country until legalities are handled.

Emergency numbers are listed on the inside front cover of this book.

MONEY

ATMS

It's increasingly easy to find *cajeros automáticos* (ATMs) in Costa Rica, even in the smallest towns. The Visa Plus network is the standard, but machines on the Cirrus network, which accepts most foreign ATM cards, can be found in larger cities and tourist towns. In these areas, ATMs also dispense US dollars, which is convenient for payments at hotels and tour agencies. Note that some machines will only accept cards held by their own customers.

CASH & CURRENCY

The Costa Rican currency is the colón (plural 'colones,' ₡), named after Cristóbal Colón (Christopher Columbus). Bills come in 500, 1000, 5000 and 10,000 notes, while coins come in denominations of 5, 10, 20, 25, 50 and 100. Note that older coins are larger and silver, while newer ones are smaller and gold-colored – this is often a source of confusion for travelers fresh off the plane.

Paying for things in US dollars should be free of hassle, and at times is encouraged since the currency is viewed as being more stable than colones (see boxed text, p352, for more on the dual currency issue). Newer US dollars (ie big heads) are preferred throughout Costa Rica.

At the time of writing, Costa Rica was about to roll out new banknotes in 2010, including two new denominations: ₡20,000 and ₡50,000. Old banknotes will subsequently be collected and destroyed, and no longer deemed legal tender. Fortunately, it should be easy enough for foreign tourists to tell the two sets apart, since the new bills will each have different colors, shapes and images than their predecessors.

CREDIT CARDS

You can expect a transaction fee on all international credit-card purchases. Holders of credit and debit cards can buy colones and sometimes US dollars in some banks, though you can expect to pay a high transaction fee. Cards are widely accepted at some midrange and most top-end hotels, as well as top-end restaurants and some travel agencies. All car-rental agencies accept credit cards.

EXCHANGING MONEY

All banks will exchange US dollars, and some will exchange euros and British pounds; other currencies are more difficult to exchange. Most banks have excruciatingly long lines, especially at the state-run institutions (Banco Nacional, Banco de Costa Rica, Banco Popular), though they don't charge commission on cash exchanges. Private banks (Banex, Banco Interfin, Scotiabank) tend to be faster. Make sure the dollar bills you want to exchange are in good condition or they may be refused.

TAXES

Travelers will notice a 13.39% sales tax at midrange and top-end hotels and restaurants, while hotels also charge an additional 3% tourist surcharge. Everybody must pay a US$26 airport tax upon leaving the country. It is payable in US dollars or in colones, and credit cards are accepted at the Juan Santamaría airport.

TIPPING

It is customary to tip the bellhop/porter (US$1 to US$5 per service) and the house-keeper (US$1 to US$2 per day) in top-end hotels, less in budget places. On guided tours, tip the guide US$5 to US$15 per person per day. Tip the tour driver about half of what you tip the guide. Naturally, tips depend upon quality of service. Taxi drivers are not normally tipped, unless some special service is provided. Top-end restaurants may add a 10% service charge onto the bill. If not, you might leave a small tip to show your appreciation, but it is not required.

TRAVELER'S CHECKS

Most banks and exchange offices will cash traveler's checks at a commission of 1% to 3%. Some hotels will accept them as payment, but check policies carefully as many hotels do not. US dollar traveler's checks are preferred. It may be difficult or impossible to change traveler's checks of other currencies.

PHOTOGRAPHY

Costa Ricans make wonderful subjects for photos. However, most people resent having cameras thrust in their faces, and some attach price tags to their mugs. As a rule,

---

DOLLARS VS COLONES

While colones are the official currency of Costa Rica, US dollars are virtually legal tender. Case in point: most ATMs in large towns and cities will dispense both currencies. However, it pays to know where and when you should be paying with each currency.

In Costa Rica you can use US dollars to pay for hotel rooms, midrange to top-end meals, admission fees for sights, tours, domestic flights, international buses, car rental, private shuttle buses and large-ticket purchase items. However, local meals and drinks, domestic bus fares, taxis and small-ticket purchase items should be paid for in colones.

Throughout this book, all of our listings for hotels, sights and activities contain prices in US dollars. For eating, drinking and entertainment listings, prices are given in colones. With regard to transportation, our use of either dollars or colones reflects the preferred currency for a given mode.

you should ask for permission if you have an inkling your subject would not approve.

Since most people use digital cameras these days, it can be quite difficult to purchase high-quality film in Costa Rica. However, most internet cafes in the country can burn your digital pictures on CD, and cheap media is available for purchase in most large towns and cities.

TELEPHONE

Public phones are found all over Costa Rica and Chip or Colibrí phone cards are available in 1000, 2000 and 3000 colón denominations. Chip cards are inserted into the phone and scanned. Colibrí cards (more common) require you to dial a toll-free number (☎ 199) and enter an access code. Instructions are provided in English or Spanish. Colibrí is the preferred card among travelers since it can be used from any phone. Cards can be found just about everywhere, including supermarkets, pharmacies, newsstands, *pulperías* (corner grocery stores) and gift shops.

The cheapest international calls from Costa Rica are direct-dialed using a phone card. To make international calls, dial '00' followed by the country code and number. Pay phones cannot receive international calls.

Make sure that no one is peeking over your shoulder when you dial your code. Some travelers have had their access numbers pilfered by thieves.

To call Costa Rica from abroad, use the country code (☎ 506) before the eight-digit number. Find other important phone numbers on the inside front cover of this book.

Due to the increasing popularity of voice-over IP services like Skype, it's sometimes possible to skip the middle man and just bring a headset along with you to an internet cafe. Ethernet connections and wireless signals are becoming more common in accommodations, so if you're traveling with a laptop you can just connect and call for pennies.

TIME

Costa Rica is six hours behind GMT, so Costa Rican time is equivalent to Central Time in North America. There is no daylight-saving time.

TOILETS

Public restrooms are rare, but most restaurants and cafes will let you use their facilities, sometimes for a small charge – never more than ₡500. Bus terminals and other major public buildings usually have toilets, also at a charge.

If you're particularly fond of toilet paper, carry it with you at all times as it is not always available. Just don't flush it down! Costa Rican plumbing is often poor and has very low pressure in all but the best hotels and buildings. Dispose of toilet paper in the rubbish bin inside the bathroom.

TOURIST INFORMATION

The government-run tourism board, the Instituto Costarricense de Turismo (ICT), has two offices in the capital (see p60) that can provide you with free maps, a master bus schedule and information on road conditions in the hinterlands. English is spoken.

Consult the ICT's flashy English-language website (www.visitcostarica.com) for information, or in the USA call the ICT's toll-free number (☎ in USA 800-343-6332) for brochures and information.

TRAVELERS WITH DISABILITIES

Independent travel is difficult for anyone with mobility problems. Although Costa Rica has an equal-opportunity law for people with disabilities, the law applies only to new or newly remodeled businesses and is loosely enforced. Therefore, very few hotels and restaurants have features specifically suited to wheelchair use. Many don't have ramps, while room or bathroom doors are rarely wide enough to accommodate a wheelchair.

Outside the buildings, streets and sidewalks are potholed and poorly paved, making wheelchair use frustrating at best. Public buses don't have provisions to carry wheelchairs, and most national parks and outdoor tourist attractions don't have trails suited to wheelchair use. Lodgings with wheelchair accessibility are indicated in the reviews with this symbol: ♿ .

The following organizations offer specially designed trips for travelers with disabilities:

Accessible Journeys (☎ in USA 800-846-4537; www.disabilitytravel.com) Organizes independent travel to Costa Rica for people with disabilities.

Vaya con Silla de Ruedas (☎ 2454-2810; www.gowithwheelchairs.com) Offers specialty trips for the wheelchair-bound traveler. The company has specially designed vans and its equipment meets international accessibility standards.

VISAS

Passport-carrying nationals of the following countries are allowed to stay for 90 days with no visa: Argentina, Canada, Israel, Japan, Panama, the USA and most Western European countries. Citizens of Australia, Iceland, Ireland, Mexico, New Zealand, Russia, South Africa and Venezuela are allowed to stay for 30 days with no visa. Others require a visa from a Costa Rican embassy or consulate.

For the latest information on visas, check the websites of the **ICT** (www.visitcostarica.com) or the **Costa Rican embassy** (www.costarica-embassy.org) in Washington, DC.

If you are in Costa Rica and need to visit your embassy or consulate, see p343 for contact information.

EXTENSIONS

Extending your stay beyond the authorized 30 or 90 days is a time-consuming hassle. It is far easier to leave the country for 72 hours and then re-enter. Otherwise, go to the office of **Migración** (Immigration; ☎ 2220-0355; ☽ 8am-4pm) in San José, opposite Channel 6, about 4km north of Parque La Sabana. Requirements for extensions change, so allow several working days.

ONWARD TICKETS

Travelers officially need onward tickets before they are allowed to enter Costa Rica. This requirement is not often checked at the airport, but travelers arriving by land should anticipate a need to show an onward ticket.

If you're heading to Panama, Nicaragua or another Central or South American country from Costa Rica, you may need an onward or round-trip ticket before you will be allowed entry into that country or even allowed to board the plane if you're flying. A quick check with the appropriate embassy – easy to do via the internet – will tell you whether the country you're heading to has an onward-ticket requirement.

WOMEN TRAVELERS

Most female travelers experience little more than a 'mi amor' (my love) or an appreciative hiss from the local men in Costa Rica. But in general, Costa Rican men consider foreign women to have looser morals and to be easier conquests than Ticas (female Costa Ricans). Men will often make flirtatious comments to single women, particularly blondes. Women traveling together are not exempt from this. The best way to deal with unwanted attention is to do what Ticas do – ignore it completely. Women who firmly resist unwanted verbal advances from men are normally treated with respect.

In small highland towns, dress is usually conservative. Women rarely wear shorts, but belly-baring tops are all the rage. On the beach, skimpy bathing suits are OK, but topless and nude bathing are not.

As in any part of the world, the possibilities of rape and assault do exist. Use your normal caution: avoid walking alone in isolated places or through city streets late at night, and skip the hitchhiking. Do not take unlicensed 'pirate' taxis (licensed taxis are red and have medallions) as there have been reports of assaults against women by unlicensed drivers.

Birth-control pills are available at most pharmacies (without a prescription), while tampons can be difficult to find in rural areas – bring some from home or stock up in San José.

TRANSPORTATION
GETTING THERE & AWAY
ENTERING THE COUNTRY
The vast majority of travelers land at the airport in San José, with a growing number arriving in Liberia.

Entering Costa Rica is usually hassle-free (with the exception of some long queues). There are no fees or taxes payable upon entering the country, though some foreign nationals will require a visa. Be aware that those who need visas cannot get them at the border. For information on visas, see opposite page.

Citizens of all nations are required to have a passport that is valid for at least six months beyond the dates of your trip. When you arrive, your passport will be stamped. The law requires that you carry your passport at all times during your stay in Costa Rica.

AIR
AIRPORTS & AIRLINES
International flights arrive at Aeropuerto Internacional Juan Santamaría (p66), 17km northwest of San José, in the town of Alajuela. As a result, an increasing number of travelers are bypassing the capital altogether, and choosing instead to strike out into the country from Alajuela.

Aeropuerto Internacional Daniel Oduber Quirós (p149) in Liberia also receives international flights from the USA and Canada. At the time of research, Liberia was being served by Air Canada, American Airlines, Continental, Delta, Northwest, United Airlines and US Airways. Private charter flights were also starting to arrive with increasing frequency from London Gatwick.

There has been a lot of talk about expanding Daniel Oduber Quirós, primarily since the airport is convenient for travelers visiting the Península de Nicoya. However, thus far progress has been extremely slow, and it will still be several years before major ground is broken. In the meantime, a few European charters have announced their intention to fly direct to Liberia, which would mean that travelers from the continent will no longer need to lay over in the USA or Canada.

Costa Rica is well connected by air to other Central and South American countries, as well as the USA. The national airline, Lacsa (part of the Central American Airline consortium Grupo TACA), flies to numerous points in the USA and Latin America, including Cuba. The Federal Aviation Administration in the USA has assessed Costa Rica's aviation authorities

TRANSPORTATION

GETTING THERE & AWAY

to be in compliance with international safety standards.

TICKETS

Airline fares are usually more expensive during the Costa Rican high season (from December through April), with December and January the most expensive months to travel.

More than one-third of all travelers to Costa Rica come from the USA, so finding a nonstop flight from Houston, Miami or New York is quite simple. Schedules and prices are competitive – a little bit of shopping around can get you a good fare.

From Canada, most travelers to Costa Rica connect through US gateway cities, though Air Canada has direct flights from Toronto.

Most flights from the UK and Europe connect either in the USA or in Mexico City, although this may change once the new airport in Liberia starts attracting more flights. High-season fares may still apply during the northern summer, even though this is the beginning of the Costa Rican rainy season.

From Australia and New Zealand, travel routes usually go through the USA or Mexico. Again, fares tend to go up in June and July even though this is the beginning of the rainy season in Costa Rica.

American Airlines, Continental, Delta, Northwest, United and US Airways have connections to Costa Rica from many Central and South American countries. Grupo TACA offers daily direct flights to Caracas, Guatemala City and San Salvador. TACA and Mexicana have daily flights to Mexico City, while both TACA and COPA have several flights a day to Panama City. Rates vary considerably on season and availability.

SEA

Cruise ships stop in Costa Rican ports and enable passengers to make a quick foray into the country. Typically, ships dock at either the Pacific port of Caldera near Puntarenas or the Caribbean port of Puerto Limón.

GETTING AROUND
AIR
SCHEDULED FLIGHTS

Costa Rica's domestic airlines are **NatureAir** (☎ 2220-3054; www.natureair.com) and **Sansa** (☎ 2290-4100; www.flysansa.com); the latter is linked with Grupo TACA.

Both airlines fly small passenger planes, and you're allocated a baggage allowance of no more than 12kg. Space is limited and demand is high in the dry season, so reserve and pay for tickets in advance.

DEPARTURE/ARRIVAL TAX

There is a US$26 departure tax on all international outbound flights, payable in cash (US dollars or colones, or a mix of the two). At the Juan Santamaría airport you can pay with credit cards, and Banco de Costa Rica has an ATM (on the Plus system) by the departure-tax station. Note that you will not be allowed through airport security without paying.

At the time of research, the government had recently declared a US$15 tax on international inbound flights, though this is included in the price of your ticket. The fee was designed to replace the 3% hotel tax, which didn't capture the increasing amount of condominium and other private rentals.

◥ CLIMATE CHANGE & TRAVEL

Every form of transportation that relies on carbon-based fuel generates CO_2, the main cause of human-induced climate change. Modern travel is dependent on planes and while they might use less fuel per kilometer per person than most cars, they travel much greater distances. It's not just CO_2 emissions from aircraft that are the problem. The altitude at which aircraft emit gases (including CO_2) and particles contributes significantly to their total climate change impact. The Intergovernmental Panel on Climate Change believes aviation is responsible for 4.9% of climate change – double the effect of its CO_2 emissions alone.

Lonely Planet regards travel as a global benefit. We encourage the use of more climate-friendly travel modes where possible and, together with other concerned partners across many industries, we support the carbon offset scheme run by ClimateCare. Websites such as climatecare.org use 'carbon calculators' that allow people to offset the greenhouse gases they are responsible for with contributions to portfolios of climate-friendly initiatives throughout the developing world. Lonely Planet offsets the carbon footprint of all staff and author travel.

In Costa Rica schedules change constantly and delays are frequent because of inclement weather. Be patient: Costa Rica has small planes and big storms – you don't want to be in them at the same time. You should not arrange a domestic flight that makes a tight connection with an international flight back home.

All domestic flights originate and terminate at San José. See also the domestic air routes map, p358.

CHARTERS

If you're limited by time rather than money, chartering a private plane is by far the quickest way to travel around the country. It takes on average 45 to 90 minutes to fly to most destinations, though weather conditions can significantly speed up or delay travel time.

While there are a good number of charter companies serving Costa Rica, the most reputable in terms of safety is the domestic carrier, **NatureAir** (☎ 2220-3054; www.natureair.com). **Alfa Romeo Aero Taxi**

(www.alfaromeoair.com) also gets good marks. You can book either directly through the company, through a tour agency or even through your accommodations, especially if it's a high-end place.

For a King Air capable of seating one to seven passengers, you can expect to pay anywhere from US$850 to US$2250. For a Twin Otter holding one to 19 passengers, the price range is US$1750 to US$4000.

Be aware that luggage space is extremely limited, so pack light if you're planning on chartering private planes.

BICYCLE & MOTORCYCLE

Some cyclists claim that the steep, narrow, winding and potholed roads and aggressive Costa Rican drivers add up to a poor cycling experience. This may be true of the main roads, but there are numerous less-trafficked roads that offer plenty of adventure – from winding and scenic mountain paths with sweeping views to rugged trails that take riders through streams and by volcanoes.

Outfitters in Costa Rica and the USA can organize multiday mountain-biking trips around Costa Rica that cover stretches of highland and beach. Gear is provided on trips organized by local companies, but US outfitters require that you bring your own.

Most international airlines will fly your bike as a piece of checked baggage if you box it (remember to pad it well, because the box is liable to be roughly handled). Some airlines might charge you an extra handling fee.

You can rent mountain bikes in almost any tourist town, but the condition of the equipment varies. Another option is to buy a decent bike and sell it back at a reduced rate at the end of your trip. It is advisable to bring your own helmet and water bottle as the selection of such personalized items may be wider in your home country.

For a monthly fee, **Trail Source** (www.trailsource.com) can provide you with information on trails all over Costa Rica and the world.

The following companies organize biking and motorcycling tours in Costa Rica:

Backroads (☎ in USA 510-527-1555, 800-462-2848; www.backroads.com) Offers a variety

DOMESTIC AIR ROUTES

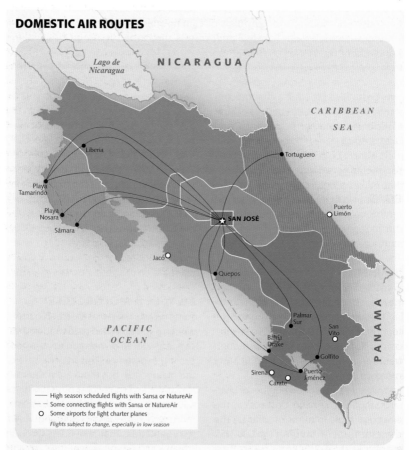

- High season scheduled flights with Sansa or NatureAir
- - Some connecting flights with Sansa or NatureAir
- ○ Some airports for light charter planes
- *Flights subject to change, especially in low season*

of excursion including a six-day cycling trip around Arenal and the Pacific coast.

Coast to Coast Adventures (☎ 2280-8054; www.ctocadventures.com) Everything from short biking excursions to 14-day coast-to-coast multisport trips.

Costa Rica Expeditions (☎ 2257-0766, 2222-0333; www.costaricaexpeditions.com) Multisport itineraries.

Lava Tours (☎ 2281-2458; www.lava-tours.com) Offers day trips, multiday packages and riding clinics.

MotoDiscovery (☎ in USA 800-233-6564, 830-438-7744; www.motodiscovery.com) Organizes motorcycle tours throughout the country.

Serendipity Adventures (☎ 2558-1000, in USA 734-995-0111, 800-635-2325; www.serendipityadventures.com) Creates custom biking itineraries to fit your schedule and your group.

Western Spirit Cycling (☎ in USA 800-845-2453; www.westernspirit.com) Offers a few different eight-day biking itineraries.

Wild Rider (☎ 2258-4604; www.wild-rider.com) Motorcycle tours.

BOAT

Ferries cross the Golfo de Nicoya connecting the central Pacific coast with the southern tip of the Península de Nicoya. The **Countermark ferry** (☎ 2661-1069) links the port of Puntarenas with Playa Naranjo, while the **Ferry Peninsular** (☎ 2641-0118) travels between Puntarenas and Paquera.

On the Golfo Dulce, a daily passenger ferry links Golfito with Puerto Jiménez on the Península de Osa, and a water taxi travels to and from Playa Zancudo. On the other side of the Península de Osa, water taxis connect Bahía Drake with Sierpe.

On the Caribbean coast, there is a bus and boat service that runs several times a day, linking Cariari and Tortuguero, while another links Parismina and Siquirres.

Boats also ply the canals that run along the coast from Moín to Tortuguero, although no regular service exists. A daily water taxi connects Puerto Viejo de Sarapiquí with Trinidad on the Río San Juan. The San Juan is Nicaraguan territory, so take your passport. You can try to arrange boat transportation in any of these towns for Barra del Colorado.

BUS
LOCAL BUSES
Local buses are the best way of getting around Costa Rica. You can take one just about everywhere, and they're frequent and cheap, with the longest domestic journey out of San José costing less than US$15.

San José is the transportation center for the country (see p66), though there is no central terminal. Bus offices are scattered around the city: some large bus companies have big terminals that sell tickets in advance, while others have little more than a stop – sometimes unmarked.

Normally there's room for everyone on a bus, and if there isn't, someone will squeeze you on anyhow. The exceptions are days before and after a major holiday, especially Easter, when buses are ridiculously full. Note that there are no buses from Thursday to Saturday before Easter Sunday.

There are two types of bus: *directo* and *colectivo*. The *directo* buses should go from one destination to the next with few stops, though it goes against the instincts of most Costa Rican bus drivers not to pick up every single roadside passenger. As for the *colectivo*, you know you're on one when the kids outside are outrunning your bus.

Trips longer than four hours usually include a rest stop as buses do not have toilets. Space is limited on board, so if you have to check luggage make sure that it gets loaded and that it isn't 'accidentally' given to someone else at intermediate stops. Keep your day pack with important documents on you at all times. Theft from overhead racks is rampant.

Bus schedules fluctuate wildly, so always confirm the time when you buy your ticket. If you are catching a bus that picks you up somewhere along a road, get to the roadside early. Departure times are estimated and if the bus comes early, it will leave early.

For information on departures from San José, pay a visit to the ICT office (p60) to pick up a (sort of) up-to-date copy of the master schedule, which is also available online at www.visitcostarica.com.

SHUTTLE BUSES

The tourist-van shuttle services (aka the gringo buses) are an alternative to the standard intercity buses. Shuttles are provided by **Grayline's Fantasy Bus** (☎ 2220-2126; www.graylinecostarica.com) and **Interbus** (☎ 2283-5573; www.interbusonline.com). Both companies run overland transportation from San José to the most popular destinations, as well as directly between other destinations (see their websites for the comprehensive list). These services will pick you up at your hotel and reservations can be made online, or through local travel agencies and hotel owners.

CAR

Renting a car is a wonderful way of touring Costa Rica, especially if your time in the country is limited. The freedom and flexibility of having your own wheels allows you to break free from the shackles of public transportation, and to move around the country at your own pace. While it will definitely take you a couple of spins behind the wheel to get accustomed to the road rules, on the whole, driving in Costa Rica is a relatively safe proposition.

If you plan to drive in Costa Rica, your driver's license from home is normally accepted for up to 90 days. Many places will also accept an International Driving Permit (IDP), issued by the automobile association in your country of origin. After 90 days, however, you will need to get a Costa Rican driver's license.

Gasoline (petrol) and diesel are widely available, and 24-hour service stations dot the entire stretch of the Interamericana. The price of gas is about US$0.75 per liter, although it can fluctuate to more than US$1 per liter. In more remote areas, fuel will likely be more expensive and might be sold from a drum at the neighborhood *pulpería* – look for signs that say *'Se vende gasolina'* ('We sell gas'). Spare parts may be hard to find, especially for vehicles with sophisticated electronics and emissions-control systems.

HIRE & INSURANCE

Most car-rental agencies can be found in San José and in popular tourist destinations on the Pacific coast. Car rental is not cheap, but if you are going to be doing even a small amount of driving, invest in a 4WD. Many agencies will insist on a 4WD for extended travel, especially in the rainy season, when driving through rivers is a matter of course. In fact, ordinary cars are pointless as soon as you leave the Interamericana.

To rent a car you need a valid driver's license, a major credit card and a passport. The minimum age for car rental is 21. Carefully inspect rented cars for minor damage and make sure that any damage is noted on the rental agreement. If your car breaks down, call the rental company. Don't attempt to get the car fixed yourself – most companies won't reimburse expenses without prior authorization.

Prices vary considerably, but on average you can expect to pay about US$350 to US$650 per week for an SUV, including *kilometraje libre* (unlimited mileage), and as little as US$200 per week for a standard car. Basic insurance will cost an additional US$15 to US$25 per day, and rental companies won't rent you a car without it. The roads in Costa Rica are rough and rugged, meaning that minor accidents or car damage are common. On top of this, you can pay an extra fee (about US$10 to US$15 per day) for a Collision Damage Waiver, or CDW, which covers the driver and a third party with a US$750 to US$1500 deductible.

Above and beyond this, you can purchase full insurance (about US$30 to US$50 per day), which is expensive, but well worth it. Note that if you pay basic insurance with a gold or platinum credit card, the company will usually take responsibility for damages to the car, in which case you can forego the cost of the full insurance. Make sure you verify this with your credit card company ahead of time.

Finally, note that most insurance policies do not cover damages caused by flooding or driving through a river (even though this is sometimes necessary in Costa Rica!), so be aware of the extent of your policy.

Rental rates fluctuate wildly, so make sure you shop around before you commit to anything. Some agencies offer discounts if you reserve online or if you rent for long periods of time. Note that rental offices at the airport charge a 12% fee in addition to regular rates.

Thieves can easily recognize rental cars, and many thefts have occurred from them. *Never* leave anything in sight in a parked car – nothing! – and remove all luggage from the trunk overnight. Park the car in a guarded parking lot rather than on the street. We cannot stress enough how many readers write us letters each year detailing thefts from their cars.

All of the major international car-rental agencies have outlets in Costa Rica, but you can usually get a better deal from one of the local companies:

Adobe (☎ 2259-4242, in USA 800-769-8422; www.adobecar.com) Reader-recommended with offices in Liberia, Tamarindo and Quepos.

Dollar (☎ 2443-2950, in USA 866-767-8651; www.dollarcostarica.com) One of the cheapest companies in Costa Rica with offices in both airports.

Poas (☎ 2442-6178, in USA 888-607-7627; www.carentals.com) Service centers in Liberia, Tamarindo, La Fortuna and Guápiles.

Solid (☎ 2442-6000; www.solidcarrental.com) The only agency with offices in Puerto Jiménez and Golfito.

ROAD CONDITIONS & HAZARDS

The roads vary from quite good (the Interamericana) to barely passable (just about everywhere else). Even the good ones can suffer from landslides, sudden flooding and fog. Most roads are single-lane and winding, lacking hard shoulders; others are dirt-and-mud affairs that climb mountains and traverse rivers.

Drive defensively. Always expect to come across cyclists, a broken-down vehicle, a herd of cattle, slow-moving trucks or an oxcart around the next bend. Unsigned speed bumps are placed on some stretches of road without warning. (The locals lovingly refer to them as *muertos*, 'the dead.')

Most roads (except around the major tourist towns) are inadequately signed and will require at least one stop to ask for directions. Always ask about road conditions before setting out, especially in the rainy season; a number of roads become impassable in the rainy season.

ROAD RULES

There are speed limits of 100km/h or less on all primary roads and 60km/h or less on secondary roads. Traffic police use radars, and speed limits are enforced with speeding tickets. You can get a traffic ticket for not wearing a seat belt. It's illegal to stop in an intersection or make a right turn on a red. At unmarked intersections, yield to the car on your right. Driving in Costa Rica is on the right and passing is allowed only on the left.

If you are issued with a ticket, you have to pay the fine at a bank; instructions are given on the ticket. If you are driving a rental car, the rental company may be able to arrange your payment for you – the amount of the fine should be on the ticket. A portion of the money from these fines goes to a children's charity.

Police have no right to ask for money, and shouldn't confiscate a car, unless: the driver cannot produce a license and ownership papers; the car lacks license plates; the driver is drunk; or the driver has been involved in an accident causing serious injury. (For more on what to do when in an accident, see p351).

If you are driving and see oncoming cars with headlights flashing, it often means that there is a road problem or a radar speed trap ahead. Slow down immediately.

LOCAL TRANSPORTATION
BUS

Local buses operate chiefly in San José, connecting urban and suburban areas. Most local buses pick up passengers on the street and on main roads. The vehicles in service are usually converted school buses imported from the USA, and they are often packed.

TAXI

In San José taxis have meters, called *marías,* but many drivers try to get out of using them, particularly if you don't

THE CASE OF THE FLAT TIRE & THE DISAPPEARING LUGGAGE

A serious scam is under way on the streets around Aeropuerto Internacional Juan Santamaría. Many readers have reported similar incidents, so take precautions to ensure this doesn't happen to you. Here's how it goes…

After picking up a rental car and driving out of the city, you notice that it has a flat tire. You pull over to try to fix it. Some friendly locals, noticing that a visitor to their fair land is in distress, pull over to help out. There is inevitably some confusion with the changing of the tire, and everybody is involved in figuring it out, but eventually the car repair is successfully accomplished and the friendly Ticos (Costa Ricans) give you a wave and drive off. That's when you get back in your car and discover that your wallet – or your luggage, or everything – is gone.

This incident has happened enough times to suggest that somebody may be tampering with rental cars to 'facilitate' these flat tires. It certainly suggests that travelers should be very wary – and aware – if somebody pulls over to help. Keep your wallet and your passport on your person whenever you get out of a car. If possible, let one person in your party stay inside the car to keep a watchful eye. In any case, lock your doors – even if you think you are going to be right outside. There's nothing like losing all your luggage to put a damper on a vacation.

USING TAXIS IN REMOTE AREAS

Taxis are considered a form of public transportation in remote areas that lack good public transportation networks. They can be hired by the hour, the half-day or full day, or you can arrange a flat fee for a trip. Meters are not used on long trips, so arrange the fare ahead of time. Fares can fluctuate due to worse-than-expected road conditions and bad weather in tough-to-reach places.

The condition of taxis varies from basic sedans held together by rust, to fully equipped 4WDs with air-con. In some cases, taxis are pick-up trucks with seats built into the back. Most towns will have at least one licensed taxi, but in some remote villages you may have to get rides from whoever is offering – ask at the local *pulpería* (corner grocery store).

speak Spanish. With that said, it is illegal not to use the meter, so don't be afraid to point this out if you feel you're about to be scammed. Outside of San José, however, most taxis don't have meters and fares tend to be agreed upon in advance – some bargaining is quite acceptable.

In some towns, there are *colectivos* (taxis that several passengers can share). Although *colectivos* are becoming increasingly difficult to find, the basic principle is that the driver charges a flat fee (usually about US$0.50) to take passengers from one end of town to the other.

In rural areas, 4WDs are often used as taxis and are a popular means for surfers (and their boards) to travel from their accommodations to the break. Prices vary wildly depending on how touristy the area is, though generally speaking a 10-minute ride should cost between US$5 and US$15.

Taxi drivers are not normally tipped unless they assist with your luggage or have provided an above-average service. However, owing to the increasing number of North American travelers, don't be surprised if drivers in tourist towns are quick to hold out their palm.

↘ GLOSSARY

almuerzo ejecutivo – literally 'executive lunch'; a more expensive version of a set meal or *casado*

avenida – avenue

bahía – bay
barrio – district or neighborhood
batido – fresh fruit drink, similar to a smoothie
bocas – small savory dishes served in bars
bomba – short, funny verse; also means 'gas station' and 'bomb'
bosque – forest
bosque nuboso – cloud forest
boyero – oxcart driver
buena nota – excellent, OK; literally 'good note'

cabaña – cabin; also known as a *cabina*
cajero automático – ATM
calle – street
campesino – peasant, farmer or person who works in agriculture
carreta – colorfully painted wooden oxcart, now a form of folk art
carretera – road
casado – inexpensive set meal; also means 'married'
casita – cottage or apartment
catedral – cathedral
cerro – mountain or hill
cerveza – beer
ceviche – local dish of raw, marinated seafood
Chepe – affectionate nickname for José; also used when referring to San José
ciudad – city
colectivo – bus, minivan or car operating as a shared taxi
colegio – school

colón – Costa Rican unit of currency; plural *colones*
comida típica – typical local food
concha – shell
conquistador – conqueror
cordillera – mountain range
correo – mail service
Costarricense – Costa Rican; see also *Tico/a*

Dios – God
directo – direct; refers to long-distance bus with few stops

edificio – building
estación – station, eg ranger station or bus station; also means 'season'
estadio – stadium

farmacia – pharmacy
fauna silvestre – wildlife
fiesta – party or festival
finca – farm or plantation
fútbol – soccer (football)

gallo pinto – stir-fry of rice and beans
gasolina – gas (petrol)
gringo/a (m/f) – US or European visitor; can be affectionate or insulting, depending on the tone used
guaro – local firewater made from sugarcane

hacienda – rural estate

ICT – Instituto Costarricense de Turismo; Costa Rica Tourism Board, which provides tourist information
iglesia – church
indígena – indigenous

Interamericana – Pan-American Hwy; the nearly continuous highway running from Alaska to Chile (it breaks at the Darién Gap between Panama and Colombia)

invierno – winter; the rainy season in Costa Rica

isla – island

jardín – garden

josefino/a (m/f) – resident of San José

lago – lake

laguna – lagoon

maría – local name for taxi meter

mercado – market

mercado central – central town market

Meseta Central – Central Valley or central plateau

mestizo/a (m/f) – person of mixed descent, usually Spanish and Indian

metate – flat stone platform, used by Costa Rica's pre-Columbian populations to grind corn

migración – immigration

Minae – Ministerio de Ambiente y Energía; Ministry of Environment and Energy, in charge of the national park system

mirador – lookout point

mole – rich chocolate sauce

muelle – dock

museo – museum

niño – child

palenque – indigenous settlement

panadería – bakery

páramo – habitat characterized by highland shrub and tussock grass

parque – park

parque central – central town square or plaza

parque nacional – national park

pastelería – pastry shop

playa – beach

posada – country-style inn or guesthouse

puente – bridge

puerto – port

pulpería – corner grocery store

punta – point

pura vida – super; literally 'pure life'

quebrada – stream

queso – cheese

ranario – frog pond

rancho – small house or houselike building

refugio nacional de vida silvestre – national wildlife refuge

río – river

sabanero – cowboy from Guanacaste

selva – jungle

Semana Santa – the Christian Holy Week that precedes Easter

sendero – trail or path

serpentario – snake garden

Sinac – Sistema Nacional de Áreas de Conservación; National System of Conservation Areas

soda – informal lunch counter or inexpensive eatery

telenovela – Spanish-language soap opera

Tico/a (m/f) – Costa Rican; see also *Costarricense*

tiquismos – typical Costa Rican expressions or slang

tortuga – turtle

valle – valley

verano – summer; the dry season in Costa Rica

vida – life

vino – wine

volcán – volcano

↘ BEHIND THE SCENES

THE AUTHORS
MATTHEW D FIRESTONE

Coordinating author, This Is Costa Rica, Costa Rica's Top 25 Experiences, Costa Rica's Top Itineraries, Planning Your Trip, Central Pacific Coast, Southern Costa Rica, Costa Rica in Focus, Directory & Transport

Matthew is a trained anthropologist and epidemiologist, though he postponed his academic career to spend his youth living out of a backpack. To date he has authored more than 20 guidebooks for Lonely Planet, and covered far-flung destinations from the Darién Gap to the Dead Sea. When he's not in graduate school, out in the field or on assignment, he likes to spend his time exploring the American West with his parents, or catching up with the in-laws on the foothills of Mt Fuji.

Author thanks My family has gotten bigger since the publication of this book, so first off, I'd like to extend a warm welcome to my wonderful wife, Aki. We've traveled the world from east to west, but there is still so much more for us to discover together. And of course, I can't overlook the overwhelming support that my parents and sister have shown me over the years, which has guided me over more hurdles and around more obstacles than I care to mention. At Lonely Planet, a tip of the hat to editor extraordinaire Catherine Craddock for getting behind the steering wheel of yet another edition of Costa Rica. And finally, a sincere *muchísimas gracias* to Carolina and César, who are two of the most diligent and high-spirited authors I've ever had the privilege to work with.

CAROLINA A MIRANDA
San José, Central Valley, Caribbean Coast

Carolina has traveled Costa Rica top to bottom, east to west on numerous occasions over more than a half-dozen years. During these sojourns, she has eaten ungodly amounts of *chifrijo* (rice and beans with fried pork and salsa) and seen some of the most spectacular scenery on earth. When she isn't getting lost along jungle trails in Costa Rica,

LONELY PLANET AUTHORS

Why is our travel information the best in the world? It's simple: our authors are passionate, dedicated travelers. They don't take freebies in exchange for positive coverage so you can be sure the advice you're given is impartial. They travel widely to all the popular spots, and off the beaten track. They don't research using just the internet or phone. They discover new places not included in any other guidebook. They personally visit thousands of hotels, restaurants, palaces, trails, galleries, temples and more. They speak with dozens of locals every day to make sure you get the kind of insider knowledge only a local could tell you. They take pride in getting all the details right, and in telling it how it is. Think you can do it? Find out how at **lonelyplanet.com**.

she works as a freelance writer in New York City, where she contributes stories to *Time, Budget Travel, Travel + Leisure, Florida Travel + Life* and the public radio station WNYC. She is the author of the uncouth and saucy cultural blog C-Monster.net. Find her on Twitter at @cmonstah.

CÉSAR G SORIANO · Northern Costa Rica, Península de Nicoya

Bitten by the wanderlust bug at birth, César has based all his life decisions on the travel opportunities they would afford. Desperate to flee his Virginia hometown after college, he joined the US Army – and was promptly deployed to war-torn Bosnia and Hercegovina. As a career journalist, César landed his first dream job at *USA Today,* where he covered everything from celebrity gossip to the Iraq and Afghanistan wars. In 2006 César changed gear and became a London-based freelance writer. This is his eighth and final guidebook for Lonely Planet; in 2010 César switched careers again and is now a US Foreign Service Officer.

CONTRIBUTING AUTHORS

Dr David Goldberg wrote the Health section in Directory & Transportation. He completed his training in internal medicine and infectious diseases at Columbia-Presbyterian Medical Center in New York City, where he has also served as voluntary faculty. At present he is an infectious-diseases specialist in Scarsdale, New York, and the editor in chief of the website MDtravelhealth.com.

David Lukas wrote the Environment section in Costa Rica in Focus. He is an avid student of natural history who has traveled widely to study tropical ecosystems in locations such as Borneo and the Amazon. He has also spent several years leading natural-history tours to all corners of Costa Rica, Belize and Guatemala.

THIS BOOK

This 1st edition of *Discover Costa Rica* was researched and written by Matthew D Firestone (coordinating author), Carolina A Miranda and César G Soriano. This guidebook was commissioned in Lonely Planet's Oakland office, and produced by the following:
Commissioning Editor Catherine Craddock-Carrillo
Coordinating Editors Martine Power, Branislava Vladisavljevic
Coordinating Cartographers Mark Griffiths, Valentina Kremenchutskaya
Coordinating Layout Designer Jacqui Saunders
Managing Editors Bruce Evans, Annelies Mertens
Managing Cartographers Alison Lyall, Herman So
Managing Layout Designers Indra Kilfoyle, Celia Wood
Assisting Cartographer Jacqueline Nguyen
Cover Research Brendan Dempsey
Internal Image Research Sabrina Dalbesio

Thanks to Craig Kilburn, Rebecca Lalor, Naomi Parker, Averil Robertson

SEND US YOUR FEEDBACK

We love to hear from travelers – your comments keep us on our toes and help make our books better. Our well-traveled team reads every word on what you loved or loathed about this book. Although we cannot reply individually to postal submissions, we always guarantee that your feedback goes straight to the appropriate authors, in time for the next edition. Each person who sends us information is thanked in the next edition and the most useful submissions are rewarded with a free book.

To send us your updates – and find out about Lonely Planet events, newsletters and travel news – visit our award-winning website: lonelyplanet.com/contact.

Note: we may edit, reproduce and incorporate your comments in Lonely Planet products such as guidebooks, websites and digital products, so let us know if you don't want your comments reproduced or your name acknowledged. For a copy of our privacy policy visit lonelyplanet.com/privacy.

Internal photographs p4 Young boy with yellow balloon, Eric Wheater; p10 Red-eyed tree frog, Tom Boyden; p12 Surfer riding a wave, Mal País, Christian Aslund; p31 Young child leaning on window sill, Puerto Limón, Eric Wheater; p39 Surfers walking to the beach, Mal País, Christian Aslund; p50 Villa in San José, Imagebroker/Oliver Gerhard; p73 Central Valley coffee plantation, Annelies Mertens; p97 Travelers crossing a canopy walkway, Reserva Biológica Bosque Nuboso Monteverde, Christer Fredriksson; p165 Rainforest, rocky inlets and white-sand beach, Playa Hermosa, Paul Kennedy; p199 White-faced capuchin monkeys, Parque Nacional Manuel Antonio, Casey Mahaney; p227 Cougar, Tom Boyden; p269 Girl in carnival costume, Puerto Limón, Ian Cumming/Axiom/Aurora Photos; p300 Souvenir vendors, Parque Nacional Manuel Antonio, Carol Barrington, De/Aurora Photos; p339 Smiling children, Cahuita, Christopher Baker.

All images are copyright of the photographer unless otherwise indicated. Many of the images in this guide are available for licensing from Lonely Planet Images: www.lonelyplanetimages.com.

NOTES

↘ INDEX

INDEX

C-H

000 Map pages
000 Photograph pages

INDEX

H-I

INDEX

J-M

000 Map pages
000 Photograph pages

INDEX

M-P

INDEX

P-R

000 Map pages
000 Photograph pages

INDEX

S–T

INDEX

W-Z

GREENDEX

GOING GREEN

It seems like everyone's going 'green' these days, but how can you know which businesses are actually ecofriendly and which are simply jumping on the sustainable bandwagon?

Lonely Planet authors have selected all of the following listings because they demonstrate an active sustainable-tourism policy. Some are involved in conservation or environmental education, and many are owned and run by local and indigenous operators, thereby maintaining and preserving regional identity and culture. Some of the listings below have also been certified by the Instituto Costarricense de Turismo (ICT; Costa Rica Tourism Board; www.visitcostarica.com), which means they meet high standards of environmental sustainability, business ethics and cultural sensitivity.

We want to keep developing our sustainable-tourism content. If you think we've omitted someone who should be listed here, or if you disagree with our choices, email us at talk2us@lonelyplanet.com.au. For more information about sustainable tourism and Lonely Planet, see www.lonelyplanet.com/responsibletravel.

INDEX

MAP LEGEND

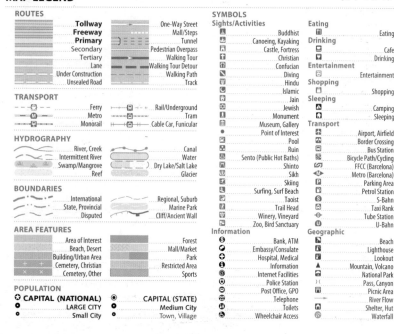

ROUTES

- Tollway
- Freeway
- Primary
- Secondary
- Tertiary
- Lane
- Under Construction
- Unsealed Road
- One-Way Street
- Mall/Steps
- Tunnel
- Pedestrian Overpass
- Walking Tour
- Walking Tour Detour
- Walking Path
- Track

TRANSPORT

- Ferry
- Metro
- Monorail
- Rail/Underground
- Tram
- Cable Car, Funicular

HYDROGRAPHY

- River, Creek
- Intermittent River
- Swamp/Mangrove
- Reef
- Canal
- Water
- Dry Lake/Salt Lake
- Glacier

BOUNDARIES

- International
- State, Provincial
- Disputed
- Regional, Suburb
- Marine Park
- Cliff/Ancient Wall

AREA FEATURES

- Area of Interest
- Beach, Desert
- Building/Urban Area
- Cemetery, Christian
- Cemetery, Other
- Forest
- Mall/Market
- Park
- Restricted Area
- Sports

POPULATION

- ◎ CAPITAL (NATIONAL)
- ● LARGE CITY
- ● Small City
- ◉ CAPITAL (STATE)
- ● Medium City
- ● Town, Village

SYMBOLS

Sights/Activities
- Buddhist
- Canoeing, Kayaking
- Castle, Fortress
- Christian
- Confucian
- Diving
- Hindu
- Islamic
- Jain
- Jewish
- Monument
- Museum, Gallery
- Point of Interest
- Pool
- Ruin
- Sento (Public Hot Baths)
- Shinto
- Sikh
- Skiing
- Surfing, Surf Beach
- Taoist
- Trail Head
- Winery, Vineyard
- Zoo, Bird Sanctuary

Information
- Bank, ATM
- Embassy/Consulate
- Hospital, Medical
- Information
- Internet Facilities
- Police Station
- Post Office, GPO
- Telephone
- Toilets
- Wheelchair Access

Eating
- Eating

Drinking
- Cafe
- Drinking

Entertainment
- Entertainment

Shopping
- Shopping

Sleeping
- Camping
- Sleeping

Transport
- Airport, Airfield
- Border Crossing
- Bus Station
- Bicycle Path/Cycling
- FFCC (Barcelona)
- Metro (Barcelona)
- Parking Area
- Petrol Station
- S-Bahn
- Taxi Rank
- Tube Station
- U-Bahn

Geographic
- Beach
- Lighthouse
- Lookout
- Mountain, Volcano
- National Park
- Pass, Canyon
- Picnic Area
- River Flow
- Shelter, Hut
- Waterfall

LONELY PLANET OFFICES

Australia
Head Office
Locked Bag 1, Footscray, Victoria 3011
☎ 03 8379 8000, fax 03 8379 8111
talk2us@lonelyplanet.com.au

USA
150 Linden St, Oakland, CA 94607
☎ 510 250 6400, toll free 800 275 8555,
fax 510 893 8572
info@lonelyplanet.com

UK
2nd fl, 186 City Rd,
London EC1V 2NT
☎ 020 7106 2100, fax 020 7106 2101
go@lonelyplanet.co.uk

Published by Lonely Planet Publications Pty Ltd
ABN 36 005 607 983

Printed by Toppan Security Printing Pte. Ltd.
Printed in Singapore